DINOSAURS
A GLOBAL VIEW

© Halle

DINOSAURS
A GLOBAL VIEW

SYLVIA J. CZERKAS

STEPHEN A. CZERKAS

Scientific Advisor
EVERETT C. OLSON Ph.D

Illustrations by
DOUGLAS HENDERSON

MARK HALLETT

JOHN SIBBICK

Produced by
MARTYN DEAN

DRAGON'S WORLD

FRONTISPIECE

Two Allosaurus *are in a confrontation that began with mutual intimidation, but could end in fierce bloodshed.*

Dragon's World Ltd
Limpsfield
Surrey RH 8 0DY
Great Britain

First published by Dragon's World Ltd 1990
Revised edition 1995

© Dragon's World Ltd 1990
© Text Sylvia J. and Stephen A. Czerkas 1990
© Colour artwork resides with the individual artists 1990

Producer & Designer: Martyn Dean
Editors: Emma Callery & Diana Steedman
Editorial Director: Pippa Rubinstein

Skeletal Drawings: Design by Stephen A. Czerkas, Illustration by David Nicholls and Denise Blagden

Globes & Charts: Design by Stephen A. Czerkas, Illustration by Ron Hayward

Dinosaur and Site Photography: Stephen A. Czerkas

Cover: Illustration by John Sibbick, Research Stephen A. Czerkas, Design by Martyn Dean

British Library Cataloguing in Publication Data
Czerkas, Sylvia J
  Dinosaurs.
  1. Dinosaurs
  I. Title
  567.91

ISBN 1-85028-050-9

Typeset by Tradespools, Frome, Somerset

Printed in Spain

ACKNOWLEDGEMENTS

The authors wish to thank the following for the contributions of their time and talents towards the realization of this project:

Everett C. Olson, our Chief Scientific Advisor, for giving this book the benefit of his comprehensive and profound knowledgeability in the field of palaeontology, for the countless hours of his time in reviewing the manuscript, and for giving us the pleasure of being able to work again with such a kind and exceptional human being.

Our artists, Mark Hallett, Douglas Henderson, and John Sibbick for astounding us time and again with the beauty and quality of their illustrations, and for their mutual enthusiasm for scientific content and artistic integrity.

Roger Dean and Martyn Dean, for seeing this project through from beginning to end with vision, imagination, and style.

Publisher, Hubert Schaafsma, Editors, Pippa Rubinstein and Emma Callery for their fine sense of quality.

Contributors in their areas of scientific speciality for their valuable insights:
Jose F. Bonaparte, Museo de Cinecias naturales
Sankar Chatterjee, Texas Technical University
Philip J. Currie, Tyrrell Museum of Palaeontology
Martin G. Lockley, University of Colorado, Denver
James O. Farlow, Indiana University – Perdue University
John S. McIntosh
Stuart A. Naquin
Jamie E. Powell, Universidad Nacional de Tucuman
Dale A. Russell, National Museum of Natural Sciences, Ottawa

Photographers, Martyn Dean, Douglas Henderson, Chip Clark, Richard Blue Trimarchi of Pasadena Art Works, and Veronica Tagland. Lab work by Tracy Hamby of Consolidated Media Inc. Pasadena. With thanks to National Geographic Magazine, the American Museum of Natural History, and the Yale Peabody Museum of Natural History for photography use.

For words of encouragement, our family and friends, with a special thanks to David B. Weishample and C. Barry Cox.

This book is dedicated to the staff of the Natural History Museum of Los Angeles,
especially the Director, Craig Black,
also to museums throughout the world for the education of today's children
and the preservation of our planet's history
for the children of tomorrow.

Stephen & Sylvia Czerkas 1990.

CONTENTS

Jurassic scene, a chance encounter between the giant Brachiosaurus *and* Ceratosaurus *startles a flight of* Rhamphorhynchus.

THE PLATES

FRONTISPIECE

CHAPTER I

CHAPTER II

CHAPTER III

CHAPTER IV

CHAPTER V

THE SKELETAL DRAWINGS

THE AUTHORS

Sylvia J. Czerkas, author, acted as Guest Curator for the Natural History Museum of Los Angeles County where she assembled an innovative international travelling exhibition entitled 'Dinosaurs Past and Present'. The four artists in *Global View* were included, along with other artists, in the exhibition. She co-edited, with Everett C. Olson, the exhibit's companion symposium volumes, *Dinosaurs Past and Present, Volumes I and II*. She also curated the travelling museum exhibition 'Dinosaurs, Mammoths, and Cavemen – The Art of Charles R. Knight' and co-authored a book of the same name with Donald F. Glut. Along with her husband and fellow artist, Stephen, she manages the S & S Czerkas Studios, and together they spend part of each summer season at various sites digging up dinosaurs.

Stephen A. Czerkas, author, is a sculptor and palaeontologist. His sculptural restorations of prehistoric animals are both scientifically accurate and beautifully realistic. His *Carnotaurus* and *Allosaurus* are featured in the collection of the Natural History Museum of Los Angeles County. Other life-size dinosaurs were sculpted for the California Academy of Sciences, the New Mexico Museum of Natural History, the Philadelphia Academy of Sciences, and the Museum of the Rockies. In 1987, an entire series of ten life-size models were created under his direction for the Taipei Taiwan Dinosaur Museum and Educational Centre in Taiwan.

Stephen Czerkas's sculptures appear on pages: 142, 143, 153, 174, 175, 176, 177, 231.

CHIEF ADVISOR

Chief Advisor **Everett C. Olson, Ph.D** is Professor Emeritus of Zoology at the University of California at Los Angeles. He has authored a wealth of influential scientific publications on the evolution of reptiles, the origin of mammals, and vertebrate palaeoecology. In 1987, he was the first to be awarded the Society of Vertebrate Palaeontology's highest and most distinctive honour, the Romer-Simpson Palaeontological Medal.

THE ARTISTS

Mark Hallett is a painter, writer, naturalist, and teacher, whose murals appear at the Natural History Museum of Los Angeles, the Page Museum, the San Diego Natural History Museum, and the San Diego Zoo. He has taught classes in zoological illustration at the Natural History Museum of Los Angeles County, and biomedical illustration and anatomy at Otis Art Institute in Los Angeles. His illustrations of living and extinct animal life are frequently published in books and magazines.

Mark Hallett's paintings appear on pages: 4, 57, 63, 74/75, 84, 95, 119, 121, 127, 130/131, 138/139, 155, 185, 199, 201, 203, 211, 221, 224/225.

Douglas Henderson is an artist whose illustrations are in constant demand and have appeared in numerous publications including *Maia, a Dinosaur Grows Up* by John Horner, Ph.D and James Gorman, *The Riddle of the Dinosaur* by John Nobel Wilford, and *Dawn of the Dinosaurs* by Robert. A. Long and Rose Houk. The extensive amount of time he has spent in sketching and observing nature in the Sierras amongst the giant Sequoia, his studies of fossil plants, and his daily life near Yellowstone Park allow him to produce Mesozoic landscapes that are unrivaled.

Douglas Henderson's drawings and paintings appear on pages: 18, 19, 21, 23, 24, 25, 26, 29, 31, 35, 37, 38, 41, 46, 48, 55, 61, 65, 68, 87, 88, 89, 96, 97, 99, 101, 103, 105, 106/107, 110/111, 116/117, 125, 137, 149, 157, 164/165, 169, 179, 183, 189, 194, 196, 197, 198, 202, 207, 209, 218, 219, 223, 233, 235.

John Sibbick is an artist whose work has appeared in numerous publications during the last eleven years including *The Illustrated Encyclopedia of Dinosaurs* by Dr David Norman and the *National Geographic Pop-Up Dinosaurs*. In both books, the colour paintings are entirely his. He has contributed artwork for several TV dinosaur programmes, including the BBC's *Lost Worlds Vanished Lives*. He also works regularly for museums and galleries.

John Sibbick's paintings appear on pages: 8, 20, 45, 47, 51, 67, 71, 79, 171.

CHAPTER I
A GLOBAL VIEW
INTRODUCTION

LOOKING BACK
THE CHANGING EARTH

Imagine a world where Mankind does not exist. Instead of our familiar modern civilization, visualize an entire world harmoniously balanced with nature and populated with successfully integrated animals. So lush and vibrant is this worldwide garden of Eden that many of the animals are of gigantic size unequalled before or after the great age in which they lived. This was the world of titanic reptiles, the dinosaurs.

How did these titanic reptiles come into existence? Were they the experimental failures of evolution's prehistoric past? What ultimately caused their demise? The answers to these, and many other mysterious questions about dinosaurs can be solved by studying their fossil remains, and understanding the world in which they lived. Perhaps their ancestry holds some clues to help explain their long success and eventual disappearance. Perhaps, rather than looking for the 'smoking gun' that is responsible for their demise, it is better to examine their primitive ancestors and other forms of life that existed long before the first dinosaurs appeared.

The dominance of the world by the dinosaurs in the Mesozoic Era lasted 140 million years, from late in the Triassic period 205 million years ago through the Jurassic and Cretaceous periods until 65 million years ago. Such a time span may be difficult to grasp, and yet it is only a tiny fraction of the history of life on Earth, with the very earliest forms of life, the most primitive single cells, coming into existence at least 3500 million years ago.

These single cells and all the more complex forms of life that followed, share an integrated relationship with the world in which they lived. Life has certainly changed tremendously during Earth's history but what may not be as apparent is that Earth itself has undergone vast changes which have dramatically affected life on the planet.

In order to better visualize these changes, imagine looking at Earth from outer space, using a time-lapse camera recording its history over the past 4600 million years. You would see the highly accelerated action of the changes that have occurred during Earth's history: the first oceans form from the gaseous clouds of a volcanic world; within the oceans, barren landmasses appear. These empty continents of land are not motionless, but are moving and floating across the surface of Earth, developing a reddish tone as the atmosphere containing life-supporting oxygen forms beyond the edge of the planet. The continents move away from some, only to collide into others, causing huge mountain ranges to rise up and then fall. Seas inundate the land, then drain away; glaciers and polar caps spread their white covering only to disappear again, melting back into the flooding seas; and a new colour, that of green, at first outlines and then covers the continents. You would then observe the continents collectively collide into each other forming the supercontinent, Pangaea.

A massive polar ice cap appears over much of the supercontinent overlying the South Pole. It then disappears, unleashing torrents of shallow seas which spread across much of the landmass. The continents, vibrantly coloured in greens and blues, continue to move, pulling apart from each other and distantly resembling the familiar landmasses of our present day. Polar caps again appear over both poles but then shrink to less than half their size as the continents finally assume the positions of our present globe.

Viewed from this distance, in outer space, we would see how the changing positions of the continents were accompanied by corresponding changes in climates and environments which had a direct influence on the success or failure of various forms of life. By examining these influences, particularly in those periods immediately before, during and after the age of the dinosaurs, we will better understand not only why the dinosaurs became extinct, but perhaps more importantly why they lived so successfully for 140 million years. Although the dinosaurs symbolically represent prehistoric life, they are far from being the oldest animals to inhabit Earth.

BEYOND THE WATER
NEW FRONTIERS

During the Precambrian Era, 3500 million years ago, algae and other simple, aquatic plant-like organisms began to evolve from the previously barren, lifeless void of erosional activity. Then, in the Late Silurian period of 420 million years ago, primitive plants that for so long had been restricted to an aquatic environment, began to develop vascular tissues which circulated life fluids and strengthened stems and rooting systems. These plants now had the mechanical advantage of the development of 'legs' to carry them onto the undeveloped land. They were followed by the multi-legged arthropods and other invertebrates which took advantage of this new terrestrial environment as plant life continued to develop and flourish over the next 50 million years before the higher-evolved descendants of the lobe-finned fishes first walked from their watery confines among the lush vegetation.

All terrestrial vertebrates (animals with backbones that live on the land) share a common ancestor. This creature first developed lungs which enabled it to breathe outside the boundaries of its aquatic habitat, and then limbs to assist in propelling its body across the surface of the land. One such ancestor was *Eusthenopteron*, a lobe-finned fish. Another descendant, appearing much later during the Late Devonian period about 374 million years ago, was the *Ichthyostega* with its primitive legs. It still retained characteristics that were derived from its primordial fish-like ancestor but the similarities in the shape of the skull, teeth and even fish-like tail are indications that

Ichthyostega was at a transitional stage of development. It represents an authentic missing link between the lobe-fin fish and the amphibians.

Why did creatures such as *Ichthyostega* venture onto the land? Environmental stresses had caused its ancestors to develop more advanced lungs, capable of breathing the outside air, as a defence mechanism against the seasonal, life-threatening depletion of oxygenated water and the cyclical evaporation of bodies of water in which they lived. But what brought the earliest *Ichthyostega* onto the land was not only its need to survive, but opportunism.

With the success of terrestrial vegetation, a totally new environment, complete with life-sustaining food, was now there for the taking. Having developed the ability to breathe, it was now necessary to develop the ability to move about to feed in this new terrestrial world. The modified limbs of lobe-finned fishes continued to strengthen and alter in shape until they no longer possessed what could be defined as fins. It was on primitive, sprawling little legs that animals like *Ichthyostega* crawled amid the greenery and forests of the terrestrial world, forever altering the course of vertebrate life.

It is important to consider whether the environment was capable of supporting life long before animals like *Ichthyostega* took advantage of it. Here then we have the riddle: 'Which came first, the chicken or the egg?' *Ichthyostega* represents the chicken, while the environment is the egg. In this case, the riddle can be solved and it was certainly the egg that came first. The environment allows other life forms to enter into that and reap its beneficial support.

No environment is totally stable and inactive, and any changes to it potentially create a threat to its inhabitants if they are unable to adapt. This is what determines the survival or extinction of all life. As we have seen with the lobe-fins and *Ichthyostega*, life forms are capable of evolving to benefit from changes caused by environmental stresses. This process of

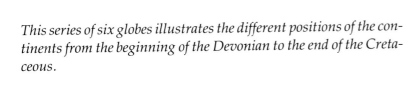

This series of six globes illustrates the different positions of the continents from the beginning of the Devonian to the end of the Cretaceous.

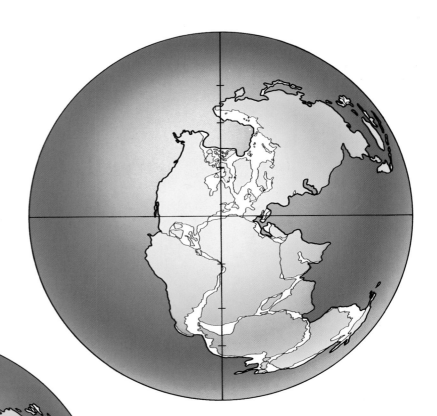

PERMIAN

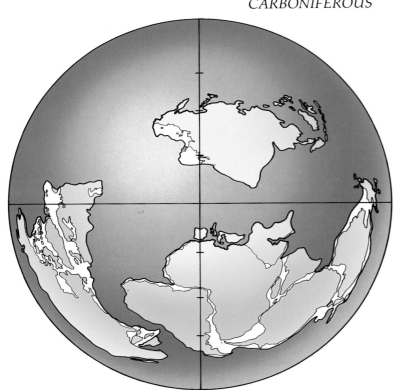

CARBONIFEROUS

EARLY DEVONIAN

EARLY DEVONIAN GLOBE
During the Early Devonian, between 408 and 387 million years ago, the continents formed two separate groups of landmasses, called Laurasia, which was in the northern hemisphere and Gondwana, which was in the southern.

CARBONIFEROUS GLOBE
During the Late Carboniferous, between 320 and 286 million years ago, Gondwana rotated northward, contacting Laurasia.

PERMIAN GLOBE
During the Late Permian, between 258 and 248 million years ago, Gondwana continued to move northward firmly uniting with Laurasia to form the supercontinent Pangaea that reached from pole to pole.

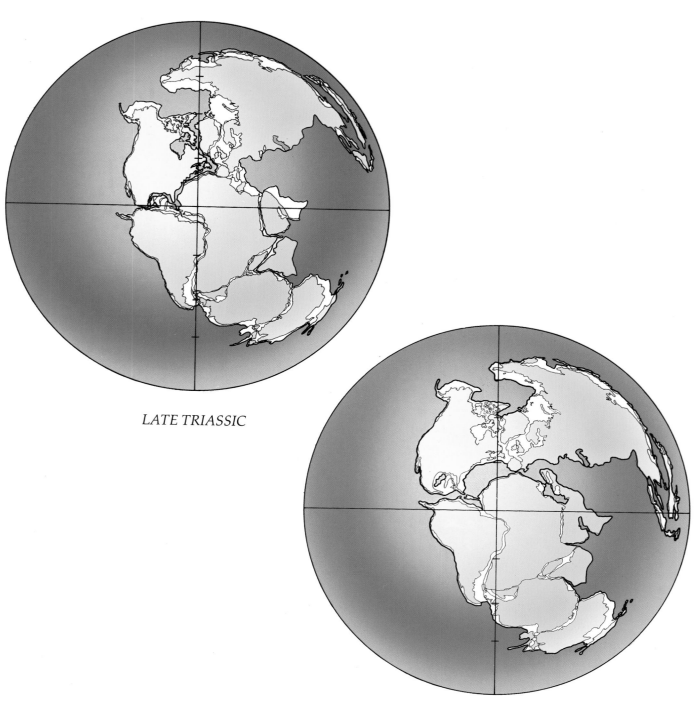

LATE TRIASSIC

LATE JURASSIC

LATE TRIASSIC GLOBE
During the Late Triassic and into the Early Jurassic, between 230 and 187 million years ago, Gondwana continued to move northward away from the southern pole.

LATE JURASSIC GLOBE
During the Late Jurassic, between 163 and 144 million years ago, an equatorial seaway appeared as the northern and southern continental landmasses separated.

LATE CRETACEOUS GLOBE
During the Late Cretaceous, between 84 and 65 million years ago, the continents continued to separate and began to assume the positions of the present day. (modified after Smith and Briden, 1977)

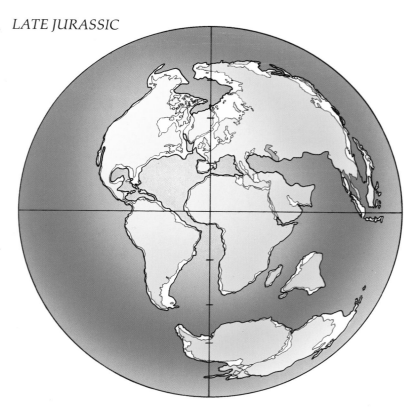

LATE CRETACEOUS

Eusthenopteron was one of the lobe-fin fishes that possessed primitive lungs which were capable of breathing air outside of the water. The lobe-fins were ancestral to the first amphibians. Eusthenopteron reached lengths of approximately 30 to 60 cms (1 to 2 ft).

Found in what is now eastern Greenland, Ichthyostega was one of the earliest amphibians that still retained many fish-like characteristics representing a missing link between the lobe-fin fish and the more advanced amphibians.

evolution is essentially a tool to aid life in its primary goal, to survive.

The descendants of animals like *Ichthyostega* continued to evolve, resulting in what we now call the Age of Amphibians. For millions of years the amphibians were prolific, with diverse, often bizarre progressions in shape and size, from the tiny to the huge. Semi-terrestrial, giant amphibians lumbered and crawled over the land but they always returned to their ancestral, aquatic habitats. Even though some of these primitive amphibians were capable of surviving on land, they were still tied to the water by their method of reproduction. The laying, incubation and hatching of the egg was still restricted to the water. The development of the egg had not exceeded beyond that of its fish-like ancestors.

Amphibian eggs are surrounded by a soft membrane that requires a watery environment for support and to prevent them from drying out. Once hatched, some amphibians continue to develop through a fully aquatic larval stage. While in this adolescent stage, a metamorphosis occurs, symbolically reliving in a single lifetime what took the earliest amphibians millions of years to achieve: the changing of the fish-like, gilled infant into an air-breathing adolescent with legs.

To become fully terrestrial and independent of their watery bind, another monumental adaptation occurred that went beyond the amphibian definition – the development of the amniotic egg. The amniotic egg could resist the injurious effects of the terrestrial world by forming a tough outer shell. With such an adaptation, some ancient amphibians crossed the line and by strict definition could no longer be considered amphibians, but were instead the first true reptiles. While strong enough to support and protect the embryo, the shell of the amniotic egg was delicate and porous enough to breathe, allowing oxygen to be absorbed into and carbon dioxide to be emitted from the egg. It contained a self-supporting environment to sustain the embryo as it developed beyond the larval

stage of its amphibious ancestors into a more mature hatchling closely resembling its parents. In addition to the nourishing yolk, the amniotic egg was composed of two unique sac-like membranes. Inside the first sac, the amnion, the embryo was surrounded in a further protective fluid. The second sac, the allantois, received the embryo's waste products as it continued to nourish from the yolk and grow.

There are some unique amphibians alive today that may reflect a transitional stage similar to what might have occurred prior to the development of the amniotic egg. These particular amphibians are little salamanders that lay tiny eggs, not necessarily in water but in moist or damp places on land. Unlike the aquatic-borne eggs of other amphibians, the terrestrial-laid eggs bypass the larval, or tadpole stages and simply hatch as small versions of their parents. Since these amphibian eggs lack the amnion and allantois they cannot be considered amniotic eggs. Speculating on the uniqueness of these terrestrial amphibian eggs, it is possible to conclude that the reptiles' immediate ancestors laid similarly primitive eggs on land before the amniotic egg evolved.

THE EARLIEST REPTILES

It is believed that some time during the Lower Carboniferous period, about 338 million years ago, the first amniotic eggs were laid on land, thereby breaking the bond to aquatic reproduction. The earliest primitive

The world's first great forests were formed by Archaeopteris trees that appeared in the Late Devonian. Ichthyostega, a small amphibian less than 1 m (3 ft) long, crawls from the water along a fallen log and enters the banks of the terrestrial world where towering trees stand as monumental columns that support a new environment.

19

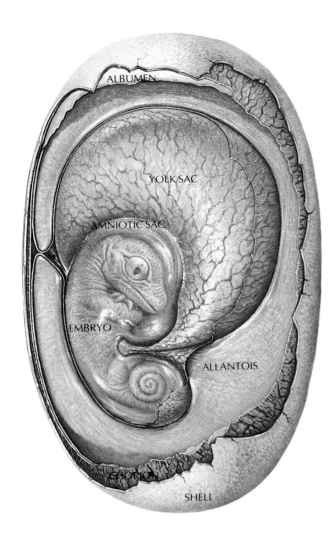

A cross-section of the amniotic egg that was the evolutionary advancement which broke the reptiles' ties to aquatic reproduction. The developing embryo is cushioned and held within the amnion. The yolk provides the embryo with nourishment while the allantois receives the embryo's waste products. The shell forms a protective outer covering.

reptiles were then free to exploit the untapped resources beyond the water's edge.

Vast forests of lycopods, huge trees related to the tiny present day clubmoss, towered to heights of 30 m (98 ft), forming a canopy of outstretched branches with clusters of long, slender leaves draping downwards. When the winds blew, the strap-like leaves of the *Siggilaria* lycopods bristled and formed an eerie blend of whistling sounds that sang hauntingly down to the world below. The undergrowth was composed of seed-ferns, tree-ferns, vines and horsetails. The ferns spread at various heights, from short, ground covering to tall trees forming soft, flowing layers of delicately detailed greenery. Thickly stalked horsetail ancestors, like *Calamites*, added a bizarre architecture to a strangely familiar, although alien, world.

Deep within these swamp jungles, sunlight streaks past the layers of foliage causing intermittent brilliant patches of light surrounded by densely shaded darkness. The intensifying heat of the morning sun causes a steamy haze to rise from the evaporating condensation that formed the night before. Lying motionless,

with its body flat and its legs splayed out to the sides, a tiny reptile called *Hylonomus*, absorbs the stimulating heat from the new day's sun. With its body temperature raised to efficient levels, the reptile's glistening eyes become alert to its immediate surroundings and patiently scan the movements of the breeze, the occasional drip of a dewdrop, as it awaits an unsuspecting victim to crawl or flitter by. In a startling burst of speed the reptile hurls forward over rocks, twigs and fallen branches, leaping into the air and landing with its jaws clenched about an insect struggling and twisting as it is carefully swallowed. With its hunger appeased, the reptile returns to the safety of its familiar surroundings.

The very earliest reptile, as yet unnamed, is from Scotland and lived about 338 million years ago, while *Hylonomus* is one of the earliest known reptiles, having lived during the Late Carboniferous period, some 300 million years ago. As tiny terrestrial lords of their vast jungle, it is fitting that their fossilized remains are often found within the castle-like walls of the petrified outer bark of *Siggilaria* lycopod tree stumps. The hollowed stumps must have provided a miniature fortress.

With the numbers of reptiles increasing, infiltration of the land increased. Competition between reptiles resulted in further adaptive changes. Changing environments promoted rapid evolution into modified shapes, sizes and specializations. The reptiles, it would seem, were on a tour of world dominance which lasted throughout the Mesozoic Era. It was a tour which suffered few challenges. Other forms of life, notably mammals, coexisted with the dinosaurs and because the mammals possessed different metabolisms and survived long after the extinction of the dinosaurs, competition and challenges for world dominance are often attributed to them. However, although mammals are quite different, it would be incorrect to depict dinosaurs and mammals as directly competing with each other.

Rather, the greatest challenge facing the dinosaurs was the physical change to the entire planet brought about by the two fundamental processes that are continuous: plate tectonics and evolution. The process of plate tectonics causes the environment to change, while evolution is the progressive adaptation of animal and plant life to those changes. The interrelationship of these two processes determine what forms of life exist and while changes brought about by evolution may be readily apparent, it is the all-encompassing changes in the physical world caused by plate tectonics that are perhaps more essential to life.

Deep within the lush lycopod forests of Siggilaria, *the crowded understorey of tree-ferns and seed-ferns is intertwined by giant* Callistophyton *vines which overhang an intrusive stalk of* Calamites. *One of the earliest reptiles,* Hylonomus, *leaps after an insectivorous meal before returning to the protection of the nearby lycopod stump.* Hylonomus *reached lengths of approximately 30 cms (1 ft).*

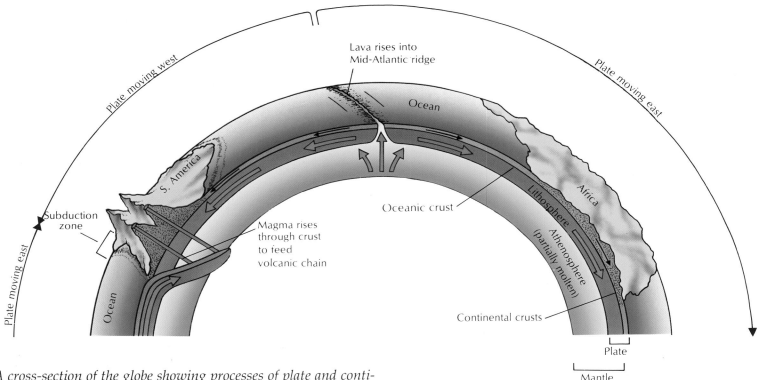

Lava rises into Mid-Atlantic ridge

Plate moving west

Plate moving east

Ocean

S. America

Subduction zone

Plate moving east

Oceanic crust

Magma rises through crust to feed volcanic chain

Ocean

Africa

Lithosphere

Athenosphere (partially molten)

Continental crusts

Plate

Mantle

A cross-section of the globe showing processes of plate and continental movement. At far left: an oceanic plate collides with a continental plate and is forced down into Earth's molten core where it is destroyed. Middle: the continents move farther apart as the oceanic plates that they rest on, separate and form the Mid-Atlantic ridge, or rift. The molten lava, which has risen to fill the gap, cools and hardens adding a new crust to the separating plates. (modified after Press and Siever, 1982)

The distribution of the lithospheric plates over the surface of the Earth. (modified after Press and Siever, 1982)

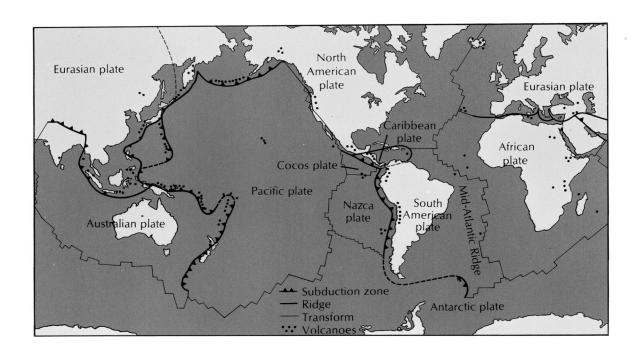

Eurasian plate

North American plate

Eurasian plate

Caribbean plate

African plate

Cocos plate

Pacific plate

Nazca plate

South American plate

Mid-Atlantic Ridge

Australian plate

▲▲ Subduction zone
— Ridge
— Transform
⋯ Volcanoes

Antarctic plate

PLATE TECTONICS
THE RESTLESS EARTH

When looking at Earth through geological time it is evident that vast physical changes have taken place altering the configuration and topography of the continents. The primary cause of these physical changes can be directly attributed to plate tectonics, which refers to the movement of the oceanic plates and continental landmasses.

The continents have undergone changes of shape and position ever since they were formed as parts of the cooler, outer crust of a molten planet. The outer crust is fractured, forming several sections called plates. Eight major plates and a number of smaller ones have been identified. All of these are moving,

Volcanic activity and mountain building are the results of plate collisions, and usually occur at plate boundaries. Chains of volcanoes can also occur as plates move over hot spots in the Earth's mantle.

being pushed, pulled and dragged along the convective currents of the molten world below. Collisions occur between the plates, resulting in spectacular topographical changes monumental in scope, but often underrated for their full significance.

When a plate moves, a series of events may take place. For example, one plate moving away from another will literally tear the crust of the Earth apart, unleashing fresh molten magma that fills the gap and forms a mountainous ridge of new protective crust. While continually separating at these rifting and division points, the continents are carried away from their original positions. The enlarged space between them eventually fills with oceanic waters.

When oceanic plates collide with continental plates, they change the very shape of the continents. Continental plates are lighter, so the denser, heavier oceanic plates are pushed downwards into the Earth's molten core, a process called subduction. This not only destroys the oceanic plate, but it can also buckle the edge

of the upper plate, forming mountain ranges along the margins of the affected continent. Volcanic activity can also be produced throughout the developing mountain range.

Mountains of even greater scope can result when two continental plates collide, forcing continents directly into each other. Enormous mountains can then be created as the edges of the impacting continents buckle upwards and are pushed to extreme heights.

Sometimes continents collide at less direct angles of impact and slide past each other. In these instances, mountain building or plate destruction may not take place. Instead, earthquakes will occur as continental breaks, or faults, shift to alleviate the accumulating stresses of the moving plates.

The circulating forces of Earth's molten interior can produce specific hot spots that melt through the plate and erupt as mountainous volcanoes. A series of volcanic mountains are produced as a plate moves over a hot spot. Should these mountains become large

Glaciation has occurred repeatedly throughout Earth's history. During the Carboniferous and Permian, Gondwana was affected by one of the most extensive periods of glaciation as it moved across the southern pole.

enough in the ocean, a line of islands is formed.

All the changes caused by the process of plate tectonics modify and alter the positions and shapes of continents and surrounding oceans and directly influence Earth's climate with global ramifications. In turn, the changing climates alter the environments that support life. Ultimately, life has reacted to the changing environments by further adaptations, selective redispersal or extinction.

MOVING CONTINENTS AND THEIR EFFECTS ON CLIMATES AND ENVIRONMENTS

The continents as they are now spread around the globe are subjected to numerous climatic influences. The frozen polar caps at the highest latitudes are in sharp contrast to the warm tropical latitudes near the Equator. In addition, the topographical features of a continent directly influence the potential climate of the

various regions that make up the continent. Together with the oceanic waters and Earth's atmosphere, these factors combine in a complex, interrelated process of events which determine what kinds of climate will occur in different parts of the globe.

It would be reasonable then to expect that as the continents moved they would have experienced changing weather conditions, producing different kinds of climates. This is exactly what happened.

The present conditions of glacial polar caps over the Arctic and Antarctic might appear to have always existed. The extreme high latitudes might also appear to automatically perpetuate the frozen zones of the North and South Poles throughout Earth's history. This may be a logical assumption, but it would be incorrect. In fact, polar ice has appeared, disappeared and reappeared during Earth's different phases. During the Mesozoic Era, there were no polar ice caps, but long before the dinosaurs, during the Carboniferous and Permian, a single vast polar cap formed over much of the southern hemisphere, while the northern pole experienced only a slight glaciation. Primarily,

Extending for miles along the horizon of what is now the Delaware Basin in Texas, are layers of mineral deposits that accumulated from evaporite seas during the Late Permian. Even after millions of years, the evaporite deposits remain as reliable climate indicators of the warm and arid conditions that once existed.

the presence or absence of polar ice caps can be attributed to the continental positions during those specific periods. Similarly, other types of climate, including tropical zones, are all affected by the positions of the continents.

During the Carboniferous and Permian periods, glacial activity was variable and restricted almost entirely to the southern hemisphere. Glaciation occurs as the heat from the sun differently affects land and water surfaces. Water surfaces heat slowly but retain their heat longer than the land. Land more rapidly reaches higher temperatures than water but is unable to retain the heat so effectively. This less efficient heat retention causes the surface of the land to cool faster, dropping far below temperatures that water may reach. Therefore, landmasses that enter the higher latitudes of the polar regions may be unable to maintain enough heat to prevent the formation of polar caps. During the Carboniferous and Permian, then, an increasing base became glacial as larger portions of the continental landmass moved over the South Pole.

Extraordinary geological events during the Permian contributed to a vast glacial expansion in the southern hemisphere that encroached beyond the polar region into subtropical latitudes as low as 30° south. Through the ages, the continents of both hemispheres had been drawn towards each other, colliding to become two supercontinents: Gondwana, in the southern hemisphere, and Laurasia, in the northern. But during the Permian, these two supercontinents joined together, forming an even greater supercontinent called Pangaea. Most of the impact was caused by Gondwana as it thrust northwards striking Laurasia at equatorial latitudes, and uplifting the continental crust into towering mountain ranges. Even while surrounded by a warm equatorial climate, these mountains rose to elevations cold enough to produce glacial ice deposits.

Pangaea continued to shift during the Late Permian, forming a single continental landmass reaching from pole to pole. The huge glacial accumulations that spread from the South Pole reduced in range, as the southernmost continental landmasses moved away from the polar region. As land approached the northern pole, a much smaller polar ice cap began to form.

Uncovered after 210 million years, large sections of fossilized tree trunks lay scattered on the deserts of Arizona as remnants of the once great forests of the Triassic.

Along with the fluctuating changes brought about by plate tectonics, climatic conditions are continuously influenced by astronomical forces. Earth's rotation around the Sun may be constant but because Earth's axis is tilted, an annual rotation produces a seasonal variance of the length and intensity of sunlight that reaches Earth. This causes the seasons to alternate between the two hemispheres, with long days in one corresponding to short days in the other.

The intensity of solar radiation is also variable depending on where it reaches Earth. The poles and higher latitudes receive less intense sunlight, while the Equator and lower latitudes receive more direct, stronger amounts of sunlight. This variability heats the oceans, continents and atmosphere, to different amounts.

Earth's atmosphere circulates in a complex relationship to the varying temperature extremes of Earth's surface. In addition, the planet's rotation deflects the atmospheric and oceanic currents from having north and south directions, forcing them into east and west circulating flows, commonly referred to as the Coriolis effect.

Throughout Earth's history, the atmosphere has circulated the globe in distinct bands, or zones, between different latitudes. These zones reflect the varying rates of heat exchange between the warmer Equator and the colder poles. These three zones, circulating in

Towering to heights of 60 m (195 ft), forests of the primitive conifer Araucarioxylon *dominated the Triassic landscape.*

each hemisphere, are known as tradewinds, westerlies and easterlies.

Tradewinds are the warmest atmospheric currents and they flow in a westerly direction from 30° north and south, towards the Equator. The tradewinds pull the moisture from the surface of the land, often leaving vast deserts in zones of near 30° latitudes. As the tradewinds continue towards the Equator, evaporative moisture is also drawn up from the warm equatorial waters, and redeposited as rainfall into tropical and subtropical zones.

Westerlies consist of generally cooler winds that are higher in latitude than the tradewinds, from approximately 30° to 60°. They flow eastwards, in the opposite direction to the tradewinds. The westerlies flow over more temperate climatic zones.

Above the westerlies, at still higher latitudes, is a third and final band of atmospheric currents called the easterlies which has the coldest circulating atmosphere and flows in a westward direction. The easterlies cover the coolest zones of the Earth, including the poles.

The scope and shape of the three atmospheric zones are variable and can increase or reduce their range according to the continental arrangements. Without the various topographical features of the continents that influence and impede the atmospheric currents, these zones would maintain more regular paths of direct circulation around the globe. However, mountain ranges and vast continental expanses can deflect atmospheric currents, expanding or reducing the range of the zones. This has a significant effect on where different kinds of climate and environment will occur within the different atmospheric zones. Each atmospheric zone produces characteristically different types of climatic conditions. Typically, the tradewinds will produce tropical climates and environments. At higher latitudes, the westerlies create sub-tropical and more temperate climates and environments. Progressively cooler easterlies reach to the poles, causing the coldest environments.

It is possible to see where different kinds of climates and environments have existed in the past by examining the different strata that have been deposited on the continents. Fossils of animals and plants found can also be good indicators, as long as they are understood well enough to be compared with living analogues. Other climatic indicators that are not organic can be even more reliably accurate. Tillites, evaporites and aeolian sandstones reveal changes that have occurred specifically due to climatic conditions.

Tillites are glacial deposits of stones that have been transported and accumulated by glacial activity. The stones and boulders that form the tillite deposits are distinctively marked by numerous scratches and grooves caused by the rubbing action during their transport. Regardless of the current climate in which tillites are found, they remain a positive testimony of when and where glacial-producing climates existed in the past.

Warm and arid climates can also leave their mark. Warming coastal lagoons and even entire epicontinental seas (see glossary) can shrink by evaporation, or periodically dry up, leaving evaporite deposits, which consist of water-soluble minerals that form sedimentary layers as the heated water continues to shrink and evaporate. The minerals that are least water soluble are deposited first, and are subsequently covered by layers of minerals which remain within the water until removed by the evaporative process. Salt and potash ultimately form the uppermost layers. Since the water-soluble minerals are deposited in a distinct pattern, it is possible to follow the deposits of water through time as they fluctuate in size and range, shrinking through evaporation or refilling from other water sources. The arid conditions that produce evaporites are generally caused by winds, and even the winds' directions are often recorded by the aeolian sandstones that were once free-flowing sand dunes around the shores of the evaporite seas.

For a more complete understanding of how the continents, climates and environments affected dinosaurs, it becomes essential to expand the scope of studies beyond just the fossilized remains of dinosaurs, and include a study of the conditions of the world in which they lived. For over 140 million years, during the Mesozoic Era, dinosaurs not only survived, but continued to evolve and change into new species.

What brought about these new and different species of dinosaurs was the natural process of evolution reacting to the changes occurring within the environments.

Before the Mesozoic, the earliest amphibians and reptiles lived within the tropical and equatorial latitudes. Cooler climates of the higher latitudes prevented these animals from venturing beyond their warmer environments. Just as today's amphibians and reptiles are ectothermic, the cold-blood amphibians and reptiles that first evolved were restricted to where they could warm and regulate their body temperature to sufficient levels. In the same way that these reptiles and all living things have specific environmental requirements, so the dinosaurs must have had their own necessities and limits. The climatic conditions of the Mesozoic must have produced temperatures that were compatible with the dinosaurs' thermoregulatory systems. Sufficient quantities of edible vegetation must also have been available as a supporting base of the food chain.

MESOZOIC LIFE

The three periods of the Mesozoic Era are called the Triassic, Jurassic and Cretaceous. During these periods the plants, like the animals, continued to evolve and modify. Plants that had been so successful through the Triassic and Jurassic were challenged by flowering plants which had enhanced modes of reproduction during the Mid-Cretaceous.

The Triassic followed a period in which glaciation fluctuated greatly within the southern hemisphere over Gondwana, ultimately shrinking and melting out of existence in a gradually warming world. With the disappearance of glacial activity, the flora within Gondwana suffered the challenging effects of a changing climate. The temperate and seasonal cooling that resulted from the presence of the southern polar ice cap had produced plants best designed for seasonal rigours. Deciduous plants like *Glossopteris*, benefited by shedding their leaves and remaining in a reduced state of torpor while winter prevailed. However, when the winter no longer brought cold extremes, and a warmer and dryer annual consistency followed, there was a dramatic adaptation of the floral environment.

Gymnosperm giants, including primitive conifers, ginkgoes and cycads dominated the Jurassic landscape. The small dinosaur, Ornitholestes *walks under a canopy of* Brachyphyllum *branches, past a cluster of stately cycads and grove of shimmering ginkgoes. Herbaceous lycopods and ferns, contribute to the understorey of plants.*

The badlands of Alberta exist today where Late Cretaceous dinosaurs and mixed hardwood forests once thrived.

By the beginning of the Triassic, the northern and southern continents of Laurasia and Gondwana had already collided along near-equatorial latitudes, creating the supercontinent, Pangaea. No longer separated by oceanic waters, the plants of Laurasia and Gondwana could interchange, and radiate throughout both hemispheres as never before. The floral exchange distributed plants that were better adapted to the consistently warm and dry climates. The entire *Glossopteris* flora of Gondwana that was so prevalent before the Triassic, became extinct and was replaced by less temperate types of plants, like the seed-fern *Dicroidium*, that were more adaptive to tropical and sub-tropical climates. Cycads, ginkgoes, conifers and other gymnosperms became the dominant plants through the Triassic, Jurassic and early part of the Cretaceous.

Vast forests of towering primitive conifers like *Araucarioxylon* formed a dense canopy of umbrella-like branches that enclosed the upper margins of the forests at heights of 45 to 60 m (146 to 195 ft). Beneath the towering trees was an understorey of ferns. Because of the warm and arid climate that prevailed, these forests were widespread from the lowlands and flood plains to the uplands, where sufficient water was available. Often though, the life-sustaining water was also destructive, causing rivers that meandered through the forests to undercut and topple the giant trees. Fallen trees, covered by sediment, became entombed and gave future prospects for fossilization. The present day deserts of Arizona in the USA have weathered away at these trees to expose them to sunlight after 210 million years. Their original woody substance is not preserved, but their exact shape and minute details were replaced as they became mineralized, often in brilliant colours.

Just as the fallen pillars of Greek or Roman architecture indicate that ancient cities were once populated with life, the fallen trees remain as petrified forests reflecting the housing of their prehistoric inhabitants.

Throughout the world, the inhabitants of these Triassic forests were mostly small, insectivorous reptiles, including procolophonids that resemble the modern horn-toads; iguana-like *Trilophosaurus*, well-adapted for climbing; other true lizards, and the remarkable gliding lizards, like *Icarosaurus* and *Kuehneosaurus* that made primitive and limited attempts to conquer the air.

On the lower edge of the forest, were wetter swamplands. *Neocalamites*, giant tree-like horsetails, grew densely along the water's shore. Bennettitales, a distant relative to cycads, was better adapted to wetter environments and ferns produced the remaining ground cover between the water and the higher forests. Within the water and along its banks were large amphibians, like metoposaurs and huge phytosaurs that lived a crocodilian lifestyle.

The *Araucarioxylon* forests lay in the humid lowlands, while above, on the dryer uplands, cycads, ginkgoes and conifers and other gymnosperms dominated the landscape. Within these uplands were the earliest dinosaurs, and the last of the mammal-like reptiles which were scarce and dwindling in numbers.

There was a broad, worldwide similarity within the fauna and, to a lesser degree, the flora of Pangaea during the Triassic, but by the end of the period, faunal replacement occurred leaving tiny mammals as a

A dominant Late Cretaceous assemblage of angiosperms surrounds a large, shallow pond which a carnivorous Albertosaurus has entered. Vine-covered oaks are in the background, a dogwood is on the bank of the left foreground, and a small magnolia and large ficus are on the right.

lingering remnant of the once thriving mammal-like reptile heritage. During this time the dinosaurs virtually replaced their own ancestors, the thecodonts, to become the dominant terrestrial vertebrates of the Mesozoic.

The Jurassic continued with the expansion of dinosaurian faunas, distributed globally with a similar consistency of types. The flora was still dominated by gymnosperms, as in the Triassic, but with more equal distribution between both hemispheres. Pangaea was still one supercontinent, but because of continual shifting, it began to separate along equatorial latitudes by the end of the Jurassic.

During the Cretaceous, the continents continued to break away from each other. The enlarging seaways separating the continents became restrictive barriers blocking the open flow of distribution that had previously placed the dinosaurs on all of the continents.

The cycads and ginkgoes that were so prevalent during the Jurassic were less prolific after the Early Cretaceous, while the conifers broadened their domi-

nance among the gymnosperms. After their mysterious appearance, the flowering plants, angiosperms, developed substantially during the Cretaceous and as a result, the gymnosperms gradually diminished in scope as the angiosperms took over a new worldwide dominance.

At the end of the Cretaceous period, 65 million years ago, the dinosaurs breathed their final breaths and from that moment the history of our planet changed. It has been thought that dinosaurs suppressed the evolution of mammals. Had the dinosaurs not died out, would the course of mammalian evolution have been altered or possibly postponed indefinitely? Would Mankind have evolved as it did? The cause of the dinosaurs' extinction suggests a significant relationship with man's own existence. Therefore, it is not surprising that numerous theories abound each year claiming to have solved the mystery of what killed the dinosaurs.

Regardless of the specifics, all extinction theories can be placed in two categories: either a gradual pro-

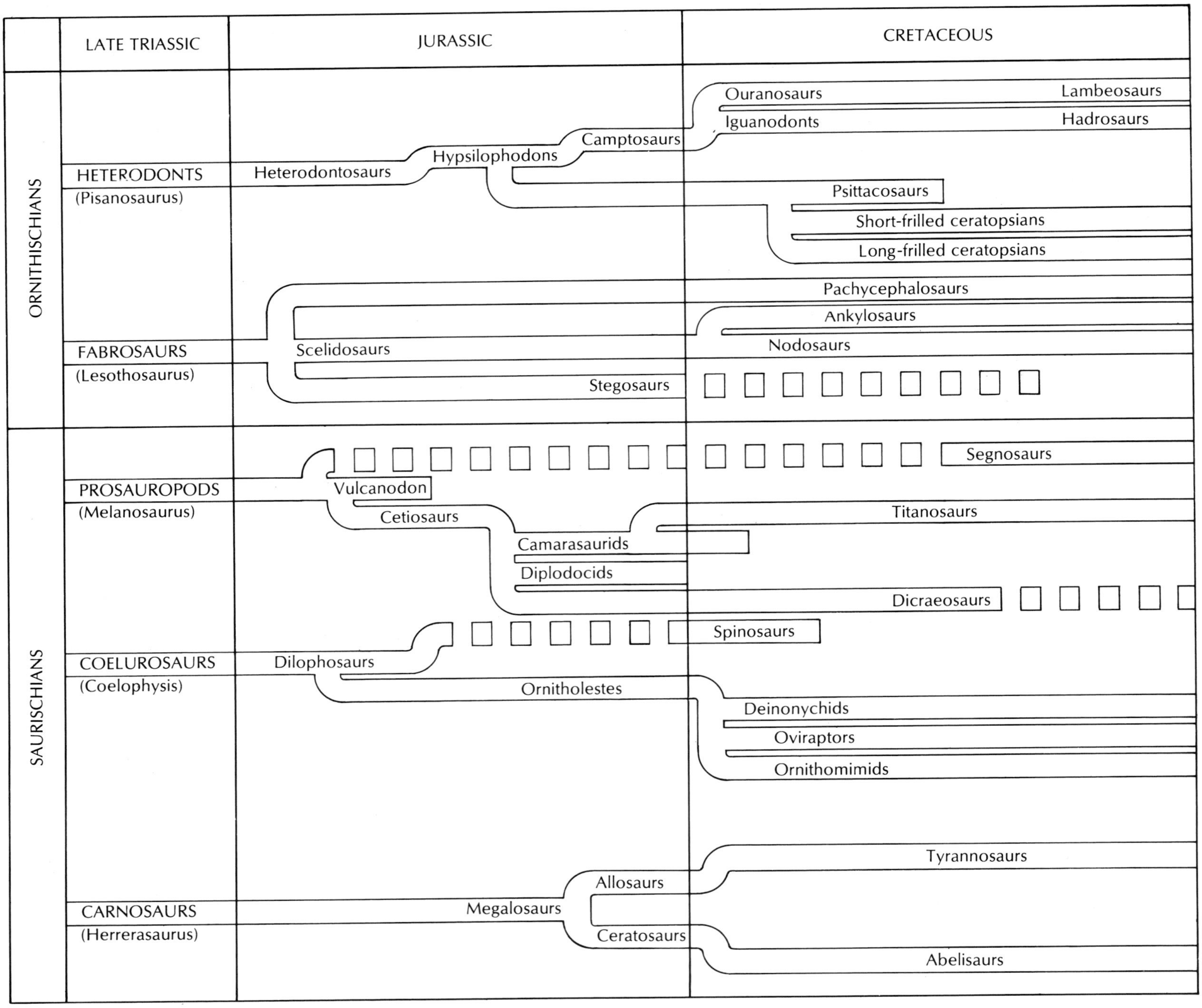

LATE TRIASSIC	JURASSIC	CRETACEOUS

ORNITHISCHIANS

Ouranosaurs — Lambeosaurs
Iguanodonts — Hadrosaurs
Camptosaurs
Hypsilophodons
HETERODONTS (Pisanosaurus) — Heterodontosaurs
Psittacosaurs
Short-frilled ceratopsians
Long-frilled ceratopsians
Pachycephalosaurs
Ankylosaurs
FABROSAURS (Lesothosaurus) — Scelidosaurs — Nodosaurs
Stegosaurs

SAURISCHIANS

Segnosaurs
PROSAUROPODS (Melanosaurus) — Vulcanodon
Cetiosaurs — Titanosaurs
Camarasaurids
Diplodocids
Dicraeosaurs
Spinosaurs
COELUROSAURS (Coelophysis) — Dilophosaurs
Ornitholestes
Deinonychids
Oviraptors
Ornithomimids
Tyrannosaurs
Allosaurs
CARNOSAURS (Herrerasaurus) — Megalosaurs
Ceratosaurs
Abelisaurs

DINOSAUR FAMILY TREE
During the Triassic, the evolution of the dinosaurs stemmed from five basic groups: fabrosaurs, heterodonts, coelurosaurs, carnosaurs, and prosauropods. This chart, or family tree, demonstrates the relationship of the different types of dinosaurs.

cess lasting perhaps millions of years, or a catastrophic event, violently ending the reign of the dinosaurs in a relatively short period of time. The emphasis on looking for a cause of the dinosaurs' extinction often neglects more significant questions: what were dinosaurs? What caused them to exist and thrive as the successful animals they were? *Dinosaurs: A Global View* aims to examine these questions and look at how and why the dinosaurs existed in harmony with an ever-changing world for 140 million years.

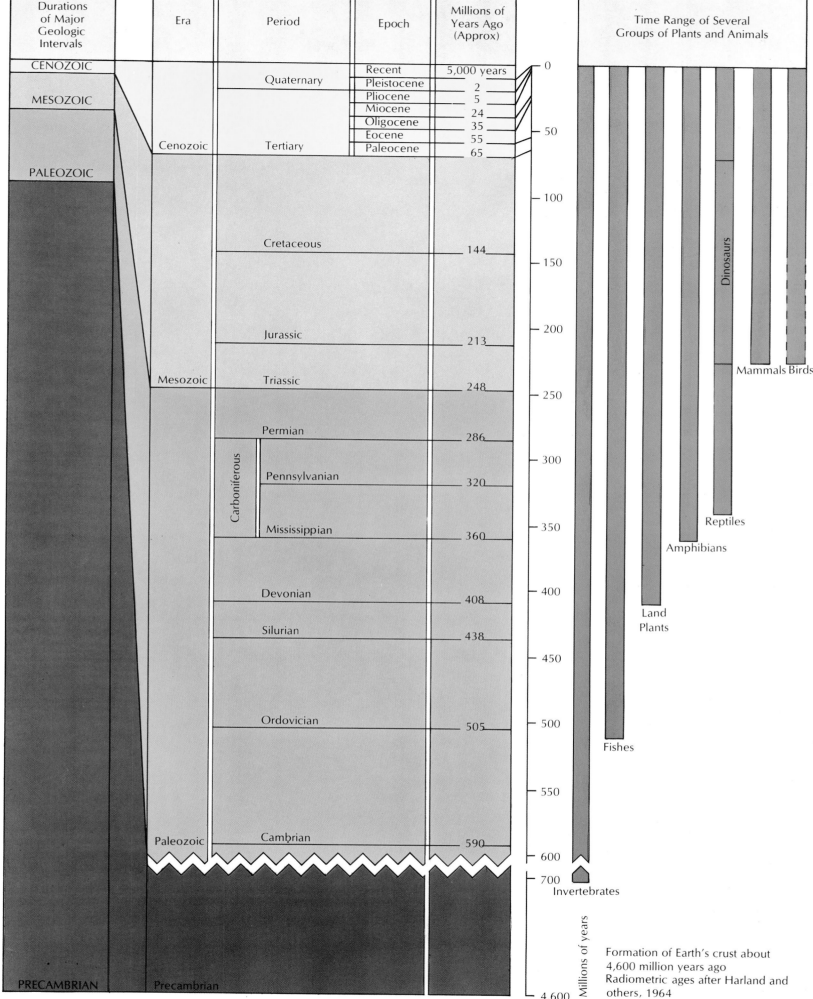

GEOLOGIC TIME SCALE

Relative Durations of Major Geologic Intervals	Era	Period	Epoch	Millions of Years Ago (Approx)
CENOZOIC	Cenozoic	Quaternary	Recent	5,000 years
			Pleistocene	2
MESOZOIC		Tertiary	Pliocene	5
			Miocene	24
PALEOZOIC			Oligocene	35
			Eocene	55
			Paleocene	65
	Mesozoic	Cretaceous		144
		Jurassic		213
		Triassic		248
	Paleozoic	Permian		286
		Carboniferous — Pennsylvanian		320
		Carboniferous — Mississippian		360
		Devonian		408
		Silurian		438
		Ordovician		505
		Cambrian		590
PRECAMBRIAN	Precambrian			4,600

Time Range of Several Groups of Plants and Animals

Dinosaurs
Mammals Birds
Reptiles
Amphibians
Land Plants
Fishes
Invertebrates

Millions of years

Formation of Earth's crust about 4,600 million years ago
Radiometric ages after Harland and others, 1964

TIME SCALE OF LIFE
Geologic time scale showing the appearance of life through time.

33

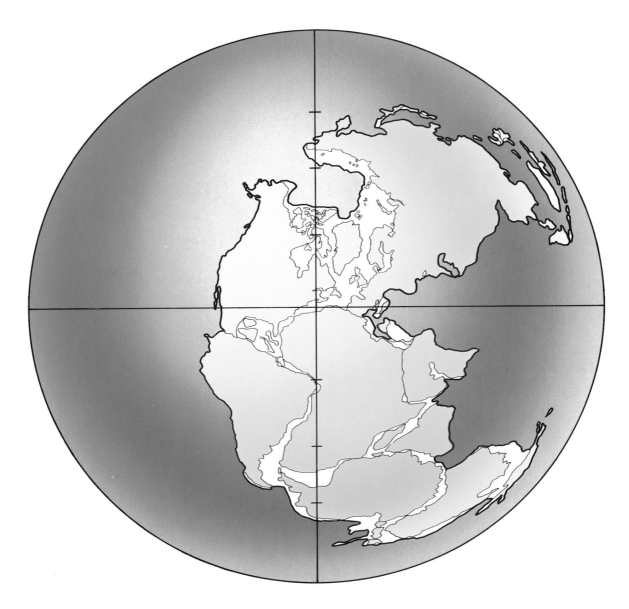

PERMIAN GLOBE
With Antarctica located over the South Pole, and much of Gondwana also within high polar latitudes, the formation of a vast glacial ice cap covered much of the continents in the southern hemisphere. The North Pole was without a glacial ice cap for most of the Permian, until the Laurasian continents moved far enough *northward to initiate the formation of glaciers which even then, remained comparatively small. The world climate consisted of colder and more temperate conditions than experienced later during the Mesozoic.*

CHAPTER II
THE PERMIAN

THE BAND OF LIFE

In order to understand the development of dinosaurs from the beginning it is essential to go back to the time before they existed to look at the conditions which prevailed during the Permian, and the sequence of events that led up to the evolution of the dinosaurs.

During the Permian, reptiles already populated the land. Amphibians, although restricted to areas near or in water, were still quite prevalent and some attained

enormous proportions. Evolution it seemed would directly advance reptiles towards the development of dinosaurs but instead it took a detour, turning towards mammal-like reptiles. Why this unexpected change occurred can be explained if one analyses the climatic and consequent environmental conditions in which the animals lived.

The Permian was a period of time during which there was a global transition of ecological extremes. Climates and environments that had lasted steadily

Bursting upwards from the silt, the bottom dwelling amphibian, Eryops, *lunges after* Orthacanthus, *a shark. In the foreground is the small amphibian* Trimerorhachis. *The approximate length of* Eryops *is 1.6 m (5 ft),* Orthacanthus *60 cms (2 ft), and* Trimerorhachis *1 m (3 ft).*

for millions of years, began to change. Throughout the equatorial zones, seasonless periods of consistently warm and wet climates modified into warm, wet and dry periods of distinct seasons. At higher latitudes, the temperate zones were similarly affected by wet and dry periods, but with cooler extremes than found in the equatorial zones. The southern hemisphere experienced the continual withdrawal of the vast glacia-

tion that, just prior to the Permian during the Late Carboniferous, had reached as far as 30° latitude. A global warming continued throughout the Permian gradually diminishing the vast southern glacier. By the end of the Permian the glacier had been reduced to a comparatively small remnant remaining over what is now Australia.

The earliest amphibians and reptiles were restricted

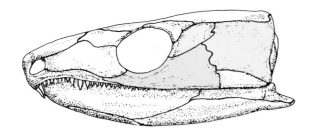

ANAPSID *(CAPTORHINUS)*

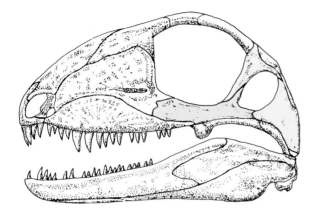

SYNAPSID *(HAPTODUS)*

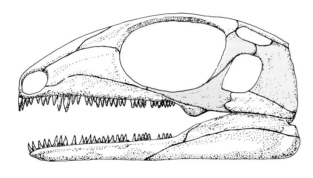

DIAPSID *(PETROLACOSAURUS)*

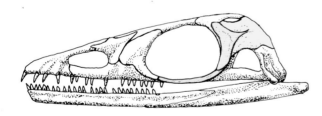

PARAPSID *(PACHYPLEUROSAURUS)*

All reptiles can be classified into one of four basic types. Anapsids are the most primitive having no openings behind the eyes. Synapsids have a temporal opening bordered by the jugal, squamosal and postorbital bones. Diapsids have two openings behind each eye, separated by the squamosal and postorbital bones. Parapsid/ euryapsid skulls have a single opening behind each eye located above the squamosal and postorbital bones. Key: Pink = jugal, Yellow = squamosal, Blue = postorbital. (Captorhinus after Romer, 1976; Haptodus after Currie, 1979; Petrolacosaurus after Reisz, 1981; Pachypleurosaurus after Carroll and Gaskill, 1985)

to equatorial zones where tropical and sub-tropical climates prevailed. As ectothermic, or 'cold-blooded' animals, they were limited to only those environments that were consistently warm enough to provide the additional source of ambient heat (see glossary), which their own metabolism could not produce. Even though plants had adapted to withstand the colder extremes of the higher latitudes, these areas remained empty of animal life. Here was a major part of the world with a completely untouched food supply (including insects). No vertebrate animal had as yet developed the necessary adaptations to allow entry and survival within these colder climates.

Isolated during the Early Permian by the climatic extremes that existed within the higher latitudes, the amphibians and reptiles nonetheless thrived in the lower, equatorial latitudes which produced consistently warm and wet, tropical and sub-tropical environments. Throughout the continental landmasses, it was only along the equatorial regions that a distinct band of life, which included terrestrial animals, existed. It extended within these latitudes from the west coast of North America, across Europe to the Ural mountains on the eastern coast of Russia. The fossil record representing the band of life is most complete in western North America and to a lesser degree in central Europe.

Throughout the band of life, the densely forested jungles were lush and overgrown with an abundance of entwined vegetation that steadily accumulated into a thick deposition of decomposing layers. Eventually this would become carbon-rich coal beds and petroleum deposits. Fallen trees, that were undermined and toppled by the eroding actions of expanding waterways, would often float along the surface of rivers and lakes. Transported by the waters' currents, log jams piled onto the banks and water-saturated trunks, branches and smaller debris of plants settled as a murky residue on the bottom of lakes and ponds.

Most of the animal life was centred around the lakes, ponds, rivers and streams, and as such was tied to an aquatic-based food web. From the water came the plants that supported the invertebrates and herbivores, and in turn, carnivores preyed upon these animals. The pattern of food sources became more complex as new forms of animals appeared, but invariably, there was a strong tie to, or dependence on, the water that initially supported the food web.

ERYOPS AND THE AQUATIC FOOD WEB

Picture the silent movement of an uprooted tree, floating in shallow water near a lakeshore, casting an ominous shadow that slowly slides over the mat of vegetation covering the lake bottom. Gazing upwards, two large, gleaming eyes shift their position as the shadow from the floating log approaches. Temporarily dulled by the darkness of the shadow and held motionless, the eyes regain a glimmering sparkle as

With a 60-cms (2-ft) long lungfish, Sagenodus, *dangling from its mouth, an* Ophiacodon *attracts other hungry reptiles of its kind.* Ophiacodon *reached lengths of 2 m (6 ft).*

the log drifts away and dim sunlight flashes back over the lake's surface. The shapeless observer lies hidden, partially covered amid the soft debris of the lake bottom. Unmoving, except for the shifting of its watching eyes and occasional emittance of small, shimmering bubbles rising to the surface, the creature patiently rests and waits.

Beyond its scope, paddles *Trimerorhachis*, a moderate-sized amphibian, almost 1 m (3 ft) long, that moves up towards the surface, and gliding near the floating log trails a primitive shark over 60 cms (2 ft) in length. With its eyes shifting forward, the shapeless observer focuses on the small shark. Erupting from a billowing cloud of rotting plant debris and sediment, broad jaws well over 30 cms (1 ft) wide, gape open and surround the startled shark. Such moments of tranquility and terror were repeated again and again for millions of years as the amphibians proliferated in their watery domain.

The large labyrinthodont amphibian, *Eryops*, was one of the 'shapeless observers' that preyed upon the smaller aquatic vertebrates, such as the primitive shark, *Orthacanthus*. Without doubt, *Eryops*' diet was diverse, randomly including any unwary fish or am-

phibian that happened to wander too close. Numerous coprolites (see glossary) associated with the fossil remains of *Eryops* have been found to contain undigested remnants of *Orthacanthus* indicating that this shark was a large and common part of the *Eryops* diet.

Eryops was a broad, bulky amphibian that reached lengths of 1.6 m (5 ft) or more. Its stocky and muscular legs allowed it to leave the confines of the water, and become semi-terrestrial. But it was an awkward hulking mass, lumbering along the beach fronts and banks of its aquatic home. Fearsome as it must have been, preying upon its aquatic food chain, *Eryops* itself fell prey to others, becoming just another part of an ever-growing food web.

The cycle of the food web was enlarging throughout the Early Permian, as more terrestrial amphibians and reptiles broadened their horizons. However, even with terrestrial capabilities, ties to aquatic food sources were strong and difficult to break. For much of the Early Permian, the larger animals remained separated from the dryer uplands, and stayed within the boundaries of the aquatic food web that was abundant in the wetter lowlands. This restriction was far from being a hindrance, for as long as the environment

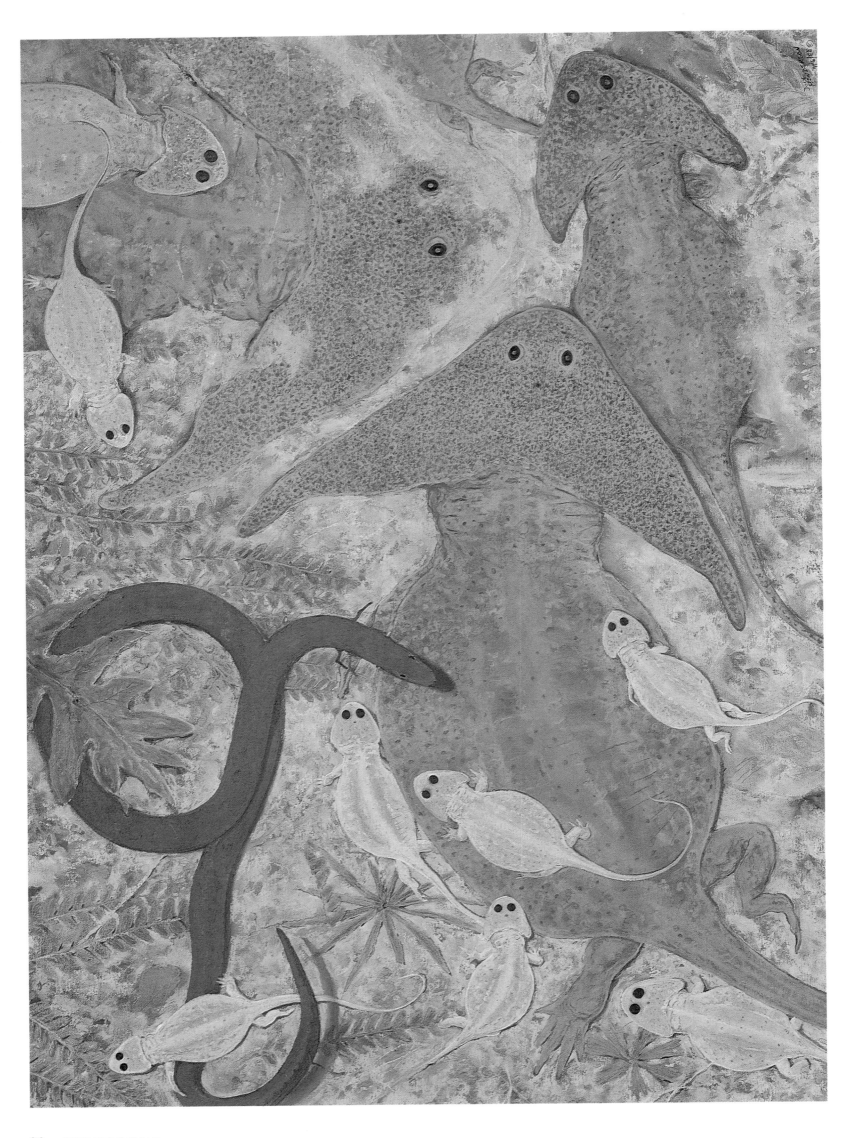

existed, so could the life it supported. While the amphibians and reptiles that survived within the aquatic-based food webs often proliferated into animals of great size, at first only small animals could break ties with the aquatic food supply. Small, insectivorous reptiles spread into different environments, away from the water and into the relatively dryer uplands. However, these carnivorous reptiles remained confined to their small size because their only available prey in the uplands consisted of insects and small invertebrates. It was only after omnivorous, and fully herbivorous, reptiles of increasingly large size invaded the dryer uplands that the larger meat-eaters had a food supply to sustain their appetites.

Meanwhile, in the lowlands, the reptiles continued to thrive and diversify. Their experimental, evolutionary adaptations allowed them to probe into previously untried environments. The similarities of their general body shape hid the fact that these early reptiles had broken into distinctly separate groups, co-existing with each other. At this time, all of the groups were definitely reptilian, but they continued to evolve along different paths while retaining distinguishing characteristics that would be used to place them into the ancestral stock from which they came. The position of certain openings in the skulls of these animals determines the group to which the animal belongs.

THE DIFFERENT TYPES OF REPTILES

Based on the manner in which the openings of the skull are located, there are four groups, or classifications into which all reptiles can be placed. The first group is called the anapsids. This is the most primitive condition, retained from its amphibious heritage, in which the rear portion of the skull behind the orbits remained solid, without additional openings.

The next group to evolve were the synapsids. Behind each orbit in this group was a single opening located between the jugal, squamosal, and postorbital. This might appear strange because it is from this

Nestled on the water's bottom of silt and plant debris are juvenile and adult Diplocaulus *with a coiled* Lysorophus. *Both* Lysorophus *and juvenile* Diplocaulus *were amphibians which could burrow within the mud and aestivate to survive droughts until rains replenished their water-holes. However, in addition to being too large, the expanded crescent-shaped skulls of adult* Diplocaulus *prevented them from being able to burrow and survive by aestivating.* Lysorophus *reached lengths of 60 cms (2 ft) and full grown* Diplocaulus *were as much as 1 m (3 ft) long.*

incredibly early group of reptiles that the ancestry of mammals began.

Independently from the development of the synapsids, arose a third group of reptiles evolving from the basal anapsid stock – the diapsids. It is from the diapsids that all other reptiles, including the dinosaurs, are derived. Diapsids' skulls are characterized by a pair of temporal openings (see glossary) behind each orbit. One opening is similarly placed to those in the synapsids, while the other opening is placed higher up, above the squamosal and postorbital.

The fourth group is a loose assemblage called the parapsids, or sometimes, the euryapsids. The origins are poorly known, but are probably derived from the early diapsids. They retain the upper openings as in the diapsid condition, but the lower openings are lost. Members of this fourth group are usually uniquely specialized for aquatic lifestyles.

The function of the temporal openings, or absence of openings, among all reptiles, relates to how and where the jaw muscles attach to the skull. Exactly why this is different in the four groups is not fully understood, but fortunately the differences remain reliable characteristics for classificiation.

EARLY PELYCOSAURS

Primitive pelycosaurs were the earliest synapsids. One of these was *Ianthasaurus*, a small insectivorous reptile, about 60 cms (2 ft) long. Experimenting in thermo-regulatory adaptations for terrestrial environments, *Ianthasaurus* evolved a high, crested sail along the length of its back. Unique and efficient, this sail might have given this small reptile the advantage of broadening its territorial range away from the aquatic food web and into the more remote uplands. While still relatively small and insectivorous, the descendants of *Ianthasaurus* became less dependent on an insect diet, increasing their preference for plants as a food source. As omnivores, they continued to increase in size from the benefits of a larger food supply. Success in this process finally led to its considerably larger descendants, like *Edaphosaurus*, which had totally adapted to a herbivorous diet.

Other primitive pelycosaurs that were insectivorous at first, became increasingly carnivorous, preying upon fish, amphibians and other reptiles found within the aquatic food web. Although many of the early pelycosaurs increased in size because of the abundance within the aquatic food web, it is interesting that a smaller, moderate-sized pelycosaur, like *Haptodus*, ventured outside the aquatic food web into different environments after *Ianthasaurus*. *Haptodus* was only

1 m (3 ft) long at best, but irrespective of its size, what was significantly missing was the development of a sail along its back. It would seem that the environmental conditions that necessitated the development of a thermoregulatory sail on *Ianthasaurus* would require a similar adaptation by *Haptodus*. Their fossil remains are found together in the Garnett quarry of Kansas, so it is likely that they co-existed at times and that *Ianthasaurus* could have been part of the *Haptodus* diet. Perhaps *Haptodus* was only a temporary intruder into this environment.

Adding to the mystery of the environmental stresses which must have been present in the newly exploited environments, is the fact that the carnivorous descendants of *Haptodus* not only increased in size along with the larger descendants of *Ianthasaurus*, but eventually, they too evolved sails.

Diverse environments probably caused the synapsids to evolve into different types of reptiles, specially adapted to different requirements. Indeed, the synapsids continued to evolve beyond the Permian. *Haptodus* and *Ianthasaurus* were only the beginning of a long, successful rule. It is, then, all the more remarkable that among the different animals found in the Garnett quarry with *Haptodus* and *Ianthasaurus*, were the earliest-known diapsids. These small reptiles under 40 cms (16 ins) long, called *Petrolacosaurus*, were on the ancestral branch leading to the dinosaurs. The Garnett quarry has produced over fifty individuals of *Petrolacosaurus*, with both partial and completely articulated skeletons.

While the development of dorsal sails along the backs of some of the larger pelycosaurs probably allowed an increased environmental range, it is unlikely that the sails were of any detriment in remaining within the wetter lowlands if the animal chose to do so. The largest sailed pelycosaurs, both herbivorous and carnivorous, are found most frequently in the lowland environments. Their fossil remains are commonly found in quarries associated with other animals and plants that are exclusively tied to lowland environments. This might indicate that these sailed, or crested, pelycosaurs belonged solely to lowland environments. However, this thought is challenged by the discovery of fossil remains of the same kinds of pelycosaurs that have been found in quarries of different environments which presumably had dryer upland characteristics.

While all the pelycosaurs had the same general body shape, not all possessed sails. It is very likely that some pelycosaurs without sails did venture beyond the original domain of their aquatic food web. However, it is significant that other types of pelycosaurs that were exclusively tied to the aquatic food web evidently did not need and therefore did not develop sails in order to remain in the lowland environments. Large pelycosaurs, such as *Ophiacodon*, reached lengths of 2 m (6 ft). *Ophiacodon* was specially adapted to a semi-aquatic lifestyle, with a definite preference for fish and other aquatic-based food. Firmly tied to the food sources available from water-borne environments, *Ophiacodon* retained its basic body shape without developing a dorsal sail, or any extra modifications for thermoregulation. The reason *Ophiacodon* did not adopt a sail could be answered simply – it did not have to if it stayed within the environment for which it was already fully suited. *Ophiacodon* was not a fully aquatic reptile, but it could swim very well when required to do so, just as virtually any reptile can if the situation calls for it. Instead, it seems more likely that *Ophiacodon* stalked along the banks and shallows of lakes and ponds. Its skull was deep and narrow, with its eyes placed high, but instead of being directly on top of the skull, as is typical on many fully aquatic hunters, the eyes were positioned on the sides of the skull. This is a more terrestrial adaptation that allowed *Ophiacodon* to have a broad range of lateral vision. This was significantly different from the bottom dwelling amphibians which had eyes positioned in their skulls for upward viewing.

Patiently waiting along the shore, or standing motionless in the shallows, it would only be a matter of time before a fish or small amphibian, visible to the *Ophiacodon* from far in the distance, gradually moved closer until the hunter had to tilt its head to one side to keep it in sight. Once the prey has moved close enough, the patient hunter splashes towards it in a sudden burst of speed. Gaping jaws dipping into the water remove a struggling lungfish flopping from side to side as it is held tightly and raised above the water. Other hungry ophiacodons approach, ready to greedily steal a mouthful. Threatening head-bobs display warnings and signs of dominance as the successful hunter stands its ground and then retreats to where it can safely eat its meal alone.

Millions of years would go by before the environments that maintained the *Ophiacodon* lifestyle show significant changes. Although commonly abundant for much of the Early Permian, the ophiacodons began to dwindle in numbers as new conditions were brought about.

Other carnivorous pelycosaurs began to increase in numbers and invade the ophiacodons' territory. A co-

The primitive anapsid, Captorhinus *is seen basking in the sun amid large fallen leaves of the seed-fern* Gigantoperis *which also towers above the reptile. Animal's length is approximately 60 cms (2 ft).*

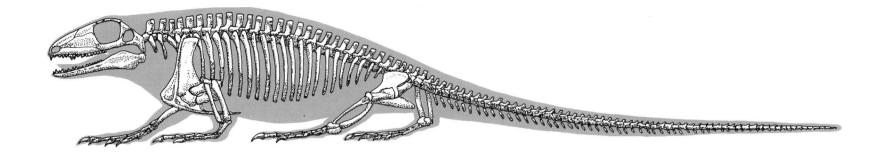

Shown is the skeleton of the synapsid, Haptodus, *which was a primitive pelycosaur without a tall sail along its back.* Haptodus *reached lengths of 60 cms (2 ft). (after Currie, 1977)*

existence at first, became a gradual competition that eventually took its toll on the *Ophiacodon* fauna.

ADVANCED PELYCOSAURS

Within the lower latitudes of the tropical and sub-tropical environments, the entire band of life that persisted during the early part of the Permian began to suffer from the effects of a gradual global warming. In part, this was caused by the changing positions of the continents. More specifically, as the landmasses moved across and past the higher latitudes of the colder Arctic regions, the vast glacial expanses began to melt and disappear. The gradual warming of Earth's climates changed the environments and the animals that lived within them. Further evolutionary adaptations became beneficial for some, and added to the specific competitions of the animals already struggling to survive the transition.

As a result of global warming, seasonal droughts constantly diminished and threatened the amphibians' environments. While this took its toll on some amphibians, others persisted in the suitable niches that still existed. Yet others adapted to withstand the new stresses of the changing environments. As if these stresses were not already bad enough, the amphibians also had to face the ever-growing onslaught of the progressing reptiles. Better suited to withstand the changing climates, the reptiles continued to expand their domain, and intrude deeper into niches once dominated by amphibians.

Fiercely powerful and competitive, the more advanced pelycosaurs became the most populous of carnivores. The development of the crested, sail-backed pelycosaurs had reached their pinnacle with *Dimetrodon*, a meat-eater, and *Edaphosaurus*, a plant-eater. Co-existing in the same environments, the sail must have provided a competitive edge. Due to the stresses associated with the changing climates there was even a terrestrial amphibian, *Platyhystrix*, that had also developed a sail as a beneficial structure.

Not all environmental niches necessitated the development of sails on its inhabitants in order to live there. Certainly, there was a great abundance of amphibians and reptiles without crests, or sails, that existed at the same time as did the crested, sail-backs. This mystery has many clues, but as many uncertainties as to exactly how and why certain animals required sails. How different were the niches where the sail-backs prospered? Perhaps the most important question is how did the sails benefit the animals that had them?

Numerous answers have been suggested over the years. While some have been incorrect, others have been half-truths and still others have been little more than silly. Utilizing the sail, literally as a sail on a boat, to carry the animal across the water is somewhat preposterous. Acting as a camouflage device is also without merit, as this could have been better achieved without any sail at all. Whatever its uses, it seems that the sail very likely had more than one function. Its large size may have been used as a form of intimidation by helping the animal to look as big as possible. This may have even been incorporated into a mating ritual, as a sexual display, to appear more attractive to its mate. But when both males and females are equipped with sails, as are the pelycosaurs, it suggests that the sexual, or defensive, visual displays were only secondary behavioural patterns.

After many years of research, the most widely accepted answer is that the sails acted as thermoregulators to assist in stabilizing the animal's body temperature, thereby maintaining a more efficient metabolism. When it is first understood that the animals in question are all ectothermic, more commonly referred to as 'cold-blooded', it becomes easier to understand how this process was achieved. Endothermic, or 'warm-blooded', animals did not exist at this time.

The difference between warm- and cold-blooded is the way the body temperature is generated. Warm-

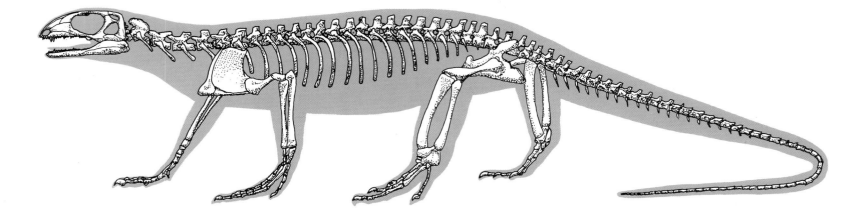

Shown is the skeleton of Petrolacosaurus, *the earliest and most primitive known diapsid. The animal's length was approximately 40 cms (16 in). (after Reisz, 1981)*

blooded animals, like today's mammals, produce their body heat from internal sources, whereas cold-blooded animals, such as amphibians and reptiles, are dependent on external environmental sources of heat.

Cold-blooded animals adjust their body temperature in any number of ways, of which basking in the sun is just one method. It is from this common method of basking that the development of the sail-backs is presumed to have originated. Basking reptiles that are trying to raise their body temperature to sufficient activity levels will position themselves, typically broadside, so as to expose as much of themselves to the sun as possible. The broad surface of the sail increased the amount of heat that was absorbed into the animal, thereby raising the animal's body temperature faster than if it was without a sail. A second benefit of the sail was the control it permitted for cooling the animal, preventing it from overheating. Too much heat at any one time can result in heat stroke and death. It is possible that a sail might have been used to prevent over-heating by positioning it so that only its narrow width was in the direct sunlight. While in this position, the heated blood could circulate from the heated mass of the body, and cool as it travelled through the thinner wall of the sail where the heat retention would be less. To exactly what extent either of these methods of thermoregulation were used by the sail-backed pelycosaurs is unknown. Nevertheless, the plausibility of either one or the other, or a combination of both methods, appears likely.

The herbivorous *Edaphosaurus* probably congregated in large numbers as a means of defence against the predacious, sail-backed *Dimetrodon*. In open clearings in the jungles, or sometimes on the sandy beaches along a large, permanent lake, such as the Waurika lake of Oklahoma, the edaphosaurs would gather and cast long shadows as they basked broadside in the sun. After achieving a sufficiently high body temperature they would become more active, but by moving only infrequently, they would appear to be resting. As the day continued, their attention would turn towards

food. Following each other in a loosely connected group, they would congregate within the lush greenery, and for hours would satisfy their appetites, cropping the leaves from the branches. Tranquil episodes of uneventful feasting would make up most of the edaphosaurs' daily routine. Inevitably, the hunger pangs of the dimetrodons would create a few brief moments of violence, after which, a peaceful normalcy would resume. Perhaps relieved, or merely unaware that a member of the group was missing, the edaphosaurs would wander off to begin anew.

For most of the first half of the Permian, the gradual global warming continued to affect the life of the planet. The equatorial-based band of life lost the stability of climates that had originally been so favourable to the amphibians and reptiles. The development of seasonal activity produced harsh weather patterns that were increasingly adverse to the animals. Instead of wet and warm periods, the seasonal extremes subjected the animals to warm, wet and *dry* periods. The loss of the consistently reliable rainfall forced the animals that lived within these environments to either relocate to areas which were suitable for their lifestyle, or stay in their original territory and adapt to the changes. The reptiles possessed the advantage of greater mobility, and an independence from the water which they frequented. The additional adaptations of various thermoregulation methods, including sails, were experiments that were often successful in prolonging the existence of particular species.

AMPHIBIANS AND SEASONAL CHANGES

Amphibians, however, had fewer options than the reptiles, and were severely limited by their inability to leave their water-based habitats. When the dry seasons became prevalent, many of these habitats would shrink in size, or disappear entirely, until the next rainy season came to replenish them. Fossil beds have

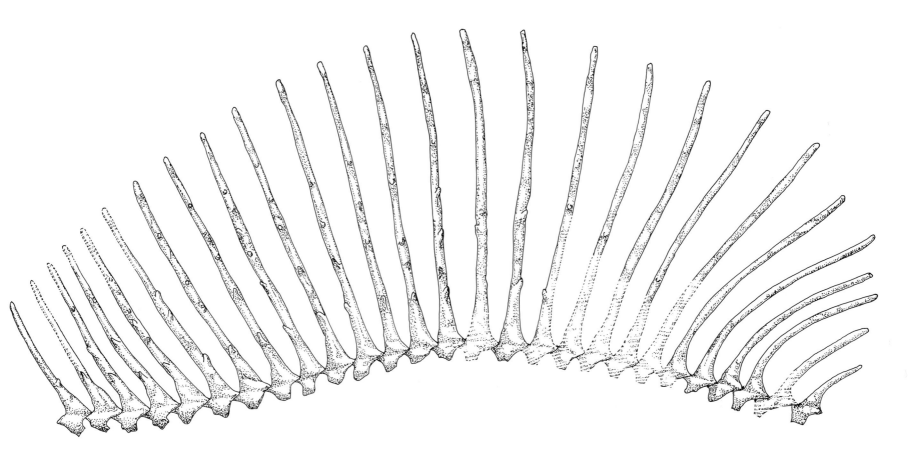

Shown 90 per cent life-size is the backbone with elongated neural spines which forms the sail along the back of the early specialized pelycosaur, Ianthasaurus. *(after Reisz and Berman, 1986)*

often revealed pockets of large concentrations of amphibians that appear to have been confined, and crammed on top of each other. Such an assemblage of fossil remains not only preserves a large collection of individuals, but records their futile attempt to resist the seasonal changes. Trapped within the confines of a rapidly evaporating pool, the ill-equipped amphibians gathered in the shrunken ponds and disappearing puddles of mud. Amphibians were continually plagued by such a fate, unlike reptiles which could travel to where healthy surroundings still existed.

Some amphibians similarly trapped in the drying mud, adopted a different method to avoid the otherwise certain death that threatened them. Rather than relocating, resilient amphibians like *Lysorophus* coiled themselves into rounded burrows in the mud, and waited until the crisis was over. This amphibian form of hibernation, called aestivation, put the animal in a protective torpor until the hard, dry ground surrounding it was once again softened into mud by the recurring rainy season. After a pond enlarged to sufficient size, the process of aestivation would end as the amphibian re-entered a new, if only temporary, world of water.

In the Hennessey quarry of Oklahoma, hundreds of coiled *Lysorophus* skeletons have been found. For them the next rainy season did not come in time. Here, as well as in other quarries, coiled specimens are preserved, trapped within their burrows, while other *Lysorophus* skeletons are found outstretched. Both are victims of insufficient rainfall. Perhaps the uncoiled

amphibians made premature attempts to return to the water. When the newly returned pond shrank still further and then disappeared these amphibians were stranded, without having been able to rebuild reserves necessary to once again aestivate. The amphibians that had returned too early perished with their bodies outstretched.

The quarry of Orlando lake in Oklahoma, reveals conditions of a semi-permanent lake that experienced seasonal drying. The community dependent on this semi-permanent lake included the reptiles, *Dimetrodon*, *Edaphosaurus*, and captorhinomorphs. There were also lungfish, such as *Gnathorhiza*; sharks, such as *Orthacanthus*; and the amphibians, *Trimerorhachis*, *Lysorophus*, and *Diplocaulus*. Of all these, *Diplocaulus* is the most numerous.

Other amphibians may have also aestivated, but not necessarily in exactly the same manner as *Lysorophus*. *Diplocaulus* was a peculiar amphibian in that as it

Around the shore of a lake (Waurika lake site of Oklahoma), sail-backed pelycosaurs warm their body temperature by basking broadside to the sun. In the foreground are two carnivores, Dimetrodon. *In the distance, around the shore of the lake, are several herbivorous* Edaphosaurus. *Clusters of* Equisetum *are spread across the shore and beneath the lowland forests of tree-ferns. Higher up, forests of* Walchia *continue across the uplands.* Dimetrodon *reached lengths of up to 3.3 m (11 ft) and* Edaphosaurus *also excelled 3 m (10 ft) in length.*

A sail-backed Dimetrodon *splashes after three* Diadectes, *while a 60-cms (2-ft) long amphibian,* Seymouria, *remains atop a fallen log. Attaining lengths of 3 m (10 ft),* Diadectes *was a reptile-like amphibian that made up much of the pelycosaurs' diet.*

matured to its full size, of over 1 m (3 ft) long, its head expanded out to the sides forming flat, recurved, horn-like projections. These may have been used as some form of defence against its predators but, more likely the projections were used to raise a meal for itself from the smaller animals which were hiding in the bottom of the lake. When necessary, the projections might have been used to help camouflage itself in the sand, or mud for additional protection. By simple twists of the head from side to side, the elongate projections of the head would rake and stir the surface of the water's bottom, dispersing tiny inhabitants. Along with undulations of the body and tail, the elongated head could then push back from side to side and toss the sand, or mud, over itself as it wiggled under cover. While projections on the head of an adult *Diplocaulus* were beneficial to its lifestyle, the adult's large size made it incapable of aestivating in burrows. However, the fossil remains of both *Lysorophus* and of tiny juvenile *Diplocaulus* are often found together, indicating that some *Diplocaulus* not only shared the seasonal hardships which caused *Lysorophus* to aestivate, but that

they, too, may have aestivated to withstand the dry spells. Unlike *Lysorophus* which could aestivate at different stages of maturity, the evidence tends to support the theory that only the young, smaller *Diplocaulus*, which had not developed the broad, lateral expansions of the skull, were capable of burrowing and aestivating.

The seasonal changes which were taking place during the Permian also brought hardship for the plantlife that was ill-equipped to withstand the changes. While

Along a shallow braided stream is a primitive upland community consisting of the amphibian Cacops *in the foreground, and herbivorous pelycosaurs,* Casea brolli *on the distant bank. Farther back is* Varanops, *also a pelycosaur, which fed mostly upon insects and small vertebrates.* Sphenophyllum *and* Equisetum *line the banks, and the araucarian,* Walchia, *towers in the background. The approximate length of* Cacops *is 50 cms (20 in),* Casea brolli *1 m (3 ft) and* Varanops *1 m (3 ft).*

During the latter part of the Early Permian in an upland forest, the primitive gorgonopsid, Watongia *encounters four* Cotylorhynchus, *which were among the largest of all pelycosaurs.* Watongia *was about 1.6 m (5 ft) long, and* Cotylorhynchus *reached lengths of 4 m (13 ft).*

some plants were adversely affected, others were aided in their development and, as a result, an increasing trend of diversification took place. As with animals, such changes are often preserved as part of the fossil record and are extremely helpful in determining what kind of climatic and environmental conditions existed. Although the exact causes of why certain conditions existed may not be easily understood, the significant facts of when and where certain types of plants lived becomes clear. In this manner, certain plants become important key fossils that can be used as a time index. Many plants that had diversified into distinct types existed only during a specific period of time. Therefore, when plant index fossils are found in association with fossils of vertebrates, a correlation between plants, animals and time can be made that forms an accurate chronology.

Gigantoperis was a specific type of seed-fern that can be used as an index fossil. So distinctive is the herringbone vein pattern on this particular plant that even the smallest of fragments containing the impression of its leaves will identify it as belonging to *Gigantoperis*. *Gigantoperis* existed during the latter part of the Early Permian, and its fossil remains have been found in geographical positions as distantly removed as Texas, in North America and in China.

In the Sid McAdams quarry, animals that are commonly associated with *Gigantoperis* include both amphibians and reptiles, some of which are difficult to define as belonging to either group. Stem reptiles such as *Captorhinus* persisted as small, primitive anapsids in parts of what is now North America. As generally lizard-like reptiles, the rather ordinary appearance of *Captorhinus* conceals what would become of its distant relatives, some of which evolved into the spiked and armoured pareiasaurs (see page 57).

Many types of amphibians were still quite prolific during the middle of the Permian and some were becoming increasingly terrestrial. *Seymouria* was a small to moderate-sized amphibian about 60 cms (2 ft) in length, and adept at moving about on land. Other 'amphibians' that existed at this time were not only very terrestrial, but in fact were close to becoming true reptiles while still retaining numerous amphibian characteristics, so their classification is very ambiguous. *Diadectes* is one of these problematic animals that while not being a true reptile, was not completely an amphibian either. The mouth of *Diadectes* was specialized with cropping teeth in front and crushing teeth at the back, probably for an omnivorous diet of plants and hard-shelled invertebrates. As a sizeable animal of nearly 3 m (10 ft), *Diadectes* was relatively inoffensive and, without doubt, a major source of food for the large carnivorous pelycosaurs. *Dimetrodon* was the largest and last of the sail-backed pelycosaurs and must have preyed heavily on the abundant *Diadectes*. Numerous other animals were also readily available to meet the dietary needs of the carnivorous reptiles. It is intriguing, then, to wonder why the sail-backed *Dimetrodon* finally became extinct, while its descendants without sails persisted into even more advanced forms.

CHRONOFAUNAS AND UPLANDS

The fossil record of vertebrates during the Permian is extensive, but yet far from being complete. As is so often the case, the available depositional strata that contain vertebrate fossils reflect only certain periods of time at various geographical locations. The monumentally destructive powers of erosion have removed all records of virtually millions of years of vertebrate life from not only different times, but different locations throughout the world.

The vertebrate-bearing strata containing the first half of the Permian is best preserved in what is now the United States of America. Elsewhere in the world, the corresponding fossil record is deficient and generally poorly preserved. While this hampers the global correlations of vertebrate life which can be made for this particular time, it is fortunate that an almost complete succession of time can be followed for the remainder of the Permian by studying strata from other parts of the world. Where the fossil record stops at a particular locality, an overlap or continuation may be preserved elsewhere. This is what happens to the middle of the Permian record. The abundant fossil remains of the Early Permian come to an abrupt end in the United States of America, but then continue from approximately the same point in time in what is now part of Russia.

Chronofaunas are ecological communities of animals that are persistent in particular environments throughout a sequence of time. It is by the comparison of such communities from different places and times that the gaps of the fossil record can sometimes be connected. Distinct communities pertaining to lowland environments are often in sharp contrast to the upland communities. The interchanges between different communities become apparent by the similarities of animals found in different environments. In the Clearfork formation of Texas, a rarely preserved upland deposit known as the *Cacops* bonebed, contained a unique community that had adapted to the upland environments. Semi-terrestrial amphibians, such as *Cacops*, and small pelycosaurs including both the insectivorous *Varanops* and herbivorous *Casea*, are conspicuously absent from the lowland environments. What this indicates is that beyond the aquatic food web of the lowland environments was a distinct assemblage of animals which had become specifically adapted, and even somewhat restricted, to the upland environments.

Initially, the animals that populated the uplands were of relatively small size. The amphibian, *Cacops*, was only about 50 cms (20 ins) in length. It was a stout creature with strong, sprawling limbs and a row of bony armour along the middle of its back. Although

Skeletons of the aquatic reptile Mesosaurus *have been found in South Africa and Brazil, South America, indicating that these continental landmasses were connected during the Middle Permian. Animal's length approximately 1 m (3 ft). (after Carroll, 1988)*

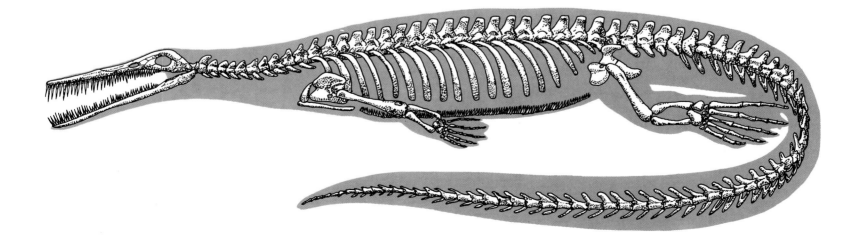

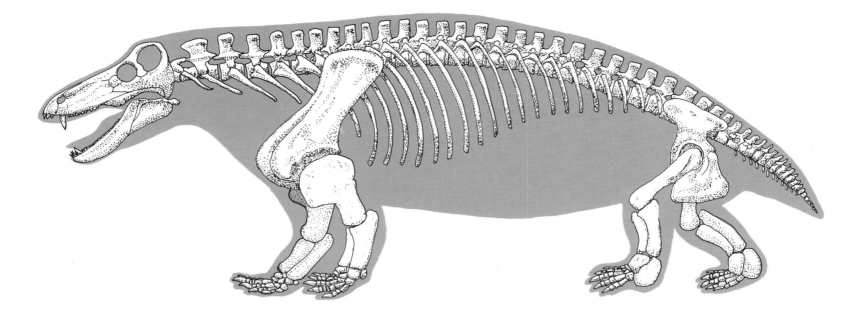

Jonkeria was a huge dinocephalian some 4.3 m (14 ft) long from the Tapinocephalus *Zone of South Africa. It may have still been to some degree carnivorous, unlike the later dinocephalians which were exclusively herbivorous. (modified after Broom, 1932)*

quite mobile across dryer terrains, *Cacops* probably frequented the streams and waterways that flowed towards the lowlands.

The small size of the upland pelycosaurs, such as *Casea brolli*, is notable in that unlike some of the considerably larger pelycosaurs that had developed tall sails on their backs, some of these small upland pely-

	RUSSIA	SOUTH AFRICA		
Upper Triassic		Stromberg	Cave Sandstone	
			Red Beds	
			Molteno	
Middle Triassic	Zone VII			
Lower Triassic	Zone VI	Upper Beaufort	Cynognathus zone	
	Zone V		(Procolophon zone) Lystrosaurus zone	
Upper Permian	Zone IV	Lower Beaufort	Cistecephalus zone	
	Zone III		Endothiodon zone	
Middle Permian	Zone II		Tapinocephalus zone	
	Zone 1		Ecca	
Lower Permian	Zone 0		Dwyka	

Comparison of the Permian and Triassic zones of Russia and South Africa.

cosaurs took on different methods of thermoregulation. Rather than expanding the height of its body into a sail, *Casea brolli* had a crestless body that was wider than it was high. This broadening of the body would later become even more pronounced in the descendants of *Casea*. As a herbivore, a large body would naturally be helpful in containing an extensive gut that could digest the eaten vegetation, but the broadness of the *Casea* body would continue to reach grotesquely short, flat and exceedingly wide proportions in its larger descendants. The broad, flattened bodies may have also contributed to thermoregulation, as did the sails on some of the earlier pelycosaurs.

It is likely that some of the pelycosaurs that existed in the uplands, and perhaps even distant continental interiors, were by necessity experimenting and adapting thermoregulation techniques that were significantly different from all the ectothermic amphibians and reptiles before them. *Varanops* was a primitive pelycosaur that persisted in the uplands along with *Cacops* and *Casea*. It is curious that not only did *Varanops* exist in the uplands, but that the next great radiation from the pelycosaurs probably arose from similar environments. *Varanops* was the earliest member of a group of pelycosaurs known as sphenacodonts. The sphenacodonts were a group of carnivorous pelycosaurs that led to the development of the mammal-like reptiles called therapsids.

Climatic conditions became increasingly adverse with the seasonal aridity that confronted the equatorial band of life. The environments of the amphibians and the reptiles diminished, causing integral parts of the food web to disappear. However, the animals of the uplands and the continental interiors at higher latitudes were not so badly affected. Instead,

Emerging from a forest of seed-ferns and araucarians, a group of dinocephalians, Estemmenosuchus, *approach a water hole. In the foreground is a gorgonopsid,* Eotitanosuchus. *Known from the Zone One of Russia,* Estemmenosuchus *is approximately 3 m (10 ft) in length, and* Eotitanosuchus *is about 2.5 m (8 ft) long.*

the changing climatic conditions may have actually assisted the development and eventual radiation of the upland communities.

The abundant fossil record of the Permian in the United States ends about half way through the period. Fortunately, though, a comparison of communities reveals that where the record stops in the United States, it slightly overlaps and continues the sequence for most of the second half of the Permian in Russia. The Chickasash formation of Oklahoma holds some of the last of the Permian animals that are preserved in the United States. Among these is *Cotylorhynchus* which was a descendant from *Casea* and the largest of all pelycosaurs reaching nearly 4 m (13 ft) in length, and *Watongia* which was a transitional animal that could no longer be considered a pelycosaur, but instead belonged to a new group of animals that would continue to become quite different from their original pelycosaur stock. This new group of animals are known as the therapsids.

Watongia and *Cotylorhynchus* probably lived in upland environments. *Cotylorhynchus* is a huge herbi-

vore. Its head was remarkably small and toothy, protruding as a hideous, undeveloped face attached to a disproportionately large, broad and squat body. Splayed out to its sides were powerful limbs and large claws designed for digging and defence. Its fairly long tail was perhaps the least offensive of what must have been a hideous reptilian beast. The sizable flesh of *Cotylorhynchus* must have had some appeal to the carnivorous *Watongia*. However, only attaining a length of 1.6 m (5 ft), *Watongia* would have had to be very cautious as it approached a *Cotylorhynchus* as a prospective meal. Certainly, other smaller animals could more easily be captured. With the powerful clawed legs that were capable of ripping roots and vegetation easily from the ground, a threatened *Cotylorhynchus* would have been far from what could be called a harmless vegetarian.

The carnivorous *Watongia* was probably one of the earliest therapsids. Its skeletal characteristics combine lingering pelycosaur traits with some unique features of an increasingly mammalian nature. This makes *Watongia* perhaps one of the earliest members of a group of therapsids known as the gorgonopsids. As the environmental stresses promoted and favoured the therapsid condition, other equally primitive therapsids may have also been evolving independently from upland pelycosaurs elsewhere across thousands of miles, reaching into Russia.

THERAPSIDS
THE NEW WAVE OF REPTILES

The climatic and environmental changes that occurred during the Early Permian eventually took its toll on the lowland, aquatic-based reptiles and amphibians by the middle of the period, or what is more correctly called the beginning of the Late Permian. The increase of the marked seasonal extremes and the subsequent loss of the comparatively more stable environments so instrumental in the success of the Early Permian reptiles and amphibians brought about not only casualties, but extinctions. The food web was thrown out of balance and disconnected. While there were lingering survivors, they were greatly reduced in numbers, living without change in the reduced remnants of their once vast and supportive environments. Other reptiles, however, did more than merely linger. They continued to evolve and adapt to the rigours of the changing world. From the synapsid line of pelycosaurs and sphenacodonts came a new wave of reptiles that would dominate the second half of the Permian and early part of the next period, the Triassic. On an ancestral path that would threaten to bypass entirely the development of the dinosaurs, the new wave of reptiles called therapsids, or mammal-like reptiles, successfully replaced other reptiles on a course of world domination which would lead not just towards true mammals, but eventually some 200 million years later, to Mankind.

As remarkable, or even miraculous, as it may seem, the fossil record clearly shows that the ancestry of all true mammals began not after the demise of the dinosaurs, but long before the first dinosaurs even existed. Any understanding of the mysterious processes that were instrumental in mammalian evolution is overshadowed by the question of how the superiority of the mammals, given their head-start of millions of years, faltered and nearly succumbed to near extinction when confronted by the origin of dinosaurs.

At the start of the Late Permian, the tendency towards mammalian traits increased within many groups of the therapsids. None of the earliest mammal-like reptiles were really mammals, but they were no longer fully reptilian either. As the different types of therapsids progressed, the more advanced mammal-like characters continued to develop. Some of the advanced therapsids lost the primitive, reptilian sprawling legs, and took on a more upright posture along the lines more typically accredited to mammals. Some may have been capable of giving live birth, and possibly could suckle their young. It is not only possible, but likely, that some advanced therapsids were even covered in pelts of hair, with protruding ears behind dog-like faces, complete with shiny, wet noses, whiskered snouts, flexible lips and panting tongues. The environmental dependence associated with ectothermy was undoubtedly lessened with the capabilities of partial, and probably in some therapsids, almost full endothermy, or 'warm-bloodedness', which distinguishes all modern mammals from reptilian definition. Among the most advanced therapsids, it would probably be far more accurate to dismiss the reptilian terminology, and simply regard them as proto-mammals.

With the earliest of the therapsids, appearances would have been quite deceiving as reptilian affinities would dominate the external look of the therapsids, and obscure their internal biological changes. The earliest known therapsids included carnivores that still closely resembled their pelycosaur and sphenacodont ancestors, but they soon diversified into omnivores, and even total herbivores. Some of these plant-eaters became larger than any animals that had previously existed.

Instead of being restricted within the lower latitudes, the therapsid range was expanded far beyond the Early Permian equatorial-based band of life. More temperate zones at latitudes as high as 70° were incorporated into the therapsid domain, and the reduction of the glacial deposits in the southern hemisphere allowed further radiation and migration into Gondwana. The fact that the therapsids could exploit the environments within higher latitudes suggests that these mammal-like reptiles possessed a greater ability to withstand climatic fluctuations than did other reptiles.

MESOSAURUS AND
CONTINENTAL CONNECTIONS

Prior to the invasion of the therapsids into the higher latitudes of the southern hemisphere, the fossil record suggests a conspicuous absence of animals there, indicating that the great southern radiation had not yet occurred. Significant fossil remains have been found of a fully aquatic reptile, *Mesosaurus*, the earliest-known reptiles to have ventured deep into the southern hemisphere. Its specialized readaptation for an aquatic way of life enabled the *Mesosaurus* to become an early immigrant. After the glaciers retreated, the aquatic low-

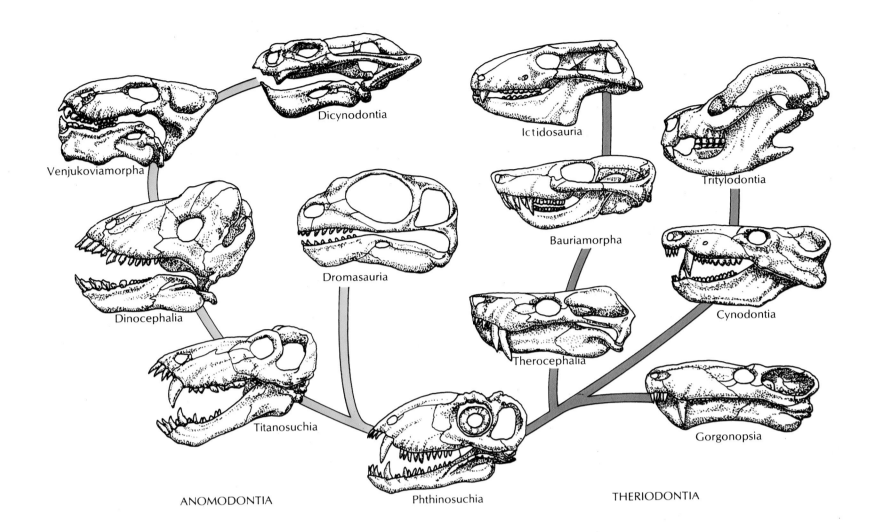

Venjukoviamorpha

Dicynodontia

Ictidosauria

Tritylodontia

Dinocephalia

Dromasauria

Bauriamorpha

Cynodontia

Titanosuchia

Therocephalia

ANOMODONTIA

Phthinosuchia

THERIODONTIA

Gorgonopsia

THERAPSID FAMILY TREE
This chart, or family tree, demonstrates how therapsids evolved. Initially, exclusive carnivores (Phthinosuchia) split into two separate groups: the Theriodontia which remained primarily carnivorous until the appearance of the last of their kind, and the Anomodontia which became herbivores early in their development. Skulls not to scale (after Romer, 1974).

lands would have been the first available environments suitable for sustaining the ectothermic reptiles. In time, the stable, warm waterways stretched further south, and with them came the unique, needle-toothed mesosaurs. The radiation of the mesosaurs is of still greater significance in that their remains are found today on two separate continents. The exacting correlations of the mesosaurs found in both South Africa and southern Brazil are clear testimony that these continental landmasses were joined together at the time the mesosaur existed. Subsequent movement of the continents have separated them by over 9600 kms (6000 miles) into what are now their current positions. A small reptile of just 1 m (3 ft) in length, the *Mesosaurus* is nonetheless a rare example of global implications.

THERAPSIDS IN RUSSIA AND AFRICA

The fossil record that continues for the remaining half of the Permian, and for much of the early part of the Triassic, is remarkably preserved in a succession of zones located in Russia and Africa. Representing both hemispheres, these zones are distinguished on the one hand by floral and faunal differences and, on the other, by abundant similarities that significantly correlate. The Russian zones are simply referred to by respective numbers, while the equivalent zones in Africa often utilize the name of a diagnostic type of animal found within each different zone. The Russian Zone One is of comparable time to the Ecca Zone in Africa. However, the Ecca Zone is virtually devoid of fossil reptiles, whereas the Russian counterpart, Zone One, contains representatives of the earliest mammal-like reptiles. Although poorly preserved and incompletely known, some very similar therapsids have also been found in the last of the fossil-bearing Permian beds in North America. But it is in Zone One that the fossil record continues with a far better representation of the great faunal changeover from pelycosaurs into therapsids.

The abrupt appearance of the therapsids is made all the more startling by their amazing diversity. Several distinct types of specialized therapsids co-existed as represented by their fossils found in Zone One. Among these were the gorgonopsids, a carnivorous group of moderately large size, superficially resembling their pelycosaur ancestors. Then there were the dinocephalians – large therapsids, some of which were of considerable stature and bulk. Initially carnivorous, dinocephalians became less predatory and later adapted to an omnivorous, and eventually an exclusively herbivorous, diet. A third group of therapsids, called the anomodonts, were also exclusively herbivorous, and became the most prolific of all therapsids. The first anomodonts were comparatively small in contrast to the gorgonopsids and dinocephalians. But as the dinocephalians became extinct, and the gorgonopsids decreased in numbers and size, the anomodont descendants increased in size.

Eventually, the mammal-like therapsids replaced their reptilian, pelycosaur ancestors. Direct competition may not have been responsible for this but rather empty niches were refilled, and environments that had previously become inhospitable to the pelycosaurs repopulated. With the absence of the recently extinct pelycosaurs, the therapsids faced little competition and were no longer prevented from invading the lowlands and radiating into new frontiers.

It is highly likely that many of the advanced therapsids shared a more gregarious and complicated social behaviour than that of the more primitive pelycosaurs, and other reptiles which continued to live alongside the mammal-like reptiles. The safety in numbers that is not entirely uncommon to reptilian behaviour probably became more structured, resulting in organized herds of beneficially co-operative animals. Herds of herbivorous therapsids probably originated long before the carnivorous therapsids benefited from the joined forces of structured packs, or prides. Unlike the simple impetus that draws a herbivore towards an edible plant, co-operative hunting is highly complex behaviour requiring a shared effort within the pack to attain the mutual goal of food for one and all. Whereas reptiles in an unstructured group might unknowingly assist one another in subduing a prey, sharing is atypical of reptilian behaviour, and it is mere coincidence if a prey becomes a meal for more than one. Before the carnivorous therapsids could develop co-operative hunting behaviour, more than cunning was necessary. Caring was also required. Levels of parental care among advanced therapsids may have assisted the bond of caring that continued into co-operative hunting. Unlike the advanced therapsids, the earliest therapsids may not have had a family structure including parental care, and were probably solitary animals which only sought others of their kind during periods of mating.

ESTEMMENOSUCHUS AND THE SKIN OF THERAPSIDS

Primitive, meat-eating gorgonopsids, such as *Eotitanosuchus* from Russia's Zone One, were probably solitary hunters. Stealth and brute force were the combined instincts that they relied on to appease their hunger. Actively searching or lying in wait for a potential prey to appear were methods that primitive therapsids could utilize. Returning to areas where animals routinely gathered, such as water holes, would offer a continual source of food for the hungry.

Dinocephalians, such as the herbivorous *Estemmenosuchus*, would instinctively approach a water hole with caution. Alert to the potential threat of a hiding gorgonopsid, an approaching herd would follow the leading bull-males that would test the area's safety and stand guard as the females and young gingerly came from behind. As much as 3 m (10 ft) long and 1.6 m (5 ft) high at the shoulders, these massive animals were crowned with a bizarre array of blunt horns on their heads. The *Estemmenosuchus* must have been powerful and foreboding beasts. Certainly quite capable of individually defending themselves, the increased safety of the herd posed an awesome obstacle for any single predator. Even a large and fierce gorgonopsid, driven by hunger, would await a relatively safe opportunity before striking an unwary member of the herd which strayed too far away, and intimidated by the imposing herd, the necessity of a meal may have been delayed and even a hungry gorgonopsid would have cowered at a safe distance to await an easier meal.

Estemmenosuchus is found in the Russian Zone One along with some of the earliest therapsids. It has the distinction of being the only known therapsid that has been preserved not only by fossilized skeletal remains, but also with its actual epidermis. This mineralized remnant of skin is fragmentary and yet its delicate and most minute details are preserved showing not only the external surface, but more importantly, the entire internal structure of the dermis. Incredibly rare and difficult to recognize, such preservation of skin has probably been lost time and time again during the process of excavating and in the preparation of the fossil

In the foreground, the primitive dinocephalian, Titanophoneus *carries a small anomodont,* Venjukovia, *in its mouth. In the distant clearing, a group of herbivorous dinocephalians,* Ulemosaurus, *cautiously watch the predator prance by as they remain basking in the sun. These therapsids are known from Zone Two of Russia. In the foreground are branches of the tree-like horsetail,* Calamites. *The approximate length of* Titanophoneus *is 2 m (6¹/₂ ft),* Venjukovia *1 m (3 ft), and* Ulemosaurus *3 m (10 ft).*

bones. Whether unpreserved or overlooked, the significance of the fossilized *Estemmenosuchus* skin reveals that this early therapsid had a more complex skin structure than scaley reptiles. Reptilian skin is characteristically simple in its internal structure and is for the most part devoid of glands. In sharp contrast, a microscopic inspection of a cross-section of the therapsid skin shows an advanced condition of numerous glands that are more indicative of a mammal-like function, such as scent-marking or perspiration. While no sign of hair is preserved, it is still remarkable that such early development among mammal-like reptiles had lost the scaley skin of typical reptiles, and adapted considerably towards an advanced mammal-like condition.

ZONE TWO OF RUSSIA AND THE *TAPINOCEPHALUS* ZONE OF AFRICA

Unlike Russia's Zone One which had no comparative fauna in the African fossil beds, Russia's Zone Two has an equivalent fauna in Africa, called the *Tapinocephalus* Zone. The appearance of this African fauna indicates that the inhospitable, or at least impenetrable, environments of the previous period, the Ecca Zone, had changed sufficiently to allow the vertebrates access into the southern hemisphere. The less severe climatic conditions were brought about, at least in part, by the movement of the continents in a northward direction and the continued diminution of the glaciers of Gondwana. At the same time a warmer climate gradually expanded farther into the southern hemisphere. Also contributing to the climatic change was the erosional destruction of a western mountain range that previously deflected the warm and wet winds from the South African regions where the *Tapinocephalus* Zones are located. As a result of the changing climatic conditions, the uninhabited territories of the southern hemisphere became more hospitable environments that awaited the immigrant faunas from the north.

The fauna of the Russian Zone Two is composed of therapsids that are very similar to some of the therapsids of the African *Tapinocephalus* Zone. The dinocephalians of Zone Two are represented by both primitive carnivores, such as *Titanophoneus*, and advanced herbivores, such as *Ulemosaurus*. Herbivorous anomodonts, including *Venjukovia*, and carnivorous gorgonopsids were also present, as were other smaller reptiles. The faunal similarities between the Russian and African zones reveal the connection and radiation of the animals onto different continents within both hemispheres. Such a broad distribution indicates the therapsids' ability to tolerate the more temperate weather conditions present within the higher latitudes. It is, therefore, not too surprising that therapsid remains have not been found in the lower latitudes of equatorial climates. For the most part, the equatorial climate may not have been as desirable for the therapsids' metabolisms that had become adapted to more temperate, and perhaps seasonally cooler, climates. This possible preference for the higher latitudinal climates might have played a major part in the therapsid distribution. But it is also quite clear that at least periodic, perhaps seasonal, migrations across the equatorial latitudes took place allowing the therapsids to become truly cosmopolitan on a global scale.

The dinocephalians were perhaps the most abundant and largest therapsids of their time. *Ulemosaurus* and its close relatives, such as the African *Moschops*, were imposing plant-eaters of considerable size. They walked on strong and muscular legs but, for the most part, retained the primitive characteristics of a sprawling gait. A partially erect gait was employed by the front limbs while the hind limbs were more directly beneath the body. Although primitive in their limb structure, even the largest dinocephalians carried their bodies above the ground when they walked or ran. Their locomotion may have looked awkward, but nonetheless it was an adequate and efficient mode of transport.

The temperate climates of Zone Two supported environments that consisted of resilient forests and vegetation which were abundant and widespread at higher latitudes. Where the therapsids are known to have existed, the weather conditions were generally of moderate warmth with a considerable annual rainfall. These conditions produced landscapes which were covered by towering primitive trees, like *Walchia*. Densely filling the understorey of the forest were seed-ferns, including *Pecopteris* and *Ullmannia*. Near the water grew *Calamites*, a tree-like ancestor of modern horsetails. Fast-moving rivers, broad lakes and ponds were also present.

It is possible that some of the herbivorous dinocephalians may have adapted to a semi-aquatic lifestyle. This would have been akin to the modern hippopotamus which spends a considerable portion of its day in the water and becomes actively terrestrial to feed on vegetation which may be some distance from the water. The behavioural patterns were no doubt as varied as were the numerous types of dinocephalians and the environmental circumstances that they lived in.

It would have been common for the dinocephalians, such as *Ulemosaurus*, to have frequented deep interiors of the forests, as well as rivers or lakes. One can imagine the occasional sight of a foraging group of *Ulemosaurus* steadily cropping the lower vegetation in the forests and then periods of calm and tranquillity, resting in the dappled shade and soft warming sunlight of a small clearing. The well-fed group of *Ulemosaurus* would lie down with their legs outstretched to their sides, content for the moment, an oblivious sense of well-being overtaking them as they busily digested the yield of the day's activities. Uneventful hours would pass by, and only when an intrusion to their solitude occurred would they become unsettled and begin to stir. Sudden glimmerings of self-concern would assess the intrusion as either a threat to their well-being or just another animal harmlessly passing by. Initially startling, the appearance of *Titanophoneus*, a primitive, pelycosaur-like, carnivorous dinocephalian and a member of the group known as brithopodids, captures the watchful eyes of the alarmed *Ulemosaurus*. A tense moment passes as the *Ulemosaurus* stand their ground. Potentially a threat, the *Titanophoneus* prances past the group. With no intent to attack this time, the *Titanophoneus* has already snapped up a small anomodont, *Venjukovia*, and is hurrying along to where it can partake its meal without disturbance.

The anomodonts of Zone Two were remarkably small herbivores, as were their counterparts from the *Tapinocephalus* Zone.

Dinocephalians were abundant in the *Tapinocephalus* Zone, and included *Tapinocephalus* itself, for which it is named, and the long-limbed *Titanosuchus*, the short-limbed *Jonkeria*, and *Moschops*. *Moschops* was remarkably similar and was no doubt closely related to *Ulemosaurus* which is found in Zone Two of Russia. Separated by over 8000 kms (5000 miles), the similar, if not identical affinities of these two animals demonstrates the incredible range of radiation of which they were capable. Yet more significant is the even higher latitudinal range of the therapsids that had moved into the southern hemisphere.

The gradual warming of the global climates further restricted the glaciers of the southern hemisphere, and extended the more temperate climates to the latitudes where the therapsids found suitable environments. Seasonally warm periods were routinely interrupted by abundant rainfall of cooler extremes. The typically deciduous *Glossopteris* flora that is so representative of Gondwana in the southern hemisphere confirms the existence of the temperate seasonal extremes.

It has been suggested that the dinocephalians, such

In the foreground are three tiny anomodonts, Eodicynodon, *which represents the earliest known dicynodont. Looming over their heads is* Moschops, *a dinocephalian much like* Ulemosaurus *of Russia. Further back on the left, a group of pareiasaurs,* Bradysaurus, *have wandered from the distant lowlands and encounter the upland dwelling dinocephalians. The approximate length of* Eodicynodon *is 30 cms (1 ft),* Moschops *3 m (10 ft), and* Bradysaurus *4 m (12 ft).*

as *Moschops*, might have been partially, or even fully endothermic, making it possible for them to withstand the stresses brought about by temperate seasonal extremes but to what extent the dinocephalians were endothermic, and thereby able to regulate their body temperature by internal biological adaptations, is indeterminable. However, the dinocephalians were still among the earliest and most primitive of therapsids, and while any trend towards actual endothermy would be important, what is of greater significance is that a move towards endothermy may very well have played a part in their global dispersal. Furthermore, the possible, if only limited, capabilities of endothermic thermoregulation, foreshadowed the more complete endothermic qualities benefiting some of the more advanced therapsids.

The large and numerous dinocephalians succeeded in global domination that was surprisingly short-lived. By the end of the Zone Two and the *Tapinocephalus* Zone, the last of the dinocephalians failed to overcome some ecological challenge which selectively brought them all to extinction. What brought about this end may have been a combination of first, direct competition from other types of animals that took over

their particular environmental habitats, and second, their inability to further adapt to the changing climates. Certainly the global climate was becoming increasingly warm during the last half of the Permian, possibly adversely affecting the dinocephalian environments.

PAREIASAURS AND DINOCEPHALIANS

Pareiasaurs were anapsid reptiles existing in both hemispheres at the same time as the dinocephalians, but the pareiasaurs survived even longer until the end of the Permian. With few exceptions, they were large animals that, at least superficially, resembled the

57

bulky, herbivorous dinocephalians. However, unlike the dinocephalians, the pareiasaurs were ornamented with bony clusters of armoured spikes that covered their body. The more primitive appearance of the pareiasaurs reflected their definite, reptilian affinities. Unquestionably, their metabolism was ectothermic and typical of most reptiles.

Exactly how the pareiasaurs co-existed with the dinocephalians poses many puzzling questions. Since they were cold-blooded, how were they capable of living in the supposedly temperate environments also populated by the presumably more advanced dinocephalians? Did they unobtrusively share, or directly compete for the food and environments that provided for the dinocephalians?

Bradysaurus was a pareiasaur, known from the *Tapinocephalus* Zone of South Africa. It is of particular note that the conditions in which the *Bradysaurus* are preserved indicate that these pareiasaurs may have had different habitats than the more abundant dinocephalians. Even though these pareiasaurs are less numerous than the dinocephalians, it is still more common to find rather complete and even articulated skeletal remains of *Bradysaurus* individuals, instead of just partial remains, such as a skull, or limb. Contrary to this, the dinocephalians are more commonly found disarticulated and their skeletal remains missing considerable portions. The discrepancy between the patterns of preservation may not only represent different behavioural patterns, but also separately exploited ecological habitats. The pareiasaurs are commonly preserved in fine clays or silts that accumulated quickly without the powerful action of fast-moving water to displace the individual bones. Also, signs of predation, so often responsible for the scattering and loss of animal remains, are notably absent. On the other hand, both fast-moving water and predation are possible factors contributing to the dinocephalian preservation patterns. If pareiasaurs and dinocephalians lived together in the same conditions more uniformity and similarities of preservation should be apparent. Perhaps not too surprisingly, this suggests the obvious: while pareiasaurs and the dinocephalians were outwardly similar, they were still very different, possessing separate needs. Even though the animals co-existed, they may have preferred different territories. The pareiasaurs may have been better suited for the warmer lowlands with calm lakes and ponds, while the dinocephalians may have preferred a more variable environment of temperature extremes as found in the forested uplands where fast-moving rivers and streams crossed through.

Herbivorous animals rarely, if ever, defend the plants and territory where they live. Separated by their own environmental preferences, the occasional intermingling of the dinocephalians and pareiasaurs would have resulted in uneventful confrontations of defensive bluffing and passive retreats. Direct competition between the two groups was limited as long as they had different environmental needs. Therefore, the extinction of the dinocephalians may have been instigated by causes other than the pareiasaurs, possibly climatic and environmental changes.

Even though the pareiasaurs existed long after the dinocephalians, they continued much as they always did, and did not become as abundant as the dinocephalians had been. Instead, the animals that multiplied and became dominant were the dicynodonts, a specialized group of anomodonts. They were the longest-lived group of mammal-like reptiles, existing for approximately 55 million years. By the Late Permian, they seem to have distributed worldwide, and their fossilized remains have been found in contemporaneous strata in South Africa, Brazil, India, China, Russia and Scotland.

DICYNODONT BEAKS AND THEROCEPHALIAN TEETH

The earliest known dicynodont fossil remains are from the very base of where the *Tapinocephalus* Zone begins, or possibly even from the last layers of the Ecca Zone. *Eodicynodon* was a very small animal, standing only several centimetres high and about 30 cms (1 ft) or so in length. Unique to the therapsids and, like all the latter dicynodonts, *Eodicynodon* had a specialized turtle-like beak used for cropping the vegetation that it ate. Also like most of the latter dicynodonts, *Eodicynodon* was equipped with a pair of tusks that could inflict further damage along with what was already a powerful and painful bite.

The superiority of the dinocephalians, such as the *Moschops* of South Africa, would hardly seem threatened by the rather innocuous looking *Eodicynodon*. Tiny in comparison, this primitive dicynodont may have lived in burrows for extra protection from both predators and environmental hardship. Its squat, little body had stubby legs that were certainly no better, and perhaps, were even more primitive than the advanced dinocephalians. However, it was the turtle-like beak that contributed to their success. The beak was a highly efficient feeding mechanism that may have allowed a greater intake of food which would have been all the more necessary if the dicynodonts were developing a level of endothermy and possessed a high metabolic rate.

It should be stressed that merely being a therapsid, or mammal-like reptile, does not automatically imply that an animal was endothermic. Indeed, the metabolic rate and development of endothermy, if any, was variable among the therapsids. However, while not totally conclusive, the likelihood is that some level of endothermy was present in at least some of the therapsids. Furthermore, it is likely that the dicynodonts were more endothermic than the dinocephalians. The high latitudes where the dicynodonts are found indicates that they would have benefited greatly from a high metabolic rate. The efficient beak would have been crucial in cropping and processing the large amounts of food that would have been necessary to sustain a higher metabolism. Also, the general body shape of the dicynodonts is quite unlike a typical reptile in that the tail is greatly reduced, the limbs are shorter and the rounded, bulky body is compact. This peculiar body shape may have contributed to the reduction of heat loss that would take place if the animal were equipped with longer appendages. All in all, the origins and success of the dicynodonts may be attributed, at least in part, to their development of a higher metabolic rate associated with some level of endothermy.

During the time that the dicynodonts were first developing, still other groups of therapsids were appearing on the scene. The therocephalians superficially resembled the gorgonopsids (see page 52). Both groups were predominantly carnivorous, but the therocephalians became more diverse to include rather large individuals, such as *Pristerognathus*, and also remarkably small animals, like *Regisaurus*, that were insectivorous.

The therocephalians first appeared in both the Russian Zone Two and the South African *Tapinocephalus* Zones. Relatively large meat-eaters were among the earliest forms, while the last of the therocephalians included only the remarkably small and medium-sized groups that had developed unique and specialized diets. The reduction in size apparently coincided with their reduction in numbers for all of their kind gradually fell victim to extinction. This occurred mostly by the end of the Permian, and then totally during the early part of the Triassic. One of the last was *Bauria*, from the Lower Triassic, which was fairly small in size. *Bauria* had become especially specialized, developing advanced dentition suitable for processing a diet of vegetation.

The decrease in size, as well as the advanced tooth structure with incipient multicusps, indicate that again, a development towards a faster metabolism and endothermy might well have been present among the therocephalians. With more advanced dentition, came an increase in the rate of processing food, a trait more typical of mammals than reptiles. Among the more advanced therocephalians, a fully developed bony, secondary palate was formed in the roof of their mouth. In similar fashion to modern mammals, their ability to breathe was therefore unimpaired while eating. A cartilaginous, unossified secondary palate might possibly have existed among the gorgonopsids but the therocephalian condition was more advanced. Also like the gorgonopsids, the therocephalians pos-

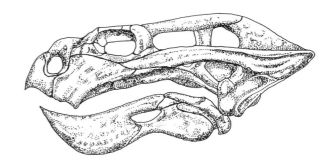

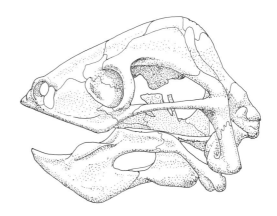

Shown are the skulls in side view of the herbivorous beaked dicynodonts, (top) Dicynodon *(length of skull is approximately 30 cms [1 ft]), and (bottom)* Cistecephalus. *These two dicynodonts signify the last two zones of the Late Permian of South Africa.* Cistecephalus *skull is shown approximately life size.*

sessed sheets of cartilage which extended from bony ridges inside their snout and increased their sense of smell.

The marked structural and biological advances that the therapsids had developed were certainly responsible for their incredible success. More than any other contemporary group of reptiles, the diverse groups of therapsids excelled in adapting to the climatic and environmental conditions prevalent during the Late Permian. However, the constant shifting of the continents and the related processes continued to influence and change the climatic conditions of the world. The environments that the therapsids had become so efficiently adapted to were threatened by instability and increasing change. They were faced with being specialized for conditions that were disappearing. Amazingly, the advanced mammal-like condition that initially benefited the therapsids may have become the incongruous characteristics that led to their downfall. This would have happened in two courses of action. First, the mammal-like metabolism, even if only partially developed, would have become less cost-effective and difficult to maintain in the increasingly warm climates that persisted. Second, the therapsids would have been confronted by competition from other types of animals, predictably fully ectothermic reptiles that

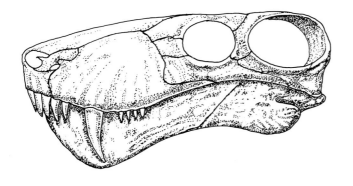
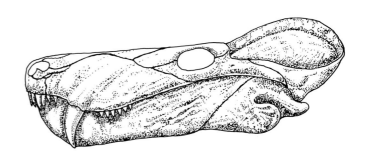

While generally resembling each other, these skulls belong to two separate groups of carnivorous therapsids: (left) Lycaenops, *a gorgonopsid (skull length approximately 20 cms [8 in]), and (right)* Pristerognathus, *a therocephalian (skull length approximately 30 cms [1 ft]). Of the two groups, the therocephalians were more diverse and advanced as there were small, as well as large members; and their mouths had bony, secondary palates and teeth that were developing multicusps. Therocephalians were therefore more like mammals than the gorgonopsids. (after Broom, 1932)*

inherently took advantage of an environment for which they were more efficiently adapted. Consequently, the therapsids were continually plagued by this ecological form of double jeopardy as the warming of the global climate continued.

The last part of the Permian is best represented in Russia's Zone Four and its counterparts in South Africa's *Endothiodon* and *Cistecephalus* Zones. The African zones are notable for the remarkable abundance of the dicynodonts which dominated a world that was previously held by the dinocephalians. None of the dicynodonts of this time were equal in size to the dinocephalian giants. The comparatively primitive *Endothiodon* was only moderately large in size, as were most of the other dicynodonts of the Late Permian, attaining only 1 m (3 ft) or so in length. In even more contrast was the remarkably small dicynodont, *Cistecephalus*, that was not much more than 30 cms (12 ins) in length. Gorgonopsids, and to a lesser extent, therocephalians were the dominant carnivores that must have preyed heavily upon the dicynodonts and other animals which were available.

GLOBAL WARMING AND EXTINCTIONS

Towards the end of the Permian, the overall size of the glaciers in the southern hemisphere fluctuated with globally deleterious effects. The temperate climates that sustained the therapsids were threatened by an increasingly warm global climate. Huge boulders littered the landscape as glacial till deposits (see glossary) were left in the wake of the retreating glaciers. But the therapsids continued to flourish as the impending doom of extinction loomed over them. Gorgonopsids, such as *Lycaenops*, would have continued

to feast on dicynodonts quite oblivious of the ecological collapse that was to confront them. Seasonal cool breezes that carried and scattered the falling autumn leaves of the *Glossopteris* flora carried no hint of the incessant change of the global climate. The apparent stability of the glaciers on the distant horizon was a deceptive image of an age that was ending.

Extinctions that occurred towards the end of the Permian may have been gradual, coming in pulses or waves of finality. Different forms of life possessed varying levels of tolerance, and would have reacted at different times relating to their particular ecological disruption. Marine life forms were decimated over several millions of years afflicting well over half, and perhaps as much as 75 to 90 percent of the sea life that existed at that time. By the end of the Permian, non-marine life forms, clearly represented by the therapsids, suffered great losses. These included all the gorgonopsids, nearly all of the therocephalians, and, to a lesser but still considerable extent, a large number of the dicynodonts. The Permian extinction also affected other types of reptiles. Pareiasaurs that had persisted for most of the Late Permian fell into nature's oblivion, extinction.

The grotesque, armour-studded pareiasaurs (see pages 57–8) are known from South Africa and Brazil, which was at that time attached to the western side of Africa. In the northern hemisphere, the pareiasaurs are also known from northern China, Scotland, and Zone Four of Russia. In the quarries of Zone Four, the

Within a temperate forest beneath a Glossopteris *tree, a gorgonopsid,* Lycaenops, *guards over its prey, a dicynodont,* Endothiodon. *The approximate length of* Lycaenops *is 1.2 m (4 ft), and* Endothiodon *1.1 m (3½ ft).*

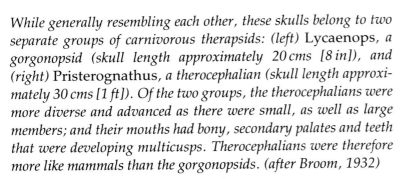

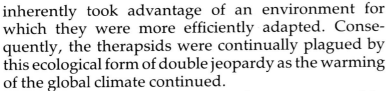

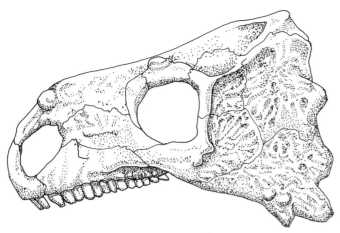

PAREIASAURUS

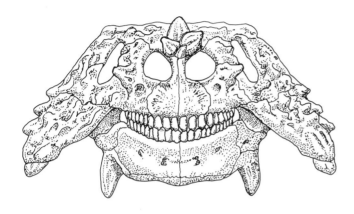

SCUTOSAURUS

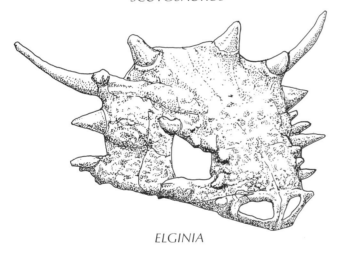

ELGINIA

Skulls of three late Permian pareiasaurs: (top) Side view of Pareiasaurus *from Brazil (length is approximately 30 cms [1 ft], (after Araujo, 1985); (middle) Front view of* Scutosaurus *with lower jaws from Russia (length and width is approximately 50 cms [20 in]), (after Kuhn, 1969); (bottom) Side view of* Elginia *from Scotland (length is approximately 20 cms [8 in]).*

pareiasaur *Scutosaurus* is found associated with one of the last and largest of gorgonopsids, *Inostrancevia*. Here, as in the southern hemisphere, the Permian extinction took its toll.

By the end of the Permian, the seasonal plants, as represented by the *Glossopteris* flora of Gondwana, were replaced by Triassic plants, like the seed-fern *Dicroidium*, that were better adapted to warmer and dryer climates. The transition of plants was pro-

tracted, and occurred in different parts of the globe at different times. Radiating from lower to higher latitudes, the pattern of floral replacement reflects the expanding climatic warming that caused the environments to change.

In the northern hemisphere during the latest part of the Permian, the movement of the continents had brought the landmasses into polar regions of the highest northern latitudes. As should be predicted by such an event, northern glacial activity occurred. And as a result, the global climate may have fluctuated, but the processes that were warming the global climate prevented the substantial expansion of glacial activity, as was previously experienced in the southern hemisphere. Instead, they prevailed in remelting this smaller northern polar icecap.

Throughout the Late Permian, the positions of the continents had shifted so as to enclose, from both the north and south, an enormous portion of the ocean. This enclosed portion of the ocean is called the Tethys Sea. Such a configuration of the continents disrupted the oceanic currents that would have otherwise maintained a stable heat exchange. Located over equatorial latitudes, the Tethys Sea continued to become warmer. The circulating currents within the Tethys Sea were restricted and did not receive the major cooling influences from the freely circulating ocean beyond. So, the gradual warming of the Tethys Sea further instigated the global climatic changes that were in progress due to other geographical and topographical conditions. An incredibly complex pattern of monumental powers were joining forces that would continue to reshape the world, bringing an end to many kinds of therapsids and setting the stage for the world of the dinosaurs to begin.

The therapsids sustained heavy losses that severely weakened their position of world dominance. After the Permian, a resurgence would occur, but this would be confronted by persistent climatic and environmental changes, as well as competition from different groups of reptiles. Even before the end of the Permian, a new group of reptiles was arising. These reptiles were not from the synapsid stock of the therapsid, mammal-like reptile ancestry, but from the diapsid lineage. One specific group of these diapsids evolved a characteristic opening in the skull located in front of the eye. This anti-orbital fenestra, as it is called, distinguishes the archosaurs, a group of reptiles that would eventually lead to the dinosaurs.

On the bottom right, a procolophon, Nyctiphruretus, *snaps at a dragonfly. On the lower left is the small amphibian,* Kotlassia. *Armour-studded pareiasaurs,* Scutosarurus, *bask in the foreground, as others in the background stray away from two of the largest gorgonopsids,* Inostrancevia, *that are approaching from the left.* Inostrancevia *reached lengths of 4.3 m (14 ft), and Scutosaurus up to 3 m (10 ft).*

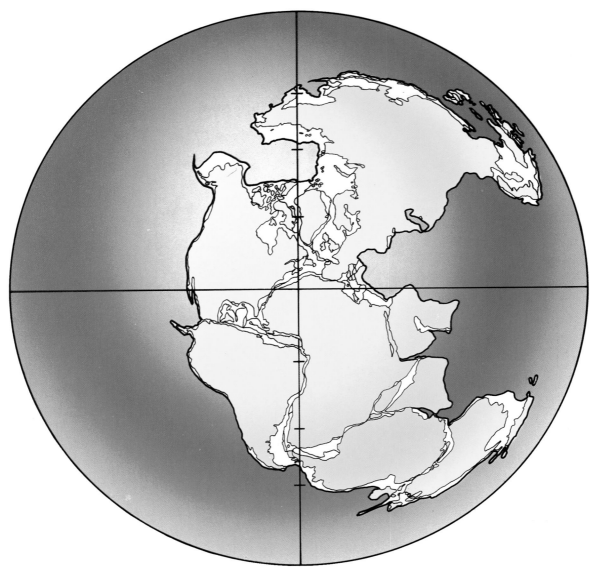

EARLY TRIASSIC GLOBE
Pangaea continued to shift northward causing the glaciers and polar ice cap of Gondwana to disappear. The world climate became warmer than it was during the Permian. Continents were connected so that animals could spread throughout Pangaea.

CHAPTER III
THE TRIASSIC
THE GREAT TRANSITION

THE COMPETITIVE EDGE

How was it possible for the comparatively advanced therapsids, animals that were well on their way to becoming truly modern mammals, to fall from world dominance and be succeeded by more 'primitive' reptiles? What enabled certain reptiles, most notably the dinosaurs, to surpass the previously dominant lineage of mammal-like reptiles? This is one of the most significant transitions to occur in the history of animal life, and almost caused the extinction of mammalian ancestry, certainly deterring its re-establishment for over 100 million years.

Lying on a tree fern stalk is a small Procolophon. *Below it is fallen debris consisting of primitive conifer leaves (podocarp) along with* Ginkgo *leaves and fruit.* Procolophon *reached lengths of approximately 30 cms (1 ft).*

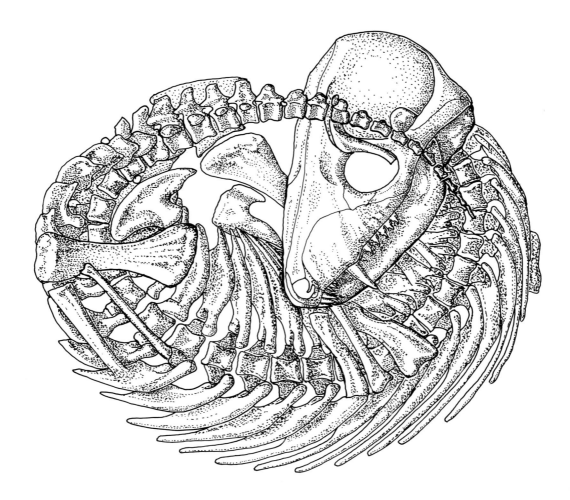

Shown life-size is a skeleton of the therapsid, Thrinaxodon, *as found in the curled up position in which it died. This mammal-like reptile is known from South Africa and Antarctica. (after Brink, 1958)*

Together the Triassic, Jurassic and Cretaceous periods formed the Mesozoic Era, a time most appropriately regarded as the 'Age of Reptiles', and it was during the Triassic period that this 'Great Transition' took place. In order to understand what brought about The Great Transition it is best to retrace the chronology of events and the particular factors that were influential at the time.

To a certain extent, the success of the therapsids during the Permian hinged upon their ability to adapt to seasonally changing environments which included periods of cool to cold winters. These climatic conditions restricted primitive, cold-blooded animals because of their dependence upon the temperature of their surroundings to maintain an active level of metabolism. Therapsids were unique as reptiles in being able to combat the cold by their ability to self-generate body heat (endothermy) to sustain an active metabolism. It was crucial to their success. However, endotherms do have to eat a comparatively large amount of food to sustain a high metabolism and in this sense, endothermy may be regarded as an expensive physiology in contrast to ectothermic physiologies which, being more directly dependent on the environment,

are less costly to maintain. While the differing physiologies have their flaws and limitations, both are effective as long as their optimal environment is stable.

But environments change and this, on a global scale, is what confronted the therapsids. Their ecological environment continued to deteriorate. While threatening the therapsids, the changing ecology became increasingly beneficial for other kinds of animals that had significantly different physical biologies, specifically the cold-blooded reptiles.

Numerous candidates lingering through the Permian were available to repopulate this changing Triassic world. Among them were diverse groups from the basic stocks of anapsid and diapsid reptiles which radiated and evolved in their attempts to exploit the dynamic, redeveloping environment. Because they possessed the 'less costly' physiology of ectothermy, allowing them to maintain an active metabolism by relying on the surrounding temperature, they were efficient exploiters of the changing climatic and environmental conditions and the Triassic world became theirs for the taking.

This competition for superiority was not a face to face battle between the therapsids and the other rep-

A cool, temperate climate prevailed in parts of South Africa where, within their den nestled among the Dicroidium flora on the upland hillsides, a protective Thrinaxodon watches over her playful pups. These mammal-like reptiles are believed to have had some degree of parental care and a social gregariousness similar to the behavioural characteristics of present-day mammals.

tiles, and while individual confrontations certainly must have occurred, it would be incorrect to imagine this competition as reptiles battling against the mammal-like therapsids in direct physical confrontation. It was rather a take-over of environments as the ecological changes favoured certain types of animals.

Some niche-holders retained their primitive characteristics, while bolder explorers ventured into new environments, developing increasingly advanced physical attributes. The anapsid *Procolophon*, had a modestly advanced pseudotemporal opening, or expanded area directly behind its orbits. These procolophons survived the Permian/Triassic extinction to become common and numerous across the globe. They were smallish animals with primitive, peg-like teeth that were best suited for a mostly herbivorous diet. Some had short spines on the back of their skull, similar to present day horned toads. As a group they were terrestrial browsers, nestling in the underbrush and fallen leaves. However, it was also to become the

fallen leaf on that surviving branch of reptiles because it failed to maintain its niche and became extinct by the end of the Triassic. Its extinction was not caused simply because it was of anapsid stock. Other anapsids took distinctly different ecological routes and continued a successful anapsid lineage. The turtles are one such lineage. By interconnecting their bony scutes into an armour-plated shell and incorporating both a terrestrial and aquatic environment, the turtles, as represented in their ancestry by *Proganochelys*, were securely established by the Late Triassic.

The success of the turtles, in contrast to the diminishing capability of the procolophons, was probably related to their ability to compete against other reptiles, including the more progressive diapsids. Primitive members of the diapsids, the lepidosaurs, were ancestors of modern snakes and lizards (including *Sphenodon*) and while these members of the lepidosaurs survive to present times, it was a more advanced group of diapsids, the thecodonts, that eventually led

67

The light of a new day's dawn reveals a community of the semi-aquatic Lystrosaurus *gathered around a water hole.*

to the dinosaurs. All thecodonts share a diagnostic characteristic in the additional opening in the skull in front of the eyes, known as the pre-orbital or anti-orbital fenestra. It identifies thecodonts as the earliest members of the Archosauria.

THRINAXODON AN ADVANCED THERAPSID

It has to be remembered that dinosaurs did not replace the therapsids. The therapsids were supplanted by a very successful pre-dinosaurian radiation of theco-donts. It is exactly how this took place that is such a quandary of evolution. How could remarkably advanced, mammal-like therapsids be taken over by the comparatively primitive reptilian thecodonts? What flaws did therapsids possess that allowed the theco-donts to surpass them in triumph?

By this time, the diversity and development of ther-apsids had reached a pinnacle, from which it seems

they could only decline. Their dwindling numbers during the Triassic included the carnivorous cyno-donts, *Thrinaxodon* and *Cynognathus*, and the vege-tarian dicynodonts, *Lystrosaurus* and *Placerias*. Fossil remains of *Thrinaxodon* have been found in South Africa and Antarctica, indicating that these land-masses were once connected when *Thrinaxodon* was alive. Whether it was restricted to the climatic con-straints of environments at high latitudes is not known, but most likely, its habitats were variable, including cooler hillsides and uplands, because it was probably equipped with an advanced mammal-like physiology that enabled it to broaden its territorial range. Evidence that it possessed such a physiology is found in specific details on its skeletal form. Modifi-cations in the positioning of the limbs allowed a more vertical posture, rather than an exclusively sprawling stance. The tail was considerably reduced in length and the rib-cage was shortened into an advanced mammalian condition which would have been necess-ary for a muscular diaphragm to assist its breathing. Its

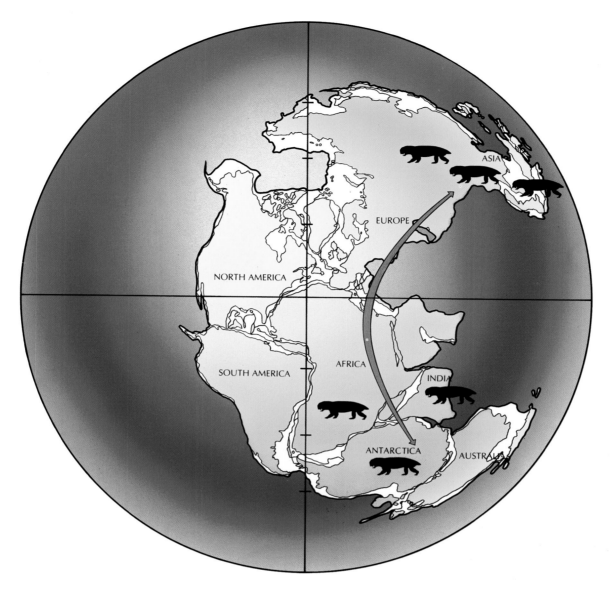

LYSTROSAURUS *DISTRIBUTION GLOBE*

The many places where fossils of Lystrosaurus *have been found indicate that the continents of Africa, India and Antarctica were joined together during the Early Triassic. Russia, China and southeast Asia must have also been connected to these Gondwanic continents for* Lystrosaurus *to have dispersed into the far east of Laurasia. Distribution routes into the northern hemisphere may have been across land bridges of northern Africa and possibly India.*

skull is reminiscent of a canine, with large, pointed teeth for grasping and efficient multi-cusped cheek teeth for cutting into its prey. Tiny openings are located in front of the snout that indicate the presence of thick, muscular lips and perhaps even sensory vibrissae, or whiskers. Rather than scales, it may well have been covered in hair and even have had primitive glands for making identifying scent markings. *Thrinaxodon* was a weasel-sized animal with a mammalian, rather than reptilian, lifestyle and temperament. Gregarious and collaborative in its social behaviour, there is no evidence to suggest that *Thrinaxodon* was a placental live-bearer of its young. There is one incredibly well-preserved fossil nodule that contains the remains of a large, mature adult and a young, remarkably small individual found side by side. It is believed that one is an adult female and the other is possibly newborn, implying that parental care might have been practised among the mammal-like cynodonts like *Thrinaxodon*. The odds against discovering such a fossil are staggering.

It is not too difficult to imagine a mother *Thrinaxodon* patiently watching over its young and active cubs. Weak, guttural cries would have called out during the mock battles of play. But nothing would seem to threaten the safety of a temporary den amid the seed-fern *Dicroidium* underneath the branches of conifers and ginkgoes that dotted the hillsides. The once dominant *Glossopteris* flora with its seasonally deciduous leaves was conspicuously absent. Environmental changes were becoming increasingly evident as a new blanket of greenery appeared across the landscape. Even as *Thrinaxodon* was gazing outward from the highest hilltop on to its surroundings, there was nothing immediately apparent to alert the therapsids to their oncoming demise.

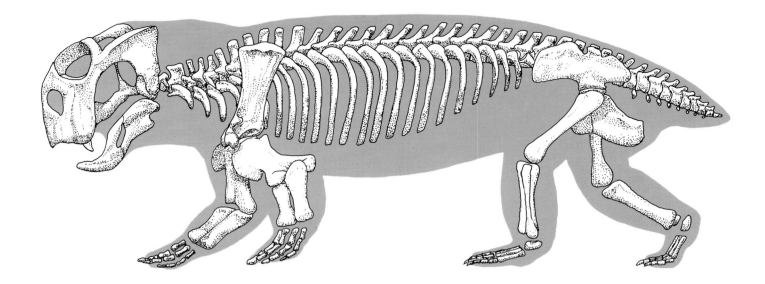

Skeleton of the herbivorous therapsid, Lystrosaurus. *Animal's length is approximately 1 m (3 ft). (after Colbert, 1980)*

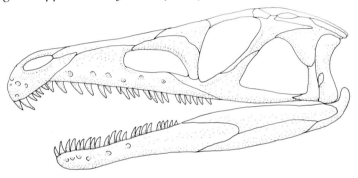

The skull of the primitive thecodont, Proterosuchus, *is approximately 15 cms (6 inches). A diapsid, as indicated by the two temporal openings behind the eye,* Proterosuchus *is also an archosaur as demonstrated by the additional opening (antiorbital fenestra) in front of the eye. (after Cruickshank, 1972)*

LYSTROSAURUS WINNING THE BATTLE

The dicynodont, *Lystrosaurus*, would have been equally unaware of any foreboding from its vantage point along the banks of rivers and lakes within the lowlands. Wallowing in the shallows or resting on the shore, a group of *Lystrosaurus* would find safety in their numbers. This small, 1-m (3-ft) long herbivore behaved similarly to the modern hippopotamus. Its awkward, stubby body was vulnerable to hungry predators, but appearances can be deceptive and like so many apparently harmless herbivores, the little *Lystrosaurus* was not to be trifled with.

A fossil quarry in Africa contained several individuals of *Lystrosaurus* that revealed the actions of one fateful day when a hungry predatory reptile met its match. The hunter was a *Proterosuchus*, one of the earliest archosaurs. It was a moderate-sized animal with a crocodilian appearance and lifestyle. Careful observation of the fossil remains of this particular *Proterosuchus* in the quarry showed that its skull had been repeatedly crushed. The only animal that could have done the crushing was the not so harmless *Lystrosaurus*. When it had to defend itself, the *Lystrosaurus* used its tusked and turtle-beaked mouth as a vicious biting vice powerfully equipped as it was with extraordinarily large jaw muscles. Perhaps the hapless hunter was first drawn precariously close to a herd while attempting to pick off a stray *Lystrosaurus*. While this procedure may have been successful sometimes, it wasn't always. Advancing towards its prey, the *Proterosuchus* must have been surrounded by a mob of stubby bodies all intent on defending themselves. Trapped and engulfed within the hord, the writhing and twisting of the doomed hunter showered waves and splashes that were dappled with drops of red. In only a few moments the lystrosaurs would retreat to safety as the *Proterosuchus* slowly sank where its body would settle on the entombing soft mud. The *Lystrosaurus* had clearly won in this brief battle against this primitive archosaur, but ultimately they were to lose the war.

The tusked and beaked Lystrosaurus *fed upon abundant vegetation, such as* Equisetum, *that surrounded the waterways.* © *National Geographic Society, used with permission.*

DISTRIBUTION OF *LYSTROSAURUS, KANNEMEYERIA* AND *CYNOGNATHUS*

The remains of *Lystrosaurus* have been found in South Africa, India and Antarctica, suggesting the distributional patterns and continental junctions existing in the Early Triassic when these locations were part of the supercontinent of Pangaea in the southern hemisphere. In the northern hemisphere, *Lystrosaurus* is known to have existed in northern Russia, China, and southeast Asia. What becomes obvious is that *Lystrosaurus* once lived on continents that are now separated by vast distances and this inter-continental distribution could only have been possible if the continents were connected in some way, enabling *Lystrosaurus* to wander freely across the unified landscape. Exactly how the continents were aligned is still a matter of great debate.

In addition to the continental land masses being joined together during the Early Triassic, Pangaea was developing a global climate seasonally warm and more uniform, bringing forth a latitudinal broadening of the tropical and sub-tropical environments with strong monsoonal conditions repeatedly prevailing from the northern and southern hemispheres. A myriad of factors worked together to change the climate. The topography of the Early Triassic world was largely lowland; mountain ranges were few and represented mostly by remnants of the North American Appalachians and Russian Ural mountain-building that had taken place in the northern hemisphere during the

71

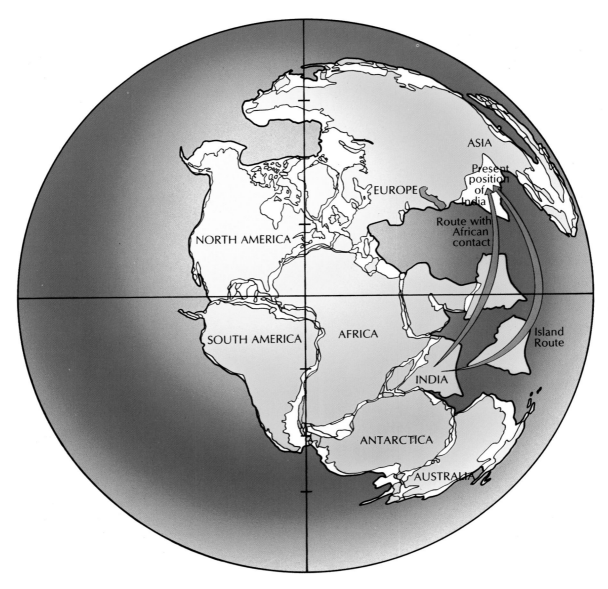

The following labels appear on the globe: ASIA, Present position of India, EUROPE, Route with African contact, NORTH AMERICA, Island Route, SOUTH AMERICA, AFRICA, INDIA, ANTARCTICA, AUSTRALIA

INDIA PLACEMENT GLOBE

The paleo-position of the continent of India has remained an unresolved matter of considerable debate. The formation of the Himalayas was caused by the continent of India colliding into Asia. But prior to this, India was thought to have first become an island continent after breaking away from Africa and Antarctica. However, the fossil evidence (including that of dinosaurs) suggests that India did not become an isolated island. Instead, it would appear that either India was always attached to Asia, or perhaps more likely, India maintained contact with the east coast of Africa as it gradually moved northwards towards its present position. Such contacts with other continents would explain the similarity of animals found in India to those of other continents, and the apparent lack of endemic animals that would have evolved if India was actually an isolated continental island.

Permian; modest hill ranges and uplands would occasionally fence their way around the broader expanses of lowlands and waterways; shallow, epicontinental seas, including the expanding Tethyan embayment, became warmer increasing the global mean temperatures. These factors, together with the accessibility of the land with its epicontinental seaways, presented no major obstacles to animals such as *Lystrosaurus* to expand their territorial range throughout Pangaea. *Lystrosaurus* were certainly not the only kind of animal to expand their territories. As the stability of the warmer climates increased, they became easier for the cold-blooded ectotherms, such as the *Proterosuchus*, to conquer and exploit.

The *Lystrosaurus* fossils of Russia and China present intriguing possibilities as to exactly how they came to exist there. Did *Lystrosaurus* simply migrate northwards gradually reaching further and further into the northern hemisphere? Or were China and Russia located closer to the southerly placed Gondwana continents, and possibly even connected to the continent of India? Or is it possible that India was not of southern hemispheric origins at all, but, instead, connected to the northern hemisphere continents of Euroasia? These possible dispersal routes present conflicting interpretations of where the continents were located, and how the consequent dispersal of animal life through the ages occurred. It is little wonder then that such questions of animal dispersal and continental positions are the controversial subjects of debate.

Animals that lived immediately after *Lystrosaurus* and *Proterosuchus* migrated throughout much of Pangaea. The carnivorous therapsid, *Cynognathus*, and the large dicynodont, *Kannemeyeria*, existed in both the northern and southern hemispheres of Pangaea. Their widespread distribution extended eastward into China, begging the question of how this distribution transpired, particularly, how did these animals reach into the distant Asian continents? Could they have migrated by way of North America to Europe and eventually reached Asia? The theory is tempting, but a shorter, and more direct route now appears to have been possible by way of East Africa directly through India and onwards to China. This recent theory is persuasive, but it challenges the long-held belief that India was part of Gondwana in the southern hemisphere, by now maintaining that India was a part of Laurasia in the northern hemisphere. Indeed, the role that India played in animal dispersal throughout the Mesozoic is easier to explain if it had been attached to Asia since the beginning of the Triassic, or even earlier.

One of the primary reasons animals wander is to satisfy their appetites. The search for food is equally compelling for herbivores and carnivores. As the lush Triassic flora changed and covered the landscape, so did the herbivores, and following the plant-eaters, came the flesh-eaters. The search for food is an extremely effective process for the wide dispersal of animals.

During the Early Triassic, the largest plant-eaters were the dicynodonts, relatives of *Lystrosaurus*, that had greatly increased in size. *Kannemeyeria*, a Late Triassic descendant, was typical of the giant dicynodonts, being up to 3 m (10 ft) in length. *Kannemeyeria* radiated into both hemispheres. Although its fossil remains have been found only in Russia and South Africa, a broader range might have been possible, as other, similar dicynodonts from later in the Triassic were extensively distributed throughout North America, India, Asia and South America.

Evidence of a broader dispersal of *Kannemeyeria* is indicated by the remains of the carnivorous wolf-like therapsid, *Cynognathus*. Because the remains of this meat-eater have been found to be associated with *Kannemeyeria* in South Africa, the *Cynognathus* fossils found in South America suggest that *Kannemeyeria* might also have been there. Using this same rationale, *Cynognathus* might have followed *Kannemeyeria* northwards into Russia. While fossil evidence is lacking, it would not be surprising if future fossil discoveries in Russia and South America reveal the presence of both of these animals.

Foraging groups, or herds of wandering tank-like *Kannemeyeria*, would have been formidable beasts for any predator to confront. Modern herding herbivores can be deadly when provoked, so it was the infirm,

young or aged members of a herd that would have been preyed upon, and it is quite possible that even the mighty *Kannemeyeria* could have fallen victim. So, while groups of *Kannemeyeria* roamed the landscape, foraging for food, occasionally a member would be overcome by hungry predators like *Cynognathus*, hunting alone or in packs.

While these therapsids maintained a broad distribution across the globe, they continued to decrease in number throughout the Triassic period. Direct competition from other reptiles may have only been incidental in their decline. A more probable cause could be related to their advanced mammal-like over-specializations and physiology. Had they been similarly equipped to the other reptiles, therapsids might not only have been able to co-exist, but might have prevented their eventual demise.

RISE OF THE THECODONTS

From amid the many different types of reptiles benefiting from the environmental changes that occurred throughout the Triassic came the uniquely specialized group of diapsids, represented by the archosaurian ancestors, the thecodonts.

Because their physiology was well adapted to the climatic changes they continued to increase in number, until they replaced the therapsids and largely dominated the Triassic world. Thecodonts were composed of highly specialized groups of archosaurs forming distinctive lineages which can be classified into four categories: Proterosuchia, Aetosauria, Parasuchia, and Pseudosuchia.

While each group possessed its own physical specializations they probably had similar if varied physiologies that produced slightly different levels of metabolism. This meant that, as a group, the thecodonts had diverse behaviour patterns and were thereby able to achieve widespread environmental exploitation. Surpassing the achievements of mammal-like reptiles, the thecodonts were to expand their

NEXT PAGE

Three Cynognathus *are seen feasting upon a dicynodont,* Kannemeyeria. *In the distance, more fortunate members of the herd move away across the rolling uplands.* Kannemeyeria *reached lengths of 3 m (10 ft), and* Cynognathus *approximately 2 m (6½ ft).*

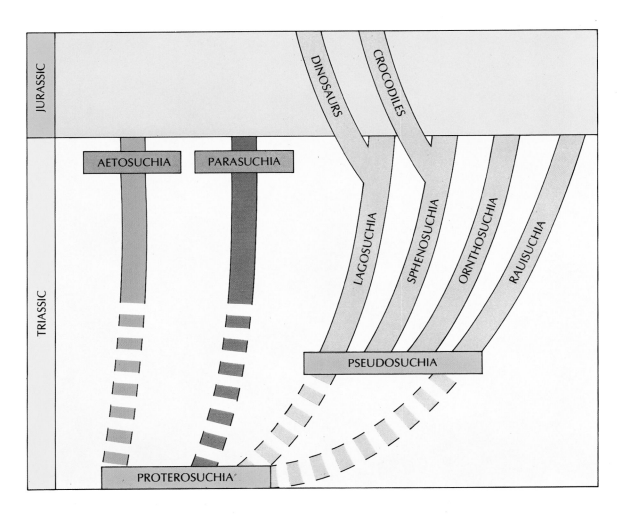

THECODONT CHART
This chart demonstrates the different paths of evolution taken on by the four basic types of thecodonts. From the beginning of the Triassic, the Proterosuchia diverged into the Aetosauria, Parasuchia and Pseudosuchia. All thecodonts failed to survive beyond the Triassic, and only the Lagosuchia and Sphenosuchia left specialized descendants that continued as either dinosaurs or crocodiles. Sub-groups within the Pseudosuchia all experimented in modes of achieving an upright limb posture. Of the four, only the Lagosuchia led to dinosaurs which successfully achieved a fully bipedal gait. The quadrupedal Ornithosuchia and Rauisuchia failed to compete. While the four-legged Sphenosuchia adapted to aquatic environments, the dinosaurs took dominance over the terrestrial world.

niches, encompassing aquatic, semi-aquatic, terrestrial, and arboreal environments. Some of them even took to the air. But as varied and widespread as the thecodonts were, not all of them were destined for success. Competition between different types resulted in the weeding out of the less efficient.

The earliest true archosaurs, including *Archosaurus* from the Late Permian, belonged to Proterosuchia, the most primitive group of thecodonts, and all the other groups of thecodonts were probably descendants from members of the Proterosuchia. Early in the Triassic they attained worldwide dispersal. Unlike their descendants, the progenitor members of the Proterosuchia all retained a sprawling limb posture and had no bony armour-scutes along the back. Basically resembling crocodiles in their general form, they probably had a limited capability of terrestrial locomotion, with a preference for aquatic environments. Early members of this group were generally of small to modest sizes, attaining a length of only 1 to 2 m (3 to 6 ft). However, certain members such as *Erythrosuchus* grew to considerable and impressive lengths of up to 5 m (16 ft). The skull of *Erythrosuchus* was nearly a full metre (3 ft) long. The 450 kg (1000 lb) of its massive body was still supported by primitive and ungainly legs that stuck outwards. On land, *Erythrosuchus* would have been a clumsy, hulking form. But as it slid from the shore into the water, its ability to move would have noticeably become more efficient and swift.

The second and third groups of thecodonts, the Aetosauria and Parasuchia, are only represented by fossils of the Late Triassic. However, they may have existed even earlier. The Aetosauria included highly specialized animals that were heavily encased in bony, armoured plates. Numerous horn-like spikes were also present on some forms, including those of *Typothorax* and *Desmatosuchus* and their body proportions resemble a typical crocodilian form. The function of the excessive array of protective bony armour becomes more understandable when the skull is examined. The skull is comparatively small, but most significant are the modifications of the teeth, lower jaws and snout.

Unlike the other thecodonts, the Aetosauria had become extremely specialized for a herbivorous diet. Smaller primitive forms such as *Neoaetosauroides* from Argentina had the teeth that were few and peg-like whereas in some advanced forms, the teeth became leaf-shaped. The most peculiar of the herbivorous modifications was the upturned snout, which appears to have been used as some sort of grubbing device. Having lost the threatening meat-eating aspects of the more typical thecodonts, the Aetosauria had also largely lost their abilities to actively defend themselves. So, to compensate for this they relied on more passive defensive tactics by using their armour covering. Considering the numerous voracious predators that could have preyed upon the Aetosauria, it is not perhaps too surprising that these armoured herbivores became extinct by the end of the Triassic.

The Parasuchia also failed to last beyond the end of the Triassic and the cause of their extinction is much more mysterious. The Parasuchia are more commonly known as the phytosaurs, and are the large, semi-aquatic carnivores that most strongly resemble crocodiles in both appearance and lifestyle. They were abundant, and widely distributed throughout the continents of the northern hemisphere in Europe, North America and India. Their conspicuous absence from the southern hemisphere may hold clues to their eventual demise. But what is so puzzling about their extinction is that they were replaced by a different thecodont lineage that converged on the phytosaurs' domain, duplicated their lifestyle and eventually succeeded them. The mimicking successors were the true crocodiles, ancestors of today's crocodiles. Why the phytosaurs failed to compete when they were so similar is simply not known, but perhaps there was the smallest difference in their physiologies which proved to be their Achilles heel.

The fourth group of thecodonts is the Pseudosuchia. It is the largest group and contains many broadly diversified archosaurs. As differences among the pseudosuchians become more obvious, some members of this group may warrant their own classifications. There are already several valid sub-divisions of classifications among the Pseudosuchia. Most of these smaller sub-divisions failed to last beyond the end of the Triassic. However, from among these groups of pseudosuchians came the separate lineages that led to crocodiles, birds, pterosaurs, and the dinosaurs.

The Pseudosuchia had spread throughout Pangaea by the early to mid-Triassic. The earliest and most primitive members are represented by *Euparkeria* of South Africa and China. It was a modest-sized reptile of about 60 cms (2 ft) in length. Its small size did not foretell of the giant offspring that were yet to come.

The skeleton of Erythrosuchus, *a large proterosuchian thecodont, is from the Early Triassic of South Africa. Animal's length is approximately 5 m (16 ft). (redrawn from Huene, 1911 and Cruickshank, 1978)*

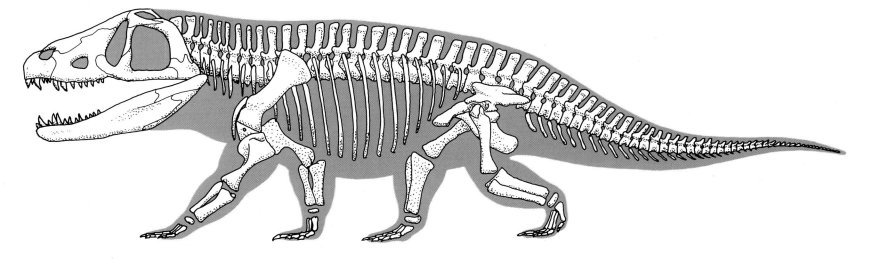

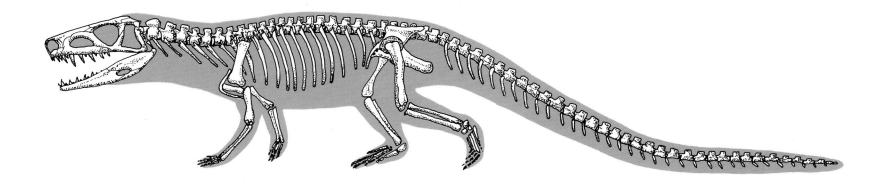

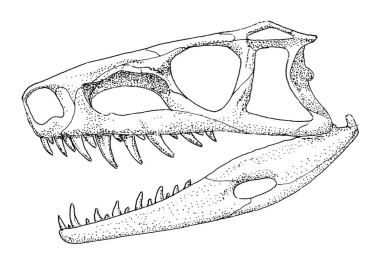

Shown is the skull (life size) and skeleton of the primitive pseudo-suchian, Euparkeria. *Animal's length is approximately 60 cms (2 ft). (skull after Ewer, 1965 and skeleton after Carroll, 1988)*

THE LEGS OF *EUPARKERIA*

Euparkeria was a progressive and specialized carnivore equipped with large, flattened teeth with tiny serrations along the edges for cutting its prey into convenient mouth-sized portions. While small invertebrates, insects and reptiles would have been part of its diet, these slashing, knife-like teeth enabled *Euparkeria* to tackle large prey that could not be swallowed whole.

When *Euparkeria* walked, it was a sinuous, fast-moving reptile that used all four of its legs. The primitive characters of its sprawling legs would have been even more obvious when *Euparkeria* lay resting on the ground with its legs outstretched to its sides. When startled, or motivated to chase after a fleeting meal, *Euparkeria* could put on an impressive burst of speed that would have raised it up onto its longer and more powerful hind legs. While running, the smaller front legs, or arms, became functionless and were held motionless against the sides of the body. With the power and speed from its hind legs alone, *Euparkeria* would have overtaken its prey, and slammed its jaws around the stunned victim, holding on without using its 'hands'.

There is a great significance associated with the fact that *Euparkeria* did not use its outstretched arms and grasping hands to catch or hold its prey. The additional movement of the front legs would cause a faster depletion of oxygen. So by not moving these limbs, the available oxygen that has passed through the lungs could sustain the hind limbs' stressful and rapid activity. Unlike the thecodonts, the therapsids did not become bipedal – even though they stood more upright, they still retained a quadrupedal gait which demonstrates differences in their physiologies.

Attempts towards bipedalism can be seen among several lizards that are living today, including the *Basiliscus*, *Hydrosaurus*, *Chlamydosaurus* and others. These reptiles are typically quadrupedal, but can run bipedally when necessary. The front legs are drawn stiffly along their sides just as *Euparkeria* could have done some 200 million years ago. This convergent behaviour could be a link between ancient and modern reptiles which represents a behavioural process that allows ectothermic reptiles to effectively conserve energy by avoiding a rapid depletion of oxygen in the bloodstream. There are no totally bipedal lizards living today. However, the unique efficiency of running on two legs reshaped the very form of the giant descendants of *Euparkeria* that were yet to come.

Running forward, Euparkeria *is shown approximately life-size.*

LAGOSUCHUS AND THE ANCESTRY OF DINOSAURS

Fossil remains have been found in Argentina, South America that belong to a progressive group of pseudo-suchians, called the Lagosuchidae. They lived after *Euparkeria*, during the Middle Triassic. Of all the known thecodonts, *Lagosuchus* of the Lagosuchidae, is the most probable ancestor of the dinosaurs. *Lagosuchus* was still a pseudosuchian and not yet a dinosaur. However, its physical characteristics are clearly on the way towards becoming dinosaurian. This can be seen particularly well in several features of the hind limbs, which are considerably more advanced than those of *Euparkeria*, creating a more efficient bipedal gait. But even *Lagosuchus* was not totally bipedal. In fact, *Lagosuchus* may still have spent most of its time on all four legs.

The degree of specialization, and yet flexibility, in the locomotion and behaviour of Lagosuchidae was essential for the development of the diverse dinosaur origins. Dinosaurs have long been designated into two separate categories divided by their hip structures. The dinosaurs that had hips resembling reptiles are called saurischians, and those with hips resembling

birds are called ornithischians. It has been suggested that the ornithischians evolved directly from the saurischians. But it is more likely that both saurischian and ornithischian dinosaurs originated independently, sharing more than one common ancestor all probably stemming from the Lagosuchidae.

As many as three or more types of lagosuchid derivatives may have played the roles of dinosaur ancestry. Prior to the transition into becoming a true dinosaur, various types of lagosuchids could have pursued distinctly separate behavioural and environmental preferences. This would result in distinctly separate species. In this manner, the varied origins of the first dinosaurs may have taken place. However, the fossil remains of these hypothetical species of Lagosuchidae are still unknown which is why the amount of behavioural versatility and lack of specialization seen in *Lagosuchus* is so important. From this evolutionary level, the Lagosuchidae could have continued to evolve into one or all of the varied origins of the dinosaurs' ancestry.

Lagosuchus was a conspicuously small reptile when compared to its gigantic dinosaurian descendants. But from humble beginnings can come great things. At a length of about 40 cms (16 ins) and weighing only a few ounces, *Lagosuchus* was an agile creature. Because of its diminutive size, lagosuchids could have been quite capable of venturing into three distinct environmental niches: terrestrial, semi-aquatic and arboreal.

Scurrying along the ground, *Lagosuchus* would be hard to follow as it darted around rocks and through the draping branches of ferns and foliage that formed the terrain. The hesitating pauses, broken with intermittent sprints of speed, would reflect its hunting behaviour. Probing around the cracks and crannies that housed insects would have prodded the potential food into revealing itself. A lunge of the head and a snap of the jaws might just successfully catch a tasty morsel. Still, the jaws would often clamp shut empty, and the hunt would go on.

Shifting its weight backwards, a standing *Lagosuchus* could have reared onto its hind legs raising its head higher for a broader field of view. Awareness of its immediate surroundings was essential to prevent it from becoming a mouthful for a larger, well hidden predator. By a quiet inspection of disturbing nearby sounds it could safely detect the presence of danger or opportunity. Any other *Lagosuchus* nearby would not have been cause for alarm. In fact, unless it were time for breeding, they may well have simply ignored members of their own kind.

Rewarded and conditioned by successful experiences from hunting on the ground, some lagosuchids may have never wandered into different niches. But others could have followed opportunities that attracted them into aquatic or arboreal environments. Preferences for the kinds of food that were found in these niches would have separated and maintained distinctly different behaviours among emerging groups within the Lagosuchidae. The arboreal invader would continue to exploit its surroundings and eventually become more adept and specialized for climbing. The aquatic niches would have had a similar modifying effect, further developing swimming abilities. Food preferences may gradually have broadened as well, to include plants as part of the diet. From such varied behaviour, which included terrestrial, aquatic, and arboreal adaptations, came the diversified origins at the very base of the dinosaurs' family tree.

STAURIKOSAURUS THE EARLIEST DINOSAUR

The transitional dinosaur ancestors immediately following *Lagosuchus* are virtually unknown. However, the appearance of the earliest-known dinosaur does come relatively soon after the time in which *Lagosuchus* lived. This step in evolution came approximately 200 million years ago, during the middle of the Triassic. While only poorly known from incomplete fossil remains, *Staurikosaurus* maintains the distinction of being the earliest dinosaur as yet discovered.

Perhaps it should not be too surprising that like *Lagosuchus*, the fossil remains of *Staurikosaurus* are also from South America, but from Brazil as well as Argentina. Does this geographical similarity imply that dinosaurs originated in South America? It is a tempting conclusion, but not necessarily correct. At this time during the Triassic, the South American continent was still connected to the African continent, and together

Shown in a quadrupedal stance is the skeleton of Lagosuchus, *which is the most probable type of ancestor for the dinosaurs from the Pseudosuchia. Animal's length is approximately 40 cms (16 ins). (after Bonaparte, 1975)*

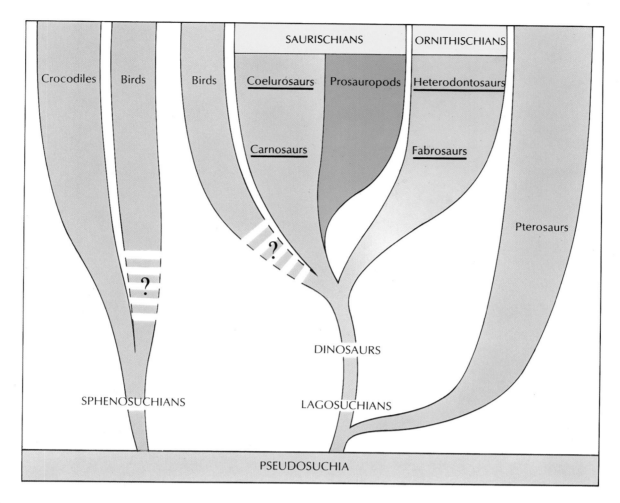

DINOSAUR CHART
*This chart demonstrates the paths of evolution taken on by the descendants of the Pseudosuchia which survived into the Triassic. Crocodiles evolved from the sphenosuchians, and dinosaurs evolved from the lagosuchians. Pterosaurs evolved from a pre-Lagosuchus pseudosuchian. The two major orders of dinosaurs, saurischians and ornithischians, split into five separate sub-orders. Saurischians consist of **1.** carnivorous short-necked carnosaurs, **2.** long-necked coelurosaurs, and **3.** herbivorous, long-necked prosauropods. The herbivorous ornithischians were either **4.** fabrosaurs with non-grinding teeth, or **5.** heterodontosaurs with grinding teeth. Birds may have evolved from either sphenosuchians or from dinosaurs during the Late Triassic.*

they formed only part of Pangaea. With the fossil record being so scantily preserved, it is more likely that *Lagosuchus* and *Staurikosaurus* did live in Africa (and perhaps elsewhere), but their fossil remains simply haven't been found as yet. Perhaps future discoveries will reveal their presence outside of South America and it is only with a much more complete fossil record that the question of where the dinosaurs originated can be answered. While the initial geographic distributions of the first dinosaurs cannot be made with certainty, it is evident that even the earliest dinosaurs had radiated broadly throughout most of Pangaea by the end of the Triassic.

Staurikosaurus was a sizeable animal reaching more than 2 m (6½ ft) in length. The sharp and pointed teeth in its jaws reveal that it was certainly a meat-eater and it may well have been almost fully bipedal. The diagnostic characteristics that make *Staurikosaurus* qualify as being considered a true dinosaur, and no longer a pseudosuchian or thecodont, can be shown by several skeletal features. The most significant of these is in the structure of the pelvis. The determination is made specifically in regards to the acetabulum, or the hip

socket, where the femur fits into the pelvis. The hip socket of thecodonts is formed by a concave, solid sheet of bone that resists the pressure from the movement of the legs. In dinosaurs, the legs are held in a more vertical stance more directly under the body and pressure from the movement of the legs is directed against the upper lip of the concave socket. Accordingly, this lip forms a ledge that becomes thicker where the stress of the femur's actions concentrate the most. The inside portion of the hip socket receives less pressure from the leg's movement, and as a result an opening appears through the bone inside the hip socket. It is the presence of this opening inside the acetabulum that represents the crossing over into becoming a true dinosaur. In *Staurikosaurus*, the opening is still relatively small, reflecting the primitive condition of this early dinosaur.

Other lesser known dinosaurs were no doubt living along with *Staurikosaurus*. Found in contemporaneous strata are the partial remains of an animal called *Spondylosoma*. It was approximately the same size, or slightly larger than *Staurikosaurus*, but *Spondylosoma* had considerably different body proportions, includ-

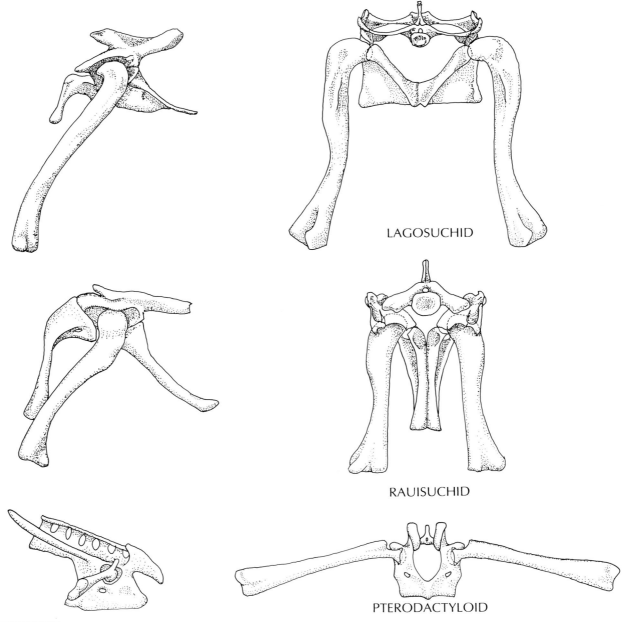

LAGOSUCHID

RAUISUCHID

PTERODACTYLOID

TYPES OF LIMB POSTURE

Comparative views of the pelvis of (top) a lagosuchid, (middle) a rauisuchid, and (bottom) a pterodactyloid as seen from the left side and rear view. Note that the acetabulum, or hip socket, is vertical on the side of the pelvis and face outwards in lagosuchids. The head of the femur is offset at right angles, to attach into the hip socket, which places the legs in an upright posture. The hip sockets are perforated in dinosaurs which evolved from lagosuchids by using this leg and hip structure. Rauisuchids achieved an upright leg posture differently, with solid hip sockets facing downward and only a slightly offset head of the femur. The leg posture of pterosaurs is oriented horizontally, splayed out to the sides. The hip sockets face out sideways and slightly upwards *as well as to the back. The sprawling posture resulted in maintaining solid, closed hip sockets. The head of the femur is slightly offset, which articulates best horizontally for quadrupedal locomotion and while flying. (top and middle after Bonaparte, 1984, and bottom redrawn after Bennett, 1990)*

Shown is the skeleton of the rauisuchian, Saurosuchus, *from Argentina. This quadrupedal pseudosuchian failed to compete against the carnivorous bipedal dinosaurs and became extinct during the Late Triassic. Animal's length is approximately 6 m (19 1/2 ft). (after Bonaparte, 1981)*

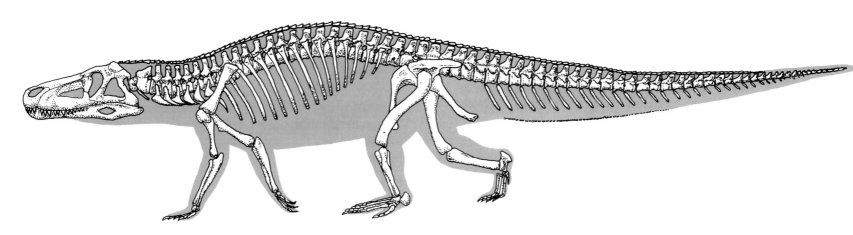

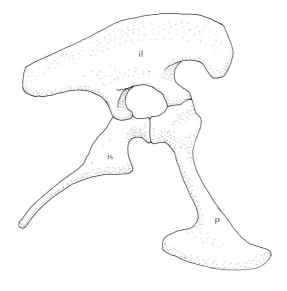

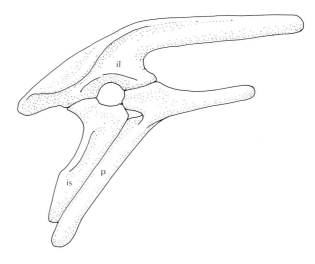

TYPES OF DINOSAUR HIPS
The pelvis, as seen from the right side, in the two orders of dino-
saurs: (left) saurischians, with the pubis facing foreward, and
(right) ornithischians, with the pubis facing backward, parallel to
the ischium. Key: il = ilium, is = ischium, p = pubis.

ing a longer back and neck. Its head appears to have been small and it probably possessed the more efficient, vertical posture characteristic of the dinosaurs. However, it may have retained a preference for walking on all four legs. The similarities seen in *Spondylosoma* appear to reflect the ancestral development of the prosauropods and sauropods, the herbivorous saurischian dinosaurs that include the long-necked giants such as the well known *Brontosaurus/Apatosaurus*. Such relationships and correlations are broad and indeed tenuous. The fragmentary and frustrating incompleteness of their fossil remains are tantalizing, providing all too small clues that can only hint at the presence of the earliest dinosaurs origins. Yet even from this sparse evidence, it appears that from the beginning there was a broadly diversified group of animals forming the origins of the dinosaurs.

RAUISUCHIANS – UPRIGHT POSTURE OF A DIFFERENT KIND

At the same time that the dinosaurs were beginning to appear, pseudosuchians and other thecodonts continued to expand in numbers. Developments occurred towards a more upright limb posture which was attempted by different methods with varying success. The primary function of an upright limb posture was to support the body more efficiently while moving about on land. Bipedalism only became possible after having achieved a more vertical limb posture. In fact, many of the early dinosaurs and progressive thecodonts retained a fully quadrupedal gait even after having achieved an upright limb posture. These quadrupedal pseudosuchians are best represented by members of the Rauisuchidae and the Ornithosuchidae.

The rauisuchids, such as *Postosuchus* and *Saurosuchus*, were the largest of the thecodonts in the last half of the Triassic. They were massive hulking quadrupeds that possessed an apparently efficient upright stance. They achieved this posture in a remarkably different manner than the other pseudosuchians and dinosaurs. The hip sockets of dinosaurs, and their closest ancestors, are located on the sides of the pelvis facing outwards. Fitting into the hip socket, the head of the femur is strongly offset, and turns inwards which vertically aligns the shaft of the femur. In sharp contrast to this, the head of the femur in rauisuchids is not greatly offset and vertical orientation was achieved by shifting the hip socket into a position facing downward, instead of outward. This was accomplished by a tilting of the entire ilium, which contains most of the hip socket, into a near horizontal alignment. The pressures from the leg pushing up and into the hip socket necessitates the primitive closed acetablum.

The ankle joints of rauisuchids also retained the primitive condition that allowed little more than a plantigrade stance – both the soles and heels of the feet touch the ground. The movement of the foot would have included a swinging outward motion similar to the way in which modern crocodiles move their feet. In comparison, dinosaur feet moved in a more direct fore and aft motion. Their ankle structure was more advanced in having a digitgrade stance, in which the back of the foot was held more vertical, and off the ground, while the toes maintained contact with the ground.

The combination of advanced and primitive characters that the rauisuchids were equipped with created essentially a fully upright limb posture. It was adequate, but inferior when faced with the superior dinosaur pelvis, hind limb and ankle structure. The

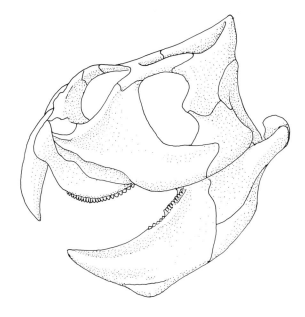

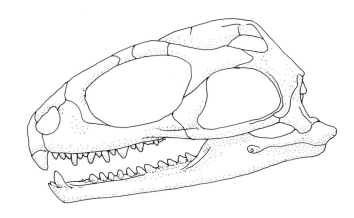

On the left is the skull of Paradapedon *shown for comparison with the distantly related* Sphenodon *of present day. Skull of* Sphenodon *is slightly reduced, and the length of the* Paradapedon *skull is about 21 cm (8 in). (Paradapedon after Chatterjee, 1974, Sphenodon after Romer, 1974)*

flaws that were instrumental in the rauisuchids' eventual demise are probably related to the manner in which they achieved their upright limb posture. Perhaps there were even further limitations that restricted their capabilities of achieving a fully bipedal stance. Numerous factors may certainly have been involved, but it is a curious fact that after the quadrupedal carnivorous pseudosuchians became extinct, all the surviving meat-eating dinosaurs were fully bipedal.

The extinction of rauisuchids is all the more surprising because of their success during most of the Triassic. They were probably descendants from the *Erythrosuchus* of the Early Triassic, which had also been the largest predator of that time. The remains of rauisuchids indicate that they were broadly distributed on every continent with the possible exceptions of Australia and Antarctica. Their voracious versatility enabled them to survive changes in the kinds of prey that they could have fed upon. First the dicynodonts,

and then later rhynchosaurs (a pre-archosaurian reptile, not a thecodont) and aetosaurs made up much of their available diet. These dangerous and powerful prey would have been formidable opponents.

ORNITHOSUCHIANS – MORE CARNIVOROUS QUADRUPEDS

Similar in appearance to the rauisuchians, the ornithosuchians were also predominantly quadrupedal. But, unlike the rauisuchians, they developed a pelvis and hip socket that followed along the lines of early dinosaurian development. The acetabulum had developed a slight opening, thereby making it possible to be considered as a dinosaur and not a thecodont. However, the retention of numerous primitive thecodont characteristics, including the outwardly directed ankle joint, seems to place it on the borderline and reflect

Standing tall on its hind legs, Staurikosaurus *gazes outward into the world of the Mesozoic. From the late Triassic of Argentina and Brazil,* Staurikosaurus *has the distinction of being the earliest known dinosaur. Animal's length is approximately 2 m (6½ ft).*

Shown below is the skeleton of the herbivorous rhynchosaur, Paradapedon, *which is about 1.5 m (5 ft) long.*

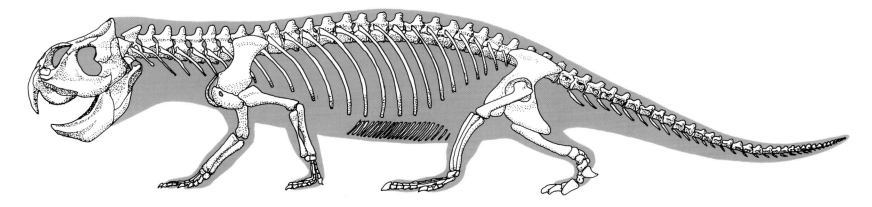

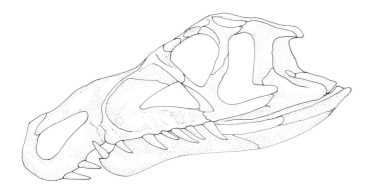
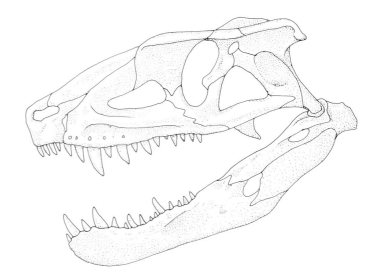

Skulls of two quadrupedal carnivorous pseudosuchians. On the left is the ornithosuchian, Riojasuchus, *and on the right is the rauisuchian,* Postosuchus. *Approximate skull lengths of* Riojasuchus *is 22 cms (9 ins) and 55 cms (22 ins) for* Postosuchus. (Riojasuchus *after Bonaparte, 1971, and* Postosuchus *after Chatterjee, 1985*)

a pre-dinosaurian condition. In comparison to the rauisuchians, the more efficient hip structure makes their smaller size and possibly more limited global distribution quite surprising.

The ornithosuchians are best represented by *Ornithosuchus* from the Elgin region of Scotland and *Riojasuchus* of South America. *Riojasuchus* was considerably smaller, growing to approximately less than half the size of its European counterpart, *Ornithosuchus*, which reached lengths of 4 m (13 ft).

As with the rauisuchians, there was a similar lifestyle between these quadrupedal meat eaters. The habitats and available range of animals to choose from as their prey was probably very much the same.

Significantly, extinction struck both of these quadrupedal carnivores by the end of the Triassic. It would seem that there must have been a distinct physiological difference, other than just a less efficient method of terrestrial locomotion, that caused the quadrupedal

carnivores to succumb to the more competitive bipedal predators. Perhaps the longer forelimbs was a costly arrangement that they would simply have been better off without. Was the reduction of the forelimbs as seen in bipeds in some way beneficial towards achieving a more productive physiology?

CROCODILES APPEAR

There is only one group of carnivorous, quadrupedal archosaurs that survived past the end of the Triassic, and throughout the rest of the Mesozoic. In fact, members of this group survived beyond the great Cretaceous extinction that ended the rule of the dinosaurs, and they are still living today. Crocodiles and alligators are these remaining survivors of an incredibly successful group which had its origins over 200 million

Shown is the skeleton of the ornithosuchian, Ornithosuchus, *from the Late Triassic of Scotland. Even with a similar hip structure to dinosaurs which allowed an upright leg posture, the ornithosuchians failed to compete and were replaced by the more efficient carnivorous bipedal dinosaurs. Animal's length is approximately 4 m (13 ft). (after Walker, 1964)*

(Right) On the outskirts of a forest that is being engulfed by shifting sand dunes, an Ornithosuchus, *walking in the sunlight catches sight of a rhynchosaur,* Paradapedon, *browsing in the shadows.*

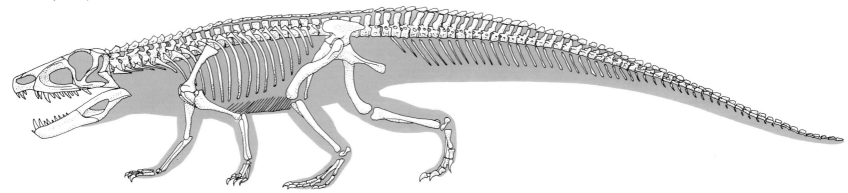

A herd of the North American dicynodonts, Placerias, *scatter from a water hole as a rauisuchian,* Postosuchus, *threatens their safety.* Placerias *reached lengths of approximately 2.5 m (8 ft), and* Postosuchus *was some 4 m (13 ft) long.*

years ago during the middle of the Triassic period.

The crocodilian ancestry arose from a thecodont relationship closely linked to the large and varied group of pseudosuchians. The beginnings of the crocodilian ancestry is represented by the Sphenosuchia which is a poorly represented group consisting of only a few known members. The earliest known member is *Gracilisuchus* from the middle of the Triassic. It was a small reptile only 60 cms (2 ft) long. The closed acetabulum and primitive limb structure reveal that it had a sprawling posture when it walked. It may have had a terrestrial lifestyle more independent from the semi-aquatic behaviour that is so common among modern crocodiles. Their small size was probably due to their inability to compete against the comparatively more advanced rauisuchians and ornithosuchians. It was this failure to compete on land which was instrumental in their eventual success in aquatic, semi-

aquatic and possibly even arboreal conditions.

The dependence upon watery environments was not restricting to the earliest of the crocodilian ancestors. In spite of their small size, their upright gait improved and a more efficient terrestrial locomotion was employed, much in the same manner as ornithosuchians and dinosaurs. Some progressive members of the Sphenosuchia had even developed an opening in their acetabulum which indicates that they had duplicated a vertical hind limb posture independently of the other thecodonts and dinosaurs.

The gracile, and remarkably long-legged sphenosuchian, *Terrestrisuchus* was equipped with hip sockets that were capable of holding the hind limbs vertically. The pelvis was quite small, but adequate to support the light weight of such a small creature of only 77 cms ($2\frac{1}{2}$ ft) in length. What is equally remarkable is the extended length of the limbs which at first

While battling its prey, a Postosuchus *hurls a juvenile armoured aetosaur,* Desmatosuchus, *high over its back. Desmatosuchus reached lengths of 5 m (16 ft).*

glance, implies an agile, swiftly moving runner. Indeed, *Terrestrisuchus* was capable of moving quite fast when necessary. It's obvious that this small animal was designed much more for mobility on the land than in the water. Even though the legs of young and small crocodilians that are living today are comparatively short, they are capable of climbing. So it is not unreasonable to surmise that *Terrestrisuchus* did too although its ability to climb, and in effect become arboreal, is not readily apparent. This is not to say that *Terrestrisuchus* was more adept to life in the trees, but only that the potential for such a lifestyle existed.

The legs of *Terrestrisuchus* were much longer than modern crocodiles. The hind legs were slightly longer than the forelimbs, but the forelimbs had not become reduced for bipedalism. Instead, they remained long, and were proportionately elongated. What this means is that the forelimbs were still largely instrumental for the locomotion of the animal, and the advanced vertical stance of the hind limbs did not automatically make the forelimbs unnecessary. On the contrary, the elongated front limbs were becoming specialized to enable an extended reach. While this could be explained as simply a modification for speed, a greater significance, that of arboreality, and the reaching from branch to branch might also be inferred.

AMID THE TREES

The importance and full significance of the arboreal capabilities of sphenosuchians, such as *Terrestrisuchus*, centres on the extremely controversial origin of birds. The ancestral link between reptiles and modern birds is undeniable. What is not so clear is exactly which reptiles modern birds evolved from.

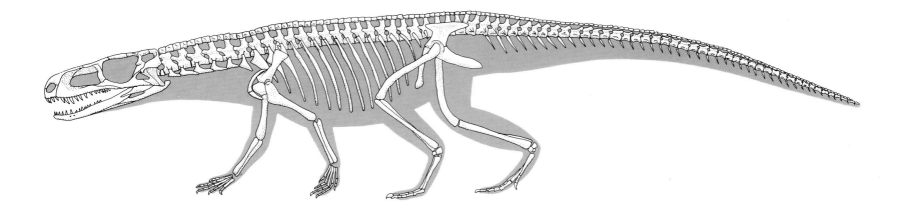

Shown in its typical quadrupedal posture is Gracilisuchus, *a primitive sphenosuchian crocodile. Animal's length is approximately 60 cms (2 ft). (after Romer, 1972)*

During much of the earlier part of this century, it was believed that the ancestors of true birds went back to before the dinosaurs, and into the thecodont transitions radiating from the Triassic. Specifically, it was suggested that the origins would have come from a pseudosuchian with crocodilian affinities.

However, in recent years, there has been a shift of opinion suggesting that modern birds are descended directly from dinosaur ancestors. But before birds could have originated from thecodonts, or for that matter even from dinosaurs, there must have been an arboreal stage that preceded the ability to fly. Only after first achieving arboreal characteristics could leaping from branch to branch turn into gliding for further distances. Modifications of the arms could then develop which would power the flapping of the wings and increase the distance travelled while still in the air.

The ancestral crocodilian, *Terrestrisuchus* possibly took one of the first steps in becoming arboreal. In addition to its having long reaching limbs, *Terrestrisuchus* also had a very long tail which would have been beneficial in clambering about the branches of trees and bushes. Then, as today, reptiles with elongated tails could utilize them as levers to brace and stabilize, in effect acting like an additional limb.

Did *Terrestrisuchus*, or some other unknown sphenosuchian, ever adapt to a fully arboreal lifestyle? It would not have been unlikely. Certainly, other enigmatic pseudosuchians did become arboreal and developed the ability to soar through the air during the Late Triassic.

Longisquama was a tiny pseudosuchian only about 12 cms (5 ins) in length. It was ornamented with a fan of plume-like scales rising high along its back. They were possibly used for thermoregulating its body temperature or to cushion its fall while leaping. A more clearly visible gliding adaptation is seen in the Late Triassic pseudosuchian, *Podopteryx*, which was also very small reaching 23 cms (9½ ins) in length. There would have been no way of knowing of its amazing gliding capabilities by examining only its skeletal remains. But in one miraculously preserved fossil there are details of the skin impressions clearly showing around the complete skeleton. The most startling fact was that the limbs, and especially the hind legs, were draped in thin webbing that could have acted as wing-like flaps. *Podopteryx* was certainly an arboreal glider. In fact, *Podopteryx* can be considered as a transitional stage of evolution that led to more advanced forms of aerodynamic flying reptiles – the pterosaurs.

The earliest known and most primitive pterosaurs are *Preondactylus*, *Peteinosaurus* and *Eudimorphodon* which were all from the Late Triassic. It has been suggested that the pterosaurs, like the dinosaurs, were descendants from a lagosuchid and they are therefore very closely related. However, the retention of five functional digits, or toes, indicates that pterosaur and *Podopteryx* ancestors must have been from a still more primitive pseudosuchian than the known *Lagosuchus*. *Lagosuchus* had reduced its fifth digit, or outer toe. This degeneration indicates that it was becoming more dinosaur-like. Therefore, pterosaur ancestry would have had to have been from a considerably earlier, pre-*Lagosuchus* level of development which had retained the fifth digit and taken to an arboreal lifestyle.

The pterosaurs' ability to fly shows that the expansion and exploitation of arboreal environments had indeed taken place with earlier, pre-flight thecodonts. Pseudosuchians definitely did invade the trees, and adapted to climbing, gliding and eventually flying. But what of *Terrestrisuchus*? Did any of these crocodilian sphenosuchians succeed in equalling what the arboreal pseudosuchians had achieved? When looking at the success of the arboreal pseudosuchians and aerial pterosaurs it would be strange if some members of the Sphenosuchia didn't also exploit those environments. Such animals should have existed, just as the thecodont/bird theory had envisaged so long ago. However, fossils can be incredibly difficult to find. The rarity of some cannot be overstated. An entire group of animals may be known from the remains of only one skeleton, or fragments and parts of a skeleton. Without these fossils there would be no direct knowledge of the animal's existence. Such a lack of discovery has hidden the existence of unquestionably arboreal sphenosuchians.

PROTOAVIS AND THE ORIGIN OF BIRDS

There has been a discovery of fragmentary remains from a bird-like creature that lived nearly 225 million years ago, during the Late Triassic. The implications from this discovery are astounding. Did birds actually evolve from thecodonts independently from any direct dinosaur ancestry? Did the origin of birds occur during the Late Jurassic, or Cretaceous, or much earlier during the Late Triassic?

The remains of this bird-like creature have been found in formations that are some 75 million years older than the Late Jurassic when the feathered *Archaeopteryx* was living (see pages 157–60). These vastly older fossils are from the fragmentary remains of at least two 'birds' that were fairly large, about the size of a crow. Besides the huge time discrepancies, the most remarkable thing about the Triassic 'birds' is that although from much earlier in time, they were considerably more advanced than *Archaeopteryx*, showing a closer relationship to modern birds. This development of advanced Triassic 'birds' would mean that the more primitive *Archaeopteryx* may not be directly related to modern birds at all, and was probably an evolutionary dead end.

The Triassic 'birds' are called *Protoavis* which means 'first bird'. Like *Archaeopteryx*, *Protoavis*, represents a transitional stage between reptiles and birds. They both still had reptilian teeth instead of toothless beaks,

although *Protoavis* had fewer teeth, and possibly a predentary bone on its lower jaw, like ornithischians, which formed the lower beak. They both still had long, only slightly modified, reptilian-style tails. Yet, in light of these convergent similarities, the *Protoavis* had a much more efficient and advanced wing structure than did the *Archaeopteryx*. The wing structure of *Archaeopteryx* is so primitive that it has long been considered to have been a poor flyer, mostly capable of gliding and not powerful flapping of its wings. But

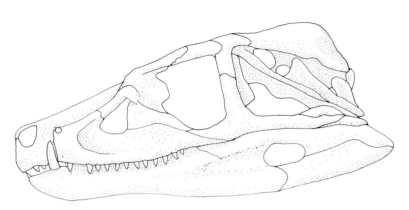

Above is the skull of Hemiprotosuchus, *a primitive terrestrial crocodilian from the Late Triassic of South America. The skull length of* Hemiprotosuchus *is approximately 19 cms (7½ in) (after Bonaparte, 1971)*

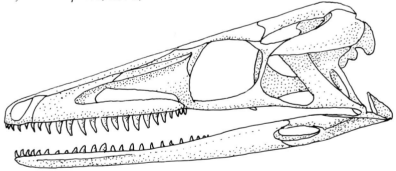

Shown is the skull (above) and skeleton (below) of the extremely gracile sphenosuchian, Terrestrisuchus. *Obviously a fast moving reptile, the light body weight, long legs and tail may have also helped* Terrestrisuchus *climb. Animal's length is approximately 77 cms (2½ ft). Skull is shown life-size (after Crush, 1984).*

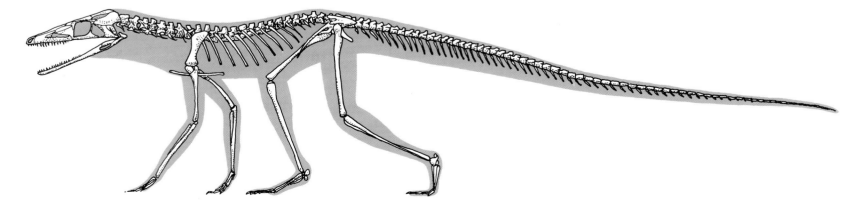

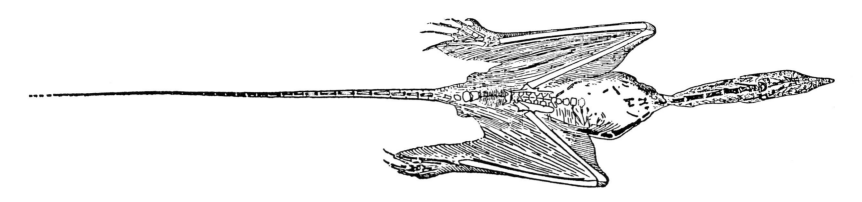

Shown life-size is the skeleton of Podopteryx *as found with impressions of its body outline and wing-like membranes. As an arboreal pseudosuchian,* Podopteryx *demonstrates an evolutionary experiment which may have led to the development of the pterosaurs. (after Sharov, 1971)*

Protoavis was indeed a powerful flyer. The development of its shoulder and chest muscles are clearly more similar to modern birds. There was a significantly larger and definite bird-like furcula (wishbone), and a sternum plate (breastbone) that had the beginnings of a small keel. The developments of these bones in particular are essential for the ability of powered flight as seen in modern birds. Also, unlike the *Archaeopteryx*, the wings of *Protoavis* show the presence of quill nodes on the bones of the forearm and hand. Typically, such quill nodes are found in modern birds that have firmly attached feathers necessary for powerful flight.

Other bird-like characteristics found in *Protoavis* that *Archaeopteryx* lacks are less obvious technical details that are found in its skull, vertebrae and limbs. Perhaps most significant are the pneumatic, or hollow, openings that are found within the limb bones of *Protoavis*. Such hollow bones are quite typical of birds and are surprisingly absent in *Archaeopteryx*. These openings are often cited as a method of lightening the bones, and weight of the animal, as a prerequisite of flight. While there may be some truth in this, the primary function of the hollow bones in birds is related to a complex evaporative cooling system that is connected to their efficient lungs and respiratory system.

HOLLOW BONES

The nature of the hollow bones of modern birds was first mentioned as early as the thirteenth century in a treatise by the Emperor Frederick II. Amazingly, since then, the processes and functions of hollow bird bones have remained largely enigmatic. In 1758 it was proven that airspaces in the limbs of birds were connected directly to the lungs via air-sacs. In fact, some birds can actually breathe through a small hole cut into the hollow openings of their limb bones. It seems odd that the significance of such early and sophisticated discoveries have been largely neglected for an acceptance of simply believing that hollow bones would make a bird lighter and therefore somehow make it easier to lift off into the air. This commonly long-held belief is almost totally erroneous. The actual reduction of the total body weight caused by the hollow openings can only account for a tiny reduction in weight loss, probably not exceeding 4 per cent of the sum total. Such a small percentage could hardly be so crucial in attaining the ability to fly. Therefore, the primary function and origins of hollow bird bones should, in theory, have evolved independently long before flight ever became possible.

Curiously enough, hollow limb bones are found in many pseudosuchians, early crocodilians, and some dinosaurs. The function then should be associated with behaviour, rather than with flight. Using modern birds as an analogue, there are two functional benefits that might be applicable to the hollow-boned reptiles of the past. First, by working as internal evaporative respiratory coolers, the additional control of body thermoregulation could have reduced the excess body heat caused by physical activity, or alleviate heat stroke brought on by the sun. Second, the lungs and respiratory system might have been more efficient than modern crocodiles and similar to modern birds, providing a more efficient oxygen intake and absorption into the bloodstream. Such conclusions may appear to be extreme as physiological differences must have been extremely varied beyond the lungs and respiratory system. However, the physical evidence that has been preserved as fossils, including hollow bones,

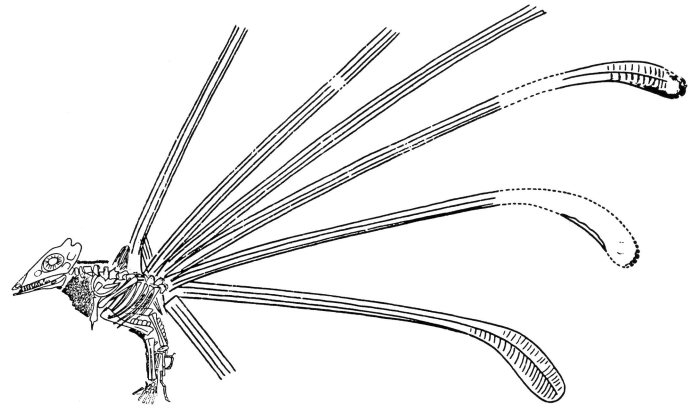

Shown life-size is the skeleton of Longisquama *as found with impression of scales around the throat and arms, and peculiar large feather-like extensions along its back. Probably an arboreal pseudosuchian,* Longisquama *may have used the elongated scaly plumes for sexual attraction, thermoregulation, and parachuting falls while jumping among the trees. (after Sharov, 1970)*

are distinct clues that not only birds, but some thecodonts and even some dinosaurs were equipped with remarkably efficient breathing systems. The success that some thecodonts and dinosaurs had over other reptiles and the mammal-like therapsids may very well have hinged, in part, on the ability to breathe more efficiently.

The similarities between *Protoavis* and *Archaeopteryx* may be due to the convergent development of feathers and the basic physical form that is necessary for flight. However, did *Protoavis* evolve from a pseudosuchian such as *Lagosuchus*, and therefore from a dinosaurian lineage? Or was it only distantly related to dinosaurs, having evolved from another, independent, pseudosuchian lineage such as the crocodilian forerunners, the sphenosuchians?

As already stated, the crocodilian ancestral link to birds has been a matter of great debate for many years, long before the discovery of *Protoavis*. However, the numerous similarities of birds with some carnivorous dinosaurs, such as their bipedal stance, tri-dactyl structure of their feet and hands, and the presence of hollow bones have led many to believe that birds have come from a dinosaur ancestor. The scientific debate has been vigorous and centred mostly upon the fossil remains of *Archaeopteryx*. However, the recent discovery of *Protoavis* has reopened the debate about the ancestry of birds.

COUNTING THE FINGERS OF DINOSAURS AND BIRDS

Evidence against the dinosaur/bird connection comes from the science of embryology. Studies on the development of chick embryos indicate that the three fingers which make up the hand of modern birds are composed of digits two, three and four. This means that birds have lost the inside and outside digits. Palaeontologists have long believed that bipedal dinosaurs lost their outside digits progressively from the fifth digit to the fourth or third digit. The fossil evidence would seem to verify that the innermost digits, including digit one (the inside 'thumb' finger), are always retained by the bipedal dinosaurs. Essentially, this means that if the dinosaur hands did retain digit one, while bird hands lost the same first digit, then birds developed from a different ancestry. If birds are not descendants of dinosaurs, then the true ancestors of modern birds must have been a thecodont of some type that had evolved in a separate and different manner than the dinosaurs.

The pseudosuchians that led towards the origins of crocodiles, notably the sphenosuchians, were potential candidates for branching off into the origins of birds. Of special significance is the hand of *Terrestrisuchus* which reveals a non-dinosaurian tendency that may homologize the crocodilian origins with that of birds. The first digit on the hand of *Terrestrisuchus* had become greatly reduced while the other four fingers remained comparatively much longer. If the embryological conclusions on birds are correct, then this process of degeneration indicating the potential loss of the first digit, is what could have taken place during the thecodont transition into the origins of birds.

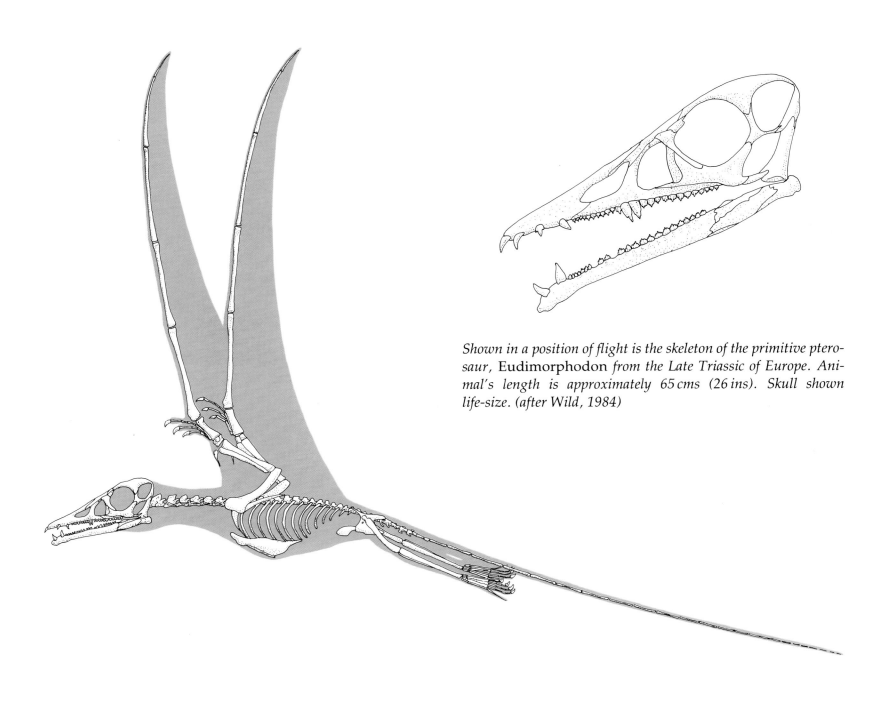

Shown in a position of flight is the skeleton of the primitive ptero-saur, Eudimorphodon *from the Late Triassic of Europe. Animal's length is approximately 65 cms (26 ins). Skull shown life-size. (after Wild, 1984)*

Perhaps it can be said that during the Late Triassic the thecodont ancestry that led towards crocodiles was closely related to the ancestral origins that led to birds. The scientific debate of bird ancestors will continue for some time to come. No doubt, *Protoavis* will add significant insights and hopefully still more future discoveries of equally informative fossils will further clarify the origins of birds and their true relationship to dinosaurs.

RETURN TO THE WATER AND AQUATIC REPTILES

Due to their inability to compete against the larger thecodonts, and still later with the carnivorous bipedal dinosaurs, the crocodilian ancestors did not maintain their terrestrial tendencies. Instead, their preferred choice of environments became more aquatic.

Another lineage of crocodilians, the protosuchians, such as *Hemiprotosuchus*, were equipped with powerful nearly upright legs. By the Late Triassic, these ancestral crocodiles closely resembled the appearance of, and probably lived the semi-aquatic lifestyle of, today's crocodiles. This readaptation and dependence on watery environments was to secure the crocodilian lineage throughout the entire Mesozoic and into present times. The warm waterways of the Mesozoic were instrumental in the success and development of many different types of reptiles.

The largest giants of the Triassic were not land animals, but in fact sea-going creatures. *Shonisaurus* was the largest of the ichthyosaurs, most of which were remarkably porpoise-like in their appearance. In general, ichthyosaurs reached only a few metres in length, but the giant *Shonisaurus* was truly of whale-sized proportions, attaining a length of 15 m (49 ft).

The origins of ichthyosaurs are virtually unknown,

The rauisuchian, Postosuchus, *passes beneath the treetops where there are two of the Triassic birds,* Protoavis. Protoavis *was approximately 60 cms (2 ft) in length and had a wingspan of 70 cms (28 ins).*

and yet their imposing dominance in the Mesozoic seaways can be traced from at least as far back as the Lower Triassic. While clearly reptiles, they were highly specialized animals which represent one of the most amazing examples of convergent body shapes and probable behaviour that can be seen among animals. The incredible preservation of their fossilized remains have often included the actual shape of the body, with outlines of the fin-like paddles and the minute details of scales. Some skeletons have even recorded tragic moments of death while in the process of giving birth. Incapable of laying eggs on land, the ichthyosaurs were ovoviviparous, retaining the eggs inside their body until fully developed, when they gave birth to live young.

From high atop the outcrops of the Sierra Nevada mountains in the Berlin Ichthyosaur State Park are the abundant fossil remains of numerous huge *Shonisaurus*. Curiously, a telling pattern of their depositional preservation reflects a behavioural similarity that is seen in the mysterious mass deaths of whales and other present day sea-going mammals. The exact causes may or may not be the same, but the uniform parallel alignment of the numerous *Shonisaurus* bodies facing the same direction are strikingly indicative of an accidental, misguided mass beaching. An entire pod of these sea-going giants followed one another to their doom. Repetitiously, their enormous bodies burst forth from waves along the shoreline. In the passing of only minutes, the weight of their hulking bodies entrapped them onto the soft sands of the beach. The twisting and writhing was futile as their heavy bodies sank only deeper into the surrounding grip of the entombing sands. Disasters such as this were probably a rare and isolated event that had little impact on the vast numbers of successfully adapted sea-going reptiles.

The warm watery environments were increasingly

95

In similar fashion to present-day whales which sometimes beach themselves, the mass deaths of these ichthyosaurs, Shonisaurus, was caused by their swimming onshore and becoming helplessly trapped on the beach.

more beneficial for reptiles throughout the Mesozoic. Even for giant amphibians, the Triassic rivers, lakes and swamps maintained suitable conditions for their survival. The metoposaurs of the Late Triassic were among the last of the successful labyrinthodont amphibian holdovers from the Permian. Resembling the Permian *Eryops*, their comparatively primitive form remained mostly unchanged throughout the ages. Perhaps because of this they were brought nearly to extinction by the more advanced semi-aquatic predacious reptiles, such as the phytosaurs (see pages 102–104) and ancestral crocodiles. It is easy to imagine that these reptiles outcompeted the metoposaurs for aquatic food, and that these broad-mouthed and wide-bodied amphibians became victims of the reptilian diet.

A steamy haze clouding over the warm ponds and lakes which housed the giant amphibians obscured the increasing numbers of reptiles moving back into the receptive watery environments. Both offensive and inoffensive thecodonts lived alongside the amphibians, sharing the stable warmth from the bodies of water. Abundant long-snouted phytosaurs were becoming more common along the banks of the water's edge. The less populous herbivorous aetosaurs, like *Typothorax*, also found refuge in the shallows of the waterways. Their broad low bodies were covered in spiked and plated bony armour resembling an elaborate carapace. But even though they were covered by an impressive form of protection, the

Resembling gigantic dolphins Shonisaurus, *the largest of ichthyosaurs, swam in an epicontinental sea where Nevada now exists. Animal's length is approximately 15 m (49 ft).*

Typothorax (and, indeed, all of the aetosaurs) failed to last beyond the end of the Triassic. It is puzzling that the aetosaurs became extinct when they did, as the origin of other kinds of armour-plated reptiles, the true turtles, marked with *Proganochelys*, occurred at approximately the same time.

EVENTS NEAR THE END
OF THE TRIASSIC

The passing of the aetosaurs was a significant part, but still only a small segment, of a much broader extinction that was affecting the animal life of the Triassic world. All the thecodonts were similarly affected, as were many other kinds of reptiles, amphibians and notably, the mammal-like therapsids. The worldwide displacement and eventual extinctions of both floral and faunal groups foreshadowed the marking of the end of the Triassic. The most notable survivors of the Triassic extinctions were the dinosaurs.

Late Triassic flora and fauna fossils found throughout the Laurasian continents reflect that a broad similarity existed from the western United States, through Europe and into the distant eastern parts of Asia. Similar climatic conditions in the southern hemisphere and connections between Gondwana and Laurasia allowed an even greater worldwide distribution. The conditions of the broad landmasses were such, that even if extinctions were at first only regional, they soon acquired global proportions.

Among the plants, the gymnosperms became more dominant, creating vast forests of titanic primitive conifers, such as *Araucarioxylon* and *Pararaucaria*. The earliest ginkgoes and cycads appeared during the Early Triassic. The primitive conifers would periodically disperse their pollen into the air. Carried by the currents of the wind, hazy yellow clouds of pollen would colour the air flooding over the landscape and beyond distant horizons. In South America, beneath the towering trunks of the *Pararaucaria*, the dappling light and shadows would occasionally flicker with the appearance of yet another new creature that ventured onto the scene. One such animal was *Pisanosaurus*, a small, seemingly insignificant reptile. Like the pollen, *Pisanosaurus* spread over the land forming the roots, and origins, of the family tree of plant-eating dinosaurs, the ornithischians.

PISANOSAURUS AND
EARLY ORNITHISCHIANS

This earliest of ornithischians was found in Late Triassic strata in Argentina. The remains of this animal were probably articulated and fairly complete prior to discovery, but unfortunately, this incredibly rare and important fossil had been ravaged by the exposure to the weathering effects of erosion. Salvaged before totally becoming the dust of oblivion, *Pisanosaurus* is known from very fragmentary and incomplete remains, including portions of the neck, back, pelvis, hind limb, scapula, hand, and most importantly, upper and lower jaws with teeth.

The teeth of *Pisanosaurus* are remarkable in that they clearly show a design that distinguishes ornithischians from other kinds of dinosaurs. The way in which the teeth of *Pisanosaurus* worked in processing its plant food was unique in that the teeth were abraded and worn down from the movement of the upper and lower jaws as they came into contact with each other. In most of the later ornithischians, this development would lead to the ability of not only cutting, but an effective way of grinding the plant food prior to digestion. Much of the success of most ornithischians can be attributed to this type of dental masticating action for processing their food.

As revealed by its non-carnivorous teeth, *Pisanosaurus* was already a progressive and very specialized dinosaur. When found, its pelvis was missing most of

A gathering of labyrinthodont amphibians, Metoposaurus, *wallow near the shore of a lake within a conifer forest.* Metoposaurus *reached lengths of 3 m (10 ft).*

the pubis and ischium that could have revealed if it had developed a fully 'bird-like' orientation, or if it still possessed a transitional stage from the saurischian lizard-style hip (see page 83). But the hip socket was definitely equipped with a perforated acetabulum. While this opening in the hip socket indicates an upright vertical stance of the hind legs, there was a peculiar transitional stage of development still present in the structure of the ankle. The ankle bones, consisting of the astragalus and calcaneum, were not totally fused onto the ends of the lower leg bones, which allowed a small amount of twisting outwards from the ankle. The direct forward and backward movement of the feet, as typically seen in dinosaurs, was not exclusively employed by *Pisanosaurus* and a slight sideways movement of its feet was still possible. This holdover from the sprawling stance of the thecodonts would continue to diminish as the ankle joints of later dinosaurs became strongly developed for a more efficient

means of support. The forelimbs are almost totally unknown, and even though *Pisanosaurus* was certainly capable of swift bipedal running, it was probably quadrupedal most of the time when it was walking.

In addition to *Pisanosaurus* in South America, there are other fragmentary remains of similarly advanced plant eaters from North America and North Africa. Unfortunately, these other fossils are known from only tiny isolated teeth and jaws. Even these minuscule remnants are significant as they reflect the broad global distribution of these ornithischian dinosaurs early in the Late Triassic world.

While *Pisanosaurus* maintains the distinction of being the earliest-known representative of the Ornithischia, it is not necessarily the most primitive. The fabrosaurs (a sub-group of ornithischian dinosaurs), as represented by *Lesothosaurus*, are from a later time in the Late Triassic. But *Lesothosaurus* is actually a more primitive ancestral sidebranch that must have pre-

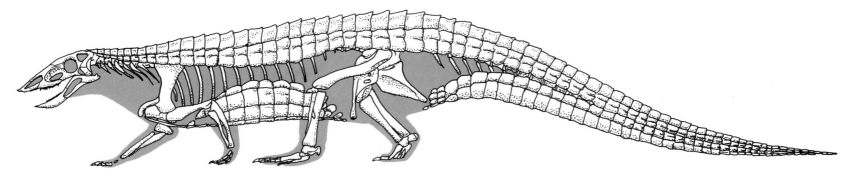

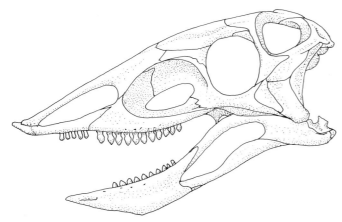

Shown with its armoured scutes is the skeleton of the aetosaur, Stagonolepis. *This peculiar thecodont was a herbivore that relied upon its bony armour for protection against predators. The snout was flattened, perhaps for grubbing for roots. Complementing this, was a pointed beak on the lower jaw. Unlike carnivores, leaf-shaped teeth were used for shearing vegetation. Animal's length is approximately 3 m (10 ft) and the skull's length is about 25 cms (10 ins). (after Walker, 1961)*

Shown from above is the skull and carapace of Proganochelys, *one of the earliest known turtles from the Late Triassic. The turtles are a long lived group of highly specialized anapsids that united bony scutes within their skin forming the characteristic armoured shell. The protection gained by the turtles' shell contributed to their successful reign while the armoured aetosaurs, which only superficially resembled turtles, dwindled into extinction by the end of the Triassic. Animal's length is approximately 1 m (3 ft). (After Jaekel, 1918)*

ceded, and then co-existed with the more progressive *Pisanosaurus*. This is an example of where being more primitive did not automatically make an animal obsolete. Primitive fabrosaurs existed long after the end of the Triassic and throughout most of the Jurassic. More advanced members would even last to the end of the Mesozoic.

A significant difference the fabrosaurs had was that the upper and lower teeth did not develop the strong contacts as seen in the abraded and worn down teeth of *Pisanosaurus*. This primitive, seemingly less effective, method of utilizing its teeth was a directional trademark that would lead to the development of an entire second branch of ornithischians. These fabrosaurs evolved in a separate, and yet parallel, direction totally independent of *Pisanosaurus* and its later descendants. All ornithischians were characteristically herbivorous, but not all had developed the ability to

Looking down past the branches of a conifer, the aetosaur Typo-thorax *is seen from above while it rests submerged in a lake's edge. Animal's length is 3–4 m (9–12 ft).*

use their teeth in the same manner when eating plants. Essentially, all types of ornithischians evolved from one of two branches, which incorporated either a primitive, non-abrading tooth action, or used an advanced, masticating, abrading tooth movement that constantly wore the teeth down with a chewing action.

While all ornithischians were herbivorous, the earliest of fabrosaurs, specifically *Lesothosaurus*, had teeth which were still in a transitional omnivorous stage indicating that small animals and insects were included in its diet. However, this distant link to its remote carnivorous ancestry was soon to be lost by the later, more advanced, ornithischians. *Lesothosaurus* also had a particular beak-like bone that joined the front tips of the lower jaws together. This bone is called the pre-dentary and is found in all ornithischians.

Unlike the fragmentary pelvis of *Pisanosaurus*, the pelvis of *Lesothosaurus* is known from virtually complete components. These clearly show that the structure of the hips had already become bird-like with the pubis facing backward along with the ischium. The acetabulum was perforated into a large opening. Also, *Lesothosaurus* had very long hind legs and much shorter front legs which indicates that it was an efficient bipedal runner. The bones of the ankle are not well known, but it is almost certain that a high degree of direct forward and backward motion was possible in the movement of the foot. The limbs were also hollow, similar to birds, indicating the possibility of a very efficient lung and respiratory system. Most of these early fabrosaurs were not more than 1 m (3 ft) in length, but other considerably larger ornithischians soon appeared.

Fabrosaurs, like all herbivores, were preyed upon by a variety of predators. Yet these ornithischians

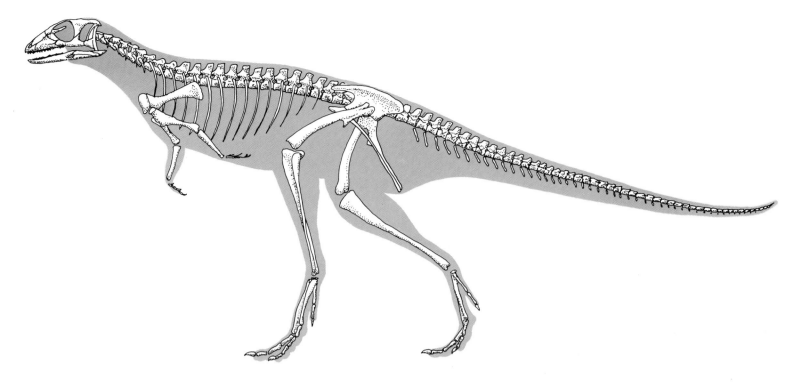

Shown above is the skeleton of the fabrosaurid, Lesothosaurus, *a fast running herbivorous dinosaur from the Late Triassic of South Africa. Animal's length is approximately 1 m (3 ft). (after Thulborn, 1972). Shown below, life-size, is the skull of* Lesothosaurus, *illustrating the small, non-grinding fabrosaurid-style teeth. On the bottom is the skull outline and jaws of* Pisanosaurus, *shown slightly reduced. The teeth of* Pisanosaurus *demonstrate the grinding, heterodont-style which led to ornithopods and ceratopsians. (*Lesothosaurus *after Thulborn, 1970, and* Pisanosaurus *after Bonaparte, 1973)*

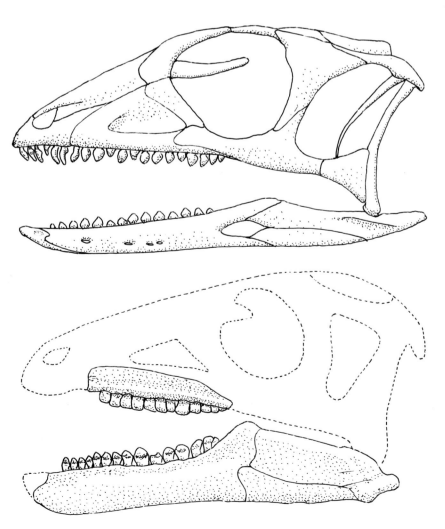

were very successful and continued to increase in numbers. Primitive carnivorous dinosaurs such as *Staurikosaurus* and the larger *Herrerasaurus* hunted the relatively defenceless early ornithischians. The last remaining thecodonts of the Late Triassic could also have included the ornithischians as part of their diet.

Phytosaurs, like *Rutiodon*, may well have hidden along the banks of rivers, passively stalking the approach of an unwary prey. Hours of a day would sometimes pass uneventfully with slowly shifting shadows and flowing movements of plants touched by an occasional breeze. The dozing eyes and attuned ears of the phytosaur patiently waited for a sign of any intruder passing through its realm. A distant rustling of leaves would have caused it to raise its eyelids into an attentive outward stare. Nearby, small heads glistening with alert eyes shifted back and forth on the edge of darkness along the bank. Cautiously, the little figures of early ornithischians, like little fabrosaurs, made their way to the water in hope of a refreshing drink. The leg muscles of the phytosaur tighten as it

Beneath a sunlit sky filled with a pollen storm of gymnosperm spores, a small Pisanosaurus *marks the beginning of the heterodont dinosaurs.* Pisanosaurus *reached lengths of approximately 1 m (3 ft).*

slowly rose, preparing itself to lunge. But the alert fabrosaurs discover its presence and scramble away to safety as the phytosaur bellows in defiance. Such encounters certainly could have taken place. But even though phytosaurs did eventually make their kills, it was the bellow and roar of phytosaurs and other sprawling thecodonts that would no longer echo throughout the Triassic lowlands.

The world during the Late Triassic was definitely changing with the ongoing extinctions of the last of the lingering mammal-like therapsids, and the reptilian thecodonts. The global climatic conditions were almost certainly responsible for initiating the demise of the therapsids. However, the extinction of the thecodonts was probably not caused as much by climatic and environmental changes, but was a result of direct competition from their progressive descendants, the dinosaurs. The less costly ectothermic physiologies that contributed to the success of the thecodonts was not enough to maintain their existence when confronted by advanced members of their own kind that had also evolved a superior mode of locomotion. The erect stance literally carried the dinosaurs into successful triumph across the continents of the globe.

COELUROSAURS BY THE THOUSANDS

The carnivorous saurischian dinosaurs were the efficient competitors that replaced the thecodonts. The presently known fossil remains of meat-eating dinosaurs probably does not represent the actual diversity that must have existed, for only a few types of predatory dinosaurs are known from the Late Triassic. The best known is *Coelophysis*, a coelurosaur (slender, long-necked theropod) from the southwestern part of the United States. Lesser known from Argentina are the carnosaurs (heavier, short-necked theropods) *Herrerasaurus* and *Frenguellisaurus* which were considerably more powerful and larger, reaching approximately 4 m (13 ft) in length.

The discovery of complete fossil skeletons are indeed extremely rare. The smaller *Coelophysis* is an astounding exception. At the Ghost Ranch in New Mexico there is a single quarry where dozens upon dozens of complete articulated skeletons of *Coelophysis* were found side by side, and jumbled on top of each other. The partial and complete remains of hundreds of them have been removed, and yet the quarry has only been partially worked out. The total number of *Coelophysis* at this mass grave site has been estimated as representing several thousand individuals.

Coelophysis was a moderate sized animal that reached lengths of between 2.5 and 3 m (8 and 10 ft). It normally stood no more than 1 m (3 ft) high. Its small stature was complemented by the fact that it was a lightly built animal. The long slender body was held up and off of the ground in a balanced horizontal stance on its powerful hind legs. The front legs were considerably shorter and probably played very little part, if any, in the role of locomotion. A neck as long, or longer than the length of the torso supported a narrow, pointed skull with small, sharp teeth lining the jaws. The limbs were hollow, and even the vertebrae were modified with pneumatic openings. So striking

The skeleton of the phytosaur, Parasuchus, *illustrates the close resemblance to the reptiles which replaced them—the crocodiles. Animal's length is approximately 2.7 m (9 ft). (after Chatterjee, 1978)*

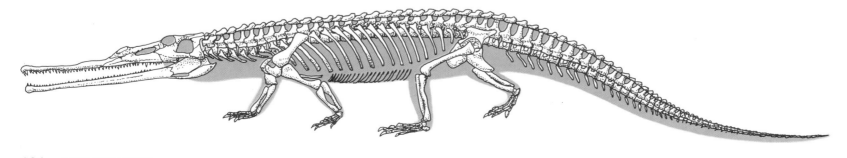

The bellows of a defiant phytosaur, Rutiodon, *sends a group of fabrosaurs running from the river banks.* Rutiodon *reached lengths of 4.5 m (15 ft).*

was the extent of the openings throughout the skeleton that the name it was so aptly given, *Coelophysis*, translates into 'hollow form'.

The abundantly populated *Coelophysis* quarry included a wide range of various sized individuals that represent different ages and stages of growth. Both males and females are included, as are the very young. The vast numbers of *Coelophysis* might very well suggest the nature of a gregarious animal in extremely large concentrations. However, the remains of small *Coelophysis* have been found within the ribs of larger individuals revealing opportunistic meals that were cannibalistic. Safety in numbers works well for many herbivores. But for the carnivorous dinosaurs, the weak or unwary of their own kind sometimes became incidental casualties of feasting.

Many unknown factors may have been responsible for the great accumulation of *Coelophysis* in this particular quarry. Even more puzzling is the cause of their death. What natural catastrophe could have been responsible for the deaths of thousands of these small dinosaurs? Could fire or floods or disease or even accidental poisoning have been responsible? The exact

cause remains a mystery.

Other dinosaurs remarkably similar to the North American *Coelophysis* have been found in South Africa, Europe, Asia and South America. The similarities in some of these cases, especially seen in *Syntarsus* from Zimbabwe in southern Africa, make them virtually indistinguishable from the well known *Coelophysis*. Most of these coelurosaurs are known from partial skeletons or fragmentary remains of isolated individuals. The coelurosaurs from South Africa are an interesting exception where the remains of over two dozen individuals are jumbled together within a remarkably small space of only a few metres in diameter. This second congregation, like the New Mexico *Coelophysis* Quarry, again suggests that these dinosaurs stayed

NEXT PAGE

A gathering of phytosaurs, Paleorhinus, *are resting on the river banks surrounded by an* Araucarioxylon *forest.* Paleorhinus *reached lengths of 3–4 m (10–13 ft).*

COELUROSAUR DISTRIBUTION GLOBE
By the Late Triassic, coelurosaurs had become widely distributed on a global scale. Fossil remains, including footprints, have been found in North America, Europe, Asia, Africa and South America. Such a broad distribution was possible because the continents were still joined together, forming Pangaea.

together in large groups.

Why would such large groups of meat-eaters stay together? Did they hunt in some collaborative fashion? What could they have been eating? Maybe co-operative hunting wasn't necessary. The communal draw may simply have been the result of feeding where the food supply was most abundant. Animals, such as *Coelophysis*, that congregated in such large numbers could not have relied solely upon hunting larger prey to satiate their hunger. Most likely, it wasn't necessary to partake in huge life and death battles.

The rivers, lakes and ponds were prominent features of the Triassic landscape. Within these waterways were abundant sources of food. Fish and invertebrates, including crustaceans, snails and insects, would have been in constant replenishing supply. Although quite efficiently bipedal on land, *Coelophysis* would have also had no problem in occasionally entering the shallows or even swimming

about in deeper waters. By hunting, or rather fishing individually, in manners similar to the feeding actions of many present day water birds, the large concentrations of *Coelophysis* could have found sufficient amounts of food, while for the most part, merely tolerating the presence of others of its own kind. Seasonal lean times when food was scarce may have prompted the gruesome preying upon their own kind.

Evidence of dinosaurs such as *Coelophysis* gathering in large numbers is also vividly recorded by their own footsteps. Literally thousands of fossil footprints have been found criss-crossing pathway over pathway. Many of the famous Connecticut Valley trackways of eastern North America are attributable to bipedal dinosaurs such as *Coelophysis*. On perhaps a single day during the Late Triassic, the soft mud flats were trod upon by hundreds of small, bipedal dinosaurs. Maybe they were heading to nearby waterways to feed or even cool their bodies from the heat of the day. The im-

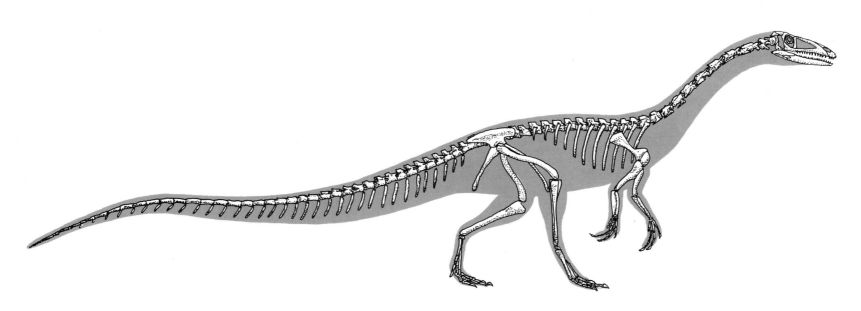

The long, lightweight skeleton of the coelurosaur, Coelophysis, *is shown in its typical bipedal stance. The small-toothed, narrow, pointed skull and long neck illustrate some basic coelurosaur characteristics. Animal's length is approximately 3 m (10 ft). (after Colbert, 1989)*

pressions of their footprints remained as the mud dried and hardened. Eventually, additional sediments accumulated over the field of tracks and preserved them from erosion. The preservation of such footprints is extremely rare because rain, wind or flowing water could have just as easily destroyed the evidence of this moment. Even more unlikely would be the discovery of one of the actual trackmakers preserved along with the footprints. Yet such an example of a remarkable fossil has been found. The bones of one of the Connecticut Valley trackmakers has been identified as belonging to a coelurosaur synonymous with the *Coelophysis* of western America.

Coelurosaurs were a unique and long-lived group of carnivorous dinosaurs that lasted from the Late Triassic to the end of the Mesozoic. The coelurosaur *Coelophysis*, along with large carnosaurs, were bipedal and had comparatively short front legs. The heavier built carnosaurs retained a relatively short neck and large, slashing teeth, while the coelurosaurs developed a significantly long neck and surprisingly small cutting teeth. The small teeth were lost entirely in some of the Cretaceous coelurosaurs which developed bird-like beaks. The retention of the long neck on coelurosaurs was characteristic of these generally smaller kinds of meat-eating dinosaurs that continued to become more diverse and specialized throughout the Mesozoic.

PROSAUROPODS
LONG-NECKED HERBIVORES

The coelurosaurs were not the only dinosaurs of the Late Triassic to have developed long necks, the prosauropods did too. This group of dinosaurs might have evolved independently of the coelurosaurs, or possibly shared an unknown ancestor which had benefited from the elongated neck. Like the carnosaurs and coelurosaurs, the prosauropods were saurischian dinosaurs. But unlike these exclusive carnivores, the prosauropods were at best only omnivorous, with an increasing preference for a totally herbivorous diet.

Unlike the bipedal carnosaurs and coelurosaurs, the normal walking posture of the prosauropods was definitely quadrupedal rather than bipedal as was once believed. Momentary rearing onto hind legs would have been possible, but actual bipedal walking was very unlikely if not impossible. The length of the backbone in prosauropods was not appreciably shortened as in the bipedal theropods. For the theropods, this shortening served to shift the body weight more centrally onto the hind legs. Even though the front legs of prosauropods were somewhat shorter than their hind legs, the robust structure and deep articulation into the joint of the shoulder (the glenoid cavity), indicates that the forelimbs also shared in supporting the weight of the body while walking or running. Four-footed fossil trackways also confirm that prosauropods were definitely quadrupedal.

The body shapes of the prosauropods were basically very similar, with a large size range reaching from 2 to 9 m (6½ to 29 ft). Smaller and more specific differences

NEXT PAGE

A large congregation of Coelophysis *enter into a river where abundant food awaits.*

in prosauropod teeth reveal different levels of adaptation and development towards becoming fully herbivorous. At least three styles of teeth represent distinct types of prosauropods. Based on the differences of the teeth and other parts of the skeleton there are four classifications that represent the currently known assortment of prosauropods, which are plateosaurs, anchisaurs, melanosaurs, and yunnanosaurs.

Plateosaurs, as represented by *Plateosaurus*, were among the most primitive types of prosauropods. *Plateosaurus* was also one of the largest, with lengths of 8 m (26 ft). The most obvious primitive feature of *Plateosaurus* was its curiously small and numerous teeth. The remarkably small size of the teeth are reminiscent of the teeth that are characteristic of *Coelophysis*. While *Plateosaurus* must have had an ancestor that was carnivorous, its small teeth reveal a transitional stage of development in which they were no longer designed for eating meat, but were modified for eating plants. The teeth of *Plateosaurus* were spatulate and leaf shaped with comparatively large serrations called denticles on the front and back edges. Meat-eating dinosaurs had much smaller serrations on their teeth which were more effective for slicing into meat, whereas the large denticles on the teeth of prosauropods were most effective for cropping leafy vegetation. Similar teeth of herbivorous lizards living today clearly show the efficiency of large denticles and the associated preference for a herbivorous diet.

Anchisaurus had fewer teeth than *Plateosaurus*. They were along the same lines of development, but of a larger size, and they did not abrade against each other. The melanosaurs such as *Riojasaurus* were the largest of the prosauropods, but unfortunately the skull and teeth are not known for this group. Finally, *Yunnanosaurus* had an advanced form of dentition which was unlike the other prosauropods in that the upper and lower jaws occluded, or contacted, while eating, and resharpened the edges as the teeth wore against each other. This advanced condition was similar to that which is seen in the later giant sauropods of the Jurassic and Cretaceous revealing a close ancestral relationship to the prosauropods that preceded them.

Whatever the style, the prosauropod primitive and advanced teeth were not capable of grinding, or masticating the plant food. Rather, they were used solely for cutting and cropping the vegetation into manoeuvrable, mouth-sized pieces that could be easily swallowed. Once inside the gizzard, or a functionally equivalent area of the stomach, the masticating process of breaking down the plant material into more easily digestible pieces was accomplished by a gastric mill of stones, called gastroliths, that ground together. Many of today's birds and reptiles, including crocodiles, utilize the same process of digestion by swallowing stones or hard objects and letting them effectively break down and process the food for a quicker and more efficient digestion.

The prosauropods were also the first plant eaters to be equipped with an elongated neck. Other planteaters, such as the ornithischians *Lesothosaurus* and *Pisanosaurus*, still had the short neck inherited from their thecodont ancestry. Presumably the obvious benefit in having the longer neck would have been to enable the prosauropods to reach a higher range of vegetation that was not exploited by short-necked herbivores. Certainly the prosauropods could have reached plants that were higher than the smaller, short-necked ornithischians. But was the development of the long neck just so that higher vegetation could be reached and incorporated into the prosauropods' diet? If so, then why did the coelurosaurs develop long necks when other meat-eaters did not? The answer may be more closely related to the animals' physiology and respiratory system rather than dietary specializations.

The bones of prosauropods were highly pneumatic, much in the same manner as they were in the coelurosaurs. The longer neck vertebrae may have originated and performed the primary function of cooling overheated blood flowing to the brain by utilizing a complex of evaporative cooling air-sacs connected to the

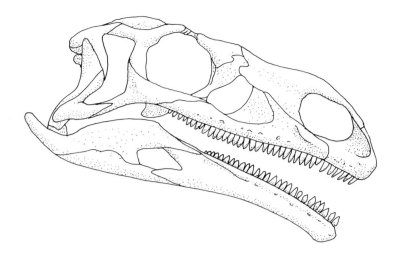

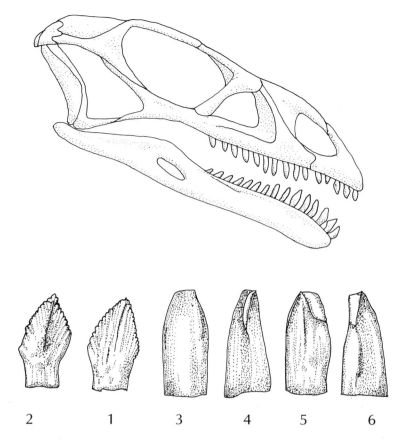

vertebrae. In this way, the origin of the long neck in coelurosaurs and prosauropods may have been to assist in thermoregulating the animal's body temperature and to avoid physical exhaustion and heatstroke. A secondary function of reaching higher vegetation still seems probable. But even with the elongated neck, the prosauropods may not have been such high browsers as is often depicted. The reason for this is seen in the lack of specialized articulation in the vertebrae that could have allowed a more upright angle and vertical posture of the neck. If it was really designed for vertically reaching high up, the cervical vertebrae at the base of the neck should have had a distinct upturned angle of articulation with the adjoining vertebra of the back. Such expected modifications in these vertebrae are conspicuously absent. The entire vertebral column is remarkably straight with only a slight arching of the back to better support the animal's weight. The neck is not modified for a vertical posture, and is instead facing straight forward from the back in a horizontal posture that, if anything, appears to slant downward.

Theoretically, the straight vertebral column of prosauropods could have been angled more vertically upwards if the animal raised the entire front of its body and tripodally balanced on its hind legs and tail. But the off-balanced distribution of weight could have been potentially injurious. When placed vertically, the shifting of body organs normally held in a horizontal posture, could put undue weight and stress on the lungs or other organs causing their functions to be impaired. Similar dysfunctions are induced in the 'hypnotizing' of alligators, sometimes dramatically demonstrated in reptile shows or magic acts. The alligator placed onto its back is not actually cast under a spell, but immobilized by the weight of its chest unnaturally pressing onto its lungs thereby causing the loss of breath. By applying such a graphic example of the danger of assuming unnatural body postures to the prosauropods, it seems more than likely that they usually remained in a horizontal quadrupedal feeding posture.

Shown are the skulls of the plateosaurs: (left) Plateosaurus *and (right)* Anchisaurus. *Also the teeth of:* **1.** Plateosaurus, *side view;* **2.** Anchisaurus, *side view; and the melanosaur,* Yunnanosaurus, *–* **3.** *side view,* **4.** *front view,* **5.** *medial, inner side view, and* **6.** *back view. As prosauropods evolved for a specialized herbivorous diet, their teeth became fewer in number, restricted more to the front of the mouth and also became larger, ridged with coarse denticles. Eventually, the teeth of melanosaurs came to resemble those of true sauropods (not to scale). (after Galton, 1985)*

The tail of prosauropods was long and heavy. The structure of the tail vertebrae reveals that they were well designed for vertical and side-to-side movement, and that its strong tail muscles could have easily powered it while swimming. The horizontal neck and body would have been well suited for the support that it could have received while floating in water. But prosauropods were not exclusively aquatic animals tied to a watery environment. They were effective terrestrial animals that would have been adept, both on land or in the water.

There was a notable process of reduction in the fingers and toes of prosauropods, for the outer two digits of the hands, and last outside digit of the hind feet degenerated in size. Huge claws were on the inside digits of the hands which were probably multifunctional in defence, grasping, digging and foraging.

During the Late Triassic, the diverse prosauropods became widely distributed throughout most of the existing landscape. Their fossil remains have been found in North America, Europe, Asia, South Amer-

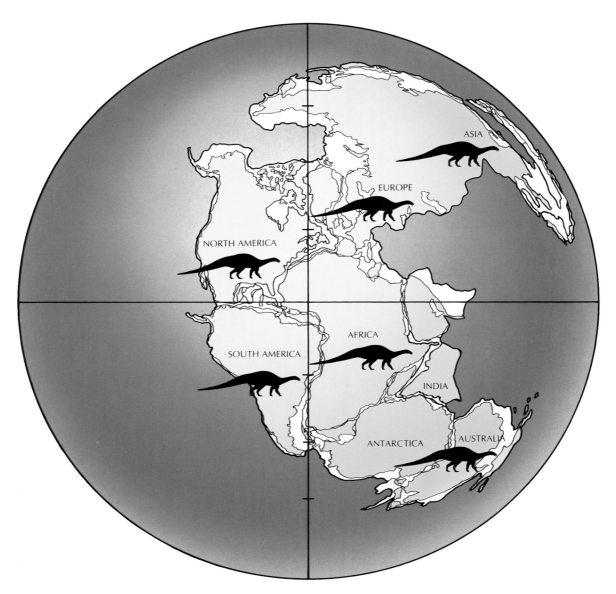

PROSAUROPOD DISTRIBUTION GLOBE
Prosauropods were probably distributed worldwide throughout Pangaea. Their fossil remains have been found in North America, Europe, Asia, Africa, South America and Australia. Their presence in Antarctica and India is suggested by the available routes which led to Australia.

ica, South Africa and Australia. The numerous skeletons and fossil trackways indicate that these animals were to some extent gregarious, and possibly herding animals which were the dominant members of the dinosaur takeover.

One remarkable discovery in Argentina revealed the beautifully preserved skeletons of several baby prosauropods, which are called *Mussaurus*. Fully articulated, uncrushed and mostly complete, their tiny bodies reached a length of only 20–30 cms (8–12 ins). Their skulls demonstrate typical baby proportions with large eyes and short faces. The skulls are only about 3 cms (1 in) long. The tiny babies were found closely huddled together in what, undoubtedly, was once their nest. Some of them were outstretched on their sides, and others were crouched over with their legs folded underneath while lying on their bellies in their final resting position. Undisturbed in these positions for some 200 million years, the delicate skeletons

are incredibly preserved with some of the tiniest bones of the feet intact, and their mouths still glistening with sharp, needle-like teeth.

What caused the death of these baby prosauropods is not known. Perhaps they were left unattended without parental care. Possibly they died from disease, or from too much heat on an excessively hot afternoon. These are only possible speculations. Answers as to the cause of death are rarely preserved, and incredibly difficult to interpret from the fossil evidence.

A SINGLE BONE OR FOOTPRINT SCARCITY IN THE FOSSIL RECORD

Fossils can often raise questions that may never be answered. The sheer magic of discovering fossils as

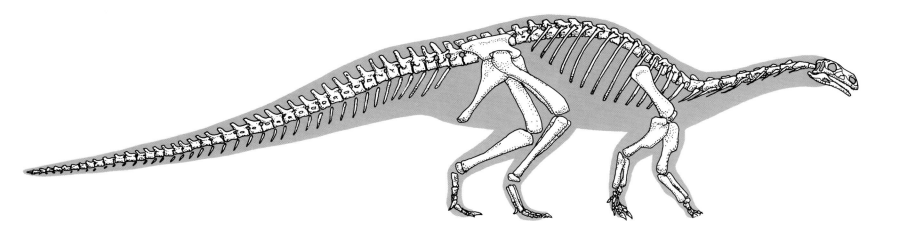

The skeleton of the prosauropod, Plateosaurus, *is shown in its naturally quadrupedal walking pose. This long-necked saurischian was among the earliest herbivores which eventually led to the sauropods. Animal's length is approximately 8 m (26 ft). (after Galton, 1976)*

extraordinary as the baby prosauropods in Argentina can be put into a proper significance when it is realized that the thousands, if not millions, of dinosaurs that lived at any one time can sometimes be represented by only a single skeleton, a small fragment of a bone, or possibly not at all.

The exceptional discovery of the thousands of *Coelophysis* in the western part of North America is complemented by a staggering array of nearby fossil trackways from large congregations of these same kinds of dinosaurs. Trackways identical to these have also been found on the eastern part of North America, and yet the skeletons of these trackmakers are almost totally missing, being represented by only bone fragments of two individuals. Certainly, as the trackways reveal, coelurosaurs were just as prevalent in the east as they were in the west. If not for the random preservation of the passing moments of a day in which these dinosaurs trod across the muddy flats, or even the fragments of their fossil bones, there would be no known record of their having ever existed there at all.

The earliest dinosaurs do appear to have existed on virtually all of the continental landmasses by the Late Triassic. Antarctica is a possible exception where no Triassic dinosaurs have as yet been discovered. This may be due to either an actual restricted exclusion by unsuitable environmental conditions, or preservational factors that have prevented the fossil evidence from being preserved. Most likely, the fossils of Triassic dinosaurs simply haven't been found there as yet due to the incredible difficulty of collecting fossils in the now frozen world of Antarctica.

The fossil record of dinosaurs in Australia may add some insight to the possible absence of Triassic dinosaurs in Antarctica for Australia and Antarctica were joined together from at least the Permian until the Late

Cetaceous. The fossils of Triassic dinosaurs in Australia are exceedingly rare. They are only represented by the partial limb of a prosauropod, *Agrosaurus*, and the surprisingly large footprints of an unknown bipedal carnosaur that left a stride of nearly 2 m (6 ft) on feet that were at least 46 cms (18½ ins) in length. Preservational factors are clearly responsible for the near total absence and poor representation of these and other Australian dinosaurs from the Triassic. Since prosauropods and theropods did radiate into Australia, as shown by the admittedly scant fossil evidence, it seems probable that such dinosaurs may well have been in a fair abundance which was simply not preserved in the fossil record. Along with the saurischians, it also seems probable that some of the early types of ornithischians, such as *Pisanosaurus* from South America or *Lesothosaurus* from South Africa, may also have ventured further southeast into Australia. During the Late Triassic, Antarctica was connected beneath Australia on the east, with southern Africa and the bottom tip of South America on the west. In this configuration, it may well have been impossible for the dinosaurs of Australia to have crossed over into that continent from Africa or South America without having first ventured onto the soil of Antarctica which bridged these continents. Therefore, it can be safely said that even by the Late Triassic, the dinosaurs had dispersed worldwide onto virtually all of the continents. From this moment there were global dinosaurs.

NEXT PAGE

Walking along the ledge of a water hole, a group of Plateosaurus *pass by.*

Held between two fingertips is the skull of a prosauropod hatchling, Mussaurus. *Found in Argentina, the total length of this baby dinosaur is only about 30 cms (1 ft). Its parent may have been between 6 and 9 m (20 and 30 ft) long. Specimen in the Collections of the Universidad Nacional de Tucuman.*

BENEATH THE FEET OF DINOSAURS THE FIRST MAMMALS

By the end of the Triassic, the age of giant dinosaurs had begun. The transition that lasted millions of years before this moment saw the explosive radiation of first the thecodonts, and then their eventual elimination and takeover by the dinosaurs. While this was happening, the mammal-like therapsids had fallen gradually over the edge of extinction. The last lingering survivors of the therapsids were more like modern mammals then ever before. One of these animals was *Diarthrognathus* which was so advanced in almost becoming a true mammal that its diminutive size seemingly contradicts its remarkably high evolutionary level of development. Other animals evolved from creatures such as *Diarthrognathus* during the Late Triassic. Coexisting with *Diarthrognathus* and equally small in stature, they, however, had lost their diagnostic reptilian characters entirely, sufficiently qualifying

On the left is the skull of the Late Triassic mammal, Morganucodon, *enlarged approximately six times. On the right is the same shown actual life-size. Descendants of this tiny mammal persisted as small inhabitants throughout the age of dinosaurs. (after Kermack, Mussett, and Rigney, 1981)*

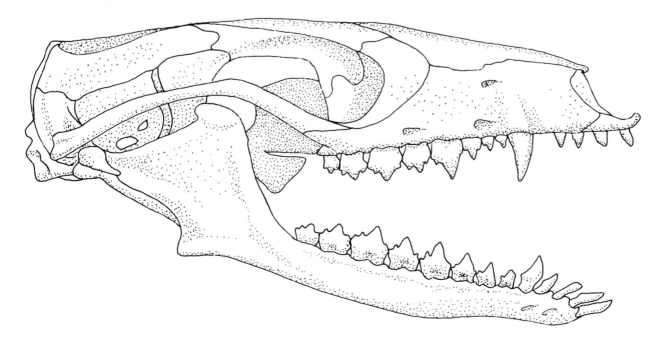

Scurrying about the leaf-litter of ginkgoes and ferns, two Diarthrognathus *have come upon a potential meal consisting of a cockroach,* Blabera atropos. *Remarkably mammal-like, these therapsids (ictidosaurs) bordered on the line of mammalian definition.*

them as the first true mammals. The tiny *Morganucodon* has this remarkable distinction. Such animals as *Diarthrognathus* and *Morganucodon* were small in size, but not necessarily in numbers or global distribution. *Morganucodon* is represented by thousands of teeth, jaws, skull fragments and other skeletal remains found mostly in South Wales. Other remains of this earliest type of true mammal are known from the distantly removed lands of China and South Africa.

Incredible as it may seem, the global distribution of the earliest mammals may well have matched the success of the dinosaurs that had also radiated across the world's landscape. However, it was the dinosaurs that dominated the world, increasing in diversity and reaching titanic proportions in size. For the following 140 million years, the mammals that had evolved from ancestors such as *Morganucodon*, would remain small and under the feet of the Mesozoic monsters.

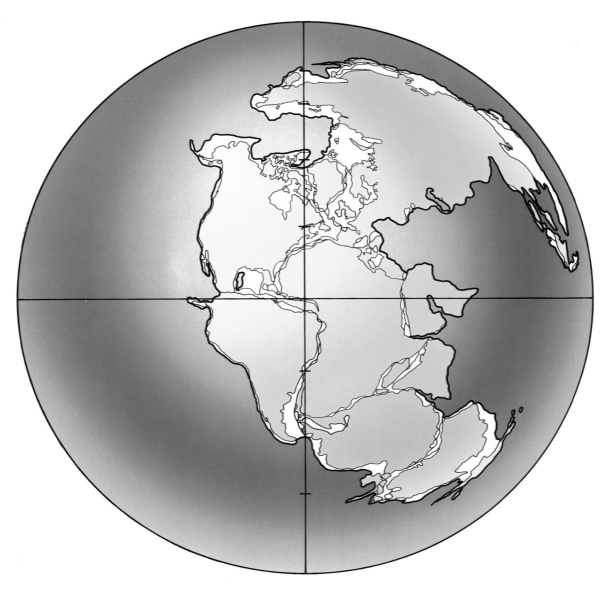

EARLY JURASSIC GLOBE
As Pangaea gradually moved northward, the increasingly warm global climate resulted in less seasonal extremes. Seasons lacked the cold or temperate winter conditions and alternated between hot, dry summers and hot, wet winters. High latitudes consisted mostly of sub-tropical conditions, unlike the temperate zones present there today. Pangaea was still connected which allowed dinosaurs to spread throughout the continents.

Thrashing about within the ferns beneath a conifer forest, two large Dilophosaurus, *double-crested coelurosaurs, grapple over a captured* Scutellosaurus, *a small fabrosaur, as another flees to safety. The animals are known from the southwestern state of Arizona in the United States of America. Length of* Dilophosaurus *is approximately 6 m (19^1/$_2$ ft), and* Scutellosaurus *is about 1.3 m (4 ft) long.*

CHAPTER IV
THE JURASSIC
TITAN REPTILES DOMINATE THE WORLD

THE PROSAUROPOD TRANSITION

At the transition from the Triassic period into the Jurassic the dinosaurs dramatically took over the void that was created by the extinction of the therapsids.

The decline and fall of the therapsids almost brought the evolution of mammals to a premature end. Their tiny, but significant, descendants would survive beyond the Triassic but for the next 140 millions years they were the diminutive, secondary characters in the world of the dinosaurs.

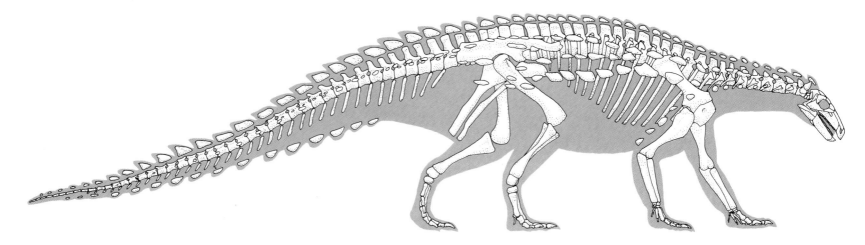

The Scelidosaurus *skeleton is shown with the probable arrangement of armoured scutes. This was one of the largest ornithischians of the Early Jurassic. It was equipped with fabrosaur-like teeth and was an early ancestor related to other armoured dinosaurs, such as stegosaurs, ankylosaurs, and perhaps most closely to the nodosaurs.* Scelidosaurus *is known from Arizona, in the United States of America, England and possibly Portugal.* Scelidosaurus *reached lengths of approximately 4 m (13 ft). (after Paul, 1987)*

The Early Jurassic was the beginning of this age of giants. Unlike any time before, no creature that walked on Earth had grown to such immense size. This gigantism reflected their unique physiologies and their environmental conditions, but not all dinosaurs became giants and their range in size from the very small to the titanic contributed to their dominance of the world.

The long-necked prosauropods of the Late Triassic had continued to evolve into ever larger variations of their kind. By the beginning of the Jurassic, some prosauropods, such as *Vulcanodon*, became the transitional predecessor of the true sauropod giants. The remains of *Vulcanodon* are known from Zimbabwe in southern Africa. The skull and many other parts of the skeleton have not yet been discovered, but the sections of *Vulcanodon's* skeleton that have been found represent an animal of considerable size, over 10 m (32 ft) in length.

As might be expected, the bones of *Vulcanodon* were not just larger versions of smaller prosauropod bones. Some of the bones possessed subtle modifications that had developed as a direct result of dealing with the problem of increased size and weight. This was necessary in order to compensate for the mechanical limitations seen in the more primitive skeletal structure of the ancestral prosauropods. The pelvis of prosauropods was connected onto only three sacral vertebrae which fused together between both ilia into a rigid, supportive bar. Still more primitive dinosaurs and other reptiles had incorporated only one or two sacral vertebrae into their pelvis. However, *Vulcanodon* was at the threshold of becoming a more advanced dinosaur, a true sauropod, capable of dealing with the problems of being a giant. The pelvis of *Vulcanodon* was attached to not just three, but at least four sacral vertebrae, however the ilia appear to have been only slightly enlarged and lengthened. These characteristics, along with the comparatively straight and robust nature of the limbs of *Vulcanodon*, indicate this animal could support itself on legs that were capable of being held more vertically beneath the body. The sprawling limb posture associated with reptiles was altered to a more upright stance in dinosaurs, as an adjustment to the stresses of locomotion and to provide support for the weight of the body.

There is more to becoming a giant than simply continuing to grow. The complexities of so doing can literally change the animal's anatomy and biology. Sustaining enough food and nourishment, regulating the body temperature and supporting the ponderous weight are only a few of the basic problems. Indeed there may be almost as many disadvantages as advantages. The safety than can be associated with the intimidating strength and imposing size were often lost when confronted and matched by giant predators.

SMALL ARMOURED FABROSAURS AND CRESTED COELUROSAURS

Some smaller dinosaurs which had descended from the Late Triassic ornithischian fabrosaurs continued to remain small animals growing to only about 1 m (3 ft) in length. *Scutellosaurus* was such a dinosaur. It was primarily quadrupedal, rarely rising on to its hind legs, except in momentary bursts of speed. Unlike the ancestral fabrosaurs, *Scutellosaurus* had evolved a protective covering of bony nodules that ornamented its body and tail. Otherwise a nearly defenceless herbivore, *Scutellosaurus* must have fallen victim to the contemporary carnivorous dinosaurs. The fossil remains of *Scutellosaurus* are known from the same strata as the predatory long-necked, slender coelurosaur, *Dilophosaurus*, found in the Kayenta formations of Arizona. Together, *Scutellosaurus* and *Dilophosaurus*, represent two of the earliest known dinosaurs of the Jurassic in North America.

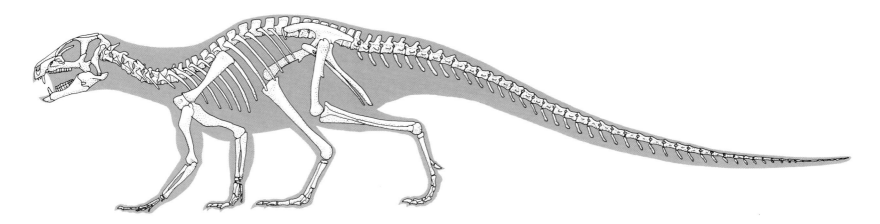

Dilophosaurus is a peculiar coelurosaur in several ways. It reached lengths of 6 m (19½ ft), twice the size of its Triassic ancestors. But even though there was a 100 per cent increase in size, *Dilophosaurus* retained a weaker and more primitive hip structure than its earlier relative, *Coelophysis* (see pages 104–112). The pelvis of *Dilophosaurus* was equipped with only four sacral vertebrae while the smaller *Coelophysis* possessed five vertebrae that strenghthened its pelvis. How *Dilophosaurus* compensated for its weaker pelvis might be explained as an adaption for a more aquatic lifestyle where the water would have helped support the weight of its body. Like *Coelophysis*, it could have been an efficient swimmer. However, it is doubtful that *Dilophosaurus* would have been restricted to a watery environment, because its hind legs were strong and well proportioned enough for bipedal locomotion. The feet were equipped with advanced modifications of structural support as seen in many later bipedal dinosaurs. While *Dilophosaurus* possessed a unique combination of primitive and advanced characters, it was still a fleet-of-foot dinosaur, capable of agile and sinuous movement.

The most obvious characteristic of *Dilophosaurus* was the presence of two tall, thin crests of bone that adorned the upper length of its skull. Why these bony crests developed is not readily apparent. Their function could not have been offensive for their delicate structure would have made them easily damaged if struck during a battle. A visual display for attracting a mate seems to be a possible function, although it may have also been used for thermoregulating or even some other unknown function. Whatever its purpose, its ornamental crests make *Dilophosaurus* one of the most bizarre-looking of all dinosaurs.

Smaller coelurosaurs, about half the size of *Dilophosaurus*, are also known from the Kayenta formation. They resemble the Triassic *Coelophysis*, but are more similar to the *Dilophosaurus* in that they also had two fragile crests of bone on top of their skulls. Since these coelurosaurs had proportionately smaller crests it would first appear that they might represent younger stages of the larger and more elaborately crested *Dilophosaurus*. However, a greater extent of fusion in many skeletal elements of the smaller, crested coelurosaurs

Heterodontosaurus was a primitive ornithopod equipped with grinding cheek teeth and peculiar fangs located in the front of the mouth. Bipedal locomotion may have been possible at times, although its large forelimbs indicate that it was often quadrupedal while walking and foraging. The hind feet had four clawed toes and the comparatively long hands had curved, pointed claws revealing its primitive hypsilophodont characteristics. Heterodontosaurus is known from southern Africa and it reached lengths of approximately 1.3 m (4 ft). (after Santa-Luca, 1980)

may indicate that they were actually fully grown adults. In contrast, the larger *Dilophosaurus* had less developed fusion in the same bones, and this would imply that its maximum stage of growth had not been reached. Perhaps then, there were two distinct crested coelurosaurs of different sizes that co-existed during the Early Jurassic.

LARGE FABROSAURS WITH ARMOUR AND SMALL ORNITHOPODS

The adaptive development of different dinosaurs resulted in an increasing number of distinct species. Some remained small in stature, such as the fabrosaur *Scutellosaurus*, but larger relatives of this ornithischian, such as *Scelidosaurus*, had evolved and co-existed with its smaller ancestors. *Scelidosaurus* was an armour-studded ornithischian that reached modest proportions, 4 m (13 ft) long. However, the increase in size resulted in no additional modifications to the teeth of this large herbivore. They retained the original fabrosaurid condition of a non-grinding action and most of the cropping action was taken over by its turtle-like beak. The additional breakdown of its food may have been assisted by gastroliths (see page 112).

Scelidosaurus was found during the middle of the last century and has the distinction of being one of the earliest dinosaurs to have been described. Remarkably preserved, the almost complete skeleton was articulated and covered by most of the armoured scutes that would have been embedded in its skin. The lower portions of the arms and the tip of the snout were missing. But even with the almost complete state of its preservation, *Scelidosaurus* has remained an enigmatic animal that has created more questions than answers.

The sediments in which the *Scelidosaurus* was found reveal that it had been entombed some distance from where it had lived. Its limp, lifeless form had been transported, probably floating on the course of a river that fed into the ocean where tidal currents carried it out to sea. Fossils of aquatic reptiles, including ichthyosaurs and plesiosaurs, are found in the same sediments, confirming that the *Scelidosaurus* was accidentally brought to rest among the denizens of the deep. Having been carried out to sea, what remains obscure is exactly in what kind of environment *Scelidosaurus* lived.

It is not clear whether the descendants of *Scelidosaurus* were closer to the armour-plated stegosaurs of the Jurassic or to the armoured and nodule-covered ankylosaurs of the Cretaceous. While both the stegosaurs and ankylosaurs were derived from a fabrosaur ancestry, *Scelidosaurus* shares primitive characteristics that may apply to either of the armoured relatives.

The original discovery of *Scelidosaurus* has been augmented by additional specimens, increasing the understanding of this puzzling dinosaur. All of the *Scelidosaurus* fossils were thought to have been restricted to regions of southern England and perhaps Portugal. But recently, the re-analysis of isolated armour scutes from the Kayenta formations of Arizona revealed that they did not belong to aetosaurs of the Late Triassic as was once believed. Rather, the distinctive, concave shape of the inner side of these scutes and their general morphology match precisely the armour of the European *Scelidosaurus*. With such proper identification, the geographical distribution of this dinosaur has been extended to the western extremities of Laurasia. Perhaps future discoveries will show that these armoured herbivores also spread eastwards to China as did the Triassic plateosaurs and other kinds of fabrosaurids. The presence of *Scelidosaurus* in the Kayenta resolves the problem of whether this formation represents the end of the Triassic or the beginning of the Jurassic. The removal of the incorrectly identified aetosaurs, and inclusion of *Scelidosaurus*, supports the belief that the Kayenta formation represents the Early Jurassic of North America.

Whether or not *Scelidosaurus* made its way into the southern hemisphere is still unknown. During the Late Triassic, fabrosaurs ventured to the southern regions of Africa, but there were also other kinds of ornithischians discovered in the Early Jurassic formations of southern Africa. They belonged to a separate lineage known as the ornithopods which were descended from the *Pisanosaurus* ancestry of herbivorous dinosaurs that chewed their food. Abraded and worn teeth show that *Heterodontosaurus* from Africa continued to develop the ability to chew its food, rather than simply cut or tear it. Yet, even with the apparent efficiency of its method of eating, *Heterodontosaurus*

remained a small dinosaur only 1 m (3 ft) or so in length. Its small size is comparable to the armoured *Scutellosaurus*. The hind legs were long and powerful, supporting most of the animal's weight, but the arms and hands were larger and more robustly structured for stronger muscles. This probably indicates quadrupedal locomotion, as well as foraging and other grasping functions. Larger relatives of *Heterodontosaurus* are as yet unknown from the same period.

THE GIANT CETIOSAUR SAUROPODS APPEAR

The fossil record of dinosaurs during the early and middle parts of the Jurassic is incomplete and leaves broad gaps of knowledge about the actual diversity of dinosaurs during this period. Even though relatively few dinosaurs are as yet known from the Early Jurassic, it is clear that the coelurosaurs and theropods showed a tendency towards gigantism. The fabrosaurs and ornithopods also increased in size, but not to the extent as seen in the long-necked herbivores, the sauropods. These true giants of the Mesozoic had become well established early in the Jurassic. The basal stock of the earliest sauropods belonged to an abundant, yet comparatively primitive family, known as the Cetiosauridae.

Included within the cetiosaurs are two groups of sauropods that achieved different stages of evolutionary development. The significant differences are most clearly seen in the height of the vertebral arch and spines that are attached to the centrum, or base of each vertebra. Such a primitive condition is seen in *Lapparentosaurus* from Madagascar, and *Volkherimeria* from Patagonia in South America. The vertebrae of both of these sauropods were comparatively short in height and unspecialized in design with simple, laterally flattened, neural spines. The more advanced cetiosaurs continued to develop taller vertebrae along with more complex structural modifications, such as extra laminae, or wall-like ridges, that buttressed the neural spines. The two known members of the primitive stage of cetiosaurs are from landmasses that were in fairly close proximity. The more advanced cetiosaurs are better represented by several members from widely separated geographical regions indicating the extensive territorial range that these sauropods occupied.

From the southern hemisphere, are the primitive cetiosaurs, *Lapparentosaurus* and *Volkherimeria*, as well as the comparatively more advanced cetiosaurs, *Amygdalodon* and *Patagosaurus* from South America, and *Rhoetosaurus* from Australia. Other similarly advanced cetiosaurs are known from the northern hemisphere including *Haplocanthosaurus* from the United States in the west, *Cetiosaurus* from England to the east, *Barapasaurus* still further east from India, and *Shunosaurus* from Asia in the distant east. This broad east to west and north to south distribution of the

With their necks outstretched horizontally, a group of Patagosaurus, *cetiosaur giants, wander through a clearing in their search for food.* Patagosaurus *is known from Argentina, and is typical of the many cetiosaurs that existed throughout the world.* Patagosaurus *reached lengths of approximately 16 m (52 ft).*

cetiosaurs clearly reflects the success of the sauropods in becoming globally cosmopolitan. It also reflects a global range of similar environments conducive to the development of these monolithic beasts.

The lack of fossil remains of cetiosaurs from Africa and Antarctica does not necessarily imply their absence. The presence of *Rhoetosaurus*, known only from Australia, suggests that similar cetiosaurs had distribution pathways that probably crossed Antarctica, Africa, South America, and Australia. Therefore, while cetiosaurs are still unknown in Africa and Antarctica, the future discovery of their fossil remains on these two continents would not be unlikely.

All the cetiosaurs shared the primitive, or ancestral condition, of having robust, spatulate teeth. The physical appearance of the cetiosaurs was probably similar throughout the group and was typical of the basic and unspecialized sauropod form. The neck was of moderate length and held mostly in a horizontal position. However, and in contrast to the extremely long-necked sauropods that were yet to come, the vertebrae of the neck were still relatively short in length which may have allowed some extra degree of flexibility. Cetiosaurs such as *Patagosaurus*, were typical of the sauropod condition, and would have normally

walked with their neck outstretched like a balanced beam projecting from the body.

The Asian cetiosaur, *Shunosaurus*, had developed one notable characteristic that was atypical of sauropods. On the tip of the tail a fused mass of bone was carried that formed a functional club which could have been used in the animal's defence against the predatory giants. The ability to utilize the tail as a weapon of defence has long been thought to have been possible among sauropods. It is not uncommon among many living reptiles to use their tails in this way, but the tail club on *Shunosaurus* gives the first tangible evidence that sauropods did in fact use their tails as such.

Sauropods were wandering animals, always searching for fresh sources of food and suitable environments. During their search there was the continuous threat of hungry theropods. Even the largest of them would have had to have been wary and alert to oncoming intruders. *Shunosaurus*, as well as other sauropods, may have been gregarious and had a complex social behaviour that added extra protection to the individual members forming a group (or herd), but even their awesome size and intimidating numbers could not have made them invulnerable from attack.

THE QUARRY OF DASHANPU

Based upon fossil evidence from the Dashanpu Quarry in China, the following scenario may have taken place. The shadows from oncoming clouds darkened the time of day with a calm grayness that brought with it a scent of moisture in the air. Instinct led the powerful legs supporting the heavy sauropod forms across the landscape. A distant roar of thunder vibrated the air as the sound passed by, and drops of rain began to fall. The dullness of the dust-covered scales began to sparkle in the fresh dots of falling rain. But an uneasy tension built throughout the herd as it continued on its way. Necks and tails rose high, anticipating defensive postures. Two hidden theropod forms sprang from the greenery, immediately encircling a startled *Shunosaurus* which had lagged behind the herd. The sauropod raised its head as high as it could, just as the large, toothed jaws snapped shut beneath it. The initial moment of surprise had passed and the sauropod began to pivot in circles, swinging its tail from side to side. Rebuffed, hesitating, and looking for an opportune moment to strike, the theropods followed after the *Shunosaurus*. Pausing too long, as the armour-spiked tail club flails through the air, one of the theropods is struck off balance and stumbles to the ground. Leaving their companion behind, the other members of the sauropod herd hurriedly moved away to safety as the battle disappeared from their view.

They had survived this attack, but a distant and ominous rumbling grew louder and louder. A more awesome threat to their safety had accumulated after falling from the sky. The channelled plain that the sauropods had entered would soon become a ravine of death and destruction. Helpless and trapped, the *Shunosaurus* herd toppled under a raging wall of oncoming water, mud, stone and debris. The flash flood carried the lifeless sauropods downstream and blanketed them in their final sleep under an entombing aggregate of soil.

At least ten skeletons of *Shunosaurus* have been discovered together in a mass grave of nature's making. Their once tumbled and torn bodies were not the only dinosaurs that were caught in the calamity. More than a hundred dinosaur skeletons have been discovered, revealing a large concentration of previously unknown and exceedingly rare dinosaurs of the Middle Jurassic. The extensive excavation is known as the Dashanpu Quarry, located in the Zigong province of China. The assortment of dinosaurs found along with the remains of the sauropods include carnivorous saurischians from both carnosaur and coelurosaur affinities, and ornithischians of grinding and non-grinding

tooth development. Adding to the wealth of this quarry is the preservation of non-dinosaurian animals, including winged pterosaurs and various fish. Surprisingly, there was also a representative of the labyrinthodonts, the giant flat-headed amphibians which until only recently were thought to have become extinct during the Triassic. Huge, fallen trees, tens of metres in length, are also beautifully preserved with their tiniest details replaced by vivid, multicoloured crystalline minerals.

The 4-m (13-ft) long carnosaur *Gasosaurus* from the Dashanpu Quarry is significant in having a primitive, if not ancestral, relationship that led to the larger allosaurs of the Late Jurassic. A very similar condition is also seen in the contemporary Middle Jurassic *Piatnitzkysaurus* from Argentina, South America which demonstrates that these carnosaurs had a wide dispersal reaching into both hemispheres.

Also from the same quarry in China was *Yandusaurus*, a small hypsilophodont ornithischian with grinding teeth. Only 1–2 m (3–6 ft) long, it was an agile herbivore that could have been a fast runner when necessary. The forelimbs were much shorter than the hind legs, but were still capable of being used during locomotion and helped support the animal when it was walking slowly or foraging for food.

Hypsilophodonts became varied and globally distributed during the Jurassic. Related to *Yandusaurus* was the Late Jurassic *Dryosaurus* from North America and the co-generic *Dysalotosaurus* from East Africa. The presence of these two closely-related hypsilophodonts suggests that a land connection still existed between the North American and African continents, at least until some time during the Late Jurassic when the continents that had formed Pangaea were separating.

A 4-m (13-ft) long descendant of the fabrosaurs was also present in the Dashanpu Quarry. It was a heavy beast of moderate size that must have been exclusively quadrupedal. No shortening of the forelimbs had occurred, and they had remained rather long and very robust. Perhaps most significant were the small flat plates and spikes of bony armour that are associated with this unusual dinosaur. The unique dermal armour identified it as a primitive stegosaur, called *Huayangosaurus*. Other characteristics of the teeth, skull, and post-cranial details of the body also clearly show primitive stages transitionally shared with the armour-plated stegosaurs best known from the Late Jurassic.

It had been thought that the stegosaurs were of European origins. This concept was based upon fragmentary remains of another Middle Jurassic stegosaur, *Lexovisaurus* known from England and France. However, the discovery of *Huayangosaurus* now suggests that the stegosaurs had their origins in Eastern Asia, and that they radiated westward across Europe into North America, and spread to the south entering East Africa.

As yet, *Huayangosaurus* is the most primitive of the stegosaurs. It is also among the best known, repre-

sented by several nearly complete individuals all found in the Dashanpu Quarry. Unfortunately, none of the specimens have a complete assortment of the dermal plates and spikes which could have provided insights as to how they were arranged on the animal. Both the plates and spikes are rather small which probably reflects their primitive development. However, most notable is the absence of paired plates which would have substantiated the long held belief that there were two, symmetrical rows of plates running along the upper length of the animal's neck, back and tail. Many plates are missing from each specimen but nevertheless, not one has been found with a matching pair of plates leaving the question of how they were arranged unanswered.

The shapes of the armour plates of *Huayangosaurus* are interesting as they reveal the manner in which the plates grew and developed their narrow, flattened form. The condition prior to becoming a plate is simply that of a spike, much like those that were on the tail. The change to plate first occurred with the back edge of the spike developing a ridge that rose from the bottom to the top of the spike. The ridge continued to lengthen into a narrow sheet of bone that would eventually obscure the initial spike. On some spikes that lengthened backwards, the front edge also formed a ridge extending into a fan-like sheet of bone furthering its thin, plate-like appearance. From observing this process, it could be seen that the primitive stegosaurs prior to *Huayangosaurus* possessed only spikes that rose from nodules of bone in the reptiles' skin. Perhaps future discoveries will reveal this kind of primitive stegosaur.

With the possible exceptions of *Scelidosaurus* and *Scutellosaurus*, the fossil record has yet to reveal the Early Jurassic ancestors that led to the development of *Huayangosaurus* and the latter stegosaurs. Also missing is the shared ancestry of fabrosaurs which at some point split into other armoured dinosaurs, the ankylosaurs and the nodosaurs. The stegosaurs, ankylosaurs

127

and nodosaurs are all related having come from the small, non-grinding toothed fabrosaurs. But their unknown ancestors had split into two, if not three separate lineages, probably early in the Jurassic. *Scelidosaurus* was closer to the nodosaurs than the ankylosaurs. However, even this relationship sheds little light on how and where the groups of armoured dinosaurs originated.

NODOSAURS AND LAND CONNECTIONS

While the stegosaurs can be traced back as far as the Middle Jurassic, to *Huayangosaurus*, the known representatives of the ankylosaurs and nodosaurs are almost exclusively from the later Cretaceous Period. There are only a few exceptions which are extremely fragmentary, yet diagnostic. Among the most conclusive is *Sarcolestes* which is the earliest representative of the nodosaurs and comes from the Middle Jurassic of England. *Sarcolestes* is known only from a partial lower jaw with teeth, and a dermal plate that in life was imbedded on the side of the animal's mouth. The huge gap of unknown ankylosaur, nodosaur and even stegosaur ancestors is a significant indication of the abundant kinds of dinosaurs that have been lost in time.

The Middle and Upper Jurassic nodosaurs, including *Sarcolestes*, are known only from Europe and they are absent from the abundant and well-known Jurassic faunas from North America, Asia and East Africa. Their lack of representation cannot explain or confirm their absence from other parts of the world, but it does suggest a regional confinement not broken until after the end of the Jurassic. The isolation, if it indeed really existed, might have been caused by topographical features that formed barriers. Epicontinental seaways flooded over much of Europe during the Middle and Late Jurassic creating several large islands and occasional archipelagos. These scattered islands could have acted as filtering routes of distribution that, while allowing the interchange of select groups of dinosaurs, hampered the movement of others, such as the nodosaurs.

The close similarity of dinosaurs known from the Late Jurassic of East Africa and western North America indicates that a land connection and dispersal routes were present allowing an inter-continental radiation. What is more vague, though, is how these continents were joined together. The archipelagos that occasionally connected Europe to North America may have allowed intermittent contact that could then have reached further onto the African continent. But if this was the main, or primary route of dispersal, then the absence of nodosaurs from these adjacent regions is all the more difficult to explain unless there was another route. It seems more likely that a larger, and more stable land connection, incorporated Central and South America which was adjacent to Africa and North America at that time.

Contemporaneous periods of the Late Jurassic are represented by the Morrison Formation in the United States, and the Tendaguru Formation in Tanzania, near the east coast of Africa. The deposition in the Tendaguru Formation incorporates alternating layers of dinosaur-bearing fresh water sediments and salt water marine sediments containing shells from squid-like ammonites, as well as corals. Wet and dry seasons alternated annually. The corals are associated with the remains of an abundant, invertebrate fauna which together indicate that a stable, warm climate existed year round, in spite of being located in higher latitudes. From this evidence, it may be seen that the marine sediments formed along the edge of a shallow, epicontinental sea that encroached upon the lagoons and shoreline of the coast. Sand bars separated the lagoons from the open sea, and overlapping deltaic sands shifted and accumulated at the journey's end of large rivers. Within these deltaic floodplains, abundant remains of sauropods, stegosaurs, other ornithischians, theropods and pterosaurs were deposited during a period that lasted hundreds, possibly even thousands, of years.

SAUROPODS WITH HORIZONTAL OR VERTICAL NECKS?

At least four distinct kinds of sauropods have been found in Tendaguru. Two of these, *Brachiosaurus* and *Barosaurus*, are also known from the Morrison Formation of North America. Also from Tendaguru are *Dicraeosaurus* and *Tornieria* which may have had exclusive southern affinities. All of these sauropods were descended from the basal stock of cetiosaurs, but each had different specialized levels of development. There were long-necked and comparatively short-necked sauropods, some had short front legs while others had long and tall front legs. Two distinct kinds of teeth lined the mouths of these giant plant eaters. Sauropod teeth were either of the robust and spatulate type, or slender, pencil-like rods. Even the nose of sauropods can be categorized into two separate types, depending on its structure and placement. Such diagnostic features can be compared to sauropods known throughout the world, and can indicate the relationships and distribution of these dinosaurs.

Brachiosaurus is a remarkable sauropod that retained some primitive characters in addition to advanced specializations. It retained the primitive condition of robust, spatulate teeth and the nasal opening was large and moved high up on its head. In a surprising reversal, the forelimbs increased in size becoming even longer than the hind legs. And most amazing, was the neck of *Brachiosaurus* which had become elongated to enormous proportions at least 10 m (32½ ft) long.

Other sauropods, such as *Barosaurus*, had also deve-

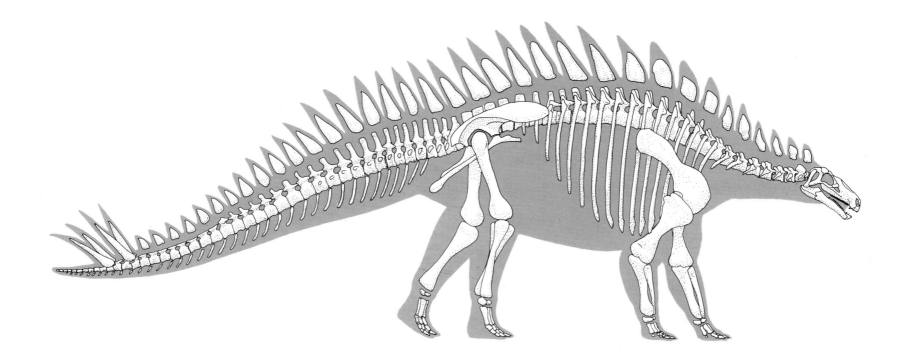

Huayangosaurus is the most primitive stegosaur as yet discovered. Several skeletons are known which demonstrate its comparatively large forelimbs, small pointed plates and spikes. Huayangosaurus is from China, and reached lengths of approximately 4 m (13 ft). (after Zhou, 1984)

loped incredibly long necks. Yet, these two long-necked sauropods were only distantly related. Unlike *Brachiosaurus*, the teeth of *Barosaurus* were slender, cylindrical rods. The nasal opening of *Barosaurus* was also quite different, being much smaller and even higher on top of the skull, almost directly above the eyes. The forelimbs were slightly elongated but only about three-fourths as much compared to *Brachiosaurus*. Even the huge, long necks were different in their construction. Certainly these were two very different kinds of sauropods.

The most significant differences in the necks can be seen in the shapes of the vertebrae in the shoulder region, and the length of the necks. Typically the primitive condition, as seen on cetiosaurs, is that each vertebra has one neural spine that rises to a summit on top of each vertebra. In life, the neural spines were the points of attachment for thick, rope-like ligaments that supported the neck, back and tail. *Brachiosaurus* retained the pattern of having only one neural spine on each vertebra. But the vertebrae located in the neck and the front part of the body on *Barosaurus* had split into two neural spines. This is surprising as it was *Brachiosaurus* which had the longer neck. Was there then, a functional advantage or disadvantage of having two neural spines for the ligaments and muscles to attach onto? Why were these two sauropods so similar in having such long necks, and at the same time so different from each other?

From a mechanical viewpoint, the vertebrae of the neck, back and tail can be compared with suspension bridges and cranes that are controlled by cables just like the ligaments and muscles attached to the neural spines on the vertebrae of sauropods. From this it can be seen that the placement of the cables, or ligaments, determines not only the amount of strength, but also the ability and range of movement that was possible.

The relatively high, single spines on *Brachiosaurus* would have given the ligaments greater leverage, best suited for supporting the neck in an elevated posture. In contrast, the deep division between the two neural spines on the *Barosaurus* vertebrae allowed the ligaments to extend farther down, filling the space between the spines. The extended low placement of the ligaments in the groove between the spines would have allowed the neck to move downward with greater ease. So, it would appear that single-spined and double-spined sauropods had necks that were suited for different functions. The single-spined *Brachiosaurus* was best designed for holding its neck high in an upright position, whereas *Barosaurus* had a greater range of movement and was better designed for lowering its long neck. But although there must have been a relationship between the sauropods' necks, their range of movement and the animals' abilities to feed themselves, why did two, such very different kinds of neck develop? The answers can be found in other parts of the animals' anatomy.

The longer than normal forelimbs of *Brachiosaurus*

NEXT PAGE

Two Dicraeosaurus *leave the water, startling a crocodile. In the distance, groups of this Gondwanic sauropod remain on the shore and others feed in the water. Found only in the Tendaguru quarry of Africa,* Dicraeosaurus *is a peculiar diplodocid with a comparatively short neck and tall neural spines.* Dicraeosaurus *reached lengths of approximately 20 m (65 ft).*

The skeleton of Brachiosaurus *is shown compared to a 2.7-m (9-ft) tall elephant, 1.8-m (6-ft) tall man and 3-m scale bar. The slight upward slant and natural horizontal orientation of the neck demonstrates the normal posture in which it was held. The height of the neck is caused by disproportionately long front legs and not the neck itself which was incapable of being raised into a totally vertical posture. Maximum height that the head could reach is about 9 m (29 ft) and the total length of* Brachiosaurus *is approximately 19 m (62 ft). (modified after Janensch 1950 and Paul 1988)*

would have automatically raised the front of its body, neck and head higher than other sauropods that had shorter front legs. The enlarged front legs are an unusual modification that must have resulted in response to the animal's need to raise its head higher. A similar development of large front legs also occurs in *Cetiosaurus* from Morocco, in north western Africa, but the neck of this cetiosaur was considerably shorter. Even so, *Cetiosaurus* had a higher reach than other sauropods which had shorter front legs. So, in this case it would appear that long forelimbs allowed the neck to be held in an elevated position, but the elongation of the neck was a separate development.

Ordinarily, most animals with short necks have vertebrae that are also short and flexible. Longer necks may include a few extra vertebrae, but most of the lengthening process is produced by the actual elongation of each individual vertebra. This places the joints of the neck much farther apart, reducing the amount of flexibility. In order to counteract this restriction, the shape of the vertebrae is usually modified so that the angle of the articulation surfaces is changed from a straight, perpendicular alignment into a bevelled, slanted angle. This redirects the shape of the neck and its range of mobility.

One would expect to see modifications such as these

in the neck vertebrae of sauropods. But, surprisingly, they are absent in *Brachiosaurus* and *Barosaurus* for the sauropod neck is generally a straight extension from the backbone of the animal. It is remarkable that the structural modifications that would have allowed the neck to be pulled back into a more vertical posture never developed in sauropods. An elongated, more vertical, neck would lift the animal's head higher. More importantly, it would have been extremely helpful in redistributing the weight of the neck more centrally. Such a pose would almost seem to have been a necessity in that it would alleviate so much of the burdensome weight of the neck. In fact, other kinds of dinosaurs, including carnivorous theropods and herbivorous ornithopods, did have modified necks that could be pulled back into a more vertical angle to alleviate much of the burden of supporting a heavy, outstretched head. But if sauropods were incapable of holding their necks in a vertical posture, there must be reasons to explain how and why they carried their necks horizontally. It is all the more puzzling because of all the dinosaurs that should have been able to lift their necks into a near vertical position, sauropods would appear to have had the greatest need and potential benefits from such a posture.

TEETH AND NOSES
HIGH OR LOW BROWSERS

It is possible that the kinds of teeth and noses of sauropods may help give an understanding of the mysterious manner in which the necks were used and how they worked. There are definitely two kinds of sauropod teeth which can be correlated to the animal's nasal structure and its position. Robust spatulate teeth are

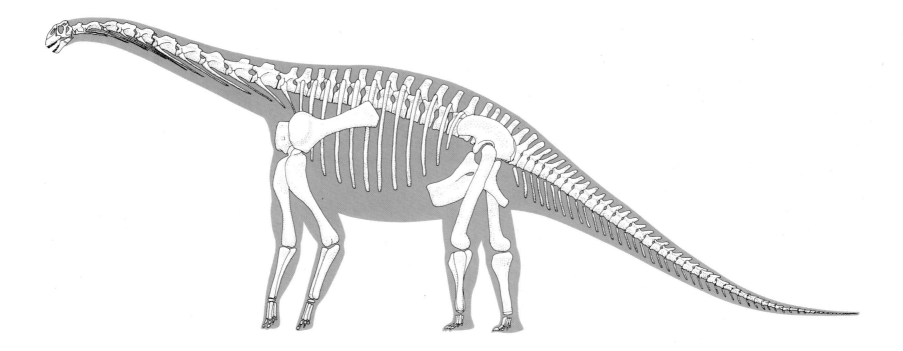

The virtually complete skeletal remains of a huge Cetiosaurus *from Morocco demonstrates the high-browsing capability associated with sauropods that have spatulate teeth. Despite its having a relatively short neck (compared to brachiosaurids), the unusually long front legs of this cetiosaur accounts for the upward slant of the neck which places the head higher than peg-toothed, low-browsing sauropods. The maximum height and length of* Cetiosaurus *is approximately 6 m (19¹/₂ ft) high and 16 m (52 ft) long. (modified from Monbaron, 1983)*

typically found in sauropods that have rather large nasal openings located fairly high up on the top of the skull. Slender, cylindrical, peg-like teeth belong to those that have small, recessed nasal openings even higher on the back of the skull almost directly above the orbits, or openings for the eyes. This condition is seen time and time again, regardless of the length of the neck. The extremely long-necked *Barosaurus* was equipped with slender teeth and small, highly-placed nasal openings in the same manner as *Dicraeosaurus* which had one of the shortest necks among the sauropods. This is especially important because it indicates that short-necked sauropods such as *Dicraeosaurus*, also had teeth that were specialized for a unique diet and food source of plants that must have been low enough to the ground for the animal to still be able to reach it. This being the case, with a suitable food source available within the lower limits and grasp of *Dicraeosaurus*, it is difficult to reconcile the idea that *Barosaurus* needed its exceptionally long neck to reach a similar food source higher up. Despite its long neck, even *Barosaurus* could have just as easily, if not more so, fed upon plants that were lower down and closer to the ground. Certainly the articulation of its neck was aptly designed for such behaviour.

With every step forward while walking towards vegetation, the sauropods with their horizontally held necks would have been able to reach a fairly sizeable area of potential food sources by simply moving their necks from side to side and up and down. It may be heretical to dismiss the popular view of these sauropods as giant reptilian giraffes that fed upon the tops of trees. But when closely examined, the evidence as revealed by sauropods like *Barosaurus* and *Dicraeosaurus* squarely confronts such a characterization.

The high position of the nostrils has been cited as a possible aquatic adaptation which would allow the giant sauropod to remain deeply submerged and hidden while breathing with its raised nose barely protruding from the water. At first, this appears to have validity since other aquatic reptiles, notably alligators and crocodiles, have elevated nostrils that can perform exactly such a function. But, as critics have correctly pointed out, it would have been impossible for the lungs of a long-necked sauropod to withstand the huge amounts of water pressure, and breathe properly at such great depths. Such thinking resulted in a backlash, sauropods were then regarded as being only terrestrial animals.

Certainly, sauropods were quite capable of moving about on dry land. Abundant examples of fossilized sauropod trackways clearly show their ability to have walked across the landscape. But rare examples of trackways that were made by sauropods as they swam across the shallows and polled themselves along on their front legs give testimony to the fact that sauropods were not restricted to either the land or water, and moved freely into either environment.

As to why the nostrils were located so high on top of the head, it is necessary to realize where the flaw in the original aquatic scenario occurred. As often depicted, the totally submerged sauropod is shown breathing through its nostrils, attempting to pump oxygen far down a vertically aligned neck. The main problem

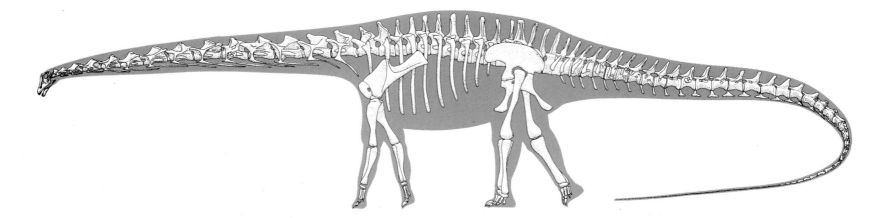

The skeleton of Diplodocus *typifies that of a low-browsing, peg-toothed sauropod. Despite having a long neck, the articulations of the vertebrae indicate that it was normally held in a horizontal posture with modifications that were best suited for bringing the neck lower to the ground. Vertical orientation of the neck was not possible.* Diplodocus *reached lengths of approximately 27 m (88 ft). (modified from Holland, 1905)*

with this scenario lies in the orientation of the neck which, if held vertically, places the body too deeply underwater. It also assumes that the depth of the water is the same as the animal's height. However, a viable alternative becomes apparent when the neck is held outstretched horizontally in a naturally articulated posture. Regardless of the water's depth, in this position the nose could have been easily held above the surface of the water while the entire mouth was placed into the water to drink, or feed on aquatic plants. Breathing would not have been hampered because the neck and body would have floated near the surface of the water. The air-sacs in the vertebrae may even have added to the animal's buoyancy, helping to support its weight while in the water. The additional support of the neck while floating in the water could explain, at least to some extent, why sauropod vertebrae were not modified for a more vertical orientation. While in the water, the articulation of the neck was functional in its horizontal pose. But still, it must be remembered that sauropods were far from being totally aquatic animals, and certainly even those with the longest of necks, were quite capable of leaving the water and walking across the land. The huge bulk of the animal with its outstretched neck looming forward, and tail carried high off the ground must have been an awesome sight.

It would seem, then, that the slender, peg-toothed sauropods were beautifully designed for feeding low to the ground, and perhaps consumed aquatic vegetation. Yet, this may not have been the limit of their food gathering capabilities. Although they were 'low browsing' animals, the horizontally held neck also allowed a sizeable side to side range in which the animal could find the food of its choice. The dinosaur's size alone would have meant it could raise its head several

metres into the air. So, it is quite possible that any vegetation within its grasp could have been a potential food source.

Other kinds of sauropods are relatively 'high browsers'. Certain sauropods, such as *Brachiosaurus* and the shorter necked *Cetiosaurus* from Morocco, had modifications that increased their eating range considerably higher than any peg-toothed sauropod. Primarily this was achieved by the increase in the length of the forelimbs, and not the neck. In similar fashion to the necks of the low-browsing sauropods, the neck remained as a straight extension from the backbone. But the longer front legs raised the front of the body, in effect increasing the angle of the vertebrae column, and lifting the neck and head higher into the air.

As with the low-browsing sauropods, there are anatomical features of the teeth and nasal developments in the skull that give a basis for determining whether there were adaptations for either low, or high, browsing.

Brachiosaurus was quite unlike the low-browsing sauropods and must have had a different kind of food source and behaviour pattern. Of course, some overlap in their lifestyle was shared, but the differences between the teeth indicate that *Brachiosaurus*, as well as other sauropods with robust, spatulate teeth, fed on a different kind of vegetation than that of the low-browsing sauropods. It seems reasonable to think that the sturdy, cropping capabilities of the *Brachiosaurus* teeth would have been capable of shearing through much tougher vegetation than the more delicate, peg-toothed, low-browsing sauropods. The two kinds of sauropod teeth therefore show that the preferred food sources were located in separate areas.

The peculiar nose of *Brachiosaurus* was greatly modified from its ancestral condition, and it was quite different from that of peg-toothed sauropods. This suggests that the nose had a different type of function, beneficial to the animal's lifestyle. The specialized function of the brachiosaur nose is not as easy to interpret as the aquatic, low-browsing kind. Was *Brachiosaurus* capable of using its nose in a similar fashion adapting to an aquatic setting? It is very likely that *Bra-*

chiosaurus did upon occasion enter into the water. Nothing should have prevented this, as it probably would have had many beneficial qualities, such as cooling off and thermoregulating the body temperature. The problem in identifying the specialized function of the brachiosaur-style nose is made more difficult because it is not clear exactly where the nostrils were located. Unlike the peg-toothed sauropods which have a small, but definite location of the nasal opening, the nasal opening on robust, spatulate-toothed sauropods is a very large space in which the nostrils could have been located anywhere. There just isn't any conclusive way to know the exact location of the nostrils, except by the discovery of a mummified skull complete with skin impressions including details of the actual nose. Only such a fabulously preserved fossil could finally resolve where the nostrils were located on these kinds of sauropods. As yet, such a fossil has not been discovered. But in time, knowing what to look for may reveal not just the nose, but even the face of a sauropod.

In *Brachiosaurus*, the expanded overall size of the nasal opening in the skull implies an increase in the available sensitive tissues that determine the animal's ability to smell. If this is so, then a terrestrial behaviour, with an increased ability to smell the proper vegetation seems likely. Analogous comparisons with bulbous, or enlarged uplifted nasal bones found on some modern reptiles, correlate such development to the presence of fleshy, ornamental horns and knobby protuberances. Perhaps *Brachiosaurus*, or other large-nosed sauropods, had nasal crests ornamenting their faces.

SAUROPOD DISTRIBUTION

The broad diversity of sauropods reflects their success in adapting to different situations within various environments. This adaptability allowed certain sauropods to increase their territory by radiating across continental landmasses. It is not too surprising that sauropods like *Brachiosaurus* and *Barosaurus* are found in regions of both Africa and North America. But why the other contemporary sauropods didn't share a similar geographical range remains a complex and unsettled problem. How was it that *Brachiosaurus* and *Barosaurus* were more successful migrants than other sauropods? And what parts of the world did they originally come from? It would seem that *Dicraeosaurus* and *Torneria* were limited to Africa in the southern hemisphere during the Late Jurassic. Perhaps, then, *Brachiosaurus* and *Barosaurus* were migrants from continents of the northern hemisphere.

The Late Jurassic Morrison formations of North America have yielded fossil remains of probably the most famous of dinosaurs: *Apatosaurus* (which is more popularly known as *Brontosaurus*), *Diplodocus* and *Camarasaurus*. The slender, peg-like teeth and small,

high location of the nostrils show that *Apatosaurus* and *Diplodocus* were related to *Barosaurus*. On the other hand, *Camarasaurus*, which had robust, spatulate teeth and a prominent large nose, was related to *Brachiosaurus*. Noticeably, *Apatosaurus*, *Diplodocus* and *Camarasaurus* are absent from the Tendaguru Formations of Africa indicating that they were probably limited to the western part of the northern hemisphere.

The types of sauropods known from the eastern part of the northern hemisphere, more specifically China and the surrounding regions of Asia, are again different as they represent an entirely separate fauna unlike those of the Tendaguru and Morrison. Fossil remains of sauropods are quite abundant in China, being widely distributed in quarries throughout the vast countryside. What is unique about all of these Asian sauropods is that they apparently belonged exclusively to the robust, spatulate-toothed forms. As yet, not a single sauropod discovered in China pertains to the slender, peg-toothed sauropods. The incredibly long-necked *Mamenchisaurus* was originally thought to have had peg-style teeth along with other features shared with *Diplodocus*. Until recently, the well-preserved, articulated skeletons of *Mamenchisaurus* have not included skulls or teeth which would provide more exact evidence of which group of sauropods it really belonged in. Was *Mamenchisaurus* the only known peg-toothed sauropod in China? Perhaps not. An associated skull has now been found, one that is believed to belong to *Mamenchisaurus*, and it has robust, spatulate teeth.

In some ways it would have been even more of a surprise if *Mamenchisaurus* really did have slender, peg-style teeth. Not only would it be the only sauropod in China so equipped, but this would contradict its otherwise very close relationship to other sauropods which share many similar skeletal features. As all the other Asian sauropods, including *Omeisaurus* and *Euhelopus*, are known to have skulls with robust, spatulate teeth, the total absence of sauropods with slender, peg-teeth in China is significant. Such an absence reflects the origins, geographical limits of distribution, and ecological conditions of the environments in which they lived.

Because the primitive, or ancestral, condition of tooth structure as inherited from the prosauropods was a robust, spatulate form, it is difficult, if not impossible, to determine exactly which part of the world the spatulate-toothed sauropods originated in. They apparently had a global distribution from very early in their history. But the absence of peg-toothed sauropods in Asia indicates that they had their origins in either Africa and adjoining regions to the south, or perhaps in North America.

Even though the primitive, spatulate-toothed sauropods abounded on virtually every continent, it is interesting that some of the Asian sauropods share strong affinities with *Brachiosaurus* of Africa and North America. The nose of sauropods such as *Omeisaurus*, *Euhelopus* and probably *Mamenchisaurus* had reached a

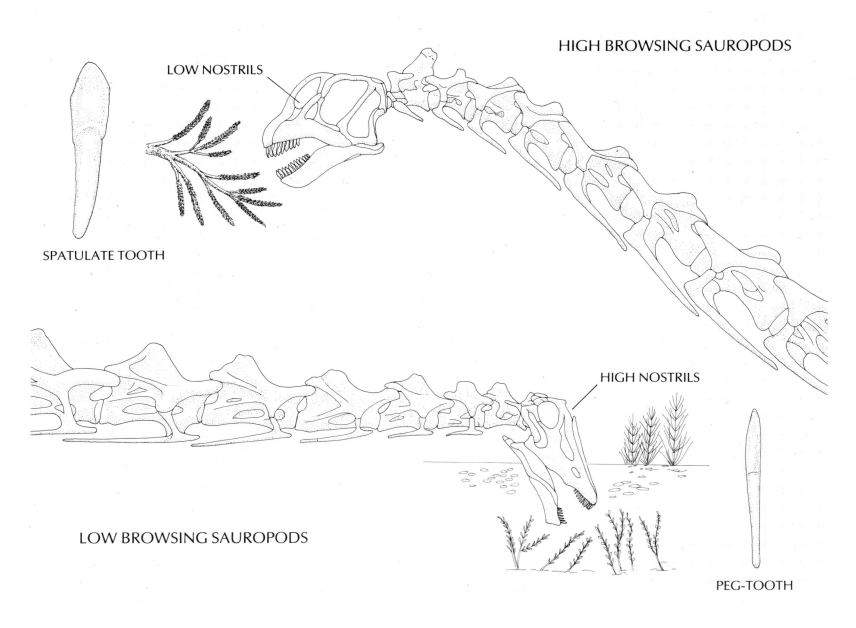

LOW NOSTRILS

SPATULATE TOOTH

HIGH NOSTRILS

LOW BROWSING SAUROPODS

PEG-TOOTH

SAUROPOD TEETH AND NOSES – EATING STYLES

Spatulate-toothed sauropods had a tendency to eat tougher vegetation that grew several metres above the ground, in contrast to the peg-toothed sauropods which had a preference for aquatic plants and softer vegetation that was low to the ground. The angle in which the heads were carried on the necks illustrates how the food source was approached. Nostrils of peg-toothed sauropods were located high on the back of the skull so that while feeding in water only the mouth was submerged and breathing remained unimpaired. Nostrils of spatulate-toothed sauropods were located much lower on the front of the skull.

transitional stage of enlargement approaching the development seen on *Brachiosaurus*. The forelimbs of *Euhelopus* were extremely elongated, nearly reaching the same proportions of *Brachiosaurus*. Their enormously elongated necks were also similar with a low, single neural spine on each vertebra. What all this may mean is that the ancestry and distribution of *Brachiosaurus* started in Asia and from there spread into the southern continents, specifically Africa, and further north-west into North America. *Barosaurus*, on the other hand, had no affinities to the east and was prob-

ably an immigrant in Africa that came from North America.

Why only *Barosaurus* migrated as far as Africa, and the other peg-toothed sauropods were constrained to mostly North America, and possibly adjoining parts of Europe, may reflect the presence of geographical barriers such as mountain ranges, desolate deserts or ocean ways. Direct competition between both kinds of sauropods for food sources may only have played a small part in restricting the peg-toothed sauropods from broadening their domain more globally into Asia. Rather, the specialization of the peg-toothed sauropods' diet may well have limited their distribution. So, different types of vegetation might have encouraged or restricted the dispersal of the wandering peg-toothed sauropods.

Attracted by the stench of a bloated Apatosaurus *body, two* Ceratosaurus *approach the carcass to feast on the opportunistic meal.*

PROBLEMS OF STEGOSAUR PLATE ARRANGEMENTS

Sauropods were the largest terrestrial animals that have ever existed. They were also the dominant herbivores of the Jurassic. During that time there were many other kinds of dinosaurs that ate plants but whereas the sauropods were saurischians, all the other herbivores were ornithischians. The tail-spiked and armour-plated stegosaurs were the next largest herbivores – still large giants but not on the same scale as the sauropods. Hypsilophodonts were still smaller in size, although they played an important part in the development of the herbivorous dinosaurs that would appear during the Cretaceous.

The stegosaurs were a varied group of dinosaurs that possessed an array of spikes and thin, narrow,

armour plates of bone arranged along the length of their backbone. These ornate forms of armament were not attached to the vertebrae or other bones of the skeleton. Instead, the spikes and plates would have been deeply embedded within the skin of the animal, being held firmly upright. Because they were not connected to other bones there are no articulating surfaces to help palaeontologists guide their placement back into their natural position. The spikes and plates usually do not remain in their natural positions after the death of the animal, and fall away from the rest of the skeleton. Once detached, the interpretation of exactly where they belong on the animal becomes extremely difficult, if not nearly impossible. Occasionally, a stegosaur has been found with only a small displacement of the spikes and plates, providing a better guide for the correct interpretation of the arrangement. Even with

Pterosaurs soar past an adult and juvenile Mamenchisaurus. *Once considered to be a diplodocid, a recently discovered skull attributed to* Mamenchisaurus *now indicates that this sauropod had spatulate teeth. Length of the neck is 10 m (32¹/₂ ft) and the animal's total length is approximately 22 m (71¹/₂ ft).*

the finest and best preserved skeletons of stegosaurs, however, the exact arrangement has been a seemingly unresolvable puzzle for over a hundred years, when the first stegosaur was discovered.

Various possibilities of what stegosaurs may have looked like have been suggested time and time again, but none with total acceptance. Spiked ankles and a turtle-like carapace (or shell) with numerous spines randomly protruding may have seemed logical when it was presented back in the late 1890s. Indeed, such an arrangement of spines and armour plating would have been an efficient design. But efficient or not, it would only have been conjection, and nothing more than a logical assumption based on an idealized interpretation of the spikes' and plates' possible function. In short, only a guess.

Due to the lack of fossils that could give sufficient

evidence, still other wildly speculative guesses were made. Numerous rows of sharp-edged plates across the width of the body followed by a multiple-spiked tail was a slightly more accurate suggestion made in the late nineteenth century. Although it was the first hypothesis to at least accurately position the thin, bony plates upright on the body, it suffered greatly from overkill.

Then, some years later, an almost totally complete and articulated stegosaur was discovered. Its death pose was twisted and contorted, missing only the last parts of its tail. But – and most importantly – the bony,

139

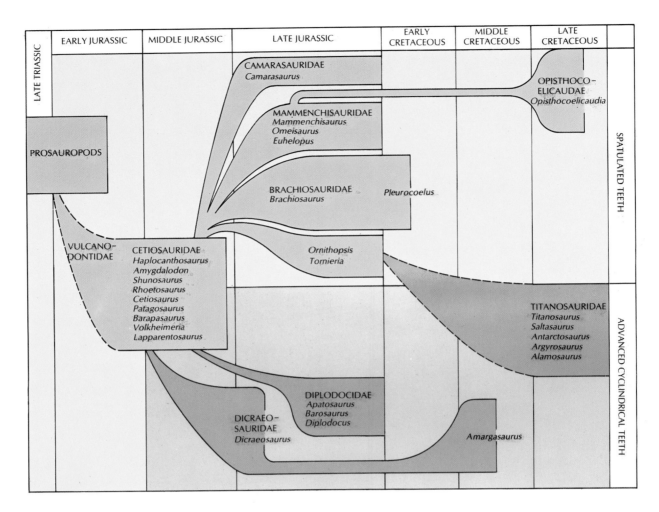

| LATE TRIASSIC | EARLY JURASSIC | MIDDLE JURASSIC | LATE JURASSIC | EARLY CRETACEOUS | MIDDLE CRETACEOUS | LATE CRETACEOUS | |

SAUROPOD PHYLOGENY CHART

The basal family of cetiosaurid sauropods evolved from the vulca-nodontid offshoot of the prosauropods. Different kinds of sauropods evolved from the cetiosaurs with either spatulate teeth or cylindrical peg-like teeth. Most of the sauropods became extinct at the end of the Jurassic. The most notable survivors were the titanosaurs which lasted until the end of the Cretaceous. The cylindrical teeth of titanosaurs appear to have evolved independently from other peg-toothed sauropods.

armour plates were remarkably undisturbed, remaining close to their original positions above the vertebrae of the neck, back and tail. With the discovery of this stegosaur skeleton there was finally tangible evidence to work with. This particular stegosaur remains the most complete and informative specimen ever discovered and it was from it that it was realized that the plates were arranged running only on top of the length of the backbone.

Stegosaurus stenops, a North American stegosaur, has therefore been a strong influence on the interpretation of how the spikes and plates on virtually all the other kinds of stegosaurs known from around the world were arranged. While this is an acceptably proper procedure, it should be remembered that stegosaurs from other parts of the world had different kinds of armour plates and spines reflecting various levels of development. So the function, as well as the arrangement, of the plates and spines may have been somewhat different to those of the North American *Stegosaurus*.

No doubt, there was some degree of defensive quality given by the plates and spines but there may have been other functions as well. In order to better understand these, it is all the more important to know exactly where and how the plates and spines were arranged. Here again, this brings *Stegosaurus* back into consideration as a rosetta stone to help in deciphering the mysteries of the stegosaurs. However, there has been a stumbling block in the translation for over a hundred years. The interpretation of this remarkably complete specimen of *Stegosaurus* centred upon whether the two rows of armour plates were either in a paired, or an alternating pattern.

The position of the plates, as found on this *Stegosaurus*, revealed that some plates on the front of the animal had portions that overlapped. This strongly suggested that the plates were either in an alternating pattern or that matched pairs existed. However, out of the seventeen plates that were found, no two were the same size and could not be considered as a matched pair. This was tangible evidence as preserved in the rock. The opposing argument suggested that the alternating pattern was only an illusion created by postmortem movements and shifting. But, while such distorting movements are possible, the disparity of

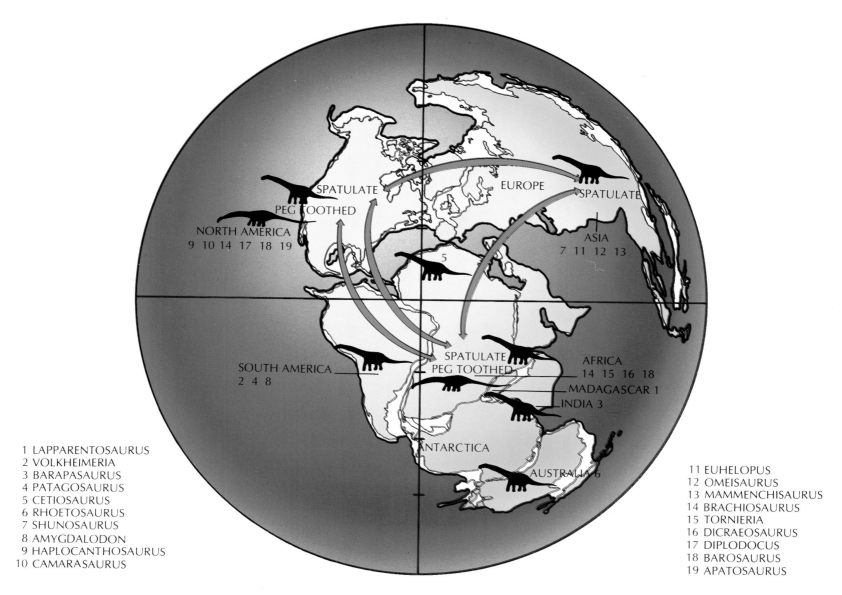

1 LAPPARENTOSAURUS
2 VOLKHEIMERIA
3 BARAPASAURUS
4 PATAGOSAURUS
5 CETIOSAURUS
6 RHOETOSAURUS
7 SHUNOSAURUS
8 AMYGDALODON
9 HAPLOCANTHOSAURUS
10 CAMARASAURUS

11 EUHELOPUS
12 OMEISAURUS
13 MAMMENCHISAURUS
14 BRACHIOSAURUS
15 TORNIERIA
16 DICRAEOSAURUS
17 DIPLODOCUS
18 BAROSAURUS
19 APATOSAURUS

SAUROPOD DISTRIBUTION GLOBE
During the Jurassic, sauropods had achieved a global distribution. However, sauropods with spatulate teeth were more broadly dispersed than peg-toothed sauropods which may have failed to populate Asia during this time.

sizes and the regularity of the spacing suggested that in this case it was unlikely.

Additional information on the positioning of these plates came from logical analogies. Because stegosaurs are dinosaurs which share their ancestry with thecodonts, it was suggested that like many thecodonts which had two paired rows of armoured scutes, so it was with their descendant *Stegosaurus*. Also, it was observed that a condition of alternating plates was unnatural: it was never seen in reptiles which had two or more rows of armour scutes. So, the tangible fossil evidence supporting the concept of two rows in an alternating pattern was overwhelmed by sound logic in favour of a paired arrangement. With this conflicting information, the exact arrangement of the stegosaur plates and spines remained in question.

Perhaps no suitable answer has been achieved because the question itself is in error. It may be that there was only one row, and not two rows in the first place. This would eliminate the concern about the so-called unnatural condition of alternating rows. In fact, the thecodont relationship has recently lost merit because it is now known that at least some thecodonts had only one row of armoured scutes running along the length of their backbone. This shouldn't be too sur-

prising, as other kinds of dinosaurs have only a single row of scutes adorning their backs, as seen on the carnivore *Ceratosaurus*. So the argument for having two rows, paired or otherwise, becomes a moot point. Still, if there was only one row of plates on *Stegosaurus*, an explanation is needed for the apparent alternating pattern of plates as they were preserved in the fossil.

Close examination of the most complete skeleton of *Stegosaurus* reveals that each plate as found has a larger or smaller size next to it, and that the bottom of each plate has a base progressively different in shape from the next. Even though some plates were found with the upper portions overlapping, it is significant that none of the bases were found overlapping. This is important because it is only if the bases overlapped that evidence would be offered for two separate rows, regardless if any of the upper parts of the plates overlapped or not. Curiously, only the plates which had bases that were wide, short in length, and asymmetrical were overlapping as seen in the intact fossil stegosaur.

141

The four views of this model of Stegosaurus *illustrates how the single row of plates would look. Note that the plates over the neck and shoulders overlap in the side view, and that the same plates slant alternately outwards as seen in the top and front views. Also note that these diagonally-held plates, like each of the remaining plates, originate from the midline of the animal, thereby representing one row.*

A knowledge of the structure of these plates leads to a more informed discussion as to how they were positioned. The shape of each plate's base is different from the first to the last in the series. The first few plates over the neck have narrow bases; the following ones, located over the back of the neck and front half of the body over the shoulders, have bases that are wider and asymmetrical, being larger on one side than the other. These plates are nearly three times the length of their short, wide bases. The bases of the remaining plates over the back quickly reduce in width, becoming quite narrow. Unlike the wide, short-based plates, the remaining ones on the back and tail have bases that are virtually as long as the total length of the plate. These structural differences must relate to the manner in which they were held in the animal's body as it was the bases which attached the plates into the fleshy hide.

All of the bases show distinct rugosity where collagenous tissues (see glossary) within the skin attached onto them. This rugose area of attachment is especially high on the narrow-based plates over the back and tail indicating that they were deeply and firmly embedded into a heightened crest of flesh above the vertebrae. The symmetrical nature of these bases indicates that they were held directly upwards. However, the offset asymmetrical development of the other bases clearly shows that they were held upwards and at a slight slant outwards. This outward slant was necessary because the plates were longer than the bases supporting them. If not for the opposite slanting of these particular plates, the expanded portions would have collided into adjacent plates in front or behind.

So it is demonstrated that it is the opposite slanting of these plates which accounts for the alternating pattern seen in the fossil skeleton of *Stegosaurus*. In fact, when the total length of this particular stegosaur is restored it confirms that the plates were arranged in one row down the mid-line of the animal's back. All seventeen plates comfortably fit the available space above the vertebrae leaving adequate room for the tail spikes

Only the plates over the neck and shoulder on Stegosaurus *are held in an alternating slanted pattern.*

near the tip of the tail. The seventeen plates on this skeleton of *Stegosaurus* is the largest number of plates found directly associated with this kind of stegosaur. Because the last half of the tail was not preserved, it was believed that additional plates were also lost. However, more complete tails of other stegosaurs suggest that no plates were missing.

In life, then, *Stegosaurus* appears to have been a fabulously crested dinosaur with a single row of narrow plates that crowned the length of the animal. The plates over the shoulder region were not just vertical, but held in a slanted position that created an alternating pattern even though these, as all of the plates, rose directly from the mid-line of the animal's back. So, if this accurately represents the arrangement of the *Stegosaurus* plates, then this may be a guide for interpreting the appearance of the other kinds of stegosaurs from different parts of the world. It also determines the possible functions that could have been available to the animal.

POSSIBLE FUNCTIONS OF STEGOSAUR PLATES AND SPIKES

Possible functions of stegosaur plates and spikes include visual display, defensive and offensive armament, and thermoregulation of the body temperature. The plates probably had more than one function, and there is a degree of validity to each of these possibilities. The North American *Stegosaurus* had reached the peak of plate development, and was unique among stegosaurs from different parts of the world which all had much smaller plates. The functions, as well as efficiency, therefore, must have been variable among the stegosaurs.

In terms of visual display, the plates could have provided an attraction between males and females. Perhaps they played some part in showing the maturity of the animal and therefore its attractiveness to potential mates. This is certainly logical but there is no sure way

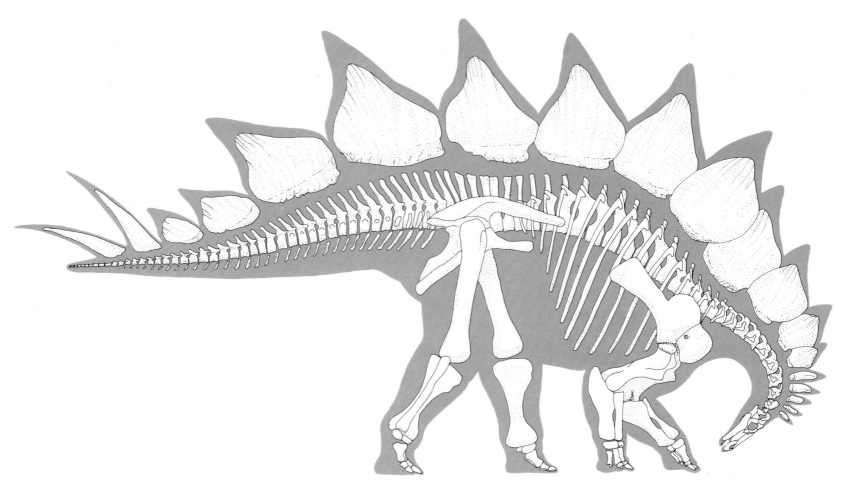

The skeleton of Stegosaurus *is shown in a defensive pose with its neck and head bent downward, and tail held high. The head was protected by the plates along the neck, and while circling away from an attacking theropod, the powerful spike-tipped tail would have been swung vigorously at the predator.* Stegosaurus *reached lengths of approximately 6 m (19¹/₂ ft).*

to determine the sex of the animals, as it appears that both male and female stegosaurs were equipped with equally sizeable plates. So visual display for attracting a mate seems unlikely. Other characteristics such as a colour change may have been utilized to indicate desires and availability. Such periodic changes in colour is fairly common among many reptiles, but can be only conjectural for stegosaurs and other dinosaurs.

Visual display may have had some defensive qualities by simply making the animal appear to be more massive than it really was. Intimidation plays a vital role in reptilian confrontations where reptiles stand as tall as possible, lifting their head and tail, and even bloating their bodies with air in the hopes of bluffing their way to a safe resolution. Stegosaurs were far from helpless, and probably used non-lethal intimidation mostly for domination over other males.

When confronted by carnivorous dinosaurs, a *Stegosaurus* must have been a dangerous opponent. The tail spikes could have been swung wildly upwards, and from side to side. It can be seen quite clearly from the structure of the vertebrae and the areas where the muscles were attached that *Stegosaurus* had incredibly powerful tail muscles, especially suited to movement from side to side. So, undoubtedly, the tail spikes were highly functional, defensive weapons. In life,

these tail spikes were covered by a tough, horn-like sheath that would have increased their length. Often they were more than 50 cms (1¹/₂ ft) long and in one species from North America, *Stegosaurus longispinus*, the tail spikes were like giant, slender needles over 1 m (3 ft) in length. *Stegosaurus sulcatus* was another aberrant form from North America that had incredibly stout tail spikes that must have acted as huge, pointed war clubs.

The use of the plates, which are modified spikes, is more difficult to interpret. Recently, it has been suggested that the plates may have been able to move from side to side thus shifting the armament into the face of a would be attacker. This concept is whimsical conjecture based on logic more than fact. Such idealizations go beyond the tangible fossil evidence and ignore conflicting data. This takes a real animal and embellishes it until it becomes a creature of fantasy and science-fiction. The suggestion that the narrow bases of the plates acted like a hinge, pulled from either side by muscles in the skin does not account for the fact that many plates had bases that were wide and not designed to be mobile. The different shapes of the bases and the extent of the rugosity conclusively shows that they were deeply embedded into a collagenous mass of tissues that attached the plates firmly beneath the skin. There were no special modifications for muscularly controlled mobility. Mobile plates would add little to the animal's defence beyond that of stationary plates because virtually the entire sides of the animal would remain vulnerable. For stegosaurs which had modest or small plates, such proposed

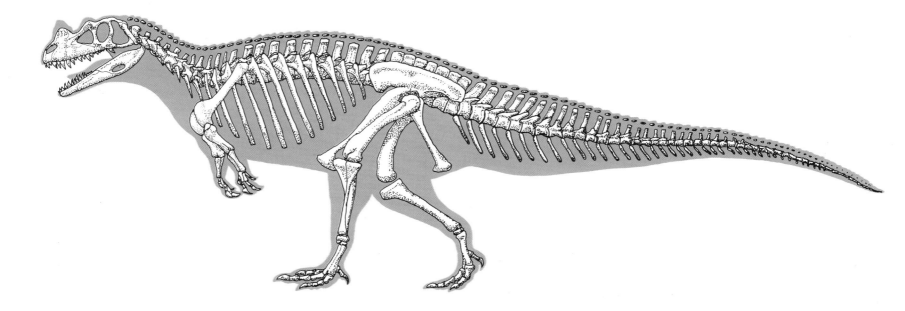

movement from side to side would obviously be futile.

Of course, the giant serrated fence of the bony armour on *Stegosaurus* may have added protection along the entire length of the animal simply by being there. But an interesting observation may offer a reason as to why the pattern of plates over the neck and shoulder region existed. When an animal is attacked it can be readily killed by a choking grasp of the predator's jaws around the neck, or a quick crushing blow to the head. Modern reptiles often use the latter mode of behaviour. *Stegosaurus*, with its notably small skull and its remarkably small brain, still had to defend what there was. Thrashing tail spikes and armour plates would be futile if the predator walked around to the front and with a bite to the head secured its meal. Such brief battles probably did happen, and this could be why the neck and shoulder plates were held at a slight slant outwards. When threatened, a stegosaur need only bend its neck downwards hiding its head beneath its protective neck which had a thick, tough skin lined with a mosaic of bony ossicles for extra defence. By bending its head down and back the offset plates with the extra lengths would have fanned out across the full curvature of the neck leaving no gaps that would be an easy target.

The other kinds of stegosaurs from different parts of the world were not as elaborately equipped with huge plates as on the North American *Stegosaurus*. Instead, the plates were comparatively small and spine-like, as seen on *Huayangosaurus* and *Tuojiangosaurus*, both from China. This is likely a transitory stage of development from a primitive ancestral condition into a more specialized or advanced one. Originally, in the most primitive stegosaurs, the bony armour probably looked much like the multi-spiked crest that adorns many modern day lizards of the iguana family. But the smaller spines were not better designed for defence by becoming plate-like. If the pointed spines evolved for a better form of defence, then why didn't they simply

Skeletons of Ceratosaurus *are more scarce than its North American contemporary,* Allosaurus. *Hands with four fingers, and a nasal horn distinguishes it from other theropods of the Late Jurassic. This rare theropod shares some primitive characteristics with the Cretaceous Gondwanic group of theropods, the abelisaurs, which suggests that* Ceratosaurus *was an immigrant from the southern hemisphere.* Ceratosaurus *reached lengths of approximately 6 m (19¹/₂ ft). (after Gilmore, 1920)*

increase in size without changing their shape? This might well indicate that defence was not the primary cause for the evolution of spines into flat plates. Some other function may have been also involved.

STEGOSAUR PLATES AS THERMOREGULATORS

Thermoregulation has long been suspected as being a function of the flattened plates. This theory is mostly based on the fact that the bone is highly vascular and grooved indicating the presence of a network of blood vessels. Whether thermoregulation was achieved by additional cooling or warming, or both, depends greatly on the shape and the pattern in which the plates are arranged.

None of the known stegosaurs are more complete than the North American *Stegosaurus*. This has caused virtually all of the other kinds to be reconstructed according to the traditional belief that two rows of plates existed, and not by the evidence given by the fossils. They may actually have looked quite different than was once supposed since, as already discussed, one row now appears to be a viable alternative. This being the case, if all stegosaurs had only one row of plates, it becomes a little easier to understand how the plates may have been used to regulate the body temperature.

Studies utilizing a wind tunnel have shown that an alternating pattern would contribute a cooling effect by a naturally forced convection channelling the wind

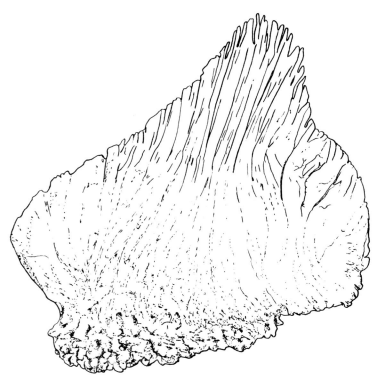

TYPES OF STEGOSAUR PLATES
Primitive stegosaurs have more spike-like plates than do the advanced stegosaurs which have narrow broadened plates. (left) The dorsal (back) plate of Huayangosaurus, (middle) anterior plate of Stegosaurus with a short, wide asymmetrical base, (right) tail plate of Stegosaurus with a long, narrow symmetrical base. Different kinds of bases indicate how they were positioned on the body, either slanted or directly upright.

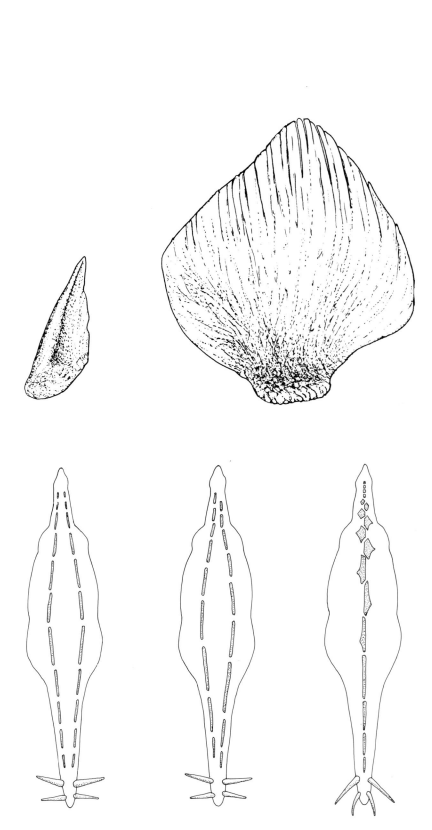

STEGOSAUR PLATES DIAGRAM
Viewed from the top, the patterns of plate arrangement on a Stegosaurus depict: (left) two rows paired, (middle) two rows alternating, and (right) one row with alternating plates over the neck and shoulders.

more surface area than the paired arrangement. Paired plates would have heated only the one row facing the sun while leaving the other row cooler in the shadows.

If thermoregulation was truly a function of the plates then either arrangement of two rows would be limited. Constant cooling from an alternating pattern would be a strange adaptation for an ectothermic animal and would imply that *Stegosaurus* was warm-blooded. However, *Stegosaurus* may actually have been cold-blooded because a single row of plates possesses the best control of both heating and cooling. This would have given a cold-blooded animal the most benefits.

A cold-blooded animal depends upon its ability to absorb extra heat from its environmental surroundings or dissipate it when the body becomes overheated. Unlike two row arrangements, a single row pattern would have been more efficient. When facing broadside into the sun, especially with the neck bent downward, there would be hardly any shadows falling onto the plates, thereby allowing the maximum absorption of the heat from the sunlight. The narrowness of the plates would have allowed them to gain heat more rapidly than the bulk of the animal's body, and the blood circulating through the plates could have re-entered the body thereby raising the overall temperature. When overheated, the *Stegosaurus* could

across the surface of the plates. This evidence was used to suggest that two rows of alternating plates was perhaps more likely to be correct than two rows of paired plates because the matched pairs would not respond to temperature changes as quickly. If the stegosaur was trying to warm itself facing broadside into the sunlight, the alternating pattern would expose

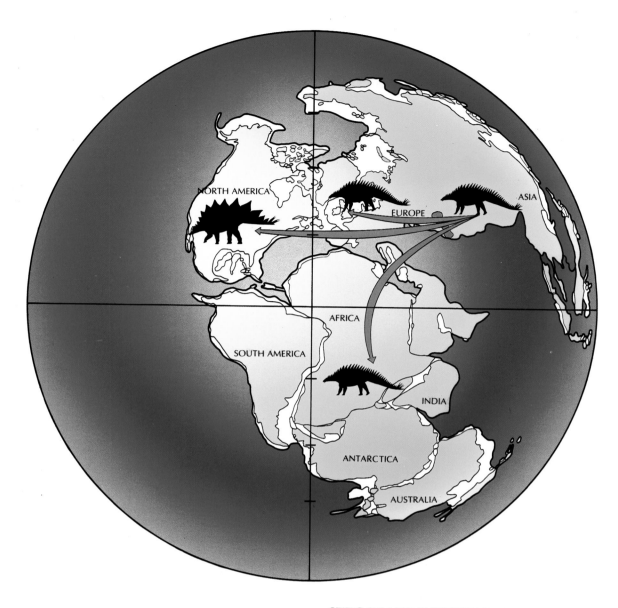

STEGOSAUR DISTRIBUTION GLOBE
Stegosaurs may have evolved in Asia and dispersed to the west into Africa, Europe and North America. The most primitive stegosaurs are known from China. Kentrosaurus of Africa may have been an immigrant Tuojiangosaurus *from China.* Stegosaurus *has the largest plates of any stegosaur, and is known only from the western states of America.*

have faced away from the sunlight exposing only the minimal surface area of the plates' edge. This also would place the head of the animal into shade from its own body. In this position, the slanted plates over the neck and shoulder region could have created a cooling, forced convection of air as demonstrated by the wind tunnel tests on plates that were in an alternating pattern. With these plates cooled, the blood would have entred back into the body, cooling the front part of the animal first. Perhaps this was necessary to bring aid quickly to where it would do the most good, preventing damage to overheated vital organs, nervous system, and brain.

It seems plausible, then, that a single row of plates on *Stegosaurus* was a very efficient thermoregulator, and a magnificent adaptation for a cold-blooded animal to function better within its environment. The small-plated stegosaurs may have been less efficient thermoregulators partly because of their primitive stage of development. However, their use as thermoregulating devices would help explain why the plate-like shapes evolved from pointed spines in the first place.

STEGOSAUR SPIKES, LOCOMOTION AND FEEDING

The tail spikes on stegosaurs retained their primitive condition, which was best designed for defensive actions. Primitive stegosaurs may have had more than four tail spikes, but *Stegosaurus* was limited to four. The largely incomplete and scattered remains of *Stegosaurus ungulatus* was found with eight 'devil's spines' as they were originally referred to when first discovered in 1879. Often this particular species is portrayed with eight spikes arranged in four pairs. This is incorrect, because other specimens have been found since then with clusters of only four spikes. The arrangement of the tail spikes may have been in a single row, but it is possible that they were arranged in pairs pointing slightly outwards.

147

Some of the more primitive stegosaurs were also equipped with spikes that had peculiar long, flattened bases. When first discovered with *Kentrosaurus* from East Africa, it was proposed that such a flat base must have made contact with a similarly flat part of a bone such as the back of the ilium. So *Kentrosaurus* is often portrayed with an extra pair of spikes pointing backwards from its hips. *Tuojiangosaurus* from China closely resembles *Kentrosaurus*, and it was also equipped with two broad flat-based spines. However, on *Tuojiangosaurus*, these spines were found resting in place over the back of each shoulder blade, pointing backwards. So, it is likely that *Kentrosaurus* was like *Tuojiangosaurus* and had shoulder spines, not hip spines. This, along with other similarities of the skeleton, and tooth structure indicate that *Kentrosaurus* may have been an immigrant in Africa, originally coming from Asia.

The different kinds of stegosaurs became specialized in various ways. But all were exclusively quadrupedal animals that needed the use of their robust and strongly built front legs to help support their ponderous, heavy weight. Stegosaurs were not designed for rearing up, or bipedal locomotion. The presence of deeply socketed shoulder joints indicate that the forelimbs were crucial to the locomotion and support of the animal. The hind limbs were much larger, but not constructed for bipedal locomotion. From the structure of the body and legs, it can be seen that stegosaurs were quadrupeds which must have eaten vegetation that was low to the ground.

The articulations and shape of the neck vertebrae of stegosaurs indicate that they were best designed for a lower, downward range of movement. The neck was limited from being able to reach up much beyond a horizontal position. This limited range of movement, together with a downwardly curved backbone, are modifications that brought the head low to the ground within easy reach of short shrubbery and low-growing vegetation.

Despite their fairly large size, stegosaurs had teeth that were along the fabrosaurid line of development, but even more diminutive. The teeth did not assist much, if any, in the mastication of food. Perhaps stegosaurs had powerful digestive systems and even gastroliths that countered the ineffectiveness of their tiny teeth.

HERBIVORES WITH GRINDING TEETH

Ornithopods existed alongside stegosaurs and sauropods during the Jurassic. Also herbivorous dinosaurs, they continued to develop grinding teeth inherited from hypsilophodonts such as *Heterdontosaurus* and *Pisanosaurus*. *Camptosaurus* was one such ornithopod which has been found intermingled with the remains of stegosaurs and sauropods. Moderately sized, usually no bigger than stegosaurs, *Camptosaurus* was a

rather generalized but very important forerunner of its kind. No elaborate armour or tremendously long neck or tail had developed on *Camptosaurus*. Superficially resembling the basic reptilian body form, *Camptosaurus* was, however, more specialized than it may at first appear. Despite its generalized form and lack of obvious defensive characteristics, the efficiency of its grinding teeth contributed to the success of its descendants.

Unlike stegosaurs, the neck of *Camptosaurus* was aligned in an upward curvature. This may have been an adaptation so that the increasingly large and heavy heads that ornithopods developed were more efficiently supported. For the sake of comparison, sauropods oddly did not evolve in this way, even though they theoretically should have. The extra flexibility of the *Camptosaurus* neck may also reflect a greater capability of finding its food. Although *Camptosaurus* was not necessarily a habitual biped, it could easily raise itself on its hind legs rearing up to feed on taller plants or it could move about without being obliged to use its forelimbs. In part this was accomplished by the ossified bony tendons which developed along the back to add strength to the backbone. Unlike the mandatory quadrupedal stegosaurs, the front legs of *Camptosaurus* were smaller and much less developed for walking. Despite this, *Camptosaurus* was still quite capable of remaining on all fours when it so desired.

Camptosaurus has a broader global distribution than *Stegosaurus* with which it is often found in North America. Remains are also known from England, where it was previously called *Cumnoria*. This suggests that a land bridge was still connecting North America to Europe during the Late Jurassic. Perhaps *Stegosaurus* will also be found someday in Europe, but for now it appears that it was isolated far in the west. Hypsilophodonts have been found in North America and East Africa, again implying that a land bridge must have existed which allowed *Dryosaurus* and its African counterpart, previously known as *Dysaltosaurus*, to have such a global distribution. Hypsilophodonts and other ornithopods, like *Camptosaurus*, were broadly distributed across the northern hemisphere and somewhat into the southern hemisphere.

THEROPODS – COELUROSAURS AND CARNOSAURS

Preying upon the herbivorous dinosaurs were the smaller coelurosaurs and the larger, more massive carnosaurs. While both groups of theropods continued to diversify into different kinds of genera and species, the coelurosaurs remained lightly built and agile. Staying totally bipedal, some coelurosaurs such as *Ornitholestes*, developed large arms and grasping hands. This is in sharp contrast to the carnosaurs, like *Allosaurus*, which tended towards a reduction in the size of the forelimbs.

The few types of coelurosaurs that are known from

A group of stegosaurs enter a clearing as they approach a water hole. Abundant remains of the North American Stegosaurus suggests that they may have been gregarious, staying together as further protection against the onslaught of predacious theropods.

the Jurassic indicates that they are rare animals, poorly represented in the fossil record. Consequently, their geographic distribution and ancestral development during this period is largely unknown.

By the Late Jurassic, *Ornitholestes* from North America had become more advanced and specialized for different behaviours to those of the earlier primitive coelurosaurs, like *Coelophysis* from the Late Triassic. The skull of *Ornitholestes* was not as long as *Coelophysis*, and was higher as well as more robust overall. Even the teeth were larger and more strongly built.

In the Middle Jurassic, a possible coelurosaur from England is *Proceratosaurus*, which is known only from a partially complete skull. Most of the upper part of the skull is missing, but there is enough preserved to reveal the presence of what could have been a nasal horn or crest that once ornamented it.

Another coelurosaur, *Elaphrosaurus*, is known from an almost complete skeleton that is lacking its skull. However, the similarity seen between the skeletons of *Elaphrosaurus* and *Dilophosaurus* suggests that *Elaphrosaurus* may have had a crested skull similar to that of

Dilophosaurus. What is amazing, though, is the length of time between these two dinosaurs: from the beginning to nearly the end of the Jurassic. *Elaphrosaurus* is from the Late Jurassic Tendaguru formations of East Africa, and is known to have existed more than 30 million years later than *Dilophosaurus*.

The carnosaurs are far better represented than the coelurosaurs in the fossil record which reveals that they had a global distribution of a highly varied assemblage. But their origins and patterns of evolution through the Early Jurassic are virtually unknown. It is not until the middle of the Jurassic that sufficient remains of carnosaurs become well known. *Eustreptospondylus*, *Gasosaurus* and *Piatnitzkysaurus* are among the earliest carnosaurs known from the Middle Jurassic of England, China and South America, respectively. They share primitive characteristics that foreshadow the development of the giant predator, *Allosaurus*. While still generally resembling *Allosaurus*, the many carnosaurs of the Jurassic became uniquely specialized in different regions of the world.

The average length of most allosaurs which have been found, is 6 to 7 m (19½ to 23 ft). However, scarcer remains of larger individuals indicate that allosaurs grew to much larger lengths. The partial remains of the theropod, *Epanterias*, were once thought to belong to a sauropod because of their large size. But *Epanterias* was in fact an enormous allosaur which attained lengths of 14 m (45½ ft), or more. It was also among the last of the allosaurs during the Late Jurassic.

Allosaurus itself is almost exclusively known from the Morrison formation of North America, but there are fragmentary fossils which indicate that it may also have ventured into Europe and the Tendaguru formations of East Africa. Although *Allosaurus* may have been limited to these regions, there were similar carnosaurs that had evolved their own characteristics on all continents.

In Europe, there was *Megalosaurus*, which was generally a more primitive form. *Metriacanthosaurus* was also from Europe, and it was peculiar in having developed vertebrae along the back with fairly tall neural spines which in life must have supported a prominent narrow crest. Still farther east, in China, there were *Szechuanosaurus*, *Yangchuanosaurus* and *Jiangjunmiaosaurus*. Each was crowned with decorative ornamentation along the upper length of its skull. *Jiangjunmiaosaurus* had a prominent single bony crest extending above and behind its nose. *Yangchuanosaurus* was more like *Allosaurus* with two separate knobby ridges extending back from the nose, but unlike *Allosaurus* the ridges were much more pronounced. Over all, each generally resembled *Allosaurus* in their basic forms being large headed with short upturned necks, and totally bipedal with forelimbs markedly reduced in size. Unfortunately, the preservation of completely intact hands are for the most part missing on these theropods. *Allosaurus* is known to have had three fingers on each hand, and these carnosaurs probably also had three fingers equipped with large, recurved talons. This, if true, is important because it reflects the tendency of advanced carnosaurs to have shorter forelimbs with the consequent loss of fingers. Perhaps some primitive allosaur-like carnosaurs or megalosaurs (also carnosaurs) were still equipped with four fingers, but by the Late Jurassic, most of their descendants were reduced to having only three. At least one archaic carnosaur, *Ceratosaurus*, was still in a transitory stage, possessing a rudimentary fourth finger. *Ceratosaurus* was a primitive holdover that lived along with *Allosaurus* in North America. Huge teeth some 15 cms (6 ins) long and similar to those of *Ceratosaurus* are known from Tendaguru, in East Africa.

Ceratosaurus is different from *Allosaurus* in many subtle morphological features of its skeleton. But it is easily distinguished by the presence of a large, prominent, narrow bony horn core just behind its nose.

Carnosaurs are not as well known from the southern hemisphere. This is probably due to preservational factors more than any real absence. Fragmentary remains of allosaur-like theropods are known from Antarctica and Australia which despite their scarcity are testimony of their global distribution.

THE DINOSAUR NATIONAL MONUMENT AND THE CLEVELAND-LLOYD QUARRY

Isolated fossil bones, partial remains and complete skeletons are scarce but always exciting, adding significant information to the knowledge of the prehistoric world. It is all the more thrilling when extensive fossil bonebeds are discovered with numerous individuals which increases the available information. Many such quarries are known throughout the world. Several are from the Morrison formation of North America and probably the best known is the Dinosaur National Monument located in north-east Utah.

The Late Jurassic ornithopod Camptosaurus *is a primitive iguanodont known from North America and Europe. It was primarily quadrupedal, although occasional rearing onto its hind legs may have been possible.* Camptosaurus *reached lengths of approximately 7 m (23 ft).*

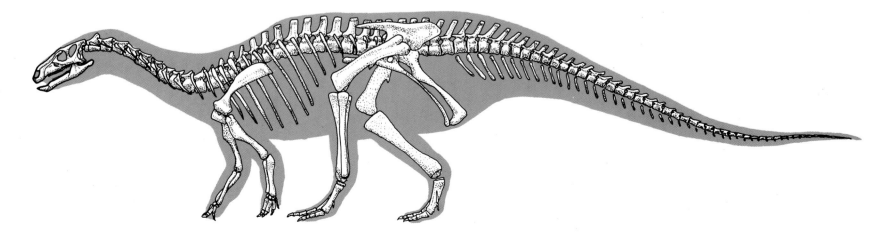

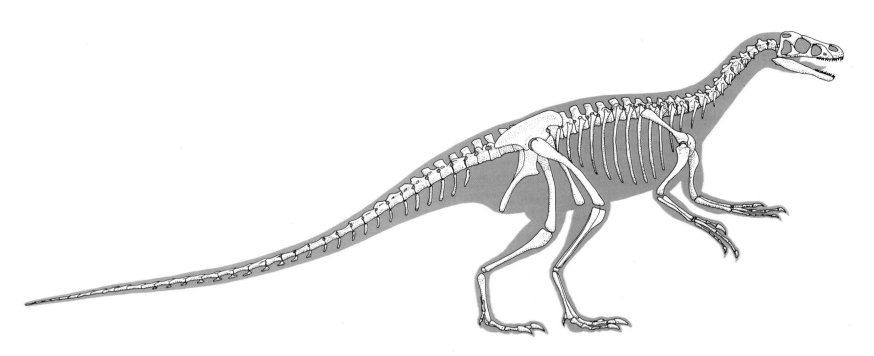

Ornitholestes *was a Late Jurassic coelurosaur from North America. Hollow vertebrae and a long neck demonstrate its coelurosaur affinities, while the short skull and jaws lined with robust teeth, and large grasping hands reflect a specialized development.* Ornitholestes *reached lengths of approximately 2 m (6½ ft). (after Osborn, 1916)*

Lesser known, but no less significant, are the Cleveland-Lloyd quarry in central Utah; Dry Mesa and Garden Park in Colorado, and, in Wyoming, Quarry 13, the Bone Cabin and Howe quarry. From these and still other sites have come hundreds of individual dinosaurs.

The Dinosaur National Monument is unique in having a broad representation of almost all of the different types of dinosaurs that are known to have lived during the Late Jurassic. Within a coarse conglomerate of pebbles and small stones are the entangled remains of many of the best known dinosaurs. The remains of *Allosaurus* and *Stegosaurus*, and sauropods including *Barosaurus*, *Diplodocus* and *Apatosaurus* (which is best known by its popular, though incorrect name *Brontosaurus*) have been revealed on an uplifted wall of stone. The surrounding matrix, being made up of small coarse stones, reveals that the bodies of these dinosaurs were carried along a powerful and fast-moving river and eventually came to rest on the bank along the bend of channels that quickly entombed them to form a shrine within the earth. Successive layers show that periodic catastrophes plagued these dinosaurs preserving their remains through the vast expanse of time to be revealed once again in a monument to their existence.

Unlike the broad diversity of dinosaurs found in the Dinosaur National Monument, the Cleveland-Lloyd Quarry has a highly disproportionate number of *Allosaurs* and remarkably few other kinds of dinosaurs. Also, with only few exceptions, the bones are totally disarticulated and randomly scattered. Close examination reveals a variety of growth stages among the allosaurs in this quarry, including fully mature adults that would have been some 12 m (39 ft) long and intermediate stages ranging down to a juvenile that was only 3 m (10 ft) long. Such an age range indicates that these allosaurs were either, to some extent, gregarious, or

that they at least tolerated the presence of their own kind.

Exactly how and why they all came to rest in this quarry is quite mystifying and uncertain. It is possible that it was a natural trap for predatory dinosaurs. Tiny shells of snail-like gastropods and other fossils suggest that this was once an area of shallow, calm, slow-moving water. Perhaps an allosaur came upon a mired herbivore in the murky sediments that appeared to be an easily available meal. Attempting to feast upon the bait, the allosaur struggled to maintain its foothold, sinking more into the grip of the sludge beneath it. The water-saturated silts may have taken on a consistency of a deadly quicksand bog. The scent of the dead attracted other opportunistic and hungry allosaurs of all sizes. Gorging themselves, they struggled to secure a full belly while ignoring the dangers of becoming mired, in turn becoming another lure to an unwary predator. In time, the remaining flesh of the bodies disintegrated and the loosened bones were tossed and spread by the constant gentle rolling action of the water. Many of the bones in the quarry show signs of predation, and some even show clean breaks as if trampled and broken either soon after or during the last moments of life.

An egg, complete with an embryo is also remarkably preserved here. It has two shell layers which resulted from its not being laid at the proper time, and instead was retained in the body where another shell layer formed. The pathology of multiple-layered shells is known to happen in some modern reptiles, but not birds (see page 18).

151

The behaviour as proposed for the predator trap at the Cleveland-Lloyd Quarry should not suggest that carnivorous dinosaurs fed exclusively upon carrion. On the contrary, they were most assuredly highly capable, voracious hunters. But just as almost every modern day hunter will take an opportunistic meal from an animal that was killed or died from another source, so too would a hungry carnivorous dinosaur. Predatory dinosaurs probably had to have a level of sophistication in their manners of hunting. Cunning perhaps more than brute force was necessary to effectively secure a meal without becoming hurt or wounded in the process. Waiting in lairs hidden along travelled paths would have been more cost effective than actively searching for potential prey. But predatory dinosaurs were capable of actively stalking after and vigorously confronting their prey.

TIDAL FLATS, SHORELINES, AND SAUROPOD TRACKS

The evidence revealed from fossil trackways strongly suggest that sauropods were gregarious and often moved about in groups. In addition, from the evidence seen in trackways from South America, it is possible that the younger sub-adults and juveniles may have been protected in the centre of a group with the larger, fully-matured adults walking along the outside. One remarkably extensive trackway along the Purgatoire River in Colorado has large and shallow tracks forming long parallel trails left by individuals that were walking along what would have been the shore of a large lake. These, among many other examples, clearly show that sauropods were fully capable of being terrestrial animals walking unhindered without any additional support from water. Still other footprints at this site form trackways that cross over the shallow trails. They continue to become deeper and deeper as the weight of the sauropods pushed further down into the increasingly soft and muddy soil as they approached and entered the water. Further evidence that this, indeed, was a trackway of a sauropod entering into a lake is seen in the accidental casualties that suffered under the enormous pressure and great weight on each footstep from the massive sauropod which probably weighed as much as 20–40 tons. Found directly underneath the fossil footprints were the victims of the killer sauropod feet – crushed clams.

As seen from their trackways, the sauropods' range of behaviour was as variable as modern day elephants. Both were fully capable as terrestrial animals, but they were also quite comfortable in aquatic situations. But were the sauropods more tied to the water than elephants? Tangible evidence is elusive in demonstrating what the behavioural limits and preferences really were. Here again, beyond the tangible evidence, any logical extrapolations are often no more than unproveable conjecture. However, from the sauropod trackways that have been preserved along what was shorelines and broad tidal flats of lakes and lagoons it is clearly seen that sauropods did, at least upon occasions, if not habitually, seek out an aquatic domain in which to live. That bones are so often found in fluvial sediments also indicates that they frequented waterways and rivers, although an even broader terrestrial range was almost certainly utilized by the sauropods as they wandered in search of food.

Often associated with sauropod trackways are the theropod tracks ranging from pathways made by single individuals to several closely knit trails that may have been made by carnosaurs moving together as a group, or pack. The parallel orientation of these numerous carnosaurs' tracks suggest that they not only fre-

The skeleton of Yangchuanosaurus *from the Late Jurassic possesses slightly elongated neural spines over the back and hips. At first, this Asian predator superficially resembles the North American* Allosaurus, *but it is probably closer related to the European* Metriacanthosaurus *which has even taller neural spines.* Yangchuanosaurus *reached lengths of approximately 8 m (26 ft).*

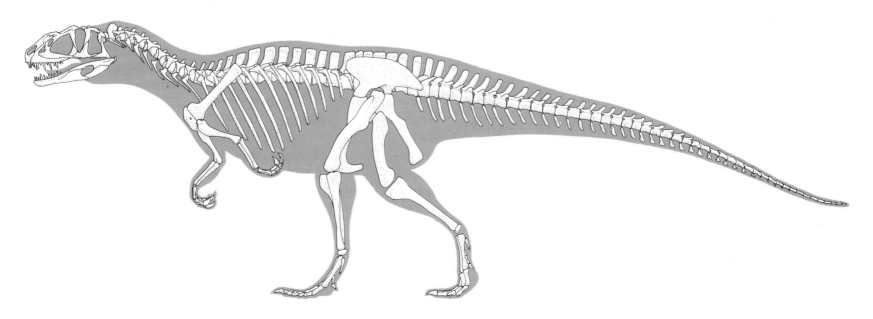

A confrontation between two Allosaurus *probably consisted of bluffing intimidation with bellowing and taunting bobbing actions of the head. More violent behaviour could have occurred if the intimidation failed to produce a submissive opponent.* Allosaurus *reached lengths of approximately 12 m (39 ft).*

quented the same shorelines as did the sauropods, but that sometimes they formed fiercesome packs of co-operative hunters. One trackway in Bolivia recorded as many as thirty-two theropods that moved along an ocean shoreline probably *en masse* as a hunting party in pursuit of a herd of sauropods.

STUCK IN THE MUD

Sauropods could easily have enjoyed the benefits of aquatic environments, and no doubt they did. Along with these benefits, though, natural dangers plagued them. The Howe Quarry appears to have recorded one such occurrence that brought members of a herd of sauropods, probably barosaurs, to a tragic end. Perhaps a seasonal drought was partly to blame. In any case, while the beasts were crossing over some mud flats, the feet of some unlucky sauropods dug too deeply within the soft and sticky mud. Unable to lift their legs free from the muddy bog, their struggling became futile and they only worked themselves deeper and deeper. Other sauropods still standing on dryer and harder ground nearby were helpless in freeing the stranded sauropods even if they had the mind

to do so. Several became victims helplessly trapped together straining and reeling until the heat from the sun and exhaustion finally overcame them. Preserved in the quarry was an incredible mass of jumbled bones, many parts of skeletons were still articulated in what looked like torn and broken sections. Some of the bones appeared to have been trampled and broken. Surrounded by the awesome maze of skeletal remains, twelve legs and feet were found, still articulated and preserved, standing upright. These telltale limbs, trapped in their final steps, remained as they were while the decimated bodies above the entombing mud collapsed, leaving the jumbled heap of bones. Perhaps this scenario is an accurate account for the death and preservation of these sauropods found in the Howe Quarry. Such accidents were probably rare events, but even today it is known to happen to elephants, which are intelligent animals, and to other ponderous, water-loving animals which have had the misfortune of trying to cross over mud that is too deeply saturated.

SAUROPOD GIANTS

The Dry Mesa Quarry is a rich site which is still actively being worked and is revealing a wealth of dinosaur bones. Along with approximately a hundred tons of bones that have been removed from the quarry, the most interesting aspect of the site is the awesome size of many of the dinosaurs that have been found within it. Discovered here was *Torvosaurus*, a huge megalosaur-like theropod as big or bigger than any known allosaur. It had primitive characteristics as compared to *Allosaurus* and probably shared affinities with European theropods. However, the largest giants of the quarry were the sauropods. Even for sauropods these were exceptionally gigantic.

Appropriate names befitting these giant sauropods from Dry Mesa became popularized as *Supersaurus* and *Ultrasaurus*. Two huge scapulocoracoids, or shoulder blades, were found from separate individuals of *Supersaurus*. The first one had a shoulder blade that was just a little under 2.5 m (8 ft) in length. This is nearly 1 m (3 ft) longer than a typical shoulder blade of a large, full grown *Diplodocus* which would have had a total length of some 30 m (97½ ft). The second *Supersaurus* shoulder blade found was even larger than the first. Then a third shoulder blade was found which was just about as long as the second. Both were 2.75 m (9 ft) long. The third specimen belonged to a different kind of sauropod and was dubbed the *Ultrasaurus*. From the shape of the scapula it appears that *Ultrasaurus* was related to *Brachiosaurus*. *Supersaurus* was more like *Diplodocus* or *Barosaurus*. In either case, the size of these animals was gigantic. A pelvis of *Supersaurus* was discovered that was nearly 2 m (6 ft) long as well as high. *Supersaurus* could have been more than 40 m (130 ft) long.

As gigantic as the Dry Mesa sauropods were they still weren't necessarily the largest. The discovery in New Mexico of another diplodocus-like sauropod, *Seismosaurus*, certainly rivals them in size. Enormous footprints in Texas, Morocco and Argentina indicate that there were other sauropods which could have been still larger. The measurement of the length of the footprints made by the rounded, elephantine-like hind feet in the trackway from Morocco was 115 cms (46 ins) wide. It is interesting to note that these tracks were preserved along with ripple marks caused by the repetitive wave motions of water, and mud cracks that were caused by the drying heat of the sun. Nearby, at least four separate trackways were found made by similarly huge sauropods that were floating and swimming about, using only half their front feet occasionally to pole themselves along.

From the evidence given by the fossil trackways of swimming sauropods it is impossible to interpret accu-

Based upon trackways composed of only manus (hand) prints, the skeleton of Apatosaurus (Brontosaurus) *is shown demonstrating how sauropods swam using their front legs to assist in pulling themselves along. The neck was supported as it floated outstretched in the water. The bulk of the body and tail floated which aligned the vertebral column horizontally to the surface of the water. Undulating motions of the tail would have propelled the animal through the water. While swimming, the weight of the neck caused the animal's centre of balance to shift forwards from the hind legs to the front legs. This redistribution of weight enabled the front legs to 'walk' across the water's bottom until the animal floated into deeper waters.* Apatosaurus *reached lengths of 25 m (80 ft).*

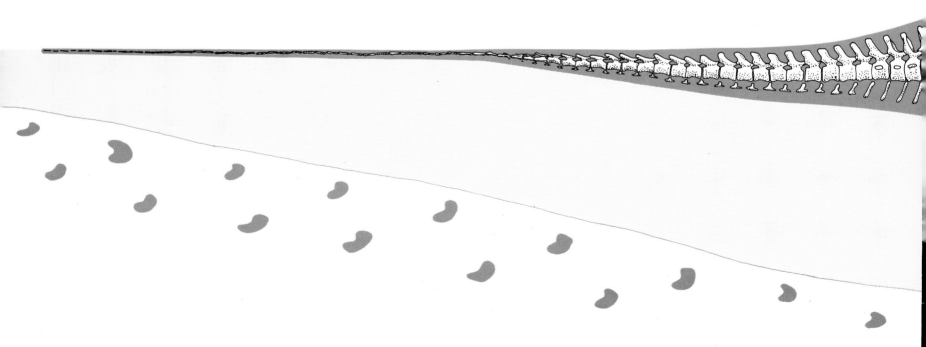

This aerial view depicts the conditions of a Late Jurassic landscape which preserved numerous dinosaurs as found at the Dinosaur National Monument. Powerful currents of a large river transported and deposited the bodies of dinosaurs along the banks within a bend of the river where they became preserved as fossils.

rately the full scope of the aquatic potential and range that they may have taken advantage of. For example, just how far out into the deep water could sauropods have floated and controllably manoeuvred about? Certainly crossing vast seaways was impossible. However, they may have been able to cross over fairly deep water of lakes and even swim along the coastal shorelines of oceans. Although sauropods were capable of aquatic behaviour, they should be considered as only semi-aquatic, as in fact they were, at least partially, terrestrial animals.

Other Mesozoic reptiles, which were not dinosaurs, continued to exploit aquatic environments exclusively. Plesiosaurs and ichthyosaurs were the true giants of the Jurassic seas. Their remains are often found in sediments laid down in coastal seaways adjacent to separated landmasses and chains of islands across much of Laurasia and Gondwana.

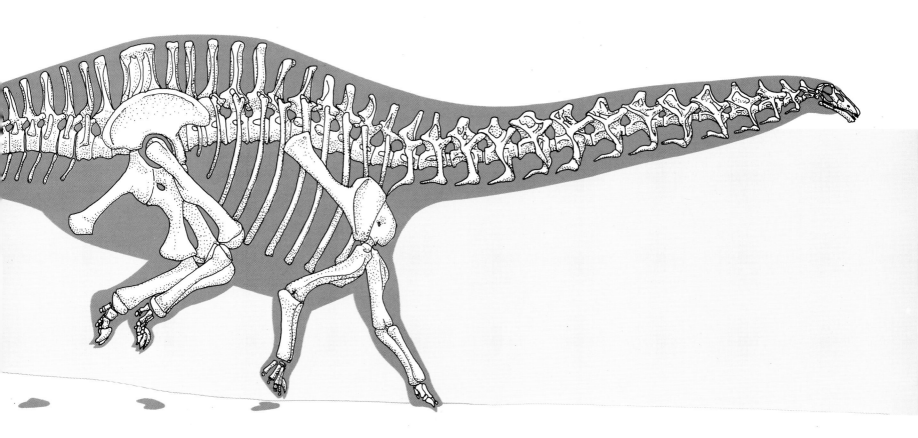

intact, and articulated, but there were no definite traces of its musculature or skin. However, found within the rib-cage of one *Compsognathus* was a surprising bonus in the guise of the last meal which this animal had eaten. The meal consisted of a long-tailed lizard that was swallowed whole. It was still mostly articulated, folded over and over again within the body cavity of the *Compsognathus*.

Obviously well fed, it is difficult to explain what could have caused the death of this *Compsognathus*. Many possibilities exist, but the evidence is too inconclusive to support any one particular theory. It was not killed by another predator, as its completeness shows no indications of having been fed upon, and it seems very unlikely that the lizard could have inflicted a fatal wound upon the attacking *Compsognathus*. Nor does it appear that this *Compsognathus* swallowed more than it could handle. Another specimen, found in France, of a slightly larger *Compsognathus*, was discovered in virtually the same condition and in practically the same pose, but without any trace of stomach contents that could have contributed to its death. Possibly, then, the deaths of these two *Compsognathus* were caused by environmental factors.

View of sauropod trackways along the Purgatoire River, Colorado. The erosional forces of the present day river have exposed the footprints which were originally made along mud flats near the edge of a lake during the Late Jurassic. Note the people near the trackways for scale.

THE LAST MEAL OF COMPSOGNATHUS

Lagoon-like basins located between coral reefs and coastal shorelines accumulated layers of fine grained limestone deposits which have preserved astonishing details of the many animals that once lived near the arid, warm tropical conditions of central Europe. In contrast to the monstrous size of the sauropods and other huge dinosaurs are the delicate, tiny bones of the smallest of dinosaurs and an assortment of flying reptiles found within the layers of limestone. Often completely articulated, some specimens have even left impressions of their soft anatomy and actual appearance.

Found in a Bavarian limestone quarry of Central Europe was *Compsognathus*, among the smallest of all the known dinosaurs. It was a coelurosaur less than 1 m (3 ft) or so in length. The remains were beautifully

THE SKIN OF PTEROSAURS

In the Bavarian quarry where *Compsognathus* was found, different strata contained small flying reptiles, including various kinds of pterosaurs. Often the preservation is so perfect that the shape of the wing membranes and other parts of the body are clearly seen: for example, a diamond-shaped tail flap was on the tip of the long tail of *Rhamphorhynchus*. No scales have been found on any pterosaurs but a smooth, leathery skin formed the membrane of the wing. Although short, hair-like structures have been tentatively identified on parts of the body of at least one pterosaur specimen, this determination has been challenged. It would be extraordinary for a reptile to have such a structure, but not impossible. However, this remains unresolved because this particular fossil is poorly preserved.

Better specimens may be necessary to demonstrate that pterosaurs had hairy bodies. One specimen from much later, from the Lower Cretaceous of Brazil, is so perfectly preserved that it not only has the surface texture of the skin, but also the internal structure of the actual epidermis itself. Only a fragment of a wing was found, but it was enough to show that the skin was remarkably thin – approximately 1 mm thick. The surface of the skin had tiny criss-crossing wrinkles that were strikingly reminiscent of human skin. When a cross section was analyzed under a microscope, it was seen that directly beneath the skin was a layer including capillaries, and still lower, was another layer with what appears to be muscle fibres. This remarkable preservation gives insights as to how the wings of pterosaurs may have been used in assisting the animal's

Three allosaurs trail after a lone Diplodocus *crossing over mud flats of a floodplain. Based upon trackways, packs of theropods may have hunted occasionally in a loosely structured and co-operative manner.*

thermoregulation. While resting with the wings outstretched and facing the sun, the capillaries filled with blood, circulating beneath the skin which could have absorbed additional heat. While flying, the naked skin could have lost the excess body heat which would have been created by the strenuous energetic activity, and thus prevent suffering from heat stroke. This cooling function would be similar to that of flying bats, where the contact with cooler air on the wings can reduce the temperature of the blood circulating through the membranes of the wings. Together with the air-sacs in the bones and their large breastbone, or sternal plate, it appears that pterosaurs had an extremely efficient lung development and flight capabilities that were comparable to modern birds.

ARCHAEOPTERYX BIRD OR DINOSAUR?

Preserved in the same limestone deposits that revealed *Compsognathus* and many pterosaurs was the most astonishing fossil of all, *Archaeopteryx*. Since its first discovery in the mid-nineteenth century, *Archaeopteryx* has created shock waves of scientific debate and controversies. Unlike pterosaurs, *Archaeopteryx* had wings and a long tail that were adorned with feathers. Although clearly bird-like, *Archaeopteryx* has a combination of reptilian and bird-like characteristics. Whereas it had functionally aerodynamic flight feathers, the mouth of *Archaeopteryx* was lined with repti-

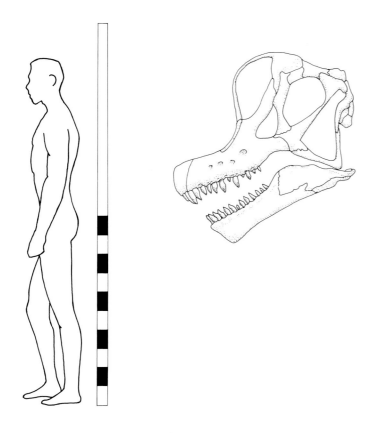

The metre-long skull of Ultrasaurus *(based on* Brachiosaurus*) is shown compared to a 1.8-m (6-ft) tall man. The scale bar is in metres and feet. Even larger than* Brachiosaurus, *the brachiosaurid* Ultrasaurus *reached an approximate length of 24 m (78 ft) and height of 11 m (36 ft).*

lian teeth, it had hands still equipped with grasping claws, and had a long, reptilian-style tail. Numerous other, lesser obvious, characteristics also displayed the reptilian and bird relationship. Questions of precisely which reptiles were ancestral to *Archaeopteryx*, and whether or not *Archaeopteryx* was indeed ancestral to modern day birds have remained unresolved matters of much debate.

With the possible exception of *Protoavis* from the Triassic, *Archaeopteryx* is the earliest known bird. However, regardless of any relationship between the two, there must still be undiscovered ancestors of *Archaeopteryx*, and hopefully they will shed more light on understanding the origins of birds. Whether or not *Archaeopteryx* was actually ancestral to modern day birds or just an evolutionary dead end remains to be seen.

The state of development seen in *Archaeopteryx* reveals many insights about the animal itself. Surprisingly, it was still equipped with many primitive features that *Protoavis*, and even pterosaurs, had either lost or modified into more advanced, avian-like characters. Why *Archaeopteryx* did not possess hollow bones and an avian-style air-sac system of breathing is difficult to account for. The absence of a large bony sternum seems to indicate that it had only a less effective reptilian lung development, and comparatively weak wing muscles.

Archaeopteryx is often regarded as a feathered dinosaur for without its feathers it could be regarded as a theropod and not a bird. However, this is not necessarily true because it has features in the skeleton that are bird-like. The teeth are not so much similar to theropods, as they are to crocodilians. The backward-oriented pubis is unlike most theropods, although still quite unlike that of true birds. The large arms and disproportionate long hands of *Archaeopteryx* should easily draw attention to its aberrant theropod characteristics. Judging from only its skeletal features, then, *Archaeopteryx* may well be a theropod, but hardly normal.

The long arms and large grasping hands are in themselves indications that *Archaeopteryx* was possibly arboreal, a trait predictably essential for the development of flight. Recent studies have also shown that the claws on the hands of *Archaeopteryx* resemble those of climbing animals. The general consensus is that *Archaeopteryx* was probably a primitive aberrant theropod that was capable of climbing and powered flight more advanced than gliding, but possibly incapable of sustained prolonged flapping.

DRIED IN THE SUN

The remarkable preservation of *Archaeopteryx* complete with its feathers, pterosaurs with skin imprints, and the articulated *Compsognathus* that have been found in the slabs of limestone from lagoonal deposits are the result of unique circumstances. It is possible that the pterosaurs and *Archaeopteryx* specimens had been blown, perhaps by storms, into the water where they were overcome and drowned. Another possibility may be more likely for some of the more remarkable specimens. For example, a death near the shoreline may have resulted in dehydration and the natural mummification of small animals. While still held together by the dried tissues of the body it could have been possible for water, perhaps from tides or storms, to have lifted a small carcass and transported it out into deeper water where it would eventually settle on the bottom of the lagoon. A rare occurrence to be sure, this would nevertheless account for some of the peculiar aspects of the remarkably preserved fossils.

The mummified anatomy would tend to be resistant to the disturbances caused by water currents or wave actions. Predatory fish may have been less likely to attempt feeding upon the carcass thereby avoiding any subsequent dismemberment. Perhaps most suggestive of mummification is the typically backward-pulled position of the neck and head that occurs from the ligaments drying along the top of the neck. A fresh body floating in the water would have ligaments that hadn't dried out and were still relatively loose. The water would keep them from shrinking any further or pulling the neck and head back over the body into the common death pose. Such a backward-

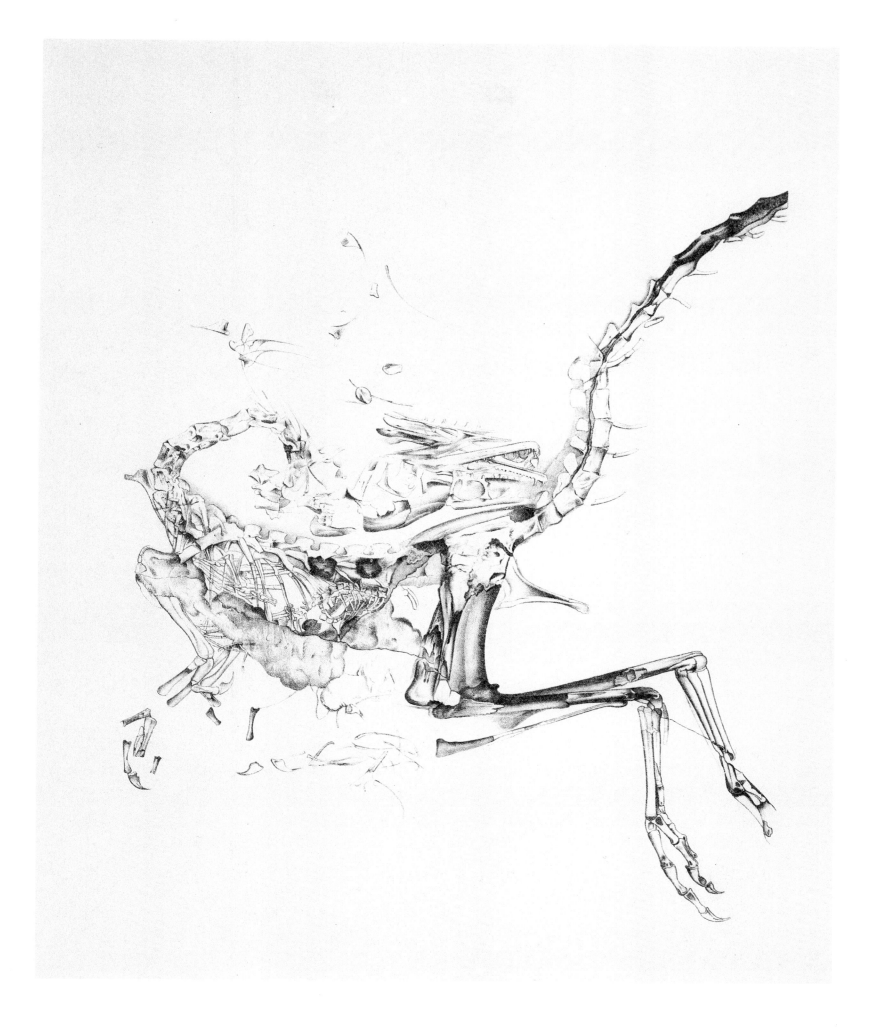

Compsognathus *was found in the lithographic limestone of Bavaria, southern Germany. Having died soon after its last meal, the skeleton of the lizard* Bavarisaurus *was found within the rib-cage of the small theropod. The approximate length of* Compsognathus *is 60 cms (2 ft).*

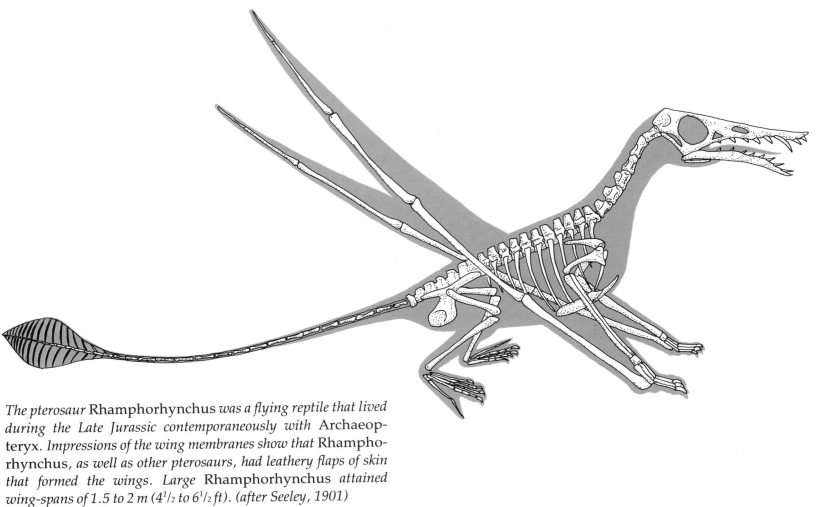

The pterosaur Rhamphorhynchus *was a flying reptile that lived during the Late Jurassic contemporaneously with* Archaeopteryx. *Impressions of the wing membranes show that* Rhamphorhynchus, *as well as other pterosaurs, had leathery flaps of skin that formed the wings. Large* Rhamphorhynchus *attained wing-spans of 1.5 to 2 m ($4^1/_2$ to $6^1/_2$ ft). (after Seeley, 1901)*

orientation of the head invariably happens in arid conditions that allow prolonged drying, but would be most improbable on a submerged animal that was not already in such a position. So, the state of preservation of *Archaeopteryx*, among other animals, might in part be attributable to their having become mummified before their final burial at sea.

INSTABILITY OF THE LATE JURASSIC

Beyond the lagoons which collected the remains of *Archaeopteryx*, *Compsognathus* and pterosaurs, there were the coral reefs that bordered the coastline and the vast open waters of the Tethys Sea. Throughout the Jurassic, the continents of Gondwana in the southern hemisphere remained connected. As one huge landmass, it gradually pulled apart from the Laurasian continents of the northern hemisphere. As a result, the Tethys Sea continued to spread westward across the gaping rifts caused by the separation between the African continent and the North American, European landmass. South America was also breaking away from North America and was probably the last connection with the northern Laurasian landmass. During this rifting away from North America, the formation of the Gulf of Mexico developed, leaving great deposits of evaporites along the Gulf of Mexico and lower parts of Texas.

The sea level fluctuated and rose during the Jurassic which caused the expansion of epicontinental seas that flooded across large areas of North America and Europe. Water from the Pacific Ocean inundated most of the western United States and parts of southern Canada creating an inland sea known as the Sundance. By the Late Jurassic, large mountain chains, known as the Nevadian orogeny, were uplifting and spreading northwards across the western United States. This tectonic activity elevated the land, draining the water of the Sundance Sea northward into a much smaller inland sea. The Morrison formation accumulated over the drained lands that were left by the displacement and removal of the Sundance Sea. Powerful rivers, broad lakes and swamps were abundant in the region of the Morrison formation: either wet or arid conditions existed, perhaps seasonally, as indicated by the presence of caliche nodules (see glossary) which can form in such conditions.

Arid conditions also were accompanied by deposits of evaporites which formed along much of the coastline bordering the Tethys Sea. The increased presence of the Tethys Sea probably had an impact in further changing the climate into the warmer, tropical conditions that affected much of the world. The overall global climate was warm and wet without extreme temperature changes between the lower latitudes which were mostly tropical, and the upper latitudes which were mostly subtropical. A gymnosperm flora prevailed throughout the world which appears to have been suited for warm climates.

The different kinds of floral assemblages found in the lower and higher latitudes indicates that higher latitudes were less tropical for tropical cycads are less

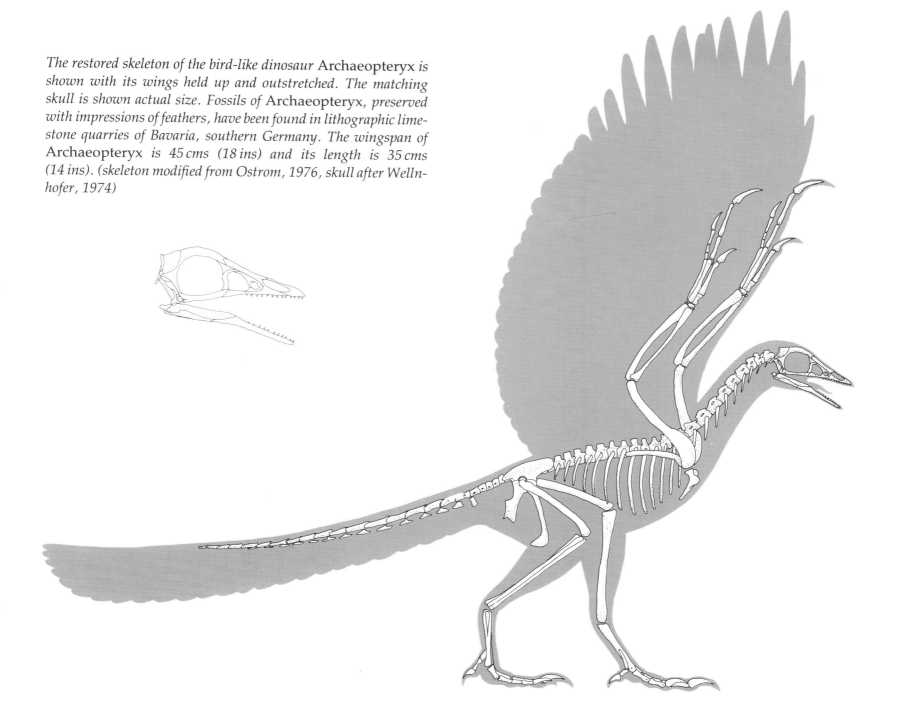

The restored skeleton of the bird-like dinosaur Archaeopteryx *is shown with its wings held up and outstretched. The matching skull is shown actual size. Fossils of* Archaeopteryx, *preserved with impressions of feathers, have been found in lithographic limestone quarries of Bavaria, southern Germany. The wingspan of* Archaeopteryx *is 45 cms (18 ins) and its length is 35 cms (14 ins). (skeleton modified from Ostrom, 1976, skull after Wellnhofer, 1974)*

numerous there. However, some ferns which could not tolerate frost and extreme cold proliferated where the cycads did not. Different regions of the world were no doubt unique with different topographies that influenced various climatic conditions. The presence or absence of mountain ranges, or broad seaways for example could either block or stimulate climatic circulation. Parts of Asia may have been affected in such a manner which caused cooler conditions and a corresponding decline of some trees that were adapted to warmer climates.

The end of the Jurassic did not experience global extinctions as severe as those of the Permian or Triassic. Aquatic forms such as ammonites went through a crisis that greatly reduced their numbers, but still they rapidly recovered. Ichthyosaurs and plesiosaurs were similarly affected, and were greatly diminished in numbers, but did not become totally extinct. Dinosaurs were not affected by any substantial extinctions that would have threatened their existence throughout the globe. Instead, regional displacement rather than actual annihilation occurred.

The abundant sauropods of the Morrison Formation in North America began to disappear from this region, and other parts of the world. The elaborate bony armour that appeared to be so efficient for the stegosaurs did not enable them to last beyond the Jurassic in North America. Surprisingly, in contrast, the supposedly defenceless camptosaurs (see pages 148,150) continued to evolve into still more advanced iguanodont-like ornithopods. It was more by replacement that descendants with derived levels of development affected the kinds of Late Jurassic dinosaurs. Climatic changes and competition from more capable forms of dinosaurs upset the stability of the dinosaurian world. Regions once populated by vast numbers of dinosaurs were changing. Many kinds, no doubt, totally died off, while others vanished only in some territories and did not actually become extinct. The Jurassic dinosaurs were being greatly affected by the changing environmental conditions in different parts of the world. As a result, new kinds of dinosaurs were evolving and they would continue their global domination for the next seventy to eighty million years.

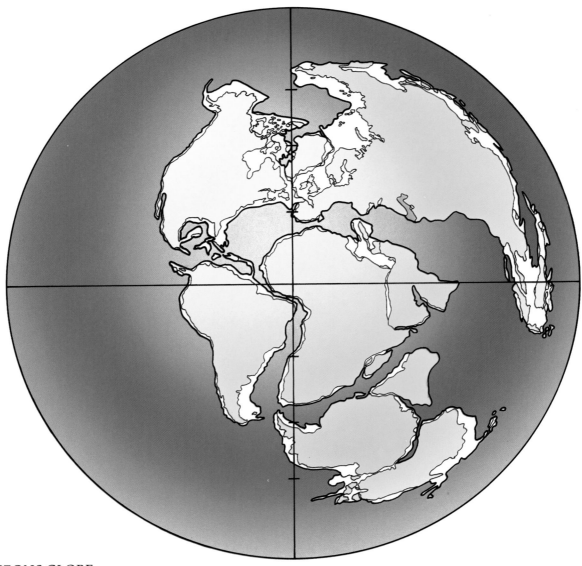

EARLY CRETACEOUS GLOBE
During the Early Cretaceous, Pangaea continued to break apart into the continental landmasses of Laurasia in the northern hemisphere and Gondwana in the southern hemisphere. Both of these supercontinents were separated by the Tethys Seaway which caused the isolated dinosaurs to evolve along different paths.

CHAPTER V
THE CRETACEOUS
THE DIFFERENT WORLDS OF DINOSAURS

WARMING CONDITIONS, SEAWAYS AND ISOLATION

In the periods before the Cretaceous, a collection of continents formed the supercontinent Pangaea, permitting the early Mesozoic dinosaurs to radiate across this vast landmass, achieving for the most part a uni-versal world of dinosaurs. However, at the end of the Jurassic period came a transformation that would divide this singular world of dinosaurs into distinctly different parts.

Gondwana, the continental landmass of the south-ern hemisphere, continued to break away and drift farther from the Laurasian continents of the northern hemisphere. The currents of the equatorial Tethys Sea spread westwards across increasingly large gaps that formed between the northern and southern supercontinents. Finally separated by this seaway, interaction ceased between the Laurasian and Gondwana continents and the subsequent isolation caused dinosaurs within both hemispheres to evolve along their different courses.

During the Cretaceous, in conjunction with the severing expanse of the Tethys Seaway, the continents of Laurasia and Gondwana were greatly affected by flooding oceanic waters which expanded between the rifting channels that appeared between continents. On a global scale, the sea level continued to rise, possibly reaching the highest level ever attained during the latter part of the earth's life history. Encroaching waters flooded farther inland with waves cutting above the coastlines and spreading across the vast interiors of continents, creating new ocean basins and seaways.

The climate of the world and its weather patterns changed under the influences of the dynamic continental topography and global circulation of the oceans' currents. During the Early Cretaceous, regional climatic zones of varying conditions existed, but the overall global climate grew increasingly warm. By the Mid-Cretaceous, the average global temperature reached a level that probably was higher than it ever has been since. Following this episode of global warming, the last half of the Cretaceous experienced a gradual temperature decline. Finally, during the Maastrichtian, which was the last stage of the Cretaceous, a significant drop in the global temperature brought an end to the Mesozoic, as well as the age of dinosaurs.

Evidence that the Cretaceous was at first remarkably warm and became progressively cooler can be found in a multitude of clues from fossils and geological events. Warm, equable climates are reflected by the extensive deposits of evaporites (see glossary) that are found across vast regions of the continental landmasses of the Early Cretaceous. Such an abundance of evaporites could only have resulted from the constant drying of continually replenishing sources of water. The presence of evaporites even at rather high latitudes is complemented by fossil coral reefs which reached latitudes as far as 30 degrees from the equator. Fossilized leaves of a tropical nature have been found in Greenland and northern Alaska which were at a possible latitude of 30 degrees during the Cretaceous. This gives startling testimony that the cooling effects commonly associated with higher latitudes were much less extreme than those which are in effect today. The tropical and sub-tropical zones were greatly expanded into the higher latitudes. During the Cretaceous, the extent of cooler temperate zones was reduced and the frozen polar regions were eliminated. The possibility of the presence of snow and ice existed only on mountains which rose to sufficiently high altitudes where a cooler atmosphere could come into effect.

So different was the climate of this Cretaceous world that not even the deepest waters of the oceans were cold. This was especially true for the middle part of the Cretaceous when the global temperature was at its greatest. Notably, during this time, large sedimentary deposits of blackened mud accumulated on the ocean floors. Such black deposits of sediment are known to occur where bottom waters have become depleted of oxygen and stagnant. This occurred when unusually poor circulation within the ocean basins failed to produce currents of freshly oxygenated water. At times when the polar regions had cold water, such as they do today, the cold oxygenated water sinks to the bottom and spreads along the sea floor as far as the equator. This circulation of cold water carrying oxygen prevents the kind of stagnation seen in the Cretaceous seas. In sharp contrast to the stagnant, black muds, the oxygen-rich deposits of sediments that are accumulated when cold waters circulate retain a light colour.

The Tethys Sea was influential in warming the global climate, and its warmth provided for an array of exclusively tropical sea life. Living in the Tethys Seaway were various forms of shelled ammonites, bottom dwelling foraminifers (see glossary) and – notably – rudists. Rudists were reef-forming molluscs that, for much of the Cretaceous, threatened the existence of corals. As a result of the powerful westward currents of the Tethys Sea, faunas that resembled those which lived in the Tethys are found on submerged seamounts as far as 1,750 kilometres (approximately 1,000 miles) west of Hawaii.

Perhaps one of the most significant indications that the Cretaceous world had an exceptionally warm climate was the continued presence and development of the dinosaurs. The climate and environmental influences which existed during the Cretaceous vividly illustrates the relationship between dinosaurs and the world they lived in. It also helps towards an understanding of the complex behaviour, physical forms, gigantism, prolonged success and ultimate extinction of the dinosaurs.

It would appear that the Cretaceous was much like the earlier parts of the Mesozoic in being ideally suited to reptiles and other animals that were ectothermic. The dinosaurs certainly must have had their own, unique, biology and like many reptiles living today, they were best suited for adapting to warm, equable climates such as those which existed during the Cretaceous and earlier parts of the Mesozoic. In such a climate, reptiles, including dinosaurs, were able to achieve the equivalency of a higher metabolism, paralleling that which is commonly associated with mammals and modern-day birds.

The advantage of being a cold-blooded reptile is dramatically seen in the reduced role of the undeniably warm-blooded (endothermic) mammals and birds that

existed during the Mesozoic. If endothermy was more efficient than ectothermy, the absence of large mammalian counterparts to the dinosaurs is difficult to explain. But if being ectothermic was a more suitable lifeforce, then other kinds of reptiles that were not dinosaurs should have been able to benefit from the same equably warm environments that supported the dinosaurs. And this is exactly what occurred. Select members of cold-blooded, non-dinosaurian reptiles evolved and adapted in some cases achieving gigantism equal to that of the dinosaurs. Monstrous crocodiles with heads nearly 2 m (6½ ft) long and a total body length of 15 m (49 ft) or more patrolled the swamps that wary dinosaurs co-habitated. Shallow seas were also alive with giant aquatic reptiles such as long-necked plesiosaurs, sinuous varanid mosasaurs (see glossary) that are related to present-day monitor lizards, and huge turtles that were larger than any turtle before or since that time. Dinosaurs had comparable metabolisms to these other reptilian giants, but the preponderance of dinosaurs indicates their superiority in this world of prehistoric reptiles.

The balance and stability of the world of dinosaurs is therefore, in part, a direct reflection of the climate and

Iguanodonts replaced the sauropods in the Early Cretaceous and became the dominant group of herbivores throughout Laurasia, and to a much lesser extent in Gondwana. Here, a small group of Iguanodonts becomes aware of a threatening theropod nearby.

environments that existed throughout the Mesozoic. As global changes occurred, the dinosaurs, as well as other contemporary animals and plants, adapted accordingly, either favourably or otherwise. There was, for example, a substantial reduction of gymnosperms corresponding to the increasing dominance of angiosperms, the flowering plants, forever altering the appearance of the landscape. But more particularly, the dinosaurs of the Cretaceous diversified still further for in addition to a progressive rise in the sea level, the Laurasian and Gondwanic continents continued to fragment.

THE LAST OF THE LAURASIAN SAUROPODS

It would appear that the great success of the sauropods during the Jurassic was coming to its end during the Early Cretaceous. In North America, most of the territories that were previously occupied by sauro-

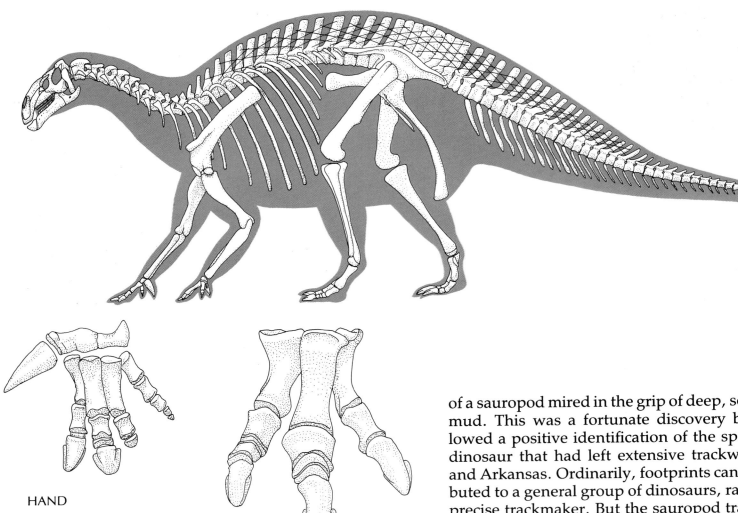

The quadrupedal stance, as shown, was a common mode of walking, but some degree of bipedality was also possible among most iguanodonts. Ossified tendons formed a lattice of long rods along the neural spines on the back and front half of the tail which were attached to powerful muscles along the neck, back and tail. Three toes were on each hind foot, while the 'hand' retained five. The first, or inner toe was modified into a prominent spike; the next three were used for support; and the outer, fifth, toe was capable of grasping, much like a thumb. Iguanodon reached lengths of approximately 10 m (32¹/₂ ft). (after Norman, 1980)

HAND

FOOT

pods had risen well above sea level, so diminishing the lake basins and floodplains known to have accommodated the Jurassic giants. The vast numbers of sauropods were greatly reduced and the few surviving descendants were apparently driven from these regions to areas further south along the coastal expanses of Texas and Arkansas.

Skeletal remains of the Lower Cretaceous sauropods are rarely found in much completeness, but partial remains of skeletons are not too uncommon. For the most part, they seem to represent a brachiosaurid relative, called *Pleurocoelus*, which was of modest to considerably large proportions. One notable discovery was that of a hind leg and foot still standing in a vertical position which preserved the final death pose of a sauropod mired in the grip of deep, soft and sticky mud. This was a fortunate discovery because it allowed a positive identification of the specific kind of dinosaur that had left extensive trackways in Texas and Arkansas. Ordinarily, footprints can only be attributed to a general group of dinosaurs, rather than the precise trackmaker. But the sauropod tracks in Texas and Arkansas show diagnostic characteristics that were found on the hind foot of the mired *Pleurocoelus*. Unlike most sauropods, *Pleurocoelus* had four claws on its hind feet, and these matched the unique four claw marks found on the footprints. In addition, the tracks made by the front feet of *Pleurocoelus* showed another distinction. Ordinarily, the front feet of sauropods were equipped with one or more prominent claw, but these tracks showed no sign of claws, even in tracks that were deeply impressed into the ground.

Together with the *Pleurocoelus* trackways found in Texas, there are numerous examples of theropods and a new kind of herbivorous dinosaur that appeared during the Early Cretaceous. The theropod tracks were probably made by *Acrocanthosaurus*. This peculiar theropod had vertebrae with fairly tall neural spines which probably supported a prominent crest along its neck, back and front half of the tail. *Altispinax* was a similarly crested theropod found in England which is known from a slightly earlier period of the Early Cretaceous. It is possible that both of these crested theropods are descendants from the group of Jurassic theropods which includes *Metriacanthosaurus* from England and *Yangchuanosaurus* from China (see page 150). Asia also had large theropods which were contemporary to the more westerly located *Altispinax* and *Acrocanthosaurus*. Impressively massive, partial remains of *Chilantaisaurus* from Inner Mongolia clearly indicate the presence in Asia of an exceptionally large, allosaurid-like theropod, possibly 13 m (42 ft) long.

Acrocanthosaurus was a large carnivore, certainly

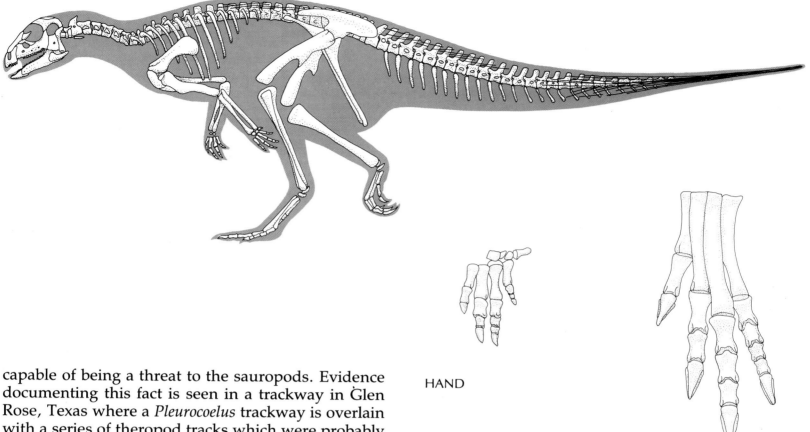

HAND

FOOT

The ornithopod, Hypsilophodon, *was an agile herbivore capable of running bipedally on its hind legs. Hypsilophodonts were more primitive than the iguanodonts, as shown by the retention of four toes on the hind feet (instead of three). The 'hands' had five fingers that were short and used mostly for support when standing quadrupedally, and perhaps also while foraging. The front feet lacked the spiked condition of the inner digit as in iguanodonts. Few ossified tendons were along the back and front of the tail, but were much more prominent along the last half of the tail.* Hypsilophodon *reached lengths of approximately 2 m (6½ ft). (after Galton, 1974)*

capable of being a threat to the sauropods. Evidence documenting this fact is seen in a trackway in Glen Rose, Texas where a *Pleurocoelus* trackway is overlain with a series of theropod tracks which were probably made by an *Acrocanthosaurus* approximately 10 m (32½ ft) or more in length. The outcome from this scenario is unknown for certain. But it is almost certain that this double trackway represents a hunting carnivore following its prey, for when the sauropod turned, so too did the theropod which followed.

The *Pleurocoelus* tracks also show that small groups of juveniles and sub-adults formed herds of nearly two dozen individuals that all moved in the same direction. Some members followed directly behind others stepping into the tracks from the ones that were leading the way. The footprints were made in tidal flats formed along lagoons that were separated from the open sea by offshore reefs. Tidal fluctuations routinely flooded the limey mud-flats, usually destroying the tracks of a day's activities. But on rare occasions, sediments were carried with the tides that covered fresh tracks preserving momentary actions in the daily life of these dinosaurs.

Sauropods were extremely mobile animals, adept at moving freely on land as well as in water. A spectacular series of trackways, literally strewn with countless numbers of sauropod tracks, was recently found in Arkansas. Most interestingly, the tracks are for the most part parallel, but directed in opposite directions. Evidently, these sauropods were moving in great numbers first in one direction and then back again from wherever they had been during the interim. Such a simple pattern only hints at the complex behavioural aspects of which sauropods were no doubt capable. Were these sauropods moving in response to the sunrise and setting sun of the day? Was this a pattern of travels to a special area in which to feed, or thermoregulate?

There is also a rare trackway in Texas of a huge *Pleurocoelus* that was made while the animal was, in effect, swimming and polling itself along only with the aid of its front legs. A single random track was made from a hind foot as the sauropod kicked downwards and shoved off with its hind leg turning and changing its course.

Certainly these sauropods were drawn towards the water, perhaps to aid in their thermoregulating, cooling their bodies of the accumulated heat from the days basking in the sun. Possibly, occasional bathing helped rid themselves of parasitic insects. The fossils of *Pleurocoelus* are more often found in sandy, inland floodplains so it is not at all unlikely that they ventured to drier plains or even wooded savannahs. But at least one specimen of *Pleurocoelus* has been found buried along the barrier of an offshore reef. Did this sauropod die while on land and was later washed into the lagoon? Or could it have died while in the lagoon

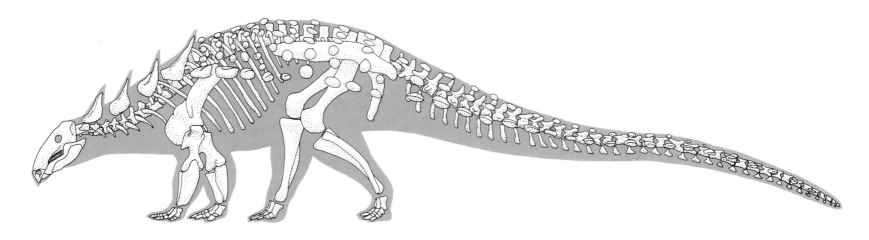

The ornithischian Sauropelta *was from North America and* belonged to the armoured group of dinosaurs called nodosaurs. *They were beaked herbivores with non-grinding, fabrosaur-like teeth. Exclusively quadrupedal, their heavy, low slung bodies were covered with a protective mosaic of ridged scutes, rounded nodes of bone, and large protruding spikes. Other Laurasian forms include* Hylaeosaurus *and* Polacanthus *from Europe. There is also the Gondwanic form* Minmi *from Australia.* Sauropelta *reached lengths of approximately 5 m (16 ft). (after Carpenter, 1984)*

itself? Either of these possibilities are likely explanations.

Pleurocoelus is one of only a few sauropods in all of Laurasia that existed into the Early Cretaceous. However, tantalizing remains of mostly incomplete skeletons and isolated bones have been found in England, indicating that at least some sauropods were lingering on in the northern hemisphere. Among them are *Dinodocus, Ornithopsis* and *Pelorosaurus.* They were possibly similar to *Pleurocoelus* in being descendants of *Brachiosaurus.*

At the time that these last few remaining sauropods were living, England was still connected to Greenland and located much closer to North America. Chains of archipelagos or even bridges of land may have still connected England and North America possibly allowing an interchange among *Pleurocoelus* and its European counterparts. But the territories that belonged to these sauropods were restrictive and certainly dwindling. The northern regions had been devoid of sauropods since the end of the Jurassic and, early in the Cretaceous, the sauropods were totally eliminated from Laurasia and the northern hemisphere.

THE RISE OF THE IGUANODONTS

What could have brought about the extinction of these Laurasian sauropods, the titans of all dinosaurs? Was there an ecological change that caused their demise? Could competition from other herbivorous dinosaurs somehow have overwhelmed them? Certainly there were regional changes that periodically affected their environments with an adverse outcome, and it seems likely that disruptive changes in the ecological balance were instrumental in wiping them out. Of the many possible factors, perhaps one of the most important clues is that of the trackways in Texas belonging to a new kind of herbivorous dinosaur. The depressions of three broad toes revealed the enigmatic trackmaker as being an iguanodont.

Iguanodonts were ornithopods that had evolved from a *Camptosaurus* ancestry which continued to improve upon the grinding tooth patterns utilized in masticating their exclusive diet of vegetation. On each jaw, the row of teeth had increased in number, enlarging the grinding surface into a long abrasive plate of continuously replaced teeth. Along with the added efficiency from the larger number of teeth there followed a significant increase in the body size of the iguanodonts, some of which grew to over 10 m (32½ ft) in length.

It might at first appear that the iguanodonts competed directly with the sauropods and simply outfed them into oblivion. This is, however, an unlikely scenario as there is no evidence that sauropods and iguanodonts fed upon the same kinds of vegetation. The different morphology between sauropod and iguanodont teeth strongly suggest that, for the most part, both groups fed upon different types of plants. So it is likely that there was little to no real competition for food which could have threatened the sauropods. Rather, it is reasonable to believe that adverse environmental changes were influential in their disappearance and subsequent replacement by the iguanodonts. As the sauropods diminished in numbers available niches were left to be filled and more efficient herbivores gradually moved in.

The largest and, coincidentally, most widely distributed of the many known kinds of iguanodonts was *Iguanodon* itself. An abundance of remarkably com-

The European Iguanodon *was an abundant prey for diverse predators. Here, the unusual theropod Baryonyx, which has a crocodile-like head, emerges on the right contemplating a larger meal than its usual diet of fish. Length of Baryonyx is approximately 9.5 m (31 ft).*

plete, often articulated *Iguanodon* skeletons have been found in Belgium and Germany. These clearly show the animal's enormous proportions and reveal curious physical characteristics which suggest some possible behavioural aspects and the physical appearance of this efficient herbivore. Quite unlike the sauropods, the neck of *Iguanodon* was fairly short and with a definite upturned curvature. It supported a rather large and heavy head reminiscent to the proportions of a modern day horse. In addition to the jaws, each of which had a prominent row of grinding teeth, there was a sharp crenulated beak on the front of its mouth used for cropping its select vegetation.

A deep, rounded body and powerful tail were often carried well above the ground by the use of only the hind legs, but also sometimes with the aid of the forelimbs. Along the sides of the neural spines of the backbone and front half of the tail was a remarkable development of bony rods, actually ossified tendons, that formed a bizarre diagonally-oriented, lattice-like structure. The front feet, or hands as the case may be, had three stout fingers attached to an elongated arch formed by the metacarpals. On the two inside fingers were blunt, pointed, oval-shaped unguals (see glos-

sary) which probably bore hoof-like sheaths in life. Together, these three fingers primarily functioned as a supportive structure while the animal was walking quadrupedally. But a fourth finger was offset from the joint of the wrist on the outside of the hand. Compared to a human hand, this offset finger was a misplaced thumb that was capable of grasping inwards from beneath rather than from above. Emanating from the opposite side of the wrist (located in the normal position of a thumb), was a prominent conical spike which was held above the ground as a threatening weapon of defence, or used as a harvesting tool for feeding. Altogether, the highly specialized hand and unique shape of the *Iguanodon* resembled a frightening combination of a crocodile (tail), a tortoise (beak), a horse (head, neck, and legs), a rooster's spur (hand spike) and a hominid thumb (grasping fourth finger).

Iguanodon were specialized herbivorous dinosaurs and perhaps it was because of their unique adap-

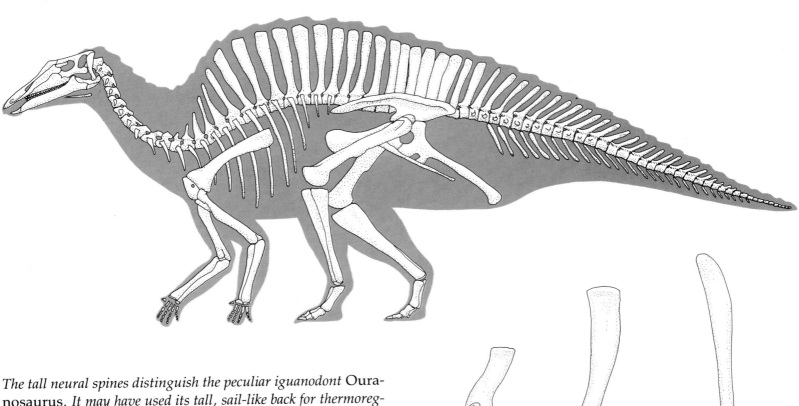

The tall neural spines distinguish the peculiar iguanodont Oura-nosaurus. It may have used its tall, sail-like back for thermoregulation in its hot, equatorial environment. Three vertebrae are shown for comparison of the height of the neural spines: (left) Iguanodon, which has a comparatively short neural spine to Ouranosaurus. (centre) Ouranosaurus, which is more than twice that of Iguanodon reaching a height of approximately 50 cms (1¹/₂ ft), or more. (right) The much larger vertebra of Spinosaurus which is reproduced at half the scale of those belonging to Iguanodon and Ouranosaurus. Total height of the Spinosaurus neural spine is approximately 1.6 m (5 ft).

Both Ouranosaurus and Spinosaurus are from similar hot, equatorial regions and exhibit tall neural spines which formed a crest as a possible adaptation to these environments. Ouranosaurus reached lengths of approximately 7 m (23 ft). (after Taquet, 1976)

tations that *Iguanodon* accomplished a wide geographical distribution and the successful replacement of the sauropods. It is reasonable to believe that adverse environmental changes were influential in the disappearance of the sauropods. To what extent *Iguanodon* was one of these adverse factors is open to speculation. However, in the absence of the sauropods, which were herbivorous saurischians, the ornithopods and other ornithischians were able to exploit the northern hemisphere. During the early Cretaceous then, and without a noticeable period of interruption, most of Laurasia became dominated by *Iguanodon* and other smaller, ornithopods.

DISTRIBUTION OF LAURASIAN ORNITHISCHIANS

There was a diversity of many other kinds of ornithischians that appeared during this time. *Vectisaurus* was

an iguanodont that had a tall-spined backbone, which was a trait taken to even greater extremes in other kinds of dinosaurs later on. *Hypsilophodon* and *Valdosaurus* were smaller ornithopods that came from Europe. *Tenontosaurus* was a close relative from North America that was considerably larger, reaching over 6 m (19¹/₂ ft) in length. There were also fabrosaurid descendants which were still equipped with tiny. nongrinding teeth that appear to have been almost functionless. Among these are poorly known enigmatic stegosaurs, represented by *Craterosaurus* from Europe, the African *Paranthodon*, and *Wuerhosaurus* of China. Other fabrosaurid forms that were not stegosaurian were the nodosaurs, *Hylaeosaurus* and *Polacanthus* from Europe, the North American *Sauropelta*, and in the southern hemisphere, *Minmi* of Australia. Also of particular note was *Yaverlandia* which comes from Europe and is the earliest-known member of another group, generally called the bone-headed dinosaurs.

The discovery of *Minmi* from Australia presents an

Where the Sahara Desert now exists, braided streams and rivers near to canopy forests of Araucaria provided the lush environments that once housed the crested Ouranosaurus and gigantic crocodiles such as Sarcosuchus which attained lengths of 10–15 m (32¹/₂–49 ft).

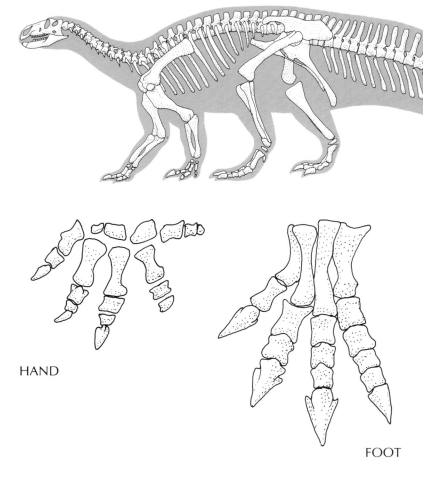

HAND

FOOT

The ornithischian Tenontosaurus *was a large hypsilophodont from North America. Superficially resembling iguanodonts, the feet of* Tenontosaurus *demonstrate its hypsilophodont affinities. Each of the hind feet retain four clawed toes, and the front feet each have five short toes with no development of a spiked inner claw.* Tenontosaurus *reached lengths of approximately 6.5 m (21 ft). (after Langston, 1974)*

inexplicable question as to how this nodosaur ventured from Laurasia to the most distant outskirts of Gondwana. Separated by thousands of kilometres, the vast distance almost becomes a secondary consideration when compared to the physical geographical barriers that had to be dealt with in crossing over from the northern continents onto the Gondwanic southern continents. The expanse of the powerful Tethys Seaway was a primary barrier that blocked the passageways between the continents in the north and south. And yet, still other ornithischians had found their way beyond the barrier of the Tethys Sea. Both hypsilophodonts and iguanodonts are also known to have made this incredible journey from Laurasia to Australia. Possible insights as to how these ornithopods, as well as *Minmi*, came to be in Australia are revealed by the numerous localities of where *Iguanodon* fossils have been found.

It is generally accepted that *Iguanodon*, as well as the hypsilophodonts, evolved in the regions of western Europe and from there they later spread onto other lands. In addition to the abundant discoveries of *Igua-*

nodon in Belgium and Germany, still other notable remains have been found in Romania, Austria, Czechoslovakia, Georgia (U.S.S.R.), England, France, Spain and Portugal. Fossil trackways that have been found in Spitzbergen give testimony to the fact that *Iguanodon* was not prevented from inhabiting the higher latitudes well above 60° north.

The European territories in which *Iguanodon* lived were composed of archipelagos which included large islands. Dispersal between these islands may have occurred only rarely along short-lived land connections within shallow seaways. Distances across vast channels were certainly restrictive. However, there is no good reason to think that *Iguanodon* was incapable of some aquatic behaviour. And intentional or accidental transport by swimming across narrow seaways, perhaps even aided by wandering currents, does not seem too unlikely to have played a part in the distribution of *Iguanodon*.

In the western part of Laurasia, the formation of a rifting zone was beginning to separate North America from Greenland during the Early Cretaceous. But the subsequent seaway that flooded into this rift had not yet totally severed the land connection and therefore it did not prevent *Iguanodon* from eventually finding its way into the United States and Mexico. Another seaway that should have been a substantial barrier had also formed across a large part of eastern Europe. This was the Turgai Straits, a broad southern extension of the Arctic Ocean which flowed to the south, connecting with the Tethys Seaway. The vast expanse of the Turgai Straits eventually flooded far across parts of western Europe. But it was the north/south extension which bordered along the margins of the Ural Mountains that separated eastern Europe from western Asia. This seaway was a considerable barrier and yet *Iguanodon* had somehow found its way across so that it could inhabit parts of Asia.

Incorporating North America and Asia into its domain, *Iguanodon* had spread completely across the length of Laurasia. But like *Minmi*, the Australian nodosaur, iguanodonts also made their way to the remote eastern territories of Gondwana. Fortunately, the discovery of additional fossil remains of iguanodonts have been found in other regions of the southern supercontinent, specifically within South America and Africa. Plotting the localities of these iguanodonts indicates the possible land connections and suggests the most likely passageways that enabled iguanodonts and *Minmi* to finally reach Australia. There are two possible options. First, they may have travelled down across a lengthy chain of land connections and archipelagos along Central America that still reached South America; second, similar connections across Spain and Portugal may have allowed at least intermittent contact with Africa. The first option appears unlikely, as no iguanodont fossils are as yet known from Central America. But this may only reflect preservational factors. However, *Iguanodon* fossils have been found in Tunisia, of northern Africa. And this is highly suggestive that the African connection with Europe was responsible for the Gondwanic invasion.

Certainly, it would have been a much shorter distance to come directly from Europe across Spain, Portugal and then onto Africa. Presumably, nodosaurs must have taken advantage of the same initial route. Once in Africa, the dispersal route was probably through South America, then eastward across Antarctica until finally reaching Australia. A more direct route across Africa and perhaps India was probably prevented by the expanding south Atlantic and Indian Oceans that had been forming as Antarctica rifted apart from these continents.

South America was also breaking away from Africa during this time. But a connection was still maintained along the coast of Brazil and the mid-western coastline of Africa. Iguanodont footprints that are known from Brazil were almost certainly made by animals that had previously come from North Africa. It seems unlikely that the iguanodont dinosaurs in Australia could have come from a distribution route other than from Africa through South America, and across Antarctica. This route would explain how the nodosaur *Minmi* came to Australia. But the presence of Australian iguanodonts that lived during a slightly later period in the Early Cretaceous will present their own peculiar distribution problems.

UNUSUAL THEROPODS AND TALL-SPINED IGUANODONTS

Along with *Iguanodon*, other kinds of dinosaurs made their way across the European/African connection. One in particular was a bizarre theropod known as *Baryonyx*. Known principally from Europe, this dinosaur appears to be a primitive spinosaur that coexisted with *Iguanodon*. Although *Baryonyx* and other spinosaurs are a poorly represented group, they may be descendants related along the lines of *Dilophosaurus* from the Early Jurassic. Fragmentary remains which may pertain to *Baryonyx* have been found in Niger, North

Africa suggesting that it, too, came across a European/African connection.

Curiously, *Baryonyx* is the earliest known spinosaur, and its primitive condition appears to have predated the characteristics for which they are named. Apparently, the neural spines on top of the vertebral column are not abnormally elongated as in the spinosaurs that came later. Nevertheless, *Baryonyx* possessed other strong similarities to spinosaurs typifying some of the incredibly strange modifications that were unique to these theropods. *Baryonyx* had an elongated skull, nearly 1 m (3 ft) long, which was remarkably low in profile for a theropod, and in some ways more indicative of crocodiles. The snout was spatulate, and the upper jaw was deeply recurved and lined with teeth that had become more conical shaped with only tiny serrations. Like the coelurosaurs, the large head was supported by a long neck. But unlike these possible ancestors, *Baryonyx* had developed a large and powerful forelimb which suggests that it was not an obligate biped and may have been capable of walking in a quadrupedal fashion. *Baryonyx* was also equipped with extremely large and powerful claws that in life would have been well over 30 cms (12 ins) long.

Altogether, what *Baryonyx* may represent is a theropod version of a crocodile, complete with a preferred diet of large, fresh-water fish. In fact, this appears to be confirmed by the presence of partly digested fish scales and teeth which were found within the rib cage of *Baryonyx*. The fish has been identified as being *Lepidotes*, which attained an average length of about 1 m (3 ft), thereby becoming a substantial meal. One can imagine a hungry *Baryonyx* using its large claws, grappling large fish from a river much like a bear might pull a salmon from the water. The highly specialized long jaws resemble that of a crocodilian, much like the modern-day gavial, which is a fish-eater. Functionally capable of similar behaviour, *Baryonyx* may have entered the water and swum to pursue its meal, catching it in its jaws. Also like crocodiles, the diet of *Baryonyx* may have been varied to include larger terrestrial animals. The sizable *Baryonyx* was nearly 10 m (32½ ft) long, and resting on all fours while lurking motionless along travelled pathways, a patient silent hunter may have sufficiently surprised its prey. Succumbing in the powerful grip of deeply penetrating claws and a suffocating clench from the vice-like jaws, even a good sized *Iguanodon* could have been brought down.

As uniquely specialized as *Baryonyx* was, its closely related descendants became even more bizarrely adapted. They lived in regions of North Africa including Egypt, Niger, Algeria and Morocco where their fossils have been discovered. Like some other kinds of dinosaurs in the same regions, the neural spines of the backbone became disproportionately tall forming a spectacular crest-like sail. On *Spinosaurus* the neural spines of the backbone were more than 1.6 m (5 ft) long. It was a monstrous animal, half again as large as *Baryonyx*, reaching nearly 15 m (49 ft) in length which makes *Spinosaurus* one of the largest theropods known

The long, low head of Deinonychus, *as well as many other parts of the body, are remarkably similar to its Mongolian counterpart,* Velociraptor.

to have ever existed.

The most intriguing aspect of *Spinosaurus* is the development of the tall crest adorning its back. Almost certainly this radical change in its body shape was more than just ornamental, and somehow related to the animal's physiological control of its body temperature. This is among the most likely of functions because other kinds of dinosaurs that lived in the same regions along with *Spinosaurus* also developed exceedingly tall crests. Therefore, it appears to have been a physical adaptation that was beneficial to living within the environmental setting of these regions. North Africa was located directly across the lowest latitudes of the equatorial belt and it may be that in this location extremely high temperatures had to be dealt with in order to exist there. Perhaps it is more than mere coincidence that there is a reptile living today, the largest agama lizard *Hydrosaurus*, which is equipped with an enormous sail-like crest caused by the elongation of the neural spines. This sail-finned lizard also lives at low equatorial latitudes in the steamy hot jungles on the islands of Indonesia and New Guinea.

The additional surface area that was created by a tall crest could have worked as a radiator to prevent the animal from overheating during the hottest times of the day. Occasional winds or being temporarily submerged in water repeatedly would have increased the efficiency of this cooling system.

Ouranosaurus was an iguanodont that has only been found in Niger, North Africa, where the predator *Spinosaurus* also existed. Also, a huge brachiosaurid sauropod, *Rebbachisaurus*, with an inordinately tall crest along its back, has been found in Morocco and Tunisia. Even though it lived slightly earlier than *Spinosaurus* and *Ouranosaurus*, the unusually tall crest along its

The agile predator Deinonychus *from North America is best known for its giant claw on each of its hind feet. Uniquely large arms and grasping hands are held close to the body, folded much like those of the wings of birds.* Deinonychus *reached lengths of approximately 3 m (10 ft).*

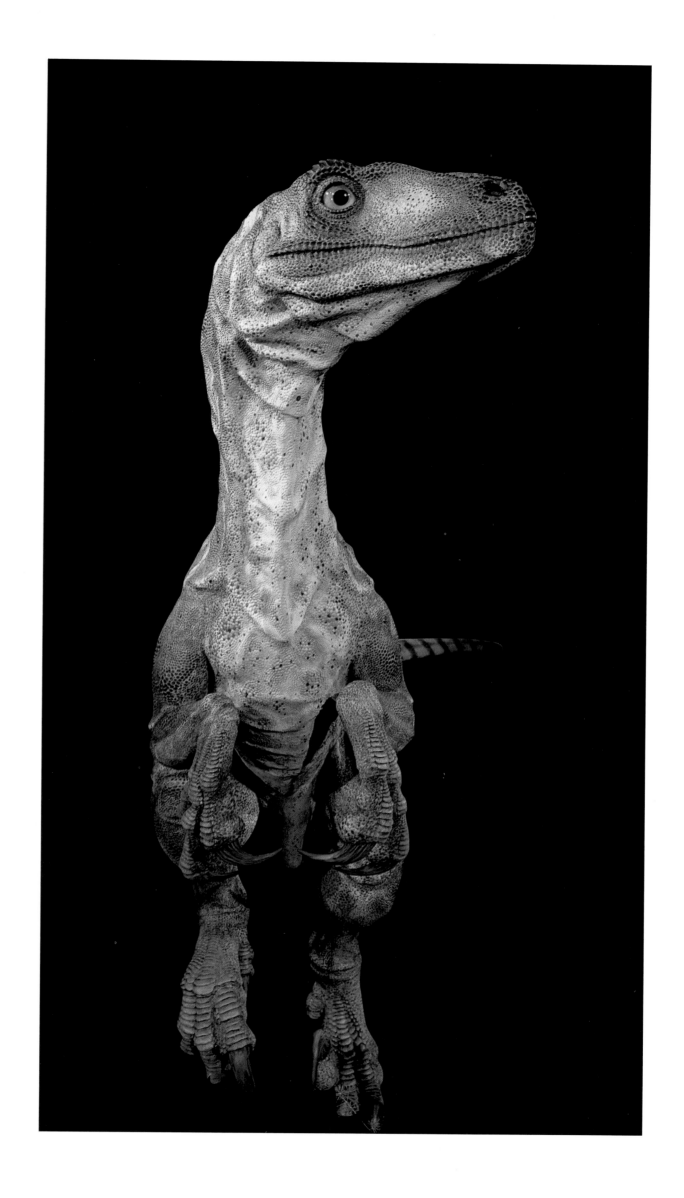

Carnotaurus is a unique theropod from Argentina which has a pair of stout horns over its eyes, and a comparatively short 'bulldog' face. Some skin impressions were found on the skull, revealing details of the actual appearance of the face.

back implies that it also had to adapt to the otherwise adverse climatic extremes of the equatorial North African territories.

The regions where these crested dinosaurs lived are presently included in the great Sahara desert, but the environment here during the Early Cretaceous was exceptionally wet and covered in a lush green landscape. Angiosperms were present, but the area was still dominated by ferns and the canopy forests of *Araucaria* that surrounded vast marshy floodplains. Meandering rivers cut their way across, forming complex deltas leading to lakes and shallow lagoons. Tidal mud flats covered with huge sauropod footprints dried and cracked from the heat of the sun. The intense heat and wet conditions made an ideal environment not only for the dinosaurs, but also for fish, turtles and crocodiles.

There was another monstrous predator that existed along with *Ouranosaurus* and *Spinosaurus*. Surprisingly, it was not a dinosaur, but a crocodile. *Sarcosuchus* reached lengths of 10–15 m (32½–49 ft) and its head alone was just a little less than 2 m (6½ ft) long.

Easily as large as, or larger than, *Spinosaurus*, it is notable that the skull of *Sarcosuchus* is like that of the modern-day gavial with a widened spatulate snout on the end of long and narrow jaws. Clearly this confirms that, like the gavial, *Sarcosuchus* had a mouth that was well adapted for catching fish. It also supports the idea that *Baryonyx* and *Spinosaurus* were indeed fish eaters. An abundance of fish must have been readily available in order to support the immense *Sarcosuchus*, as well as the additional presence of *Spinosaurus*. It is unlikely that these two predators intermingled, and they probably stayed in areas among their own kind. As with alligators living today, the deep bellowing sounds of these animals carried for miles, and although normally calling to attract a mate, the roars may have helped claim their territories and ward off potential intruders. However, occasional territorial battles could have occurred.

The enormous size of *Sarcosuchus* is a perfect example that the climate and environment was ideal for supporting cold-blooded animals. Only under the best conditions complete with stable warmth and a large food supply could a crocodile reach such huge proportions. The same is true for dinosaurs which were reptiles and basically ectothermic. Yet, even though these North African dinosaurs and crocodiles illus-

As with the skull, the rest of the skeleton of the peculiar Gondwanic theropod, Carnotaurus, has characteristics which are quite different from those of Laurasian theropods. With the discovery of this skeleton, large sections of skin were found over many parts of the body. This was the first time that this occurred among theropods and reveal what the animal would have looked like. Carnotaurus reached lengths of approximately 9 m (29½ ft).

trate a remarkably successful adaptation to the hot tropical environments, they must have possessed substantially different physiology and metabolism levels. This is to be expected as among endotherms there are mammals that are equipped with their own unique physiology and varying levels of metabolism. And so too this must have been among the dinosaurs and other reptiles.

While still being reptiles, the dinosaurs, like *Ouranosaurus* and *Spinosaurus*, possessed a physiology and metabolism that was somewhat different from that of crocodiles, like *Sarcosuchus*. This is indicated by the manner in which they adapted to the stresses of the environment that they all shared. Unlike these dinosaurs, *Sarcosuchus* did not have abnormally tall neural spines on its backbone. Just like modern crocodiles, it must have relied solely upon the cooling effects from being in the water, as well as gaping its mouth open to cool the blood as it circulated through the exposed soft inner tissues. That this was insufficient to maintain the required body temperature of the crested dinosaurs probably reflects a higher activity level than that of the crocodile. Such behaviour caused additional stress resulting in adaptive modifications that were beyond what an ordinary reptile, such as *Sarcosuchus*, might need.

Ouranosaurus was probably a herding animal, as it is not uncommon to find numerous skeletons lying close together. So far, however, its fossils have only been

found in North Africa which might mean that it was restricted to the hot environments near the equator. The same may apply to *Spinosaurus*. But the remains of *Sarcosuchus* have also been found in north-eastern Brazil which not only reaffirms the existing connection between South America and Africa, it suggests that the crested dinosaurs may have also existed there as well.

GONDWANIC SAUROPODS PREVAIL

That *Ouranosaurus* or other iguanodonts radiated throughout the rest of Gondwana is unlikely. But it is possible that at least some iguanodonts might have entered South Africa, although the fossil remains from there are inconclusive. And in a startling contrast to what had occurred in the Laurasian continents in the northern hemisphere, it is clear that the iguanodonts failed to equally dominate Gondwana in the southern hemisphere. While the sauropods in Laurasia were becoming extinct and replaced by iguanodonts, the sauropods continued to rule supreme throughout Gondwana. The intrusions made by the iguanodonts failed to replace the sauropods of Gondwana, and the rise of the ornithischians was prevented from occurring as it did in Laurasia.

Sauropods similar to *Pleurocoelus* made their way to South Africa. Fragmentary remains of other possible brachiosaurids, such as *Austrosaurus*, have even been found from near the middle of the Cretaceous of Australia. South America was densely populated by bizarre sauropods, and they probably persisted in the rest of Gondwana, including India and Antarctica.

Environmental conditions may be more responsible for the continuation of the sauropods in Gondwana rather than any direct confrontation against the iguanodonts. The most decisive determining factor might have been the isolating effects caused by the Tethys Seaway which finally separated the northern and southern continents. Without the continual influx of iguanodonts into Gondwana, the sauropods and other dinosaurs that were indigenous to the southern continents, maintained their hold over their domain resisting the limited advances of the immigrant dinosaurs from the north.

When the southern continents finally became totally separated from those of the northern hemisphere, the subsequent isolation caused two worlds of endemic dinosaurs that were unique to either hemisphere to continue evolving throughout most of the Cretaceous. The previous similarity of the same kinds of dinosaurs throughout the globe was ended. Throughout Laurasia, the iguanodonts and ornithischians continued to evolve into more advanced forms, often developing astonishing and bizarre characteristics. But in Gondwana, it was the sauropods which maintained their dominance where they, too, continued to evolve and often into incredible new forms. The same can be said for the Gondwanic theropods which due to their isolation evolved radically different endemic forms from those in Laurasia.

The Jurassic sauropod *Dicraeosaurus* has only been found in Africa, and was probably a unique species endemic to only the southern continents. *Amargasaurus* was a related form that is known from Argentina which continued to exist well into the beginning of the Cretaceous. Like *Dicraeosaurus*, the neck of *Amargasaurus* was uncharacteristically short for a sauropod, quite unlike the more typical elongated neck of *Brachiosaurus* or *Diplodocus*. *Dicraeosaurus* already had a narrow and fairly deep neck caused by two, rather tall, bifurcated neural spines on each of the cervical vertebra of the neck. This condition continued to persist on *Amargasaurus*, developing unprecedented proportions that formed an incredibly tall crest-like sail not only on the neck, but running across the length of the back as well.

In functional terms, the shorter necks of *Dicraeosaurus* and *Amargasaurus* prevented them from feeding on anything but low-growing vegetation. But the exceptionally tall crests can perhaps be best explained functionally as essential thermoregulating devices which

developed in the absence of elongated necks. The thermoregulating influences that would have been normally caused by the increased surface area of the long neck, had been compensated for by the additional increased height of the neural spines on these Gondwanic sauropods with short necks. Again, as with *Rebbachisaurus*, *Spinosaurus* and *Ouranosaurus*, the development of the incredibly tall neural spines and elaborate crests must have been an essential adaptation to aid their thermoregulation against the environmental stresses caused by the extremely hot climatic conditions during the middle parts of the Cretaceous. And so *Amargasaurus* probably lived in lush, steamy hot tropical environments not too unlike those which existed in North Africa.

LARGE-NOSED IGUANODONTS FROM THE EAST

It seems likely that by living in different regions with similar environments the dinosaurs developed convergent modifications. This would explain the tall crests on dinosaurs, like the *Amargasaurus* from Argentina, that lived some distance apart from the crested North African dinosaurs. However, there are two dinosaurs that are equipped with a peculiar adaptation which may not be so easily explained. They are both iguanodonts, *Iguanodon orientalis* from Mongolia and *Muttaburrasaurus* from Australia. These two iguanodonts lived at roughly the same time and, unlike any other iguanodonts, both possessed remarkably enlarged noses. Why such an adaptation should occur is not easily explained, and that it should happen in similar animals (both being iguanodonts), which were separated by such a great distance across both hemispheres, adds to the difficulty. Could this adaptation have evolved twice, independently in each of these iguanodonts? Or were these two iguanodonts more closely related to each other, having developed the large nasal adaptation only once, and then one migrated across into the other hemisphere? The enlarged nasal condition of these two iguanodonts may have been an environmental adaptation, increasing their sense of smell to help in distinguishing their preferred foods. There also seems to be a possible territorial relationship with lowland environments close to the sea.

These iguanodonts come from regions located in the distant far east of both hemispheres. While it is certainly possible that similar climatic conditions and environments existed in these far eastern regions, there may be reasons to believe that the iguanodonts actually evolved the large nose only once. The distribution of these particular iguanodonts would then have followed afterwards, spreading between the far east regions of both hemispheres. But if (and it should be stressed that this is a big if) the distribution occurred after these iguanodonts evolved the large nose, they would have had to travel an exceedingly long way around, heading west, down south across Africa

With a skull as much as 3 m (10 ft) in length, Kronosaurus *existed within shallow seas which covered what is now central Australia. It was one of the short-necked pliosaurs, and was among the largest of marine reptiles. The feeding behaviour of* Kronosaurus *was probably similar to that of Orca, the killer whale, in that they fed upon sizeable prey.* Kronosaurus *reached lengths of approximately 14 m (45¹/₂ ft).*

and South America and then back east again over Antarctica. Because no similar large-nosed iguanodonts are known from along this route this is an unlikely scenario, although still a possibility.

A recent discovery of spinosaur teeth from Thailand does present the possibility that there was a connection between south-east Asia and North Africa. But a shorter route might have existed if there was a chain of archipelagos stretching across south-east Asia that reached Australia. If such a connection existed this would have been a much shorter route involving only regions of the far east and it could explain the absence of these iguanodonts from the western territories. But for now, the answers to this issue must remain hypothetical and unresolved. Only with additional information from future discoveries will more light be shed on understanding how these large-nosed iguanodonts came to be where they are.

LARGE HYPSILOPHODONTS AND THEROPODS WITH GIANT CLAWS

Along with the broad success that the iguanodonts had made in their distribution throughout Laurasia

there was another fairly large ornithischian that is known from the western parts of North America. *Tenontosaurus* reached lengths between 4 and 6.5 m (13 and 21 ft) and because of the large forelimbs which were over two-thirds as long as the hind legs, *Tenontosaurus* must have usually moved about on all four legs. At first glance, then, *Tenontosaurus* might appear to be an iguanodont, but a closer inspection reveals that it was still a primitive hypsilophodont, although an exceptionally large one.

Tenontosaurus possessed qualities that were too primitive to have been inherited from the same kind of ancestor, presumably the Late Jurassic *Camptosaurus*, which led to the development of the iguanodonts. While the iguanodonts inherited advanced camptosaurid-like characteristics, such as the strongly connected bones of the wrist and the tridactyl condition of the hind feet, *Tenontosaurus* was equipped with more

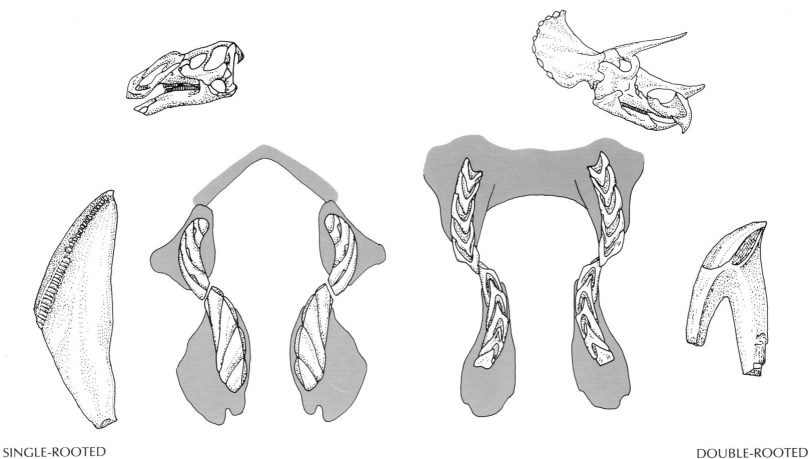

SINGLE-ROOTED

DOUBLE-ROOTED

DIAGONAL GRINDING   VERTICAL SLICING

ORNITHOPOD AND CERATOPSIAN TEETH CHART
Both iguanodonts and ceratopsians were advanced ornithischians which had complex tooth batteries that continually replaced old worn teeth with underlying new ones throughout the animal's life. Hadrosaurs and other ornithopods had single-rooted teeth, and ceratopsians had double-rooted teeth. Cross-sections of the upper and lower jaws illustrate the manner in which the teeth grew, one on top of the other, forming a constant battery of additional replacements. Note the angle at the point where the teeth made contact. The diagonal angle of the ornithopods was caused by a grinding tooth action. The vertical angle of the ceratopsians demonstrates more of a slicing action of the teeth. Individual teeth are shown actual size.

flexible elements in the wrist and hind feet that still retained four functional toes. From these details, and numerous other subtle characteristics, the hypsilophodont ancestry of *Tenontosaurus* becomes clear. *Tenontosaurus* was in effect a hypsilophodont version of an iguanodont that for a while filled a similar environmental niche. And it is perhaps largely due to its primitive condition that *Tenontosaurus* failed to compete against the intrusion of the European iguanodonts, and became extinct soon thereafter.

Other kinds of dinosaurs that were living along with *Tenontosaurus* included some of the last surviving Laurasian sauropods; the armoured nodosaur, *Sauropelta*; an early representation of the ostrich-like dinosaurs

with *Ornithomimus*; and small to moderate sized theropod predators, *Microvenator* and *Deinonychus*. Except for the theropods, none of these dinosaurs would have caused much, if any, adverse effects on *Tenontosaurus*. Among the theropods, *Microvenator*, which was only about the size of a turkey, certainly wasn't much of a threat, unless it went after the very young, or robbed the eggs from nests that were left unattended. However, not even the largest *Tenontosaurus* was safe from *Deinonychus*. Teeth from this predator are frequently found associated with the dismembered skeletal remains of *Tenontosaurus* clearly indicating that *Deinonychus* often fed upon these comparatively defenceless dinosaurs.

Deinonychus was at most only about 3 m (10 ft) long, which would make it considerably less than half the size of a full grown *Tenontosaurus*. But even though it stood little more than 1 m (3 ft) high, *Deinonychus* was a most formidable beast and capable hunter. By virtue of its slender, lightweight body and agile hind legs the animal could move swiftly. The vertebrae of the last two-thirds of its tail had been uniquely modified with long overlapping extensions of bone which reduced the normal degree of flexibility, turning it into a rigid balancing pole. In a burst of speed, *Deinonychus* would have leaped upon its prey, and with its powerful large arms and grasping fingers, clutched tightly, firming its grip while balancing itself with the use of its tail as the victim struggled. Then in a rapid flurry of thrashing strokes from the hind legs, a giant claw on each foot would have sliced its way repeatedly until the victim fell to the ground. Despite its size, the special modifications that *Deinonychus* was equipped with certainly made it a most efficient and terrifying predator. Furthermore, as terribly awesome as a single *Deinonychus* must have been, there is reason to believe that upon occasions, like a pack of relentless hyenas, this giant clawed theropod co-operatively hunted *en masse*.

AVIAN CHARACTERISTICS

Although *Deinonychus* is perhaps better known for the giant claw on each of its feet, the large hands, forelimbs and pelvis are of special interest and deserve more attention. These elements bear a striking resemblance to those of the Jurassic bird, *Archaeopteryx*. In an avian fashion and unlike typical theropods, the pubic bone slanted backwards, and the individual bones of the hand and wrist are so similar and avian in their shape that the arms were normally held close to the sides of the body, folded up like the wings of a bird. This probably represents an inherited condition from a common ancestral stock with *Archaeopteryx*. But *Deinonychus* did not continue to become more bird-like. Instead, its evolutionary course lost any tendency towards flight, becoming considerably larger and more like other theropods.

With the advent of its ability to fly, however clumsily, it is highly unlikely that the descendants of *Archaeopteryx* reverted to a fully terrestrial condition. As with modern raties, such as the ostrich, the loss of the ability to fly might cause a functional retardation and the atrophied condition of the wings. But *Deinonychus* fully retained the proportionally large hands and arms which suggest that although related to *Archaeopteryx*, its closer and more direct ancestor was still primarily terrestrial, maybe even to some extent arboreal, but not capable of flight.

Whether or not *Archaeopteryx* continued to evolve into more advanced, avian-like descendants is not known at this time. The gaps in the fossil record are still simply too large. But there are several important fossils from the Early Cretaceous that represent a broad diversity of much more advanced birds. *Ambiortus* of Central Asia possessed a keeled sternum, avian-like elongated coracoids and fused elements of the hand resembling that of modern flying birds. From England, there is *Enaliornis* which was a primitive member of flightless birds that had become specialized in swimming. Another bird is known from Las Hoyas, Spain which represents an intermediate stage, again with elongated coracoids (see glossary), but also with a considerably shortened tail that was in effect becoming fused into an avian-like pygostyle (see glossary). Impressions of feathers have been found in Australia,

and footprints made by shorebirds have been found in western Canada. Together, these examples suggest that there could have been several lineages, not necessarily having to include *Archaeopteryx*, which continued to evolve throughout the Jurassic leading towards more advanced birds. Without any doubt, all of these birds had evolved from a reptilian ancestry, but what remains unresolved is exactly which kind of reptile they, and all modern birds, are descended from. Was the ancestor dinosaurian, crocodilian or a thecodont?

The complexity of this issue can not be overstated as the fossil record is far from easy to decipher. What may often look like a bird may, in fact, not actually be a bird. Diagnostic characters and shapes of bones may become at times remarkably similar to those of unrelated animals due to a similar adaptation of behaviour. Simply because of the relatively close relationship that exists between dinosaurs, crocodiles and thecodonts, this convergent form of evolution can greatly hamper the correct identification of many fossils, leading to problems such as which particular reptiles may or may not have led towards becoming modern birds.

CROCODILES WITH MAMMAL-LIKE TEETH

To demonstrate the difficulty of identification when confronted by functionally convergent shapes, there are certain crocodiles from the lower Cretaceous which if only their teeth were found, the logical identification would place them as a mammal. Incredibly, even though not at all closely related to mammals, these crocodilians developed an atypical behaviour more like that of mammals which can chew their food.

At least five skulls of these small crocodilians with 'mammal-like' dentition were found in Malawi of south-east Central Africa. They represent highly specialized members of a terrestrial group of crocodilians called notosuchians. Unlike typical crocodiles, the eyes of the notosuchians were on the sides of the head, and together with the extreme anterior position of the nose, as well as large canine teeth, there is a striking resemblance to some of the early mammal-like reptiles of the Permian and Late Triassic. But this is only due to the adaptive qualities developed by similar behavioural lifestyles, and not because of a shared ancestry. The notosuchians were also endemic to Gondwana. Their strange evolution must be, at least in part, due to their isolation in the southern hemisphere.

LONG- AND SHORT-NECKED PLESIOSAURS

The separation of the continents must have had far less impact on the isolation of the sea-going reptiles. In fact, the resulting seaways may not have only increased the areas that provided suitable environments, but were also connected with distant seas on the opposite sides of the continents. The gradual extinction of the ichthyosaurs (see pages 94–5) continued until the last of their kind perished sometime during the middle of the Cretaceous. However, the plesiosaurs (see page 155) persisted until the very end of the Mesozoic.

There are two major groups of plesiosaurs, being the short-necked pliosaurs with large skulls, and the long-necked plesiosaurs which had small skulls. The flexible long necks of the plesiosaurs were probably of great assistance in the capture of smaller fish. In contrast, the pliosaurs' long and powerfully built jaws with large sharply pointed teeth, clearly indicate that they must have gone after sizeable prey.

Fossil skulls of the largest marine reptiles have been found in the sediments laid down at the bottom of shallow seas which covered much of central Australia. These skulls, some of which reached 3 m (10 ft) in length, belong to pliosaurs called *Kronosaurus*. Something like giant reptilian versions of killer whales, these pliosaurs were at least 14 m (45¹/₂ ft) long, and must have been the terror of the seas.

A HORNED THEROPOD FROM GONDWANA

The isolating effects on dinosaurs in Gondwana may have been responsible for the successful continuance of the sauropods and, as with the tall-spined *Amargasaurus*, the evolution in isolation often resulted in uniquely peculiar new forms of dinosaurs. Together with the evolution of the Gondwanic theropods, there was also apparently a failure. No coelurosaurs have as yet been discovered from the Cretaceous of Gondwana possibly reflecting their regional extinction in the southern hemisphere. However, the carnosaurs continued to exist, evolving in a remarkably different fashion compared to the Laurasian theropods.

Perhaps the best known of these aberrant theropods is the recently discovered *Carnotaurus* from Patagonia, Argentina. *Carnotaurus* is a member of the Abelisauridae, a newly recognized family of Gondwanic theropods which represents a lineage separate from that of the Laurasian theropods. The distant ancestral relationship may have been in a ceratosaur-like theropod during the Jurassic which, when separated from the influences of the northern continents, broke off into the aberrant evolution of the abelisaurs.

The head of *Carnotaurus* is crowned with two stout horns protruding over its eyes. Compared to more typical carnosaurs, its abnormally short and deep skull creates a brutish bull-dog appearance quite unlike any other theropod. But the truly significant differences that set *Carnotaurus* and other Gondwanic theropods apart from those of Laurasia are to be found not only in the skull, but throughout the entire skeleton. The neural spines on the neck vertebrae were extremely reduced in size, and to compensate, two separated

extensions of bone on either side of the vertebrae were raised as high as the neural spine would have normally been. This would have greatly affected how the musculature worked. Other features of the skeleton are also unique, but although different from those of other theropods, they must have performed similar functions. Among the strangest things that *Carnotaurus* had evolved was its forelimbs. Like most other theropods, the arms were greatly reduced in size. But they were also very robust and must have been extremely powerful. Most remarkable, though, was the size reduction of the bones in the forearm. They were so small that they had almost become more like bones of the wrist and hand. The hand itself was short as well, but still equipped with three, or possibly four, claws. Why such a bizarre mixture of primitive and advanced characters should have occurred is difficult to explain. Unfortunately for the sake of comparison, the arms of other Gondwanic theropods are insufficiently known as to whether or not they were modified in a similar fashion to *Carnotaurus* or had become specialized for yet other kinds of functions.

The *Carnotaurus* skeleton was found completely articulated in an exceptionally hard stone concretion. Only the hind feet, lower portions of the legs and the last half of the tail were missing due to the destructive effects of the erosion which was exposing the bones from the rock. Aside from being the most complete example of a Gondwanic theropod from the Cretaceous, *Carnotaurus* also has the distinction of being the only theropod in which skin impressions have been found over much of its body. Prior to this, only a tiny patch of theropod skin a few centimetres in diameter had ever been found. Due to the rarity and informative significance of the skin impressions, a second expedition returned to the original *Carnotaurus* quarry in the hopes of finding any additional impressions of skin that might have been overlooked during the initial excavation. Several additional sections of skin were found which, together with the first findings, represent portions across the entire length of the body, from the base of the tail, sides of the torso, shoulder, neck and even parts of the face. For the first time, the fossil impressions of skin revealed the actual appearance of a theropod dinosaur.

DISTRIBUTION OF COELUROSAURS AND 'OSTRICH' DINOSAURS WITH TEETH

The implications that there was an extinction which had wiped out the coelurosaurs of Gondwana during the Cretaceous is astounding, if it did indeed occur. Certainly, the Cretaceous sauropods had been displaced from Laurasia, but whatever caused the premature extinction of Gondwanic coelurosaurs becomes

all the more inexplicable in light of the fact that the Laurasian coelurosaurs proliferated successfully in many diverse new forms which lasted to the end of the Mesozoic. Perhaps the early demise of coelurosaurs is only an inaccurate representation due to preservational factors and reflects more the scarcity of any theropods that are as yet known from the southern hemisphere. In time, future discoveries may well prove that such an extinction did not actually occur.

As with the apparent lack of Gondwanic coelurosaurs, such broad gaps in the fossil record greatly hinder the complete understanding of the evolution of dinosaurs. But there have been remarkable, highly informative discoveries of transitional forms of dinosaurs evolving towards more advanced and specialized conditions.

One group of coelurosaurs, commonly referred to as the 'ostrich' dinosaurs, is the ornithomimids. Known best from the last half of the Cretaceous, the ornithomimids have been found only in Mongolia, parts of Asia in the far east, and in North America situated in the distant far west. No ornithomimids are as yet known from Europe or more central parts of Laurasia.

And yet, unless the ornithomimids could have somehow made their way across the Turgai seaway and all of Europe, there must have been another distribution path connecting the far east to the far west. Such a pathway could only have been across Beringia, a bridge of land that stretched over the Bering Strait between Alaska and the north-easternmost parts of Asia.

The discovery of a partial skeleton, including a fragmentary skull, has revealed the possible place of origin from which the ornithomimids first evolved and later dispersed. This primitive ancestral ornithomimid is called *Harpymimus*, and was found in Mongolia. The most significant diagnostic feature of *Harpymimus* is that, unlike all other known ornithomimids, it was still equipped with teeth. All of the more advanced ornithomimids had lost their teeth entirely and developed an ostrich-like beak to rely upon while feeding.

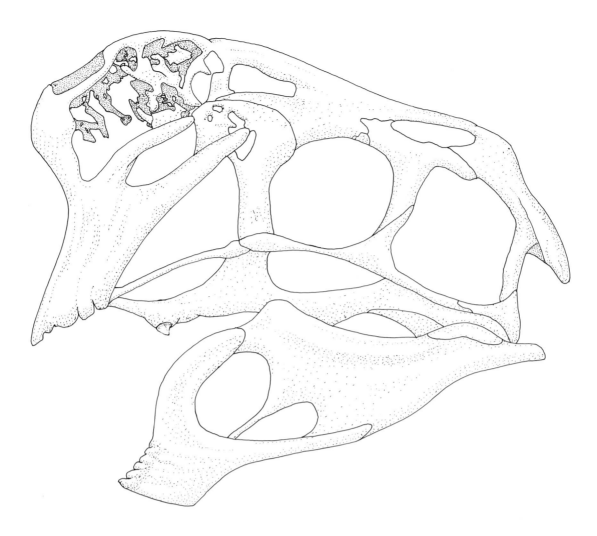

Shown ³/₄ life-size is a skull and jaw of a crested Oviraptor, *facing to the left. This peculiar theropod is one of only two kinds of omnivorous theropods (the other being the ornithomimids) which lost the teeth in their jaws and instead relied upon a beak. Unique among theropods,* Oviraptor *possessed two short teeth in its upper palate which may have been used for cracking into eggs and possibly shearing fruits.* Oviraptor *reached lengths of approximately 2.5 m (8 ft).*

But the jaws of *Harpymimus* were still at a transitory stage in which the beak had formed, but the small atrophied remnants of teeth were still present in the very front of the lower jaw. Other primitive characteristics were found to exist in the hands and feet. Only the most advanced kinds of ornithomimids are known from North America, which together with the primitive status of *Harpymimus* in Asia, suggests that the ostrich dinosaurs may have originated in Central Asia, radiated throughout that continent and migrated to North America by way of an eastern route across the land connection of Beringia.

Further evidence of these movements is suggested by an extensive series of trackways found along the Peace River in British Columbia, western Canada, from a period of time roughly contemporaneous to when *Harpymimus* existed. The trackways were made by various kinds of dinosaurs, including large theropods, advanced inguanodonts and nodosaurs. Also of note, were the tracks of shorebirds, some of which

might have been made while the animals were feeding. Conspicuously missing, however, are the footprints of ornithomimids, although in addition to skeletal remains, there are footprints of ornithomimids from Alberta, western Canada, from much later in time during the last portions of the Cretaceous. This may indicate that ornithomimids did not exist in North America earlier during the Mid-Cretaceous, and migrated from Asia at a later date.

TRACKWAYS, SWIMMING AND TENDONS

Among the most interesting of the Peace River track-

Defending itself and possibly its nest, a Protoceratops *engages in a vicious battle against an invading* Velociraptor. *The battle ended with both combatants dying in each other's grasp. The skeletons of these dinosaurs from Mongolia were found in the positions of their final death throes within desert sands that entombed them soon after their battle ended. Also shown is another potential egg-stealer,* Oviraptor, *in the background. Length of* Protoceratops *is approximately 3 m (10 ft); and* Velociraptor *is about 2 m (6¹/₂ ft).*

ways are those which were made by the advanced iguanodonts. These tracks were made by hadrosaurs, or duck-billed dinosaurs, the descendants of the iguanodonts. The daily activities and behaviour of these hadrosaurs were recorded by their footprints. When one is walking alongside, or stepping in, the actual footsteps of dinosaurs there is an eerie, almost magical sensation to such trackways. The preservation is often so good that the footprints give a feeling of having been made only recently. But the reality that they were created by creatures of so long ago conjures up only vague ghost-like images of the trackmakers, for the footprints in stone remain the only tangible testimony to their existence. The Peace River trackways include footprints known as *Amblydactylus*, which are named for the footprints only and are perhaps the earliest known representation of the ancestral stages of the hadrosaurs. The skeletons of these trackmakers are as yet unknown.

The footprints of the Peace River hadrosaurs resemble iguanodont tracks, but are shorter and broader in shape. Among at least six of the larger *Amblydactylus* trackways there are irregular crescent-shaped depressions made by the hands of the animals as they walked in a quadrupedal fashion. It would appear that at this stage of development, these hadrosaurs were still mostly quadrupedal and only partially capable of moving about on only their hind legs.

The *Amblydactylus* tracks were made in many settings that although somewhat similar, reflect different areas and environmental conditions. For example, trackways were left along the once muddy margins of the shoreline and a quiet expanse of fresh water. The fact that undulating ripple-marks caused by the water's repetitive motions were also preserved indicates that many of the tracks were made while the animals were in the water. There are also very small *Amblydactylus* footprints which must have been made by very young individuals walking along the water's edge in extremely shallow water which may have been only a few centimetres deep. Many of the trackways were made by larger animals while they were partially submerged in shallow water or floating in water that was deep enough, perhaps 2 m (6½ ft) or more, to help support the weight of the body. Such swimming may account for the absence of the handprints in many trackways.

The hadrosaurs swam in a different way than sauropods which had to poll themselves along using primarily their front legs because of the disproportionate distribution of weight on the front of the animals caused by their long neck. But the distribution of the hadrosaurs' body weight was more centrally distributed thereby allowing the larger hind legs to be used in pushing off the water's bottom, while the front legs were held higher and could have been used for occasional paddling. The hadrosaurs' hands were not equipped with webbing that would have formed a paddle-like structure idealized for swimming. Instead, the fingers were closely bound together, and the ends cloven in hoofs within a thickened curved pad on the sole of the foot.

Although the front feet were not specifically designed for swimming, they must have been of some assistance while in the water. Even many animals that are living today, which may at first appear to be exclusively terrestrial, can swim quite efficiently when it is necessary to do so. Certainly, the hoofed feet of horses and their slender lower legs are not at all designed for swimming, and yet, even they can swim. Although the hands of a hadrosaur appear to be suited best for terrestrial functions, there is no reason that they could not have been of some help while swimming.

Besides the horse, other examples of modern-day animals with unexpected aquatic abilities are elk, rhinos, and elephants, just to mention a few. The highly aquatic hippopotamus, together with these competent swimmers, can all swim without any assistance from their tails. This becomes a significant point regarding hadrosaurs because in more recent years it has become accepted by many palaeontologists that hadrosaurs were highly terrestrial animals, virtually incapable of swimming. This interpretation has been based upon the fact that along the back and front half of the tail, just above the vertebrae along the neural spines, there is a lattice-like structure of bony tendons. *Iguanodon* has two layers of these tendons on either side of the neural spines, while on hadrosaurs there are three layers on each side. This has led many to believe that the function of the bony tendons was to strengthen the back and tail so that they could be carried more easily up in the air while walking on just the hind legs. Somehow this added strength was to have caused an extra rigidity of the tail which then, having lost its suppleness, caused hadrosaurs to also lose their ability to swim. This is an overstated conclusion, as even a somewhat stiffened tail of a hadrosaur would have been far more effective for swimming than that of the tail of a horse or hippopotamus. In short, even without the use of their tails, hadrosaurs could easily have been efficient swimmers. And the presence of any large muscular tail, stiffened or otherwise, such as in hadrosaurs, could have only been of extra assistance while swimming.

Even if it is accepted that hadrosaurs could swim, the function of the ossified tendons warrants further explanation. Had the sole purpose of these bony tendons been to strengthen the back, then it is surprising that the neural spines and vertebrae which are supposedly affected do not show any additional modifications or signs of rigidity. If strength and rigidity was the desired function, then the neural spines should have become much closer together and the vertebrae themselves should also show signs of uniting or actual bonding. This is what normally occurs to the vertebrae within the pelvis because the strength and rigidity is essential in this part of the body. But this development did not occur in the back and tail of hadrosaurs. Therefore another function must have promoted the development of the ossified tendons.

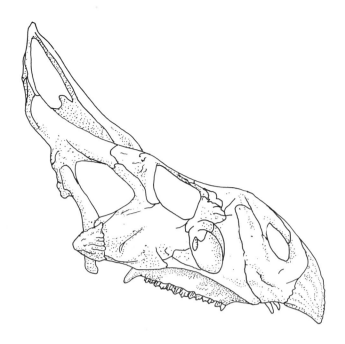

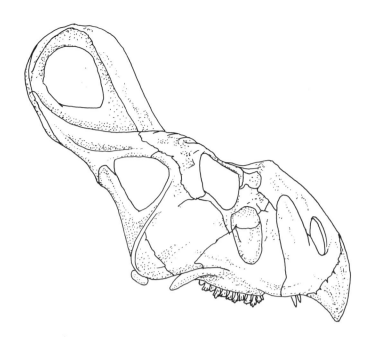

Abundant remains of Protoceratops' *skulls have demonstrated different characteristics which have been interpreted as belonging to either males or females. On the left is the skull of a female Protoceratops, which is more gracile, and lower in its profile, with a less prominent crest and a much reduced summit that supported a small horn behind its nose compared to that of the skull of a male, on the right. This is more robust, and has a taller profile with a more prominent crest and nasal horn. (after Brown and Schlaikjer, 1940)*

Tendons are not connective tissues that normally function to make a part of the body rigid. They are connective parts of muscles which become firmly attached to bones for additional strength in the muscles. The ossification process by which the tendon actually becomes bone does not necessarily instigate a rigidity in that region of the body. However, although the shape of the tendon can contribute to some immobility, simply because tendons have become ossified and turned to bone does not make the tendon totally inflexible. The long, rod-like tendons would still retain a certain amount of flexibility even if they were made of steel.

A close inspection of the hadrosaurs' bony tendons reveal that they are not perfectly rounded throughout their length, and that they become progressively oval and flattened towards one end. Like a long narrow bar that is held vertically, the increased height of the bar resists bending while the narrow width between the flattened sides remains flexible. Such a condition would not have developed in hadrosaurs unless, in addition to the increased strength, there was a necessity for movement from side to side. The bony tendons, therefore, may have contributed to some vertical strength along the backbone and tail, but the greatest power was in a lateral motion, capable of pulling the tail from side to side. The tendons and musculature that led towards the front of the animal were connected to similarly powerful muscles and nuchal ligaments (see glossary) that supported the heavy head and neck. In this manner, the ossified tendons along the back and tail of a hadrosaur confirms rather than denies its ability to swim, as recorded by many of the *Amblydactylus* Peace River trackways.

The shape of the body of hadrosaurs is not as streamlined as a crocodile, mostly due to the length of the hind legs. This might imply that they were not particularly fast swimmers, unless they were capable

of holding their arms and legs to their sides, which they probably did. In such a position, a fast moving hadrosaur that was only using its tail for propulsion would not leave any tracks in the substrate below. However, there is positive evidence in the trackways that while swimming slowly, hadrosaurs resorted to utilizing their hind legs to help push off and steer into different directions. One such trackway was made where the hadrosaur was in deep enough water that its hind feet barely reached the bottom. The heel of the foot made little to no contact while the toes pushed off more firmly leaving deeper depressions. Quite abruptly, the course of the animal shifted over a metre to the right side and then again, after a few steps back a metre or so to the left. This prehistoric version of playing hopscotch could only have occurred while floating in water, kicking off with its feet and an occasional swipe from the tail. Other extensive areas are covered by random and occasional single footprints which must have been made from swimming hadrosaurs that slowed down enough to enable them to step down and push off during a momentary pause.

The *Amblydactylus* trackways give strong indications that these hadrosaurs were gregarious and congregated in herds. A series of parallel trackways made by at least four animals walking side by side continued straight in the same direction until one hadrosaur on the end apparently stumbled, or walked around something in its way which caused it to swerve into

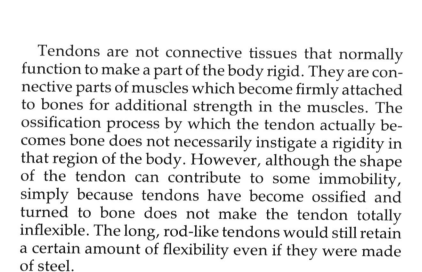

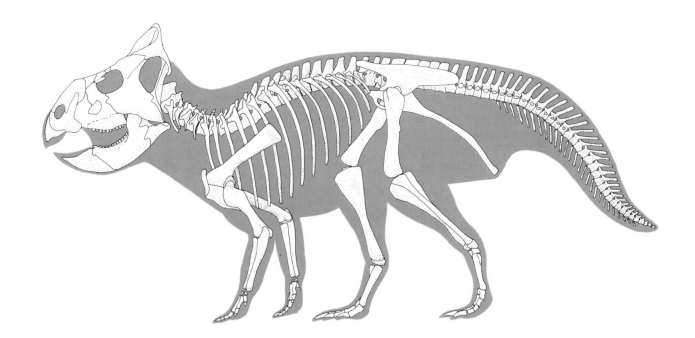

Even though Leptoceratops *lived long after* Protoceratops, *it had a shorter frill on the back of its skull and was slightly more primitive than the Asian form.* Leptoceratops *reached lengths of approximately 2 m (6½ ft). (after Russell, 1970)*

the animal next to it. In turn this second hadrosaur stepped out of line causing both of the animals next to it to also move over. Once around the obstacle, the first hadrosaur continued in its original direction, followed alongside by its temporarily disturbed members of the group. Multiple sets of trackways have also been found that were made exclusively by juvenile hadrosaurs indicating that groups of young hadrosaurs of similar age and size may have stayed together, perhaps segregated from the larger members of the herd for at least some of the time.

Along with some of the *Amblydactylus* trackways at Peace River, there were trackways made by other kinds of dinosaurs, including a rare example of a nodosaur. But most of the other dinosaurs that left their footprints here were theropods. There are some sets of theropod footprints in pathways that appear to be following after the hadrosaurs. The theropod tracks were also made in soft mud and places that were situated in fairly deep water. Apparently not afraid of entering the water, the theropods could have followed after swimming hadrosaurs. And here, the tendons and stronger muscles of the tail probably aided in the hadrosaurs' escape from the less powerfully equipped theropods.

BARRIER SEAWAYS

At about the time the *Amblydactylus* tracks were made, or sometime soon thereafter, a gradual continuous transgression of a seaway took place from the Arctic Ocean down across vast portions of the western interiors of Canada and the United States of America. This was the Mowry Seaway. And even though its waters came from the distant north arctic ocean, the blackened shales that accumulated on the bottom of this seaway are clear testimony that the northern waters were not cold. The Mowry Seaway made temporary contact with the Gulf of Mexico by the middle the Cretaceous, and after a regression it again made contact through the Mexican Gulf and onto the Tethys Seaway. The southern expansion of the Mowry Seaway had formed the great Cretaceous Interior Seaway dividing the landmass of North America until just before the end of the Mesozoic.

Other parts of Laurasia were divided by the seaways around Greenland that developed as the rifting separation of the continents took place. The Turgai Sea also spread across central Europe connecting with the Tethyan Sea which together covered much of western Europe. Barrier reefs and islands stretched across many of the coastlines forming lagoons between them and the mainland. Bordering the lagoons were broad swamps, deltas and mangroves fed by slow moving streams and rivers that crossed alluvial plains. Running across North America, alluvial fans were formed from the erosional soil carried by the runoff waters issuing from the Sevier mountains in the western United States.

BEAKS AND TEETH

The formation of Beringia probably did not occur until sometime after the middle of the Cretaceous, and Asia

Leptoceratops *is the North American counterpart to* Protoceratops *of Mongolia. Here a* Leptoceratops *is strolling through the shallows of a stream beneath a densely wooded forest of Araucaria.*

remained largely isolated from Europe to its west and North America to its east. Perhaps due to this isolation, a new kind of dinosaur had evolved in Asia. It resembled other small ornithopods except that it still had four functional toes on its hind feet. Other characteristics seem to be an odd blend of primitive and advanced development. But the most significant feature about this little dinosaur was that it had an additional bone, called the rostrum, which supported the upper beak. This counterpart to the predentary bone, which formed the lower beak in all other ornithischians, is the hallmark of all of the ceratopsian dinosaurs, better known as the horned dinosaurs. And the earliest dinosaur known to possess such a rostral bone is *Psittacosaurus* from the Middle Cretaceous of Mongolia.

The advanced, additional character of the rostral bone must have a relationship to the kinds of plants and the manner in which the ceratopsians fed upon them. Like ornithopods, the teeth of ceratopsians were heterodont which meant that they had an abrasive contact between the upper and lower jaws. The evolution leading to this development in ceratopsians had come from a much more primitive hypsilophodont ancestor that strayed from the ornithopod lifestyle. Independently of the iguanodonts and hadrosaurs, the number of teeth ceratopsians had also increased to form batteries of teeth that were constantly replaced as the older ones became worn. The primitive nature of *Psittacosaurus* is shown by the presence of only two rows of teeth in each jaw, including the erupted, fully grown teeth and the non-erupted replacement teeth located immediately below and still totally within the jaw. As the tooth replacement became more advanced in later ceratopsians, the number of replacement teeth increased by additional rows of teeth stacked upon themselves within the jaws. As many as five successive rows of teeth formed elaborate dental batteries. The dental batteries of hadrosaurs evolved in a similar fashion, having increased the number of rows of replacement teeth. In both cases, as new teeth continually grew, the worn teeth were replaced by those immediately below. Throughout the animal's life, the constant cycle of tooth replacement kept up with the abrasive action that reduced older and worn teeth.

The teeth within each row forming the dental batteries are tightly wedged together strengthening the combined surface of the teeth into a rigid abrasive plate. Hadrosaur teeth are single rooted and the diamond shape of each tooth fit together in a regimented mosaic. Ceratopsian teeth are more complex in that they have two roots overlapping the crown of the tooth directly beneath. Such a distinction between hadrosaur and ceratopsian teeth is a likely indication that they worked differently in both groups of these dinosaurs. The different kinds of functions between the teeth of these herbivores becomes apparent when jaws of the two groups are examined together. Both kinds of teeth wore down from abrading actions, but

hadrosaur teeth made contact at an angle that caused more of a grinding action. Ceratopsian teeth, however, made contact in a more parallel direction resulting in a slicing action. These different methods of eating almost certainly indicate that hadrosaurs and ceratopsians fed upon their own unique kinds of preferred vegetation.

Psittacosaurus was a very primitive ceratopsian with only a poorly developed dental battery: the single rooted teeth barely show the slightest bifurcation into two separate roots. Also, the back of the skull where the jaw musculature attached was still quite short. More advanced ceratopsians with double rooted teeth not only continued to perfect the slicing dental batteries, but the backs of their skulls also became enlarged into a frill so that the jaw muscles could become larger and more efficient. All things considered, the morphology of *Psittacosaurus* makes it a perfect ancestor for all of the later ceratopsians, except for one thing. Each of the front feet of *Psittacosaurus* are equipped with only four toes, while all other more advanced ceratopsians still had five. As features that are lost can not be passed on, this indicates that even though *Psittacosaurus* is an extremely primitive ceratopsian, it was not the direct ancestor of the ceratopsians. Although closely related, the actual ancestor must have come from a more primitive form similar to *Psittacosaurus* which had not lost its fifth finger.

Psittacosaurus was a small dinosaur that was only 1 m (3 ft) or so in length. Even with the development of the rostral bone, the primitive teeth were such that once the food had been swallowed it was still often necessary for gastroliths (see glossary) to aid in breaking the food down so that it could be properly digested. Because gastroliths are not known among the more advanced ceratopsians, the beak and teeth may have become efficient enough as to not need the help from gastroliths. These ceratopsians may have increased the efficiency of their digestive systems in part because of their larger size.

NESTS AND EGG-STEALERS

The remains of baby psittacosaurs have been found

IGUANODONT FAMILY TREE
Two kinds of iguanodonts were ancestral to the distinctly separate families of duckbills. One group consists of hollow-crested lambeosaurs which evolved from an iguanodont such as Ouranosaurus. *The other group, hadrosaurs, are flat-headed forms, with or without solid crests which evolved from the iguanodont,* Iguanodon. *These two groups of duckbills became the dominant herbivores. The iguanodonts were greatly reduced in numbers although they did persist throughout the Cretaceous in various parts of the globe. The hypsilophodonts, which also lasted to the end of the period, evolved from ancestors that were more primitive than iguanodonts such as* Camptosaurus. *Skulls shown not to scale.*

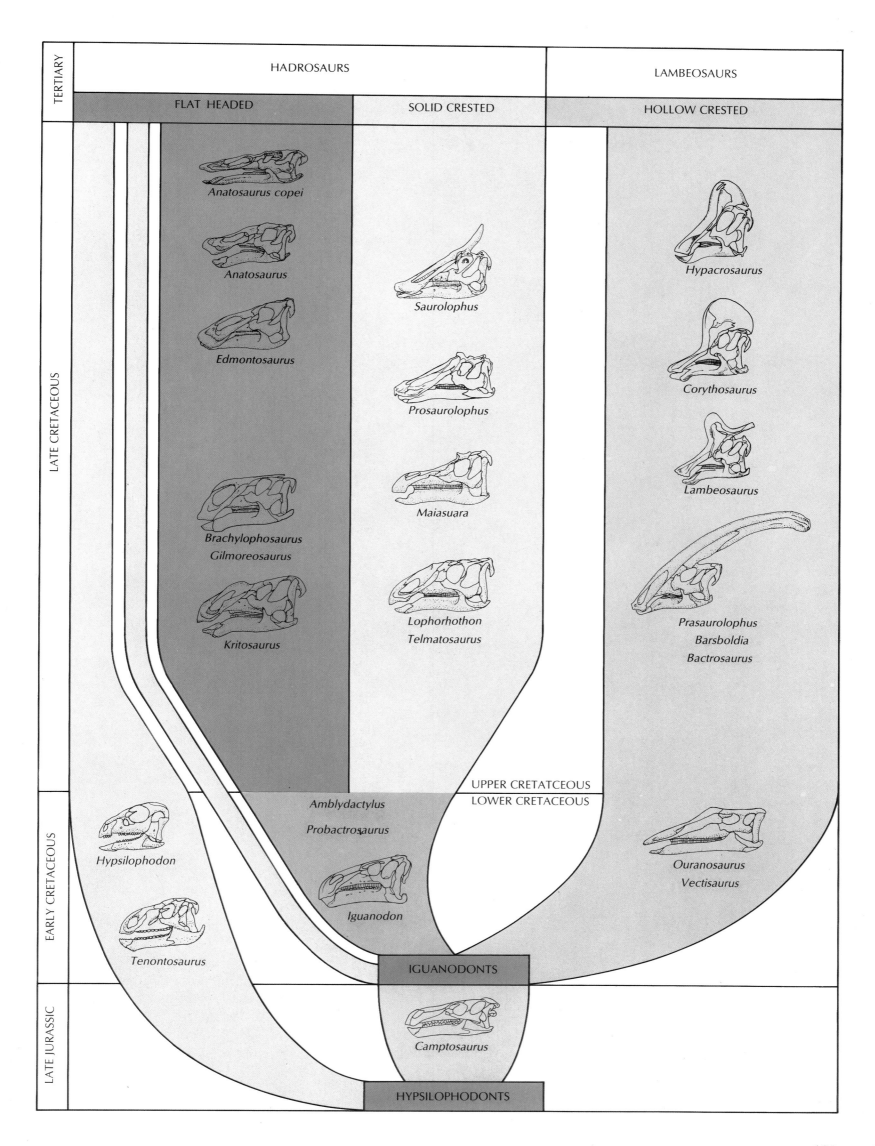

TERTIARY

HADROSAURS

LAMBEOSAURS

FLAT HEADED

SOLID CRESTED

HOLLOW CRESTED

LATE CRETACEOUS

Anatosaurus copei

Anatosaurus

Edmontosaurus

Brachylophosaurus
Gilmoreosaurus

Kritosaurus

Saurolophus

Prosaurolophus

Maiasuara

Lophorhothon
Telmatosaurus

Hypacrosaurus

Corythosaurus

Lambeosaurus

Prasaurolophus
Barsboldia
Bactrosaurus

UPPER CRETATCEOUS
LOWER CRETACEOUS

Amblydactylus
Probactrosaurus

EARLY CRETACEOUS

Hypsilophodon

Tenontosaurus

Iguanodon

Ouranosaurus
Vectisaurus

IGUANODONTS

LATE JURASSIC

Camptosaurus

HYPSILOPHODONTS

191

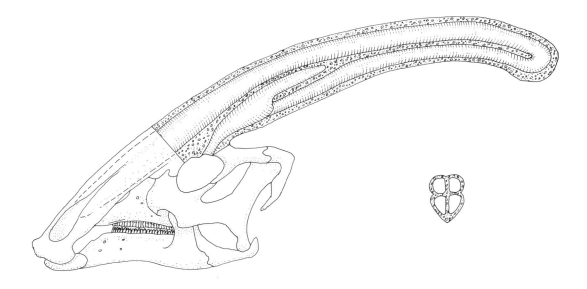

The crest of Parasaurolophus *is shown sectioned in half to illustrate the complex hollow chambers that channelled from its nasal opening and throughout its crest.*

As with all lambeosaur skulls, regardless of the shape of their crest, such hollow chambers may have been lined with tissues in which circulating overheated blood was cooled by the panting actions brought about by heavy breathing in moments of stress. Length of skull, including crest: approximately 1.8 m (6 ft).

which would have a total length of 25 cms (10 ins). The babies looked something like a combination of a scaly lizard with a parrot's head. The skull of one baby was less than 3 cms (1¼ ins) long and yet the teeth showed signs of wear suggesting that it had lived for at least a few days after it hatched. Other than possible protection from a watchful parent, the well-ossified limbs suggest that these tiny babies may have been precocial and, for the most part, had to feed and take care of themselves.

In recent years, it has become appreciated that the social behaviour and parental care among certain of today's reptiles are far more complicated than was once supposed. Croaking sounds from inside nests are known to attract the mother crocodile who assists in reopening the densely covered nest, and guards over the young while they hatch. Crocodiles have been observed using their large and powerful jaws with remarkable care, to gingerly crack the eggshell allowing the baby to emerge more easily. Even after they are hatched, the parent crocodile often stays close to its brood, and desperate croaking sounds from a baby can gain the attention of not only the parent, but other crocodiles as well, which gather close so as to protect the threatened young. One has only to imagine that these baby psittacosaurs that have been found as fossils for some reason failed to have their chirping sounds heeded in time.

The nests of dinosaurs were no doubt very attractive to a broad assortment of predators. Besides smaller carnivorous dinosaurs, other reptiles would have feasted upon the nests at any given opportunity. Varanid lizards would have dug into unattended nests and gorged themselves, swallowing egg after egg just like their living descendants, the monitor lizards, which raid nests of birds, turtles and even crocodiles. The mammals of the Mesozoic may have occasionally fed upon dinosaur eggs, but mostly their diet consisted of grubs, insects, tiny reptiles, rootlets, and vegetation. Their diminutive size and dentition was not well designed for cracking into eggshells to feed upon the eggs which were often as large or larger than the entire mammal itself.

The first dinosaurs' eggs and nests were discovered during the 1920s in Mongolia. Among them were several distinct kinds of eggs that had been laid by different kinds of dinosaurs. There were round eggs about 10 cms (4 ins) in diameter, and oval, oblong eggs from different nests that were of larger and smaller sizes ranging from less than 10 cms (4 ins) to over 15 cms (6 ins). Which kind of dinosaur had laid which kind of egg is for the most part uncertain. One small clutch may not have been dinosaurian at all, and may have belonged to some kind of crocodile. But the elongate oval eggs that have been found the most frequently probably belonged to yet another primitive ceratopsian known as *Protoceratops*. Numerous complete skeletons and scattered partial remains of *Protoceratops* were found in great abundance in areas closely associated around the nests that were filled with clusters of oblong eggs. The skeletons were of many varying sizes, representing various stages of growth. The fully adult *Protoceratops* was still of comparatively modest size for a dinosaur, rarely exceeding 3 m (10 ft) in length. Smaller sub-adults, juveniles and even tiny hatchlings were also preserved. It is quite clear that the abundant skeletons and numerous nests represented a large nesting ground and community of *Protoceratops*.

Lying directly over one of the nests filled with eggs

was a skeleton that was not of a *Protoceratops*. It belonged to one of the strangest and most enigmatic of all carnivorous dinosaurs, a theropod called *Oviraptor*. At first, it might appear that this was the true nest builder which had died while tending to its eggs. But, from the shape of the eggs a different conclusion appears to be more likely. The eggs probably belonged to a *Protoceratops* and, in this case, the *Oviraptor* might have been an intruder that had been caught while trying to raid the nest. Caught in the act and overpowered by an attentive parent, the *Oviraptor* was killed by the bone-crushing bites from the sharp beak and powerful jaws of the *Protoceratops*. Such a scenario is not at all unlikely, as *Protoceratops* was certainly not a harmless herbivore.

Yet another example of the ferocity of *Protoceratops* is seen in one of the most dramatic and remarkable of all fossils which have ever been discovered, that of two fighting dinosaurs still clutching together in their final throes of death. This time, the other victim was not an *Oviraptor*, but was instead a *Velociraptor*, a small theropod very much like *Deinonychus*. During the battle, each had become fatally wounded. And some eighty million years later, the complete, uncrushed and still articulated skeletons of the *Protoceratops* and *Velociraptor* retained virtually their exact positions in which they died. With their limbs entangled, the unrelentless beak of the *Protoceratops* was still clenched around the right forearm of the *Velociraptor*. Hopelessly caught within the beak, the theropod's flailing arms and legs clawed and slashed across the face and deep into the body of the ceratopsian.

Like *Deinonychus*, each hind foot of *Velociraptor* possessed a huge recurved claw. It was one of these claws which had found its way into the neck of the *Protoceratops* where it has remained all these years. Having first killed the ceratopsian, the mortally wounded theropod was too weak to pry itself free from the powerful grip of the closed beak, and quickly perished. Both animals were of nearly equal size, and although it will never be known for sure, it could be that the *Velociraptor* simply underestimated the power of its potential prey. Or was the *Protoceratops* defending its nest from another unlucky would-be egg-stealer?

It is curious that the *Velociraptor* of Mongolia is so remarkably similar to the North American *Deinonychus*, as 25–30 million years separated the two animals. The similarities tend to suggest that the ancestral *Deinonychus* had somehow found its way into Asia from North America during this period of time. Even though the Pacific Ocean lay between the two continents, *Deinonychus* – or its descendants – might have travelled across Beringia which formed a connecting bridge.

Similar indications that Beringia had become a land bridge that provided a passageway between the far east and west can also be seen in the distribution of the bizarre theropod, *Oviraptor*, and the earliest primitive ceratopsians. Like the ornithomimids, the origins of these dinosaurs, the oviraptors and ceratopsians, seem to have occurred during the Early Cretaceous within Asia while it was largely isolated from the rest of the world.

As with the ostrich-dinosaurs, *Oviraptor* evolved from an ancestral coelurosaur. Perhaps they were much more closely related during their earliest origins, but soon both groups had taken independent evolutionary routes. The one characteristic that they both shared was the atrophied loss of teeth and development of a beak in their place. With the major exception of the sauropods, this was the only time that members of the primarily carnivorous saurischians had adapted to a diet other than meat. The ornithomimids and oviraptors were omnivores, whose diet included a certain degree of meat as well as eggs. The omnivore status of the beak-lined jaws on these toothless dinosaurs is indicated by the fact that they had not become deeply pointed and recurved as in today's carnivorous raptorial birds. *Oviraptor* had an additional modification in its mouth quite unlike any other theropod. Two stout, conical palatal teeth (see glossary) had grown in the roof of its mouth which appear to have been used as a wedged point for crushing or piercing large fruits. They also could have been ideally suited for cracking into an egg, at a point where the insides could be swallowed without having to actually ingest the shell, which when empty of its contents was then spat out.

The few examples of *Oviraptor* skulls which are known are either that of a simple non-ornamental type, or an incredibly elaborate crested form. Reminiscent somewhat of a cassowary crest, the prominent protruberance on top of the ornamented *Oviraptor* face may have been used to help part thick foliage that it was moving through. But the primary function of the ornamental headdress may have had sexually attractive overtones and indicated a dominating status between rivaling males. As yet, there are too few examples of crested and non-crested skulls to make a positive interpretation as to whether or not this really represents differences between males and females. But such kinds of identification are rarely possible among dinosaurs.

The abundant remains of *Protoceratops* skulls is one case where there are enough examples to demonstrate a significant sexual dimorphism. Presumably, a more prominently elevated horn over the nose on the more robust skulls with larger and broadly expanded neck frills were those of males. On females, the nasal horn was much smaller while the skull was shorter with less pronounced frills. So perhaps this may have been the same situation in *Oviraptor*, where the more powerful, and ornately imposing skulls signified the threatening character and attractiveness of the male dinosaur.

Although the fossils of *Psittacosaurus* are known only from Asia, it may be significant to its apparent isolation that it lived at least ten million years earlier than *Oviraptor*, *Protoceratops* and *Velociraptor*. It may be that *Psittacosaurus* was somehow environmentally res-

Large congregations of duckbills formed herds that sometimes numbered in the thousands. Shown here, gathering along a river bank, numerous Maiasaura *refresh themselves.* Maiasaura *reached lengths of approximately 9 m (29 ft).*

During the Late Cretaceous, periodic volcanic eruptions were not uncommon in western North America due to the uplift of the Rocky Mountains, known as the Laramide Orogeny. Eruptions plagued the dinosaurs, often killing thousands at a time as shown by the mass graveyards of Maiasaura *in Montana. Also shown in the foreground are two* Quetzalcoatlus, *the largest of flying reptiles which had wing-spans of approximately 15 m(49 ft).*

tricted to Asia, or perhaps its kind had died out before it was possible to radiate across Beringia. But this was not the case with *Oviraptor* and *Protoceratops*, both of which had evidently reached North America by heading east across this northern land bridge. The western counterparts of *Oviraptor* are poorly represented, mostly by fragmentary remains belonging to animals called *Chirostenotes* and *Caenagnathus*, although these two may by synonymous. Among the primitive ceratopsians is the North American migrant, *Leptoceratops*, which is known to have existed sometime after its Mongolian relative. Even though it is remarkably similar to *Protoceratops*, this ceratopsian has a smaller neck frill and no appreciable nasal horn indicating that it may have had a closer relationship to a slightly more primitive ancestor.

DUAL ORIGINS OF DUCKBILLS

The origins and distribution patterns of the hadrosaurs are almost certainly different from those of the dinosaurs which had evolved during the isolation of Asia. The hadrosaur tracks from Peace River clearly indicate that they were already present in North America long before the formation of the Beringia passageway across to Asia. Since their ancestral iguanodonts had already become widely dispersed across Laurasia and even parts of Gondwana it is practically impossible to know exactly where the earliest hadrosaurs appeared. The paucity of fossil remains which might represent the transition from iguanodonts to hadrosaurs further complicates the mysterious origins of the duckbill dinosaurs. In addition, there is the fact that hadrosaurs appear to have evolved more than once from among the iguanodonts.

It has long been thought that all hadrosaurs were direct descendants from a single iguanodont stock, and that the crested hadrosaurs then evolved from the flat-headed forms. But in recent years it has become apparent that both kinds evolved quite independently

from each other, coming from distinctly different kinds of iguanodont ancestors. The flat-headed duckbills (the true hadrosaurs) originated from a dinosaur much like *Iguanodon*. The crested duckbills (more accurately called lambeosaurs), evolved separately from an iguanodont more like the tall-spined *Ouranosaurus*.

Curiously, it appears that hadrosaurs and lambeosaurs evolved at the same time but it is unlikely that their origins were stimulated by the same environmental pressures or opportunities. Early in their history, the two kinds of duckbills were largely segregated from each other living in different kinds of environments. Only much later in their development did a greater interaction between the two groups occur. Then soon after, the lambeosaurs underwent an early extinction, while the hadrosaurs persisted to the very end of the Cretaceous as one of the last of the dinosaurs. It is possible that because of their interaction, some degree of competition resulted which may have contributed to the demise of the lambeosaurs. But, far more likely their extinction was brought about by the loss of their own unique environments which possibly forced the last of the lambeosaurs to intermingle among the hadrosaurs until they could no longer be sustained. Since the hadrosaurs were already suited for a different environment, it may be that the prevailing conditions, different from what lambeosaurs needed, allowed them to survive longer.

Both hadrosaurs and lambeosaurs had lost the

'thumb' spike so characteristic of the more primitive iguanodonts. They had also a greatly increased number of teeth with additional rows of replacement teeth, forming large, magazine-like dental batteries. Constantly replaced throughout the life of the animal, the back up series of teeth formed as many as six rows of teeth stacked upon one another. More than fifty teeth could be in each row, making a total of more than 300 in each jaw, and over 1,200 in the entire mouth. One of the last flat-headed forms is known to have had over 1,600 teeth. As in the ceratopsians, such large dental batteries of replacement teeth became necessary because of the abrasive characteristics of their food.

Although the teeth of hadrosaurs and lambeosaurs are basically similar, there are subtle diagnostic differences. The more obvious differences between the two groups of duckbills are in the rest of their bodies, however, particularly in the structure of their skulls. The pelvises of the two groups are also quite different. This is especially evident on the end of the ischium which is always expanded into a prominent foot-like shape in lambeosaurs, whereas in hadrosaurs it remains a narrow rod to the very end. Typically, the neural spines along the back and tail are usually taller on lambeosaurs and perhaps this is an important environmental trait inherited from *Ouranosaurus*.

197

Colonial nesting grounds of hypsilophodonts were incapable of protecting their young as well as the more imposing hadrosaur giants. Once hatched, the baby hypsilophodonts left the nest, perhaps as a group trailing after a supervising parent. Length of adults were approximately 2 m (6¹/₂ ft).

HEAD CRESTS AND NOSES

The elaborate nasal crests on lambeosaurs were probably related to the environment. These bony extensions from the nasal region were bizarrely ornamental and highly varied in shape. But whether the nasal region was incredibly elongated, as in *Parasaurolophus*, or dome-shaped, as in *Corythosaurus*, the nasal structures were always hollow, and often in convoluted tube-like channels. In contrast, hadrosaurs had a much simpler and conservative nasal development.

On some hadrosaurs, such as *Maiasaura* and possibly *Telmatosaurus*, the nasal openings are still rather small and restricted much like those of *Iguanodon*. But this was a primitive holdover and most other hadrosaurs had nasal openings that were somewhat enlarged across much of the muzzle in front of the eyes. The skulls of hadrosaurs were far less orna-

mental than those of lambeosaurs. And what decorative features that there might have been appear to have had little relationship with the smelling or breathing functions of the nose. The nasal bones are raised into a modest hump on the back of the nose on the hadrosaur *Kritosaurus*, bearing a striking resemblance to the same region on the skull of the rhinoceros iguana currently living on the Haitian islands. Since the nasal hump on the skull of this iguana has a direct relationship to the stout horns that are above its nose, there is good reason to believe that *Kritosaurus* may have also had some similar horn-like ornamentation.

A sub-group of the hadrosaurs called the saurolophines reveals that the lambeosaurs were not the only duckbills with decorative ornamentation. Like other hadrosaurs, the saurolophines had a conserva-

Newly hatched Hypacrosaurus *babies are watched over by their protective parent. Only about 30 cms (1 ft) long, the hatchlings are dwarfed by the adults which were 10 m (32¹/₂ ft), or more in length.*

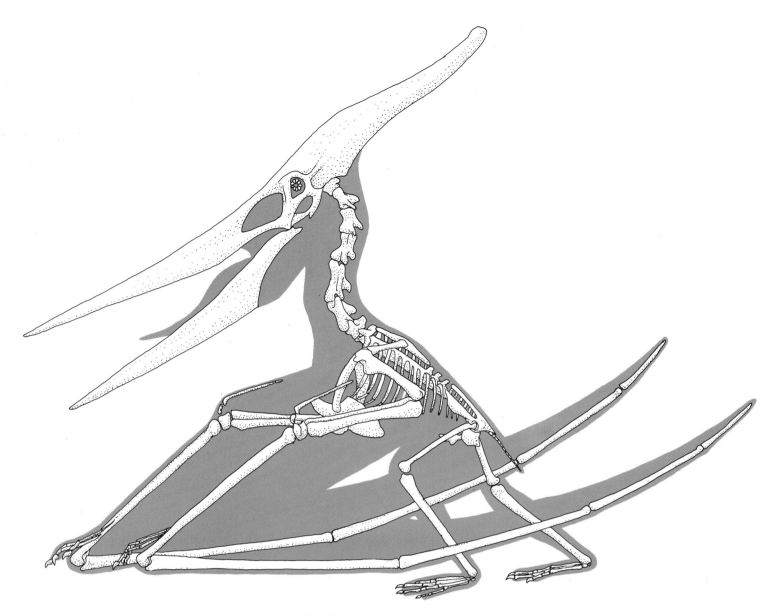

Shown in a quadrupedal stance, **Pteranodon** *used its wings to support its body while moving about on the ground. Wingspan: approximately 8 m (26 ft). (after Eaton, 1910)*

tive development of the nasal region, but they developed long bony projections from the centre of their head, just above their eyes. Superficially resembling a lambeosaur crest, the difference that distinguishes these peculiar duckbills from lambeosaurs and to the flat-headed hadrosaurs is that the saurolophine crests are not hollow, but solid bone.

Since the lambeosaurs and the hadrosaurs (including saurolophines) had such different kinds of nasal structures there have been many interpretations of the functions that they might have served. The solid spiked skulls of saurolophines clearly show that if ornamentation was the only function, there was no need for lambeosaurs to have incorporated the nasal passageway into their crests. So aside from decorative purposes there must have been other functions that the lambeosaurs needed which the hadrosaurs did not. It has been suggested that the complex inner tubing of the lambeosaurs' crests may have enlarged the sensory areas thereby increasing their sense of smell. But if this is so, then it is all the more puzzling why the hadrosaurs did not need to do this as well. Also, most reptiles 'taste' the smell through two nasal pits in the

front of the roof of the mouth. Any increased sensory tissues in the lambeosaurs' crests would have been located too far past these tasting pits to have helped much, if at all. Even though the nasal tubes are long and often overlapping they never return to the tasting pits that are located just like other reptiles, in the front of the mouth. In fact, after passing through various chambers, the nasal passageway finally leads to the back of the throat.

Another theory accounting for the overlapping tubes in the nasal chambers of *Parasolophus* is that they were an enhanced resonating chamber. By exhaling strongly and blowing back through the crest, the lambeosaur would have increased its ability to make loud sounds. This theory is largely based on the fact that the tubes resemble the structure of a musical instrument whose excessive length of tubing requires bending into a more manageable shape. But even if this is so for the *Parasaurolophus*, it hardly accounts for the different shaped crests of other kinds of lambeosaurs. Also, if such a vocalization function were the case for lambeosaurs, would this mean that the hadrosaurs were mute? Alligators and even tiny frogs can be heard for miles using only their throats. So it seems highly unlikely that hadrosaurs were silent. If hadrosaurs could vocalize using only their throats, then it is all the more

puzzling why lambeosaurs would have gone to such extremes to further enhance their vocal capabilities.

Over the years, none of the suggested solutions have very satisfactorily explained the function of the lambeosaurs' crests but to fully appreciate what this might have been, it is important to know more about the environments they lived in. To do this it is necessary to look at the kinds of plants and animals found associated with the duckbill dinosaurs, as well as analyse the sediments in which they are found to reveal the ecological conditions of the environments in which they lived. From such correlations there appears to be a significant difference between the environments of the lambeosaurs and hadrosaurs. These can be divided into the uplands and the lowlands and while they may have shared some overlapping characteristics, such as abundance of water and vegetation, the climates were probably quite different. The lowlands were closer to sea level and consequently were much hotter than the uplands, which were still quite warm and wet.

Regional preferences could be revealed according to where each kind of duckbill is found. Discoveries sug-

gest that hadrosaurs, especially those that retained the small nasal openings, preferred the uplands. They also suggest that larger modifications of the nose on more advanced hadrosaurs, especially the lambeosaurs, was in a response to their living within the hotter lowland environments. If this is so, a functional explanation of the lambeosaur crests should reflect some beneficial adaptation for these duckbills to live within the lowlands. An elaborate sound-making capability or increased sense of smell, hardly seems so essential as to have restricted them to the lowlands. But since both regions had a different climate, with the lowlands being substantially hotter, an additional thermoregulatory control is what was probably needed most by the lambeosaurs. Their tall neural spines may have contributed to this function, in the same manner as suggested for *Ouranosaurus.*

The long necked plesiosaur, Elasmosaurus, *had long teeth that interlocked around prey consisting of small fish. The plesiosaurs were cosmopolitan animals that, undeterred by barriers, radiated into regions of North America, Europe, South America and Australia.* Elasmosaurus *reached lengths of approximately 12 m (39 ft).*

However, this was mostly effective in cooling the body and did not necessarily contribute much to cooling the head and the brain of the animal. This is where the lambeosaur crest could have best been of service.

All dinosaurs, including the duckbills, had a reptilian skin incapable of perspiring and so assist in the prevention of overheating. One well known method to compensate for this is to breathe hard with an open mouth, similar to a panting dog. Crocodiles accomplish the same results by gaping their mouths wide open and letting their exposed blood-filled tissues dissipate excess heat. This method first affects their brain and then the rest of the body. The mouths of all duckbills, however, are unlike crocodiles and gaping could therefore not have been as effective. Lambeosaurs actually had shorter mouths than hadrosaurs, which would have meant they were even less effective at gaping. But if lambeosaurs 'panted' through the nasal passageways within the crests and then out the nose, all of these limitations could have been compensated for. Such 'panting' could have

been accomplished if the inner linings of the hollow crests were tissues filled with blood that circulated to the brain. Deep breathing would have increased as a natural response to either strenuous activity or the overheating of the body due to the climate. Before dangerously overheated blood flowed to the brain, though, it would have first had to pass through the linings within the crest, where it would have been cooled by the rapid circulating breaths of air. As the blood was cooled, the brain was protected from debilitating conditions that would have otherwise led to heatstroke and death. It would appear, then, that the most likely function that can explain the bizarre hollow crests on lambeosaurs can be attributed to their thermoregulatory capabilities in an elaborate method of panting through the nasal passageways.

Much of the success that the duckbill dinosaurs had can be attributed to their unique adaptations of being able to effectively 'chew' their food, as well as their ability to thermoregulate in otherwise harsh environments. But in addition to their highly specialized physical adaptations, perhaps the greatest beneficial factor was their elaborate and somewhat sophisticated methods of behaviour.

GREGARIOUS DUCKBILLS AND MASS GRAVEYARDS

Related to monitor lizards living today, Mosasaurus *was probably totally aquatic. Unlike turtles, they were incapable of coming onto the land to lay eggs. As many as forty species are known from throughout the globe. Mosasaurs reached lengths of approximately 9 m (29 ft).*

In western Montana, vast fields laden with fossil remains all pertaining to a single species of duckbill have been discovered. All of them have been identified as *Maiasaura* and it has been estimated that there are as many as 10,000 of these hadrosaurs in this extensive bone-bed. Since it appears that they all belonged to just one huge congregation of herding *Maiasaura*, this suggests that among all of the dinosaurs, it is the duckbills that became the most populous.

Such an incredible accumulation of dinosaur bones presents the question of how they came to be preserved in this prehistoric mass graveyard. Several clues from the conditions in which the bones were preserved reveal a complex sequence of events that began with a catastrophic volcanic explosion. This volcano was just one of many that often erupted during the tectonic activity of the Laramide orogeny (see glossary)

which caused the continuing formation of the Rocky Mountains. Poisonous gases, choking smoke and the ash fall from the volcano were no doubt instrumental in the death of these particular *Maiasaura*. This could easily account for the mass death, but the bones of these hadrosaurs indicate that the process of fossilization did not stop there. While covered in dirt and volcanic ash, the contorted bodies decayed until only the bones were left. It was then at this point that portions of many of the bones were destroyed while adjacent parts continued to be replaced by minerals, thus becoming fossilized. This peculiar combination of destruction and preservation left some bones, such as those of the leg, with the appearance of having been neatly split across the length of the bone. But such a violent action that would be necessary to actually split these bones certainly did not occur. It is most likely that what really happened was that the missing portions of the bones had been dissolved by the acidic conditions of the soil and ground waters. While the portions of the bones that had settled into the ground were deteriorating, the other parts that were covered by the volcanic ash began to absorb the silica from it, thus contributing to the fossilization process. This ultimately preserved the parts of the bones that had not been affected, and eaten away by the acidic soils.

It was some time, perhaps even soon after this last stage, that another event occurred. Torrential amounts of water inundated the area where the bones originally lay. Picked up and carried along in the fast moving currents of the flooding waters, the bones were transported and scattered across broad plains. In the slurry of mud, volcanic ash and bone, the heavier long bones often settled in directions parallel to the waters' flow, while smaller fragments were carried the greatest distance before coming to rest. The waters receded slowly and the heavier sediments of the mud settled around the bones. Finally, the lightest layer which consisted of the volcanic ash then settled, leaving a thin telltale layer over the surface of the bones.

Some 80 million years have elapsed since this intricate series of events entombed the thousands of hadrosaurs that had been killed by a volcano. Although this is a scenario that may account for how the animals died, there are still far greater questions that remain quite conjectural and mostly unanswered which deal with Maiasaura while they were alive. First and foremost, is the question, why were there so many? Then, did they belong to a structured herd? And how could such great numbers of hadrosaurs have found enough food to adequately fill their needs?

Some things are known for certain, such as there being a size range in these hadrosaurs that represent their ages and stages of growth. The bones within the quarry represent juveniles which would have been about 3 m (10 ft) long, and adults that reached as much as 7 m (23 ft) or more. Intermediate stages of sub-adults were also present. So overall this appears to reflect an entire community, with only the possible exception of babies and the extremely young. Exactly how close members of this community were to each other or how directly interactive they were among themselves remains highly speculative. Was there really any structure to the community? Hadrosaur trackways, such as those from the Peace River, strongly suggest that at least small groups moved about together. There also appears to be a sort of size-regulating hierarchy among duckbills where animals of similar size stayed together. But it is impossible to know if this could still apply to such large groups as in the thousands of Maiasaura.

As with living animals that form structured herds, even of thousands of individuals, there can be benefits as well as detrimental factors. The so-called safety of the herd can be somewhat misleading because casualties and victims from predator attacks still occur: it is

only because there are so many members of such herds that survival is ensured. Also, vast, structured herds normally depend on migration so that fresh supplies of food are available. It might be logical to assume that this was largely true even for the hadrosaurs, but this would depend greatly on what kinds of, and how much, vegetation the hadrosaurs fed upon. In the right conditions, some kinds of vegetation have amazing growth capabilities. If this was so with the preferred foods of hadrosaurs they may not have had to wander far before they could return again to their feeding grounds. Perhaps, then, hadrosaurs did form herds, however loosely structured, that migrated back and forth across great distances. Or maybe their environment was so lush that abundant numbers of smaller groups and even single individuals simply coexisted wandering to and fro within the same somewhat smaller and restricted feeding grounds. In either case, the real success of the hadrosaurs seems to have been in their ability to maintain the large numbers of their kind.

CARING FOR THE YOUNG

Extensive nesting grounds that are attributable to Maiasaura have also been found in western Montana. The nests are spaced at regular intervals of about 6–7 m (20–23 ft) from each other and the intervening space suggests that it was used as a passageway through the nesting grounds allowing the parents safe movement without accidentally stepping on the nests of others. It also might reflect the area that was claimed and even defended by an attendant parent.

Many modern reptiles, such as sea turtles or iguanas, and birds that are known to nest in colonies, usually show very little to no regard to nests or eggs that aren't their own. In fact, disputing battles for the most prized areas often occur. Unattended nests and eggs can be destroyed by another individual which claims the site as its own. It would be quite surprising if this wasn't also true for the hadrosaurs. The uniform spacing between the nests suggests that one of the parents stayed with the nest, possibly defending it from potential aggressors by threatening postures, including vigorous bobbing of the head, noisy chatter from its teeth and beak, bellowing and, if the intruder came too close, even painful nips from its beak.

Certainly the attending parent, if indeed such was the case, never actually sat upon the nest because its weight would surely have crushed the eggs. But if a

CERATOPSIAN FAMILY TREE
The earliest ceratopsian, Psittacosaurus, *evolved from an unknown hypsilophodont ancestor. But from somewhat more primitive ceratopsians, which are as yet unknown, two separate lineages of ceratopsians evolved into forms that possessed either long or comparatively short frills. Skulls not shown to scale.*

EVOLUTION OF THE CERATOPSIANS

SHORT FRILLED

LONG FRILLED

NORTH AMERICA

ASIA (MONGOLIA)

Triceratops

Pachyrhinosaurus

Pentaceratops

Torosaurus

Leptoceratops

Centrosaurus

Styracosaurus

Arrhinoceratops

Anchiceratops

Brachyceratops

Chasmosaurus

Protoceratops

Montanoceratops

Bagaceratops

Psittacosaurus

UPPER CRETACEOUS

LOWER CRETACEOUS

UNKNOWN HYPSILOPHODONT ANCESTOR

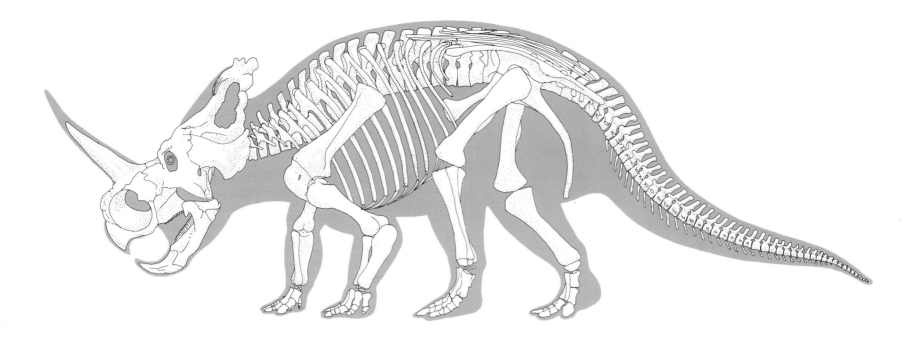

Centrosaurus was a short-frilled ceratopsian from Alberta, Western Canada. It is often found with tendon-like muscular attachments that superficially resemble spikes pointing forwards and down, on top of its frill. These attachments were connected to powerful muscles of the jaw. As with all ceratopsians, located above the hips were ossified tendons that were connected to powerful tail muscles. These tendons were also connected to strong muscles of the back and neck which supported the weight of the skull. Centrosaurus reached lengths of approximately 5.5 m (18 ft). (after Brown, 1917)

parent did tend the nest, it could have provided special care which would have prevented the nest from either becoming too hot or cold. One can envisage the parent as laying in a protective circle around the margin of the nest. The nest itself is covered by layers of decaying vegetation and soil that generate the incubating heat. As the nest becomes too hot from the strong sunlight of the day, the parent may have used itself to shade the nest, or could even have used its head or hands to remove the outer layers of vegetation from the nest thereby preventing harmful amounts of heat from damaging the eggs. There probably would have been periods when the parent hadrosaur left the nest unprotected, but the presence of any nearby duckbill would have greatly prevented predatory reptiles from venturing too close. Such encounters no doubt occurred, with some nests being raided. Also there must have been potential predators that were scared off or thrashed to death by a defensive parent. Although these attentive parental patterns of behaviour are somewhat conjectural, it seems likely that they might have occurred because such behaviour is known among living reptiles such as crocodiles.

More tangible evidence from fossils within the *Maiasaura* nests actually indicate that the hadrosaurs' parental behaviour was more complex than that of crocodiles, and in some respects may have resembled birds. Again, that such behaviour existed should not be too unlikely as the parental instincts could certainly have been just as complex as today's many larger vertebrates that care for their young.

Some of the most intriguing information comes from within one single nest where fifteen baby *Maiasaura* were found. That they were babies in the nest wasn't as significant as the fact that they were nearly three times the size that they would have been when just hatched. The skeletal remains of *Maiasaura* hatchlings found in other nests indicate that they were only about 30 cms (12 ins) long when just out of the egg. But the fifteen baby *Maiasaura* that were all found together in one nest had grown to some 90 cms (36 ins) in length. This clearly indicated that a considerable period of time had elapsed during the hadrosaurs' early life during which they still stayed within the nest. Such behaviour is virtually unknown among modern reptiles, including crocodiles which leave the nest immediately after hatching. What these fifteen partially-grown baby dinosaurs revealed for the first time is that the life behaviour of these hadrosaurs was far more complex than was previously believed possible for reptiles. It strongly suggested that the family structure of the *Maiasaura* included a higher form of parental care, perhaps even in ways more akin to that of some birds.

It seems strange to think of a baby dinosaur as being altricial (or helpless) when just hatched, let alone for any period of time thereafter. Normal reptilian growth and development which results in active, self-reliant hatchlings would appear to be far more efficient than being born rather helpless and dependent upon the parents for food and protection. And yet, if these baby *Maiasaura* actually did not venture beyond the nest, they would have had to have been fed and watched over by an attentive parent until they had grown older

Panic and death struck hundreds of Centrosaurus *as a herd attempted to cross a flooded river channel. Fossilized remains of such ceratopsians have left extensive monogeneric bonebeds which from tooth marks on the bones and shed teeth show that predatory theropods sometimes fed opportunistically upon the carcasses as they accumulated along the river banks.*

and large enough to take care of themselves. Perhaps the supervising parent could have brought vegetation to the nest so that the babies would have something to eat. But they would have had to still fend for themselves while in the nest, because it would have been impossible for the parent to use its own mouth to place food down the mouths and throat of the hungry babies. An adult beak was nearly as wide as a newly hatched *Maiasaura*. Yet if the parent didn't bring fresh vegetation to the nest could it have instead, in similar behaviour to nurturing birds, regurgitated food that it had previously swallowed into the nest, making it available for the babies to feed upon? Even if the parent held its head down within the nest offering the food within its opened beak-lined mouth, it would still have been up to the baby duckbills to feed themselves. So just how helpless were the baby duckbills, and how did they actually eat?

The baby hadrosaurs would have been safest while in the nest with a protective parent nearby. But unless the newly hatched duckbills were helpless, like most baby birds, perhaps they weren't as equally dependent on the parents' provision of food. Of course, this would mean that the baby dinosaurs would have had to have left the nest. But this doesn't mean that they couldn't also return to the nest after feeding else-

where. As for protection, a watchful parent would have been an imposing deterrent anywhere as long as it stayed near its brood. And perhaps what the baby duckbills needed the most from their parents was protection.

Since the fifteen baby *Maiasaura* were virtually all the same size this presents a unique problem. Was there no competition from among the babies themselves? It is common practice for rivalry to occur within nests of birds that produce more than one hatchling. More often than not, this sibling competition results in the death of the weaker, usually younger, birds that are last to hatch. The fifteen baby *Maiasaura* represent only a majority of the eggs that were normally laid within a single nest. As many as twenty-four or -five made up the average sized clutch in a nest. So were there nine or ten younger unfortunates that fell victim to their more powerful dominating siblings? Their tiny bodies may have been tossed outside the nest, which could explain the absence of their smaller skeletal remains being found along with the others. But the missing number in this particular nest may also reflect the casualties that perished along the journey gathering food away from the nest.

Another indication that the fifteen baby *Maiasaura* did, in fact, leave and return to the nest is their size. Having tripled their original size they were fairly large creatures with a body torso that was about as big as an average full-grown chicken. If these partially grown *Maiasaura* were still nest bound, just how big did they have to be in order to become precocial and leave the nest? It's difficult to imagine why, at nearly a metre in length, these baby hadrosaurs would not have been able to be strong enough to be on their own. And perhaps this is the key to their success, that they did not stay alone.

Even though virtually all reptiles can fend for themselves immediately after they are hatched, there is always a high mortality rate among the young. This would have also been true for the hadrosaurs. But what would have served the hatchlings best is additional protection from their concerned parents. In this regard, the level of parental care as displayed by duckbills would be a logical extension of the behaviour that is already well known to exist among crocodilians. Returning to the nest, however, would be unique among reptiles. Perhaps the increased safety for the babies and the additional stimulus for the parent to protect its brood was instigated by having such territorial behaviour and maintaining occupancy at the nest.

In addition to the rather extensive *Maiasaura* nesting grounds in western Montana there have been similar discoveries in the nearby regions of Alberta, Canada and from the distant expanse of Asia. The Canadian discoveries include partially grown individuals not much more than 60 cms (2 ft) long which have been identified as belonging to the crested lambeosaur, *Hypacrosaurus*. The identity of even smaller duckbills from Asia remains unknown except that they probably pertain to the hadrosaur line. Also from Asia, a wide variety of different kinds of baby dinosaur skeletons and partial remains have been found, including theropods, possibly belonging to the tyannosaurid, *Tarbosaurus*; ostrich-mimic ornithomimids such as *Gallimimus*; armoured ankylosaurs similar to *Saichania*; and, of course, the primitive ceratopsians, *Psittacosaurus* and *Protoceratops*. Fragmentary remains of baby theropods are also known from Montana, as are the nesting grounds of primitive hypsilophodont ornithopods, called *Orodromeus*.

It is from these nesting grounds of *Orodromeus* that a somewhat different kind of parental care from that of the *Maiasaura* hadrosaurs can be observed. A full grown *Orodromeus* was a much smaller animal than the hadrosaurs, reaching a length of only about 2 m (6½ ft). This is significant because the nests were placed about 2 m (6½ ft) apart as well, just like a scaled down version of the *Maiasaura* nesting grounds. This space between nests not only left adequate room for

the adults to move freely about but it probably marked the margins of the territory that was claimed by the nesting dinosaur.

As in the formation of the hadrosaur nesting grounds, the *Orodromeus* certainly must have gathered in large, if not huge, colonies to lay their eggs. Again like the hadrosaurs, the preferred nesting areas appear to have been on low-lying islands amid very broad, but shallow alkaline lakes. Perhaps there was some added protection afforded by these islands, but more likely and importantly, the islands provided just the right conditions which would benefit the incubation of the eggs.

It is interesting to note that not only was *Orodromeus* a much smaller and more primitive ornithischian than the hadrosaurs, but that its nesting behaviour was not as elaborately advanced. Unlike the hadrosaurs which constructed large, hollowed-out mounds to house their clutch of eggs, the hypsilophodont *Orodromeus* made a much simpler designed nest. But simple or not, much care was taken in the process. This is seen by the unique spiral pattern in which the eggs were laid. The mother probably moved slowly about in a tight circle, taking a step further after each egg was securely placed upright in the soft sandy soil. Perhaps after all the eggs were laid, the mother dinosaur carefully placed additional coverings of sand or vegetation over the clutch to help in the incubation. The spacing of the nests implies that the adults may have stayed with their nest, providing protection and tending it as necessary.

It was after the baby dinosaurs hatched that a distinctly different behavioural pattern took place. This is conclusively shown by the condition of the eggs after the young entered into the world outside. Unlike the hadrosaur nests in which the eggshells were crushed under the trampling feet and actions from the babies moving about, the emptied eggs of *Orodromeus* remained undisturbed leaving the bottom half of the shell virtually intact. Here is a case where the young had to have been fully precocial, capable of effectively moving about upon leaving the egg. In this case, why they left the nest may be in part due to the small size of the parents.

There is considerable evidence that the nests within the colonies of *Orodromeus* suffered from the attacks of nest-raiding predators. This is shown by the large numbers of teeth that were shed by small theropods while they were feasting upon the helpless prey. The most common of these predacious dinosaurs was a creature called *Troodon*. It wasn't a very large theropod, but *Troodon* was about half again as large as a full grown *Orodromeus*. Even amid an active colony of these hypsilophodonts, the terrified adults would

An underwater view of two drowned styracosaurs floating down a river. Based upon a recently discovered species from Montana called Styracosaurus makeli.

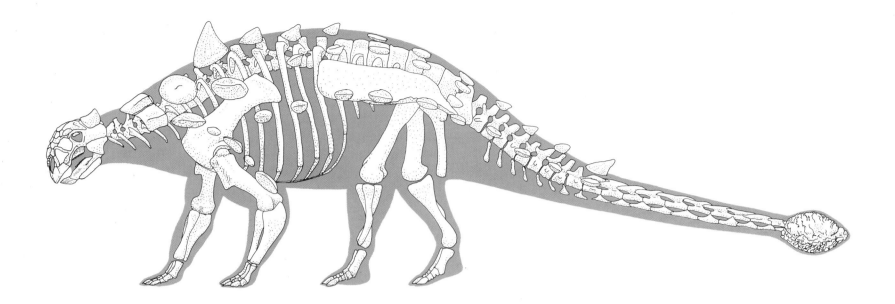

Similar to nodosaurs in having bony armour over their bodies, the ankylosaurs, such as Euoplocephalus, *are distinguished from nodosaurs in always having tail-clubs. Found in both North America and Asia, ankylosaurs may have dispersed between these two continents across the landbridge of Beringia.* Euoplocephalus *reached lengths of approximately 6 m (19½ft). (after Carpenter, 1982)*

have been quite defenceless and could have eventually been driven from their nest of unhatched eggs. There is a decisive absence of bones from adult *Orodromeus* within the nesting grounds, but scattered remains of newly hatched and very young juveniles give vivid testimony that they were often unable to flee to safety. There must have been considerable periods of time where the eggs and young were highly vulnerable and, as evidenced by a few larger tyrannosaurid teeth, even large theropods may have raided the nesting colony upon occasions.

Nesting in large colonies may have created some protection from much smaller predators, but it is clear that the adult *Orodromeus* was mostly defenceless from hungry intruders of the same size or larger. Unlike the larger hadrosaurs which could have been much more formidable opponents to smaller theropods like *Troodon*, the hypsilophodonts had to maintain a different behavioural strategy. Perhaps the adult *Orodromeus* even stayed near its nest, tending to it and protecting it as best it could. But as soon as the hatchlings emerged from the nest the best thing they could do for their survival was run. It is impossible to known from the fossil evidence as yet discovered, but it is tempting to visualize the collective young brood following its parent like baby ducks chasing after its mother across the shore and into the water.

FAST GROWING DINOSAURS?

Most reptiles living today are not especially fast growing creatures in the wild. The fact that the fifteen baby *Maiasaura* were three times the size of when they were just hatched, and still within their nest, has resulted in some speculation that they had a metabolism that was more like birds which are warm-blooded. Certainly there is no reason to assume that the hadrosaurs had metabolisms like the slowest growing, cold-blooded reptiles. But, with regard to its lungs, heart, and digestive abilities there is good reason to believe that the duckbills, and perhaps other dinosaurs, were at least comparable to the development of varanid monitor lizards or crocodiles. Monitor lizards have complex and unusually efficient lungs for a reptile, and the heart of a crocodile is, except for an open septum, extremely close to the development of a four-chambered mammalian-style heart. In fact, it would be surprising if in some ways the biological functions of at least some dinosaurs did not surpass those of these reptiles. But, and this is an important point to remember, being fully warm-blooded in the strict mammalian or even avian terminology may have been the least desirable condition for being a dinosaur. The larger a truly warm-blooded animal is, the more difficult it becomes for it to dissipate its own body heat. If it lived in

A desert sandstorm threatens Saichania, *an Asian ankylosaur from Mongolia. Such sandstorms periodically trapped dinosaurs in deep sands, where their fossilized remains were preserved, entombed through the ages. Juvenile specimens of another Asian ankylosaur, called* Pinacosaurus *which is similar to* Saichania, *were apparently either covered during a sandstorm or perhaps by a landslide from a collapsing sand dune. Length of* Saichania *is approximately 7 m (23 ft).*

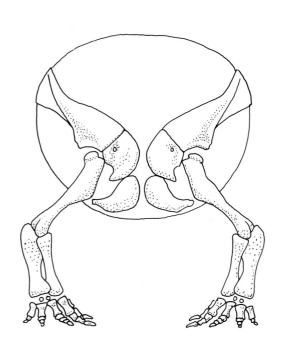

REPTILIAN HIGH WALK POSTURE

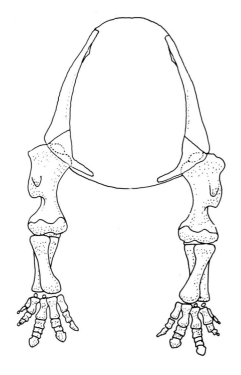

INACCURATE "MAMMALIAN" POSTURE

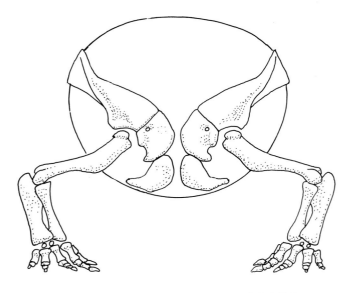

HIGH SPRAWL WALKING POSTURE

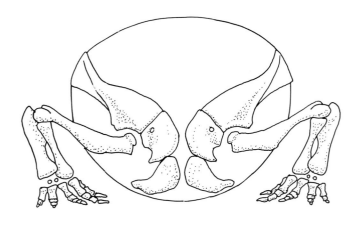

RESTING POSE

CERATOPSIAN LIMB POSTURE

The upright posture of dinosaurs' hind limbs enabled them to have a more efficient manner of locomotion while supporting the animals' weight. However, exactly how the front limbs accomplished an upright posture has remained controversial. As shown above, a popular theory suggests that the front limbs of ceratopsians (and all other quadrupedal dinosaurs) were aligned in a mammal-like posture which were held vertically underneath the animal's chest with the elbows oriented directly backwards. To achieve this posture, the front portions (coracoids) of the shoulder blades are widely separated. Opposing this concept are numerous articulated fossil specimens including horned dinosaurs, duckbills, sauropods, and armoured dinosaurs which demonstrate that the mammal-like orientation is incorrect, and that the shoulder blades met much closer together in the front of the chest.

As shown by these examples of articulated specimens, the proper leg posture works in a reptilian manner with the elbows pointed outwards through the walking cycle. With the upper arms held horizontally, the body was still capable of being held off the ground. As with modern reptiles, combined portions of the scapula and coracoid (absent in mammals) form the shoulder socket which resists the pressures exerted from the legs.

Exclusively sprawling reptiles have shallow sockets. But the deeper the socket, the better the support which in turn allows a more upright posture. Among reptiles, dinosaurs have the deepest shoulder sockets. The scapula portion of the socket faces downwards, while the coracoid portion faces outwards. Altogether, this allows the front legs to achieve a reptilian high walk posture that brought the front feet in line with the hind feet while walking. This also accounts for dinosaur trackways in which the front feet are parallel with the hind feet.

an environment that was too hot for the animal to lose its excess heat, its naturally high metabolism would have been so inefficient as to be life threatening. This would have been especially true for the larger variety of dinosaurs. As cold-blooded reptiles they would have become stable mass-homeotherms which maintained a rather constant and efficiently high body temperature. This reptilian condition could have achieved a simulated higher level of metabolism, functionally close to that of mammals and birds, but the body heat was not generated in the same manner as with these modern warm-blooded animals. Instead of generating its own heat, the mass of the dinosaur's body retained the heat that it absorbed from the environment. Why many dinosaurs became as large as they did was not just because they continued to grow throughout their lives. By becoming larger, their body mass was more capable of retaining the environmental heat. In doing so, the effectiveness of their biological functions increased as the body heat continued to stabilize. As a reptile, becoming a giant was the most efficient way in which a dinosaur could have used its environment to achieve a higher metabolism.

What of the smaller dinosaurs, and especially the young? Despite the popular image of reptiles as being dim-witted, clumsy and slow, most reptiles can be incredibly active, fast moving and even surprisingly curious animals in their optimum environmental settings. Certainly, a captive lizard placed in a cage that is too cool will not be able to actively move about, or, for that matter, even survive for very long. But if the conditions in the cage fit the natural needs of the lizard, or if the same lizard was in its natural environment, then a strikingly different and highly active behaviour would be observed. There are documented cases where reptiles, such as alligators and turtles, have been raised under optimum conditions which surpass that of their naturally wild state. The results have been a dramatic size increase and unusually fast growth. Alligators which may grow only about 30 cms (1 ft) or so a year in the wild, are known to reach lengths of 90 cms (3 ft) in only eight months, and be almost 2 m (6½ ft) long within a year and a half. This being the case, couldn't the fifteen baby *Maiasaura* have been similarly affected by the ideal Mesozoic environment, and also grown much faster than is generally thought possible for a reptile? Usually, the normally slow, or seasonal periodic growth in modern reptiles leaves a series of rings that are observable in a cross section of their teeth or bones, just like a sliced section of a tree reveals its annual growth rings. However, extensive studies of cross-sections of bones from both *Maiasaura* and *Orodromeus* have revealed that these particular dinosaurs may have been growing quite fast because there were no discernible growth rings within their bones.

REPTILES OF THE SEA AND AIR

There certainly were climatic conditions and environments ideally suited for the reptilian physiology and such stimuli also affected many of the other non-dinosaurian kinds of Mesozoic reptiles. For the most part, these other reptiles occupied the air and sea in environmental niches that the dinosaurs failed to exploit.

The air was filled by pterosaurs during the Mesozoic, most of which were generally not large. But during the Late Cretaceous, some of these flying reptiles became giants of the air just as the dinosaurs had become the giants of the land. *Pteranodon* was equipped with a wing-span of at least 7 m (23 ft), and had a bizarrely crested head with a pointed, long toothless beak. But even larger winged reptiles soared their way high among the clouds. The wing-span of *Quetzalcoatlus* may have been greater than 15 m (49 ft) across from tip to tip.

It is not known how and under what conditions the pterosaurs gave birth to their young. Although there have been a few, rare skeletons that are almost certainly those of extremely young and perhaps even infantile pterosaurs, no nests or eggs have as yet been found.

The giant reptiles of the sea are from a variety of different and unrelated kinds of animals. Ichthyosaurs, which had been so abundant earlier in the Mesozoic, had severely dwindled in numbers and became totally extinct during the middle of the Cretaceous. But many other sea-going reptiles persisted until the Mesozoic ended, including huge sea turtles, plesiosaurs and mosasaurs. With such a variety of reptiles in the seas, their existence and the enormous sizes that they attained can be attributed to the optimal environmental conditions in which they lived.

Two of the largest Cretaceous turtles are *Archelon* and *Protostega*. The huge shells that covered their backs had lost much of the solid character, typical of most turtles, and resembled more closely those of a soft shelled, leather-back turtle. One can envisage the giant *Archelon*, like present-day sea turtles, gathering perhaps by the hundreds, or even thousands upon certain stretches of shoreline where they returned to lay their eggs for generation after generation. The great commotion from the female turtles struggling up the beach and digging their nests must have attracted some predators. Even large theropods could have gone after these turtles when they were so vulnerable. While the turtles struggled to lay their eggs and then return to sea, their exhausted and weakened condition only made them more defenceless. Most of the turtles would have made their way back to the safety of the water, but, snatched in the huge jaws of a large theropod, some may have been flipped helplessly onto their backs, or simply dragged further inland to disappear in the darkness of the dinosaurs' domain.

Other sea-going reptiles, such as the mosasaurs, must have had quite different methods of giving birth than did the turtle *Archelon*. Even though the mosasaurs were reptiles, closely related to present-day monitor lizards, they had probably lost the reptilian characteristic of laying eggs. Because they were helpless and virtually unable to move over the land, they almost certainly developed the ability to retain their eggs within their body giving live birth to their young. This would have been much like the process that is known to have existed in the ichthyosaurs. Such advanced and typically un-reptilian behaviour may have also existed in the plesiosaurs, as they, too, were most likely restricted to the water.

Monstrous crocodiles like *Deinosuchus* were more typical semi-aquatic reptiles, capable of coming ashore to lay their eggs. Indications are quite strong that along with abundant food supplies, the environmental conditions that allowed a full-grown *Deinosuchus* to reach lengths of 15 m (49 ft) or more, would have also been similarly instrumental in the gigantism of the dinosaurs. With a powerfully built skull that was considerably larger than a full grown tyrannosaur, such huge crocodiles as *Deinosuchus* along the margins of rivers and swamps must have plagued dinosaurs that ventured too close, or into the same waters.

MONOGENERIC BONEBEDS, RIVER CROSSINGS AND FLASH FLOODS

Waterways throughout the Cretaceous landscape must have been capable of supporting the large numbers and diverse kinds of dinosaurs. But just as animals today can fall victim to the uncontrollable events of nature, so too did changes in the environment take their toll upon the dinosaurs. Torrential downpours of rain resulted in flash-floods which ripped across the valleys leaving destruction in their wake. Any dinosaur unlucky enough to be at the wrong place at the wrong time would have been hopelessly carried away in the violent rushing wall of water. In Alberta, Canada there are extensive bonebeds of ceratopsians that indicate these horned-dinosaurs perished in similar watery catastrophes.

At least nine such bonebeds of ceratopsians have been discovered. In each quarry, only a small percentage of bones were from other kinds of dinosaurs. The horned-dinosaurs not only dominated each site, but every bonebed was represented by a different species of ceratopsian. In each quarry, members of a single herd were somehow caught in a disaster such that the bones were, for the most part, left in a disarticulated and scattered array. Not only are the bones from the same kind of dinosaur, they also represent animals of different stages of growth.

There are at least six kinds of ceratopsians that have been identified, each from a separate bonebed. Among them are *Centrosaurus*, *Anchiceratops*, *Chasmosaurus*, *Monoclonius*, *Pachyrhinosaurus*, and *Styracosaurus*. They were all much larger and more advanced than the ancestral forms of horned dinosaurs like *Protoceratops* and *Leptoceratops* for most of them easily reached lengths of 2 m (6½ ft), and some grew even larger. The general body shape was quite similar and the increase in their size mostly resulted in the greater robustness of their bones, which became stronger to support their heavier, bulky weight. The tails of these larger ceratopsians were shorter than on most other dinosaurs, and they were not equipped with the characteristically tall neural spines that created the narrow crested tail on *Protoceratops*.

The main differences among the ceratopsians were in the features of the skull. Each ceratopsian had their own peculiar and usually quite elaborate assortment of horns which decorated their skulls. There were also considerable size differences in the skulls' bony frill that extended over the neck. Depending on which kind of horned-dinosaur it was, the frill could be either remarkably long or comparatively quite short. Regardless of size, the outer edges were always lined with some kind of ornamental, horn-like projections ranging in size from a low scalloped appearance as on *Centrosaurus*, to the long pointed backward horns of *Styracosaurus*.

Horns of varying shapes and sizes also distinguished the faces of the different kinds of ceratopsians. A single horn above the nose was always present, although it could be either quite large or small. The same is true for a pair of horns located over the eyes that protruded forward. On *Centrosaurus* these orbital horns are so small that they must have been of virtually no use in combat. But on *Chasmosaurus*, and nearly all of the later ceratopsians, the orbital horns had become large and powerful and must have been used in defence against predators, and ritual battles between rivalling males. Much smaller cheek horns stuck out from the back of the jaws. *Pachyrhinosaurus*, however, was quite unlike any other horned-dinosaur in that the top of its skull was thickened into a large convoluted mass of bone in lieu of the normal nasal and orbital horns. *Pachyrhinosaurus* was also unique in that stout horns arose from the mid-line of its frill, and further back on the top were two large horns that pointed out to the sides looking something like a Texas long-horned steer.

The nearly monogeneric bonebeds of these ceratopsians are significant not only because of the diverse kinds which are represented, but because it strongly indicates that the horned dinosaurs stayed together in large herds. Full grown adults existed along with all of the younger ceratopsians, including individuals that may have been even less than a year old. No eggs or hatchlings were found at these sites so it is doubtful that they had come together just for nesting. Many of the smallest ceratopsians that were found would have been far too immature to be con-

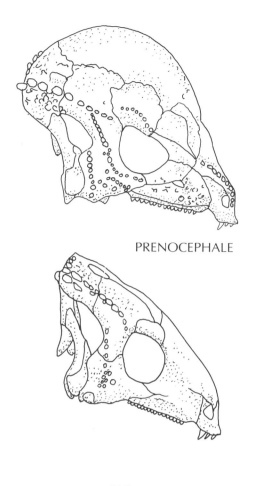

PRENOCEPHALE

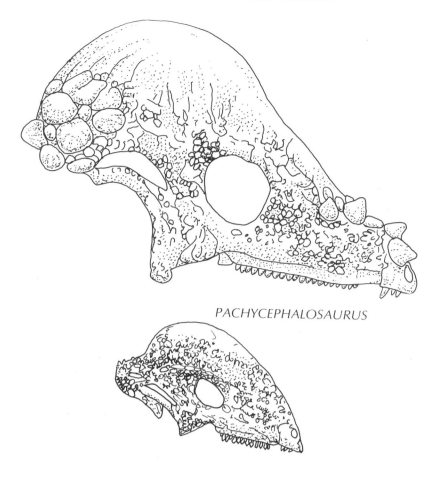

PACHYCEPHALOSAURUS

HOMALOCEPHALE

STEGOCERAS

The bone-headed pachycephalosaurs are known primarily from North America and Asia in Laurasia. During the Late Cretaceous, small forms resembling Stegoceras *were present in parts of Gondwana. These peculiar ornithischians have small fabrosaur-like teeth and broad body proportions that are still poorly known. Skulls shown are at approximate scale to each other. Length of* Pachycephalosaurus *skull is about 60 cms (2 ft).*

cerned with nesting. It is quite clear that the bonebeds were made by herds of ceratopsians occasionally confronted by some natural life-threatening event that, in one brief moment, greatly took its toll upon large numbers of a herd. The *Centrosaurus* bonebed alone may well have been made up of over 300 to 400 animals.

Droughts or disease could account for such large numbers of deaths. It appears, though, that an excess of water played the key role which threatened these horned-dinosaurs. It is conceivable that a vast flood sweeping broadly across a plain could pick up and carry isolated animals, not necessarily representing an actual herd, and later deposit their remains together in one area to form a bonebed. But, at least for the *Centrosaurus* bonebed, and possibly even for the other kinds of ceratopsian bonebeds, the cause of death was more complex and related to the herding structure of these dinosaurs. Flooding waters or largely swollen rivers certainly initiated the disasters, but the natural response for the herding ceratopsians to stay together contributed to much of their loss. It appears that in a state of panic, the ceratopsians may have even been trying to avoid the flooding waters, but when their passageway was blocked by a broad, fast moving river, they were forced into trying to swim across. Their barrel-shaped bodies may have allowed some ability to swim, but deeper and faster moving water would have increasingly hindered them. And if the channel was too wide, they may have struggled until exhausted and then were carried helplessly down the river. The herding instincts to stay together may have continually led the ceratopsians to at least try to stay together, following each other heading across the river. Perhaps many even made it safely across to the other side, but in the confusion some may have lost their sense of direction and swum in circles back and forth following hopelessly misdirected leaders in front of them. Such behaviour was not because of the limited brain capacity often attributed to the reptilian nature of the dinosaurs – such incidents and behaviour is also known to happen among many present-day herding mammals including bison and caribou.

After the ceratopsians drowned, their bodies were carried with the water's current until they were washed ashore along the bends of the river. The stench of their bloated bodies attracted predators which took the opportunity for a free meal. Huge theropods feasted upon many of the bodies, leaving their telltale tooth marks on bones that they chewed on. While gorging themselves, the theropods snapped and crushed many of the bones in their jaws and under their feet as they trampled over the ceratopsians' remains. Many of the bones probably remained on the banks and some, no doubt, were carried away in the bellies of theropods. But still enough were carried further down the river until finally they came to rest in an expansive channel cove where they were then covered by sediments which preserved them as the informative ceratopsian bonebeds.

One of the great mysteries about dinosaurs concerns the ceratopsians and their presumed isolation in North America. If the larger ceratopsians, excluding those like *Protoceratops*, actually lived only in North America then whatever caused their territorial restriction remains unresolved. Adding to the difficulty of this problem is the fact that other kinds of North American dinosaurs living during the same period did succeed in wider distributions. It has been suggested that the particular kind of vegetation that the larger ceratopsians needed to feed upon might not have been readily available in areas leading to distant lands adjacent to North America. But this seems to be a very unsatisfactory explanation because other kinds of herbivorous dinosaurs had no problem in radiating in either direction across the continental connection of Beringia. So why then couldn't these ceratopsians also make their way onto the Asian continent? In the absence of evidence that could explain otherwise, it may be that the answer to this problem is that they weren't isolated in North America. It appears more likely that Asian counterparts to these larger horned dinosaurs probably did exist. In fact, although obviously very rare, there have been recent discoveries in China that may actually prove to be the remains of ceratopsians like those of North America.

LAURASIAN ARMOURED DINOSAURS

One of the herbivorous ornithischians that made its way across Beringia and onto both Asia and North America belongs to a group known as the ankylosaurs. These were strictly quadrupedal animals that had especially thickened scaly hides along their backs, studded with various arrays of knobby and pointed bony scutes (see glossary). In many ways, the ankylosaurs closely resemble the other group of armoured dinosaurs known as nodosaurs. The most readily distinguishable difference between the two groups is the addition of the bony tail club on all ankylosaurs. The tails of nodosaurs always lack such additional armament. Both groups appear to have co-existed throughout much of the Cretaceous, although the ankylosaurs may have been more abundant during the latter part of the period.

Only two ankylosaurs are well known from North America, *Ankylosaurus* itself, and *Euoplocephalus*. Both were rather large, barrel-chested animals: *Euoplocephalus* was some 6 m (19½ ft) long and *Ankylosaurus* reached lengths of as much as 10 m (32½ ft). There are at least six known Asian counterparts to these armoured dinosaurs, some of which more closely resembled the western versions than the others. All of them, including *Sainchania*, *Pinacosaurus*, *Talarurus*, *Tarchia*, *Shamosaurus*, and *Sauroplites*, are from parts of eastern Asia, mostly within Mongolia. Most of them are from very late in the Cretaceous, except for *Shamosaurus* and *Sauroplites* which are among the earliest-known representatives of ankylosaurs, having come from the middle parts of the period. This suggests that their origins came from within Asia and that *Anklylosaurus* and *Euoplocephalus* may have migrated across Beringia from the Far East.

Evidently, the environments in which some of the Asian ankylosaurs lived were near sand dunes. Waterways, including rivers and lagoons, may have been near by, but the rather arid, desert-like conditions bordered the more vegetated areas. Wind storms no doubt shifted the margins between the environmental extremes and it appears that often dinosaurs living in these regions were caught in the moving waves of sand. This may account for such ankylosaurs as a full grown *Saichania* being entombed is soft sands. Also probably trapped during a sandstorm were several juvenile *Pinacosaurus* which huddled together hopelessly trying to wait out the storm only to be buried alive.

Even though the ankylosaurs were exclusively quadrupedal, their musculature, like hadrosaurs, developed long bony tendons for additional strength. But unlike the lattice-like pattern of iguanodonts and duckbills, the ankylosaur tendons remained in simpler linear orientation along the top of the back and last half of their tail. The front half of the tail was without any bony tendons, but this was probably due to the already powerful nature of the muscles in that area as well as the greater flexibility that was necessary to swing the tail club from side to side.

The rounded chest of ankylosaurs is strikingly similar to that which would normally be attributed to semi-aquatic animals such as the hippopotamus. The front legs are similar, too, being powerfully built but rather short with especially stubby feet. One can envisage a somewhat similar lifestyle for the ankylosaurs and hippopotamus as they were and are semi-aquatic herbivores. But any similarities in behaviour are coincidental examples of convergence.

PROBLEMS IN LIMB POSTURE

Many characteristics of dinosaurs may in some ways resemble those of modern mammals. Often stated in the popular press is the dinosaur's ability to have a

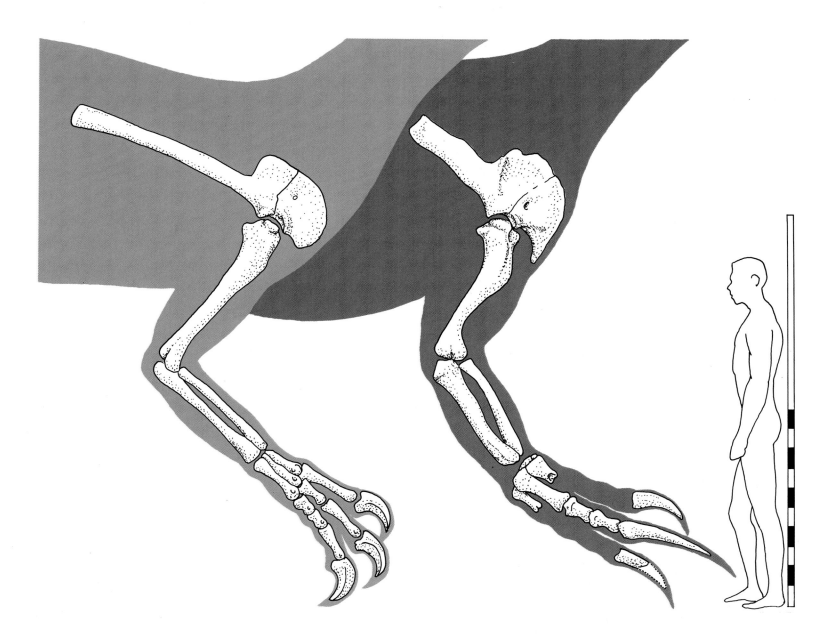

The mysterious saurischians Deinocheirus, *(left), which may be a huge ornithomimid, and* Therizinosaurus, *(right), which may be a segnosaur, are both known almost exclusively by their front limbs. Shown in scale to each other, they are compared to a figure of a full-grown man and 2 m (6¹/₂ ft) scale bar to illustrate the enormous size of these dinosaurs. Notice the size of the claws.* Therizinosaurus *has the largest claws of any known dinosaur.*

fully upright leg posture. But this is only an example of convergence. What is not readily clear is the fact that while dinosaurs certainly may have attained an upright leg posture, they did so in a reptilian manner quite unlike that of mammals. Trackways of quadrupedal dinosaurs have been cited as evidence that the forelimbs were not held out to the sides like sprawling reptiles. But even though this is for the most part correct, the angle in which the front legs were positioned and how the muscles moved them was totally reptilian and not in a typically mammalian fashion.

Dinosaurs achieved such a posture and leg movement in the front limbs by the mechanical perfection of the shoulder socket supporting the attachment of the humerus (the upper 'arm' bone). The shoulder socket, more accurately called the glenoid cavity, is composed of two bones that are closely joined together. The larger bone is the scapula, and the other is the coracoid. Only in reptiles, birds and monotremes (which are the most primitive of living mammals) does the coracoid actually form a considerable part of the articulating surface in the glenoid cavity. On all other higher forms of mammals, the coracoid is greatly

reduced in size and remains only as a small vestigial process used for a muscle attachment, and not as part of the articulating surface of the glenoid cavity. With this bone out of the way, and since the coracoid on mammals lost its original function of being part of the glenoid cavity, this allowed the front legs a greater range of movement and a vertical orientation directly underneath the body. But because reptiles, including dinosaurs, retained the coracoid as a bone which contributed to the glenoid cavity, their front legs could not possibly have functioned or been oriented in the same vertical stance as modern mammals.

But this is not to say that the dinosaurs did not achieve a reptilian version of a fully upright stance, not only with their hind legs but with their front legs as well. As stated in Chapter Three, the upright posture

Three Struthiomimus *flee from the flames of a forest fire. Charcoal strata layers found in Alberta, Canada demonstrates that naturally caused wildfires occurred during the Mesozoic, and perhaps, as today, were set aflame by lightning strikes.* Struthiomimus *reached lengths of approximately 4 m (13 ft).*

of dinosaurs' hind limbs was caused by bringing the hind legs closer to the sides of the body and, in effect, more directly beneath the animal to more efficiently support its weight. However, the front legs achieved a more upright stance by enlarging the articulating surface of both the scapula and coracoid which became thicker and more pronounced, increasing the deepness of the glenoid cavity. This portion of the scapula produced an overhanging ledge that faced more downward, while the corresponding part of the coracoid continued to face out to the side and slightly back. The same development can be seen among many heavier and more terrestrial reptiles living today, although to a much lesser extent. The advantage of a deeper glenoid cavity is quite simply that it creates a stronger mechanical support so that the front leg can have something to push up against when holding the leg more vertically. The deeper the socket, the more vertical the front leg could be held. Only reptiles with very weak and shallow development of the glenoid cavity are true sprawling creatures.

The advantage of having a greater scapular ledge has been cited as the cause which enabled quadrupedal dinosaurs to attain a mammal-like posture of the front legs in a vertical stance. But the fact that this ledge often produces only about half of the shoulder socket is dismissed without explanation. Since the coracoid of these dinosaurs clearly formed so much of the glenoid cavity then the only explanation can be that the outwardly directed part of the socket was necessary because the humerus pushed not only up into the scapula, but also inwards against the coracoid. This means that the manner in which the front legs moved was still in a reptilian style with the elbows pointing outwards throughout the forward motion of the leg. However, with the humerus supported in a nearly vertical position, only the slightest bend in the elbow would have been necessary in order to place the front feet beneath the animal and in line with the hind feet. A crouching, or resting dinosaur that was laying down would have its elbows bent, and facing outwards.

Often shimmering in bright colours, or glowing in shafts of light, the aurora borealis occurs in the skies at higher latitudes of Canada and Arctic regions, including the North Slope of Alaska. Shown are a group of wary Edmontosaurus *hadrosaurs which are cautiously standing their ground as a tyrannosaur approaches.* Edmontosaurus *reached lengths of approximately 13 m (42 ft).*

TRACKWAYS AND IMPROPERLY PLACED SHOULDER BLADES

Much of the confusion which has led to the mammal-like interpretation of the front legs of dinosaurs has been because of the narrow trackways made by quadrupedal dinosaurs, and the usually improper placement during reconstruction of the scapula and coracoid against the rib-cage. All too often the coracoids are placed much too far apart, so that the coracoid is facing almost directly forwards. This causes its articular surface of the glenoid cavity to face backwards and slightly inwards. But many exceptionally well-preserved, fully articulated skeletons have retained their original orientations which clearly demonstrates the accurate position of coracoids. In life, the coracoids would have been placed in a reptilian orientation, being extremely close together, literally joining at the middle of the animal's chest. And in this proper orientation the glenoid cavity faces downward with the portion of the scapula, and the part made up by the coracoid would face mostly outwards and only slightly back. Working in this reptilian orientation, the front legs could have easily made

trackways in which the front feet were held closely underneath the body in line with the hind feet. At least one trackway attributed to an *Iguanodon* shows the front feet as being in line with the hind feet, but elsewhere in the series, the prints left by the front feet are considerably farther out to the sides. So, it appears that because of the reptilian manner in which the forelimb worked it was possible, at least at times, for some dinosaurs to walk with their front legs angled outwards.

Since the front legs of quadrupedal dinosaurs did not move in the same manner as modern animals it is hardly possible that they could have run or galloped in the same fashion. But this does not mean that they were less efficient or incapable of moving quite fast when they wanted to. In fact, at least one documented study reveals that some of today's sprawling lizards require less energy output and are actually more efficient than modern mammals and birds of the same size. If the same was true for the dinosaurs then it is

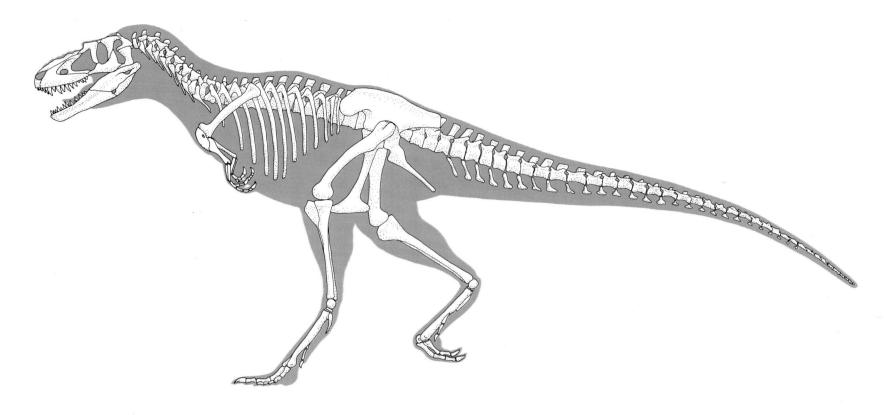

Albertosaurus is known from North America, and was a member of the Laurasian family of Cretaceous theropods called tyrannosaurs. Albertosaurus *had more gracile arms than* Tyrannosaurus, *and was slightly smaller and more slender overall. Animal's length: approximately 9 m (29 ft).*

highly probable that they had a strong endurance and could, when necessary, have been highly active, and to some degree, even rather fast moving animals.

BONE-HEADED FABROSAURS

It is an understatement to say that much of the dinosaurian world is still largely unknown and unfortunately poorly understood. Regarding their life-behaviour, body postures, physical biology and global distribution much tangible evidence exists from their fossils, but even more remains speculative awaiting further discoveries to bring new sources of data. No doubt, in the future there will be new kinds of dinosaurs discovered that today lie hidden in the rocks, totally unknown to science. Such exciting discoveries will fill in many gaps about certain kinds of dinosaurs that are at present only known by tantalizing fragmentary remains; remains that are so incomplete as to keep the shape of the animal's body an unresolved mystery.

One such group of dinosaurs is the ornithischian pachycephalosaurs, the so-called 'bone-headed' dinosaurs which descended from the fabrosaurids. The skulls of these dinosaurs give the illusion of their having been large brained creatures. But the characteristic high-brow dome shape of their skull is actually made

of solid bone, sometimes as much as 25 cms (10 ins) thick, and underneath this bony mass is where the typically small reptilian brain was housed. Around the base of the skull's dome, there are often knobby clusters and bony spikes that encircled the head like a decorative wreath. Even though the thickened dome of the skull is not an uncommon fossil in some regions, such as the Alberta badlands, the rest of the body of these peculiar dinosaurs remains largely unknown. No doubt, the thickened skull is commonly preserved because of its unusual durability. But its skeleton, or even parts thereof, are so rarely preserved that even compiling information from the partial remains of the various known species still leaves much of what the actual animal looked like a mystery.

The earliest pachycephalosaur is *Yaverlandia* which comes from the Early Cretaceous of England. From this moment on, it is conceivable that such dinosaurs spread at least through much of Laurasia. There is also a close similarity between many Late Cretaceous pachycephalosaurs from Asia and North America which suggests that their distribution interchanged between the far east and west, travelling across Beringia.

One of the largest theropods, Tyrannosaurus, *wanders across a steamy, morning's haze clouding the landscape of what is now Montana, in the United States of America. A crested* Pteranodon *soars above them in the distance.* Tyrannosaurus *reached lengths of approximately 14 m (45^1/$_2$ ft).*

The teeth of the pachycephalosaurs are surprisingly small and primitive for such large dinosaurs living so late in the Mesozoic. Once even thought to be a primitive form of ornithopod, their ancestry actually stems from even more primitive ornithischians with fabrosaurid affinities. This is also true for the armoured nodosaurs and ankylosaurs which retained similarly primitive fabrosaurid teeth. But although these dinosaurs shared a distant fabrosaurid ancestry, it appears that the pachycephalosaurs may not have had any bony scutes over their bodies. Instead what protection there was, may have been concentrated only on the thickened, spiked skull. It has been suggested that the thickened skulls of the bone-headed dinosaurs may have been used for inter-species combat where rivalling males clashed their heads together, like rutting horned rams. Such vigorous displays may have occurred, but it might be more likely that intensive shoving matches were the norm as such behaviour is quite common among reptiles. However, unless the female pachycephalosaurs were equipped with a distinctly different kind of skull, presumably less thickly developed, the function of the thick bony skull may have been for some other function.

ENIGMATIC GIANTS

There are other strange dinosaurs that are as yet poorly known by only partial remains, sometimes just a skull, pelvis or limb. Among the most surprising of these little known dinosaurs are those belonging to a group called the segnosaurs. Several individuals are known from only fragmentary remains which collectively suggest that they are aberrant descendants of prosauropods that persisted until the end of the Cretaceous. Among the currently known segnosaurs are *Segnosaurus* itself, *Erlikosaurus*, *Nanshiungosaurus* and possibly *Therizinosaurus*. These are all from Asia, but undescribed materials from Alberta that are currently under study may represent a small segnosaur. This suggests that these strangest of dinosaurs crossed over onto at least the two northern continents of the far east and west.

Totally unlike the prosauropods which led towards the evolution of the sauropods, the segnosaur lineage retained small, spatulate, peg-like teeth lining the length of their jaws, while the front of the upper snout was toothless and modified into a cropping beak. The segnosaurs are definitely saurischians because they totally lack any development of a predentary bone. Therefore, the uniquely ornithischian-like pelvis of segnosaurs which has a backward-oriented pubis is a convergent development. This was probably caused by an increased herbivorous digestive system that necessitated moving the pubis further back from the normal saurischian placement. The hind feet are equipped with four toes with long narrow claws indicating that their ancestry began not from a theropod

with three toes, but from some kind of prosauropod. The unusually wide pelvis suggests an exceptionally wide body, while the neck is of modest length and shows little tendency towards becoming like that of sauropods. Altogether, the segnosaurs remain one of the most bizarre and enigmatic of all dinosaurs.

Although some of the remains attributed to the segnosaurs are from small and modest sized animals, there is one partial front limb which, if indeed it can be attributed to the segnosaurs, represents a segnosaur of enormous sauropod-like size. This huge dinosaur is called *Therizinosaurus*, and from the rather slender shape of the forearm it appears that it may have been a semi-bipedal giant. The claws on the hand are the largest known of any dinosaur, reaching a length of some 80 cms (32 ins) or more. Only slightly recurved, the claws were definitely not raptorial (see glossary), or used for tearing into the flesh of animals. In keeping with the herbivorous diet of the segnosaurs, one can envisage the huge *Therizinosaurus* as sitting below trees using its front legs and giant claws to pull down branches of foliage so that it could then more easily feed. So if this interpretation is correct, *Therizinosaurus* (and perhaps segnosaurs in general) may have been gigantic prosauropods that had become a reptilian version of a giant ground sloth.

Yet another giant set of forelimbs is known from a dinosaur from Mongolia, known as *Deinocheirus*. Aside from only a few fragments that are mostly ribs, the rest of the animal remains unknown. The scapula and coracoid together measure over 1.5 m (5 ft) long, and the adjoining forelimb was some 2.5 m (8 ft) long. The claws alone were 30 cms (1 ft) long, powerfully built and deeply recurved. *Deinocheirus* was like *Therizinosaurus* in that they were both saurischians, but instead of coming from a prosauropod or sauropod ancestry, the *Deinocheirus* was definitely a theropod. The huge size of its arms might therefore conjure up images of a horrifying carnivorous monster, but while certainly being a monster in size, the shape of the forelimb and the scapula, in particular, closely resembles the omnivorous group of theropods, the ornithomimids. Perhaps here with *Deinocheirus* the tendency towards herbivory excelled and, as with the sauropods, the end result was a dramatic increase in size. If so, then *Deinocheirus* was the only theropod to have become a giant plant eater, paralleling the prosauropods like *Therizinosaurus*, and the sauropods.

NATURAL EVENTS OF FIRE AND LIGHTS

Other Late Cretaceous ornithomimids from Mongolia are *Gallimimus* and the somewhat peculiar *Garudimimus* which has a small, pointed crest on its skull. Outside of Asia, the only other ornithomimids are from North America which include *Ornithomimis*, *Struthiomimus* and *Dromiceiomimus*. Although these are fairly

rare dinosaurs there was at least one discovery in which two of these ostrich-mimics were found crouched together laying side by side.

It is always puzzling as to what could have caused the deaths of the same kinds of animals that are found-preserved so closely together. In this particular example, it is unlikely that they were caught in a watery disaster such as a flood because of the well-articulated state of their skeletons and orientation to each other. Another natural cause of death that occasionally threatened such dinosaurs as these was fire. Remains of forest fires preserved as distinct sedimentary layers from the Cretaceous strata have been found in the Alberta badlands. At first looking like an ordinary, thin coal seam, a closer inspection revealed that the blackened layer was made up of burnt cinders and ashes of wood and vegetation. However, neither the skeletons nor the surrounding soil showed any indications of their having been burned or necessarily related to a forest fire. But certainly, just as with the many present day animals that are caught and perish in such incidents, at times the dinosaurs probably faced the same fates.

Just as natural catastrophes such as fire and flood, have occurred throughout the ages there were other natural events that must have occurred much as they do even today. In the higher latitudes, the elaborate display of shimmering and often colourful lights caused by the earth's magnetic field resulted in an aur-

NEXT PAGE

During a fierce battle between two rutting Triceratops, *the weaker male is overcome by the dominant male which sends the defeated animal toppling over a stream bank.* Triceratops *reached lengths of approximately 9 m (29 ft).*

The pathway between points A and B demonstrates the route across Beringia in which dispersal between Asia and North America was possible for Late Cretaceous dinosaurs. Note the barriers of the Turgai Strait and the Interior Seaway. The pathway from C to D represents the dispersal route taken by duckbills heading south from North America, across the intermittent barrier of the Tethys Sea, and down into South America. In the opposite direction, travelling from D to C, the titanosaurs found their way northward back into Laurasia. The pathway from E to F allowed abelisaurs (as well as titanosaurs) in Africa to cross past the Tethys Sea and enter into Europe.

ora borealis. It seems likely then that dinosaurs found on the north slope of Alaska, such as tyrannosaurid theropods, the duckbill *Edmontosaurus* and even the ceratopsian *Pachyrhinosaurus*, all walked under the brilliant shows of light of the northern sky.

Edmontosaurus is among the largest of the hadrosaurs and its fossil remains have been found throughout much of western North America. Its presence along the north slope of Alaska is the closest placement of dinosaur fossils to Beringia which further demonstrates the distribution path which the hadrosaurs and lambeosaurs used to cross between the eastern and western continents. Closely resembling, and

possibly even co-generic with *Edmontosaurus*, is the largest known duckbill, *Shantungosaurus*. It is a huge animal, comparable to the sauropods for size, reaching a total length of 15 m (49$^1/_2$ ft). The tail of this giant duckbill was immensely powerful and deeply narrowed like a giant flattened paddle which may have been used to help swim past the broken islands or coastline of Beringia. However, this land bridge sufficiently existed for the less aquatic dinosaurs to use it.

The presence of the *Pachyrhinosaurus* so far north in Alaska also suggests that these ceratopsians and perhaps other kinds of ceratopsians could have gone still further east, across the connective landmass of Beringia and onward into Asia. Since so many kinds of dinosaurs must have done so, it would be quite inexplicable if the ceratopsians were somehow blocked at this point.

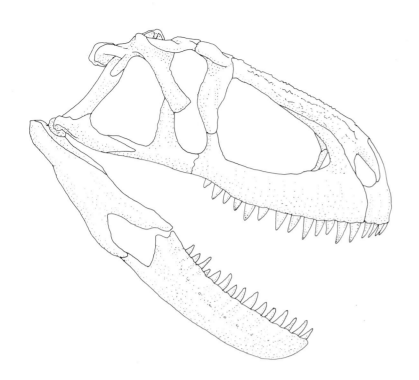

GIANT THEROPODS OF LAURASIA

Among the many large carnivorous theropods known from Asia, most appear to have strong affinities with the tyrannosaurids. One of the most primitive forms is the little known *Alioramus* which comes from near the middle of the Cretaceous. Its skull is only partially known, but is apparently quite long and low compared to later tyrannosaurs. The top of the nasal bones are peculiar to *Alioramus* which have several raised rugose curved ridges that give an ornamental appearance. From the Late Cretaceous the most abundant theropod is *Tarbosaurus* which closely resembles the infamous *Tyrannosaurus rex* of North America.

Although the centre of the tyrannosaurs' evolution is unclear (it was possibly in Asia), what is much more certain is that they represent a northern group of theropods endemic to Laurasia. It was only near the very end of the Cretaceous that they migrated onto the Gondwanic continents, of which South America was the most likely.

A greater diversity of tyrannosaurs is known from North America than from Asia. At a length of over 12 m (39 ft), *Tyrannosaurus* is certainly the largest of the carnivorous dinosaurs from the Cretaceous. It is also the closest related to, if not co-generic with, the Asian form, *Tarbosaurus*. Other tyrannosaurs from the west currently do not have such counterparts from the far east.

Daspletosaurus and *Albertosaurus* are two distinct types of tyrannosaurs of North America. Both attained lengths of some 9 m (29 ft) or more, but *Daspletosaurus* was much more robust and, in this respect, similar to *Tyrannosaurus*. Although the forelimbs are still dra-

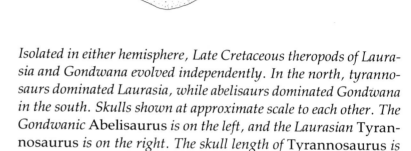

Isolated in either hemisphere, Late Cretaceous theropods of Laurasia and Gondwana evolved independently. In the north, tyrannosaurs dominated Laurasia, while abelisaurs dominated Gondwana in the south. Skulls shown at approximate scale to each other. The Gondwanic Abelisaurus *is on the left, and the Laurasian* Tyrannosaurus *is on the right. The skull length of* Tyrannosaurus *is approximately 1.3 m (4 ft).*

matically reduced in size, *Daspletosaurus* is notable for having the longest forearms among all of the tyrannosaurs.

The arms of *Tyrannosaurus*, due to their fragmentary and largely unknown status, have been in the past incorrectly reconstructed based upon the smaller and much more gracile arms of *Albertosaurus*. However, a recent discovery from Montana has now revealed that the arms of *Tyrannosaurus* are considerably more robust and must have been much stronger than previously thought. In comparison with these two larger and more heavily built tyrannosaurs, *Albertosaurus* was a more slender version which may have made it the most agile of these theropods.

Possibly the smallest of the tyrannosaurs is *Nanotyrannus*, which is known only by a skull. The fairly small size of approximately 60 cms (2 ft) in length may reflect some degree of immaturity. It is also possible that its relatively small size may reflect its primitive nature. Unlike all other tyrannosaurs from the Late Cretaceous which had more robust and thickened teeth, *Nanotyrannus* still had slender, blade-like teeth which clearly indicates its primitive status among the last of the tyrannosaurs with which it co-existed in the final days of the Mesozoic.

The distribution of the tyrannosaurs demonstrates more than the existence of the land bridges connecting continents. It also indicates that they followed specific

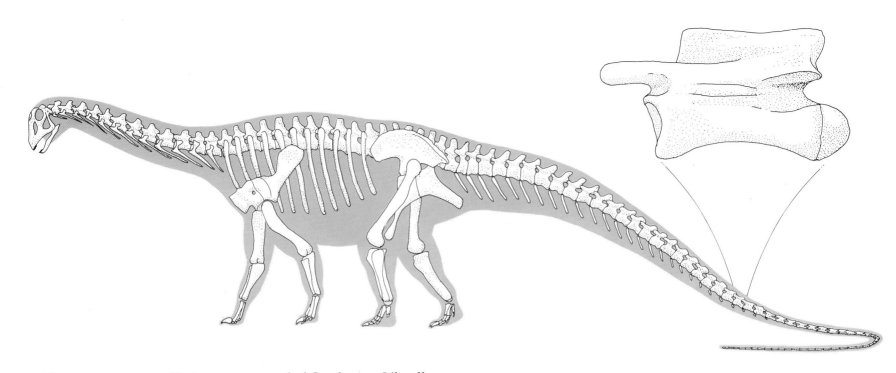

Titanosaurus was a Cretaceous sauropod of Gondwana. Like all titanosaurs, it had tail vertebrae which were deeply cupped in the front, and articulated with a rounded condyle on the back of the preceding vertebra. Titanosaurus *reached lengths of approximately 9 m (29 ft). (after Huene, 1929)*

kinds of animals which they preyed upon as their preferred food source. The great abundance of duckbills certainly must have satisfied much of the tyrannosaurs' dietary needs. As the duckbills became more widely distributed, radiating across distant lands, they continued to attract the tyrannosaurs which trailed after them. Both lambeosaurs and hadrosaurs are found in Asia and North America, so it is not surprising that tyrannosaurs are also found on each of these continents.

The positive identification of specific co-generic duckbills which are definitely known from both the far east and western continents, is as yet rarely possible. *Saurolophus* is one of the best examples of the same kinds of duckbills which were inhabiting both of these continents and it maintains the distinction of being preyed upon by tyrannosaurs in both Asia and North America. The remains of this particular duckbill which are known from Mongolia are virtually identical with those that have been found in North America. *Saurolophus* is distinguished by a prominent solid bony spike which projects backwards from the top of its skull. The bony spike may have supported a fleshy crest, much like that of the present day basilisk lizard, which is both ornamental and a contributing factor in its thermoregulation. However, the head spike was not used in its defence against the predatory theropods.

Tarbosaurus from Asia, as well as the North American *Tyrannosaurus*, *Daspletosaurus*, *Albertosaurus* and even *Nanotyrannus* must have preyed upon *Saurolophus* and the various kinds of duckbills that co-existed in their environments. However, the abun-

dance of duckbills would not have prevented any of the other kinds of dinosaurs from also becoming the prey of hungry tyrannosaurs. Surely the tyrannosaurs would have made a meal out of any animal that crossed its path. Ceratopsians were nearly as abundant as the duckbills, and they must have at times been hunted by the giant predatory tyrannosaurs.

FRILLS, AND HORNS OF OFFENCE AND DEFENCE

The elaborate array of horns and protective bony shield above the neck of the ceratopsians may have played an important function in the defence against the tyrannosaurs. It is easy to see how a confronted horned dinosaur could have used its armament to protect itself. However, the function of defence was probably only one of many functions that the horns and bony neck shield provided for the ceratopsians. The neck shield was also designed to increase the area of certain muscle attachments which increased the power of the jaws. In addition, with the head tilted down, the horns would have been more horizontal and the neck shield would have been raised higher giving the illusion of an even larger animal. Such a pose of the head may have assisted some in defence against predators, but it would have been as effective or even more so in ritualistic battles of domination between their own kind. The piercing blows of horns during such battles apparently caused terrible wounds that later healed in the neck shields of some ceratopsians such as *Pentaceratops*, *Torosaurus* and *Triceratops*. Such healed wounds indicate that vicious battles, probably between rutting males, was part of the ceratopsian lifestyle. Skulls with broken horns that continued to heal also show that battles among their own kind existed. If such wounds occurred during a battle with a tyrannosaur it is very doubtful that the ceratopsian would have been successful in living long enough to heal its wounds. So, battles between males for sexual dominance is one of the functions of the horns and neck shields. Evidence from monogeneric bonebeds indicate that different kinds of ceratopsians stayed closely together among their own kind which implies that they had little tolerance of ceratopsians of other species. Territorial disputes between different kinds of ceratopsians were probably a result of the naturally aggressive temperament of the horned dinosaurs.

The eyes of the horned dinosaurs were not directed forwards and they did not have binocular vision. Instead, the eyes faced laterally out to the sides. In some cases, as in *Triceratops*, they were blocked from looking forward by a protective ridge of bone that housed the eye. A side to side movement of the skull would have been the only way for the ceratopsians to judge the proper distance between itself and its opponent. Such movement would have also been a threatening sign of aggression, like the vigorous defensive head bobs that many present day lizards demonstrate in times of combative stress.

A battle between two ceratopsians may have consisted primarily of bluffing and encircling each other while giving threatening sideways tosses of the head. This would have been intimidating while enabling each a better view and estimate of the distance to its opponent. As the confrontation grew more intense, the heaving charge of the more aggressive horned dinosaur would burst forward against the other. The horns would have clacked loudly as the animals slammed their heads against each other. The three horns of *Ticeratops* could have locked into a position where they remained entangled during a brutal shoving match against the horns of the adversary. Such behaviour could have gone on for extensive periods of time as long as the endurance of the animals lasted. The outwardly directed elbows of the front legs would have stabilized the animals' bodies against the shoving forces while they stepped back and forth, turning around in circles. The power of such huge animals must have routinely resulted in injuries such as those seen in so many ceratopsians. Only when the weaker of the two was overcome, with its efforts thwarted, and eventually driven off did such battles finally come to an end.

It may be that the ceratopsians that suffered the battle wounds from its own kind pertain to the males of its species. But as there is little or no size distinction of the horns between male and female ceratopsians, it would appear that they were necessary weapons of defence which both sexes had to utilize against the giant predatory tyrannosaurs. It also implies that the horns as well as the neck shield may have played a thermoregulatory role for the animals. This appears to be especially likely with regards to the bony frill which has a pronounced vascular pattern, mostly on the upper surface of the shield. There, the circulating blood would have been either warmed in the sun, or cooled in the wind as the animal positioned itself appropriately.

Triceratops is often regarded as the last of its kind, and among the very last of the dinosaurs. It is interesting that the remains of *Triceratops* are known from only North America. They ranged from Alberta, Canada across the United States and even down into Mexico. As with the possible, but questionable distribution of ceratopsians across Beringia and into Asia, it is an unresolved puzzle as to whether or not the ceratopsians, and especially the last of them including *Triceratops*, could have made their way across a southern land bridge connecting North and South America during the last part of the Cretaceous.

Fragmentary remains that were described during the late 1920s may represent a ceratopsian from Argentina called *Notoceratops*. These include a few possible limb elements, and a portion of a lower jaw which is the only known diagnostic piece. If these fragments have been correctly identified, this indicates that ceratopsians did indeed migrate from the northern continents, travelling across a central American land bridge and far into South America. Unfortunately these fossils are now lost and are known mostly from a series of rather loosely drawn sketches. Due to the fragmentary condition of the jaw there have been some doubts raised about whether it pertains to a ceratopsian or perhaps a duckbill dinosaur. In either case, this would still suggest a migration of northern dinosaurs that eventually populated this part of Gondwana. What could resolve this problem remains hidden deep within the jaw. The sketches, as well as a written description, indicate that there was still a series of teeth held in place within the jaw. But neither of the references provide a clear enough description of the teeth for a positive identification. But because ceratopsian teeth are so distinctively different from those of a duckbill, even a single tooth should have revealed which kind of dinosaur the jaw was from. It is doubtful, then, that the original inspection could have resulted in such an obvious error. Yet until the missing jaw can be found and re-examined the mystery of South American ceratopsians remains unresolved.

DUCKBILLS MIGRATE SOUTH

Other kinds of northern dinosaurs found in South America make it not unlikely that some of the last ceratopsians ventured south. The most notable of these immigrants are the hadrosaurs *Secernosaurus* and *Kritosaurus*, and possibly a lambeosaur with tall spines that is as yet unnamed. The skeletal remains of these dinosaurs are rather fragmentary, but clearly are those of duckbills. Numerous fossil trackways attributed to duckbills are further evidence of their presence throughout much of South America. The sudden appearance of these fossils during the last few million years of the Cretaceous can best be explained as representing a wave of northern immigrants that ventured into South America across a chain of islands, or an actual land bridge, across Central America.

Other Late Cretaceous dinosaurs that emigrated from Laurasia into the southern hemisphere may include the armour-studded nodosaurs which have been found on the coast of California and the distantly remote regions of Antarctica. The bone-headed pachycephalosaurs may also be immigrants from the northern hemisphere as they are represented by *Majungatholus* from Madagascar and possibly by undescribed forms from South America. Based upon fragmentary fossils, there are clues that it is likely that the huge tyrannosaurs followed as far as South America trailing after the southward bound duckbills and other relocated dinosaurs.

ABELISAURS RADIATE NORTHWARDS

The tyrannosaurs then, may well have entered into South America during the latest part of the Cretaceous. If they did, together with all of the immigrating dinosaurs from the north, they were entering into a different world still alive with sauropods. Also, in the southern hemisphere there were uniquely different kinds of theropods which had evolved independent of the influences of the tyrannosaurs in the northern hemisphere. These Gondwanic theropods were the abelisaurs, the relatives of the aberrant horned *Carnotaurus* from South America.

Comparatively little is known about the abelisaurs although they were the dominant predatory theropods probably throughout Gondwana for virtually the entire Cretaceous. The Early Cretaceous *Carnotaurus* is by far the most completely preserved and best known of the abelisaurs. Partial skulls and vertebrae of later abelisaurs are known from Argentina, as well as India and the southern part of France. From Argentina there is a huge fragmentary skull of *Abelisaurus* which is as big as most tyrannosaur skulls, reaching nearly 1 m (3 ft) in length. Unlike *Carnotaurus*, the skull of *Abelisaurus* does not have prominent horns above its eyes, and its muzzle is not as short compared to the bull-dog look of the horned theropod. *Genyodectes* is another large theropod from Argentina which is almost certainly an abelisaur. It is known by only fragmentary parts of the skull, which share similar characteristics with *Carnotaurus*.

From India, another probable abelisaur is also known from a partial skull. The classification of this animal, called *Indosuchus*, has been very difficult in the past because of the few abelisaurs that were available for comparison. However, new discoveries during recent years have shed more light on this problematical theropod. It is clearly not a tyrannosaur as was supposed earlier and it appears that *Indosuchus* is not a Laurasian form, but instead represents a Gondwanic theropod.

Even though the fossil record is comparatively sparse for the Cretaceous theropods within the southern hemisphere, there are indications that the evolution of the abelisaurs produced a highly diversified array that spread throughout Gondwana. The abelisaurs became the dominant predatory theropods in the southern hemisphere, taking over the roles not only of the larger carnosaurs, but also as smaller theropods that were functionally equivalent to the coelurosaurs. This is rather astonishing because of the remarkable diversification and success of the coelurosaurs that prevailed in Laurasia. But, perhaps due to some competitive edge that the abelisaurs had over the coelurosaurs, the abelisaurs apparently displaced even the smaller theropods with their own variations.

Originally described as a coelurosaur, *Noasaurus*, known from Argentina, is actually a peculiar small abelisaur. Its true affinities were not realized until after the discovery of *Carnotaurus* which more clearly demonstrated the aberrant, and yet consistent diagnostic features of the abelisaurs. The skull of *Noasaurus* is rather small, being little more than 10 cms (4 ins) long. There is a large claw which may be from its foot and might have been used in a similar fashion as those on the feet of *Deinonychus* and *Velociraptor*. Although the claw is similar to the Laurasian theropods in its unusually large size, it is shaped quite differently reflecting a convergence of form which evolved in Gondwana.

The distribution of the abelisaurs must have been restricted to the continents of the southern hemisphere throughout most of their evolution during nearly the entire Cretaceous. It was only during perhaps the last few million years before the end of the Mesozoic that the isolation was broken. As with the faunal interchange that brought many of the last Laurasian dinosaurs south onto Gondwana soil, there was also a migrational wave from the southern continents dispersing into the northern world of Laurasia.

An upper jaw bone attributed to a migrant abelisaur is known from southern France. The most likely migratory route which could have allowed the abelisaurs to reach this part of Europe would have begun in the northernmost regions of Africa. The abelisaurs then would have had to bypass the Tethys Sea by travelling across chains of islands or connective stretches of land that emerged over what would have been parts of either Spain or Italy. Other kinds of dinosaurs must have also made similar journeys north from Africa and into Europe.

SAUROPODS RETURN TO LAURASIA

The most notable Gondwanic dinosaurs that migrated into Europe belong to a group of sauropods known as the titanosaurs. The isolation between the northern and southern continents produced dramatically different evolutionary pathways among the sauropods. The

Among the very last of the dinosaurs, a baby Titanosaurus *gazes outward into the last days of the Cretaceous world. Shown approximately life-size.*

sauropods of Laurasia had become virtually extinct, displaced by the ornithischians. But the southern sauropods had continued to flourish and evolve huge and bizarre new forms lasting until the very end of the Mesozoic. Some of the sauropods probably migrated into Europe along the same northern routes that the abelisaurs found in France must have taken. The titanosaur *Hypselosaurus* is known from Spain as well as France where not only bones, but sizeable eggs which are attributed to them have been found. Other titanosaurs are known from Hungary and Transylvania in Romania, which are called *Magyarosaurus*. Further evidence of the northward migration into Europe by the titanosaurs is seen by the presence of *Macrurosaurus* in England.

The titanosaurs also migrated northwards into North America along the same Central American connection that allowed the duckbills to enter South America. These titanosaurs were huge beasts of the genus *Alamosaurus*. One specimen from Utah has a forelimb that is nearly 3 m (10 ft) long. Other, mostly fragmentary, remains of these sauropods are also known from New Mexico but the titanosaurs are not known to have reached farther north than central Utah and southwest Wyoming. A barrier, if indeed there was one, could have been due to any number of environmental restrictions. One of these might have been the pre-established presence of the ornithischians, which could have prevented the titanosaurs from venturing any farther north. There are several dinosaurs known to have co-existed with the intruding *Alamosaurus*, which include the ceratopsians *Torosaurus* and *Pentaceratops*, the hadrosaur *Kritosaurus* and tyrannosaurs.

It is significant that the titanosaurs were most likely unsuccessful in migrating farther north across Canada and even Alaska. Unless they did this and continued across Beringia, the few extremely problematical sauropods that are known from Asia must have come along another, entirely different, route. It is, of course, possible that the Asian sauropods were already indigenous to this part of the world throughout the Cretaceous. But this is very doubtful. What little is known strongly suggests that they have affinities to sauropods from Gondwana, and if they didn't come from the western route across Beringia, they must have come from the north-eastern route from Africa. As with the titanosaurs that ventured from Africa into Europe, still other sauropods may have continued this migration eastward across Russia, and India, and other parts of Asia, including Mongolia.

The Late Cretaceous sauropods from Asia are very poorly represented, mostly by isolated bones. Many have been attributed to the titanosaurs but two partial skulls from Mongolia might belong to another group of Gondwanic sauropods, the dicraeosaurs. The assignment of these skulls of *Nemegtosaurus* and *Quaesitosaurus* is possibly correct, as dicraeosaurs like *Amargasaurus* are known to have existed well into the Cretaceous. It is also possible that these skulls belong to titanosaurs. Although, the skulls of titanosaurs are poorly known, represented by only a few rare, fragmentary pieces, there is enough known to indicate that the titanosaurs had skulls that resembled those of the dicraeosaurs in many ways. So until more is known about the missing bodies of these sauropod skulls from Mongolia, and some complete titanosaurs' skulls are found, a more precise comparison and identification cannot be made.

Other questionable titanosaurs are known from China, and Laos in south-east Asia. The most complete skeleton of a Late Cretaceous sauropod from Asia is another Mongolian form called *Opisthocoelicaudia*. Only the neck and skull are missing from this peculiar sauropod. In some ways *Opisthocoelicaudia* resembles the titanosaurs in such features as the rectangular expanded portion of the coracoid that is unique among titanosaurs. But it lacks the most diagnostic characteristic of the titanosaurs which is the ball and socket articulation of the tail vertebrae where the deeply cupped socket faces forward to receive the backward directed, rounded condyle. The reverse of this condition occurs in the tail of *Opisthocoelicaudia* in which the cupped socket faces backward and the condyle forward. No other known sauropod has such a tail with rounded condyles facing forwards, and its classification remains uncertain. This strange manner in which the tail vertebrae articulate has been explained as being stronger and more restrictive of movement which may have assisted the animal in holding its tail horizontally above the ground. Regardless if this is so, why such a development occurred only in this sauropod remains quite inexplicable.

The titanosaurs are the most enigmatic of all the sauropods. They were the dominant herbivores of Gondwana during the Cretaceous and not only did they continue to survive long after all the Laurasian sauropods had died out, they also proliferated, evolving into different forms that are in some ways strikingly similar to some ornithischians. These various forms included possibly the largest of all sauropods as well as some of the smallest. Some comparatively gracile forms had slender, long legs, but most had very robust, stout legs with rather stubby feet. The necks of some titanosaurs may have been fairly long, but many had necks that were much shorter than the typically long-necked sauropods from Laurasia.

The teeth of titanosaurs are of particular interest because they are apparently much more like the peg-toothed Jurassic sauropods than those with the heavily broad and spatulate teeth. This similarity in the structure of the teeth does not necessarily reflect a characteristic trait inherited from the Jurassic ancestors that led towards the titanosaur line of evolution. It is much more likely that the titanosaurs evolved the more slender, peg-like teeth totally independently from other kinds of sauropods with such specialized teeth. This means that the evolution of slender peg-like teeth actually occurred twice between two totally different kinds of sauropods. First, they evolved during the Jurassic among the diplodocids with animals like *Diplodocus*, *Apatosaurus*, and *Barosaurus*. Then again for a second time, during the Early Cretaceous, the titanosaurs continued to lose the primitive robust and spatulate condition of their teeth becoming modified more and more like the teeth of diplodocids. This is clearly an example of a parallel evolution brought about independently by the similar eating habits of two distinctly different groups of sauropods.

Based upon the evidence of the peg-like teeth, it would appear that the titanosaurs fed upon soft, low-growing vegetation, probably aquatic plants, much like the diplodocids are believed to have done. This is further substantiated by the exceptionally wide, scoop-like jaws that are lined with teeth only along the length of the front margins. This condition, which is developed as much or even more so than on diplodocids, would have functioned like a broad shovel gathering large mouthfuls of vegetation with each bite. This would have been most effective, especially while feeding upon soft aquatic plants. While the food was

in the mouth, the excess water could have been strained through sieve-like spaces between the teeth. Also like diplodocids, the nostrils were placed very far back on the skull so that the entire muzzle could be immersed under water to gather floating vegetation without getting the nose soaked or the animal's breathing impaired. The relatively shorter necks of most titanosaurs is again a rather clear indication that they were not browsers among the tree tops, and instead preferred vegetation that was much lower to the ground.

The short feet and shanks of even the largest titanosaurs, such as *Antarctosaurus*, are similar in proportion to semi-aquatic animals like the hippopotamus. Their rounded rib-cage formed a broad body that was rather low slung which, again, is reminiscent of what would be expected of an animal that spent considerable time in a watery environment. As with all sauropods, however, this should not be interpreted as being a restrictive condition preventing them from being quite adept and even surprisingly agile while moving about on dry land. There is, of course, some degree of physical limitation that occurs as any animal becomes larger. But, as with even the largest of elephants, rhinoceros and hippopotamus, their giant size does not hinder their surefootedness or hamper them from becoming surprisingly fast and agile when it is necessary for them to do so. Likewise, there is no reason to think that simply because of their size these huge sauropods were slow moving, sluggish waddlers. Nor did their great size restrict them to being supported within water. Indeed, there is a series of fossil trackways from Argentina that were made by gigantic titanosaurs, possibly *Antarctosaurus*, which

233

walked side by side on all fours across what was then a large mud flat. The tracks of the hind feet were among the largest ever recorded reaching nearly 1 m (3 ft) in diameter.

Many titanosaurs besides the giant *Antarctosaurus* are known from South America including *Laplatasaurus*, *Argyrosaurus* and *Titanosaurus*. But perhaps the strangest of all is *Saltasaurus* which, like most of these other titanosaurs, is known from Argentina. *Neuquensaurus* is also closely related to *Saltasaurus*. It is *Saltasaurus*, however, that is definitely known to have bony armour, which was previously believed to have been very uncharacteristic of sauropods.

Before the discovery of *Saltasaurus*, peculiar bony scutes and knobbly dermal bones had been found in Argentina and India which, with doubts, had been attributed to ankylosaurs under the names *Loricosaurus* and *Lametasaurus* respectively. It is now quite clear that they are not from ankylosaurs but instead are from armoured titanosaurs. Still other bony scutes of armour from titanosaurs have been reported from Spain. It appears likely, then, that many if not most of the titanosaurs were equipped with at least some degree of bony armour.

It is unfortunate that the armour scutes and other dermal bones of *Saltasaurus* were found mostly in a scattered disarray, not in their natural positions. The large variability in the sizes and shapes of the bony armour makes it exceptionally difficult to place the scutes in their original positions on the body. It appears that some areas of the body were covered by large sheets of skin containing a layer of very small round and sometimes polygonal nodes of bone. Larger rounded scutes, sometimes with flat surfaces and sometimes with pointed conical surfaces, were probably placed in random rosettes or linear rows that stretched across the width of the upper neck, body and tail. Still larger conical nodes of bones were held deeply within the skin by collagenous tissues firmly attached to the rugose underlying bases. These larger, conical nodes of bone may have been located along the back, or even along the sides of the tail. A matched pair of very large, bulbous, multi-pointed mass of bones could have been located most anywhere along the back of the animal. It is tempting to think that the convergent development of the bony armour on *Saltasaurus* matched the ankylosaurs with a titanosaur version of a tail club composed of these paired, large, multi-pointed, dermal bones. However, only the future discovery of better preserved specimens with the skin armour still in its natural positions can reveal what these titanosaurs must have really looked like.

The titanosaurs are known to have spread across most of Gondwana, including South America, Africa, Madagascar and India. In Africa, they are represented by *Aegyptosaurus* from Egypt, as well as several other unnamed animals from the desert wastelands of the Sahara and other regions of that continent. *Titanosaurus* itself is known not only from South America, but also from India, and possibly Madagascar. Fossil remains of titanosaurs have not as yet been found on the continents of Antarctica and Australia, but this may be due to preservational factors and the practical difficulties of exploration which have so far prevented such discoveries. It would not be too surprising if titanosaurs are found on these other continents because South America was probably still connected at its southernmost tip, allowing a passageway onto the combined continental landmass of Antarctica and Australia.

The titanosaurs are also noted for several nesting sites which have been discovered, complete with eggs. Titanosaur eggs have long been known from France, but significant deposits of extremely large nesting grounds are known from Argentina and India. The eggs are usually about 20 cms (8 ins) in diameter and because of their large size they certainly must have been laid by titanosaurs. They are often in clutches of approximately a dozen, and, as with the duckbills, the distance between the nests indicates that these sauropods nested in huge colonies.

A partial skeleton of a baby titanosaur has been discovered among the nesting grounds from India. There is a tragic foreshadowing that this baby sauropod failed to live long enough to grow into the giant like so many of its kind did in earlier times. During the short period of time that this baby dinosaur was alive, its large glinting eyes took a glimpse at a world that was ending. Soon after it had closed its eyelids forever, the world of the dinosaurs collapsed into extinction.

ABRUPT EXTINCTION
AN EXTRATERRESTRIAL CAUSE?

The extinction of the dinosaurs is by far the most controversial mystery of these once magnificent prehistoric animals. Countless theories have been proposed as possible solutions to what may have finally caused the downfall of the dinosaurs. Many of these are flawed because they cannot account for all of the various forms of life that became extinct along with the dinosaurs, making the issue remarkably complex. Whatever caused the death of the dinosaurs must also explain the extinction not only of non-dinosaurian reptiles, such as the winged pterosaurs, or aquatic mosasaurs and plesiosaurs, but also certain kinds of snail-like molluscs, gastropods, bivalves, and particular kinds of plankton among the tiniest of living organisms.

At first, it may not be readily apparent that there is any common denominator that is shared by all of these animals, but such a characteristic does exist. It provides the greatest clue for understanding why this major extinction occurred: they were all animals best adapted for living within stable, warm, tropical and sub-tropical environments.

All of the animals that died out at the end of the Mesozoic, from the giant dinosaurs to the miniscule plankton, were dependent upon the global climatic

conditions which created their environments. From this observation, the most complete and effective way for them all to have become extinct was to disrupt the climatic conditions so that their environments were lethally altered or, in effect, destroyed. Exactly how this deadly climatic metamorphosis was brought about remains controversially speculative, but the fact that it did happen is constantly being shown by the fossil record and sequence of geologic events.

Basically, there are two possible ways in which the extinctions could have been brought about. Either it was a gradual process that took place over an extended period of time, or there was an abrupt cataclysm. Adding to the confusion and controversy is the fact that there is evidence which can be interpreted as being from either a fast or slow process. During the 1980s, much evidence was produced supporting the concept of an apocalyptic disaster brought about by an extraterrestrial object slamming into the earth. A huge comet, meteor or asteroid as much as 9.5 kms (6 miles) in diameter is thought to have crashed into the earth, forming a crater some twenty times larger than itself. Upon impact, the astral bolide (see glossary) is thought to have been pulverized into minute granular particles that shot back into the atmosphere in a gigantic fiery plume. Then, these shattered, dust-like particles from outer space dispersed in darkening clouds that eventually rained down and settled upon the earth. The highly congested atmosphere is then be-

lieved to have become even worse because of worldwide fires set aflame by the impact, which blocked the sunlight for so long as to cool the global climate and virtually shut down the process of photosynthesis. During the aftermath of the impact, the Cretaceous extinctions are supposed to have occurred.

It is certainly possible that the earth could have been struck by a bolide from outer space, at the time of the extinction, but even if it did, it may not necessarily have been the major cause of the Cretaceous extinction. It is reasonable to believe that the earth has been struck time and time again by extremely large meteorites. And huge asteroids have been recorded as passing by, missing the planet. But if such a disaster actually occurred as interpreted by the impact scenario it is difficult to believe that such a disaster could have been so selective in the kinds of life that it killed, and surprising that anything could have lived through such a devastating calamity.

While being dramatically convincing at first, the impact scenario has problems and hinges to a great extent upon the abnormally high amounts of iridium which have been found in the sedimentary layer marking the transition of the Cretaceous-Tertiary (Paleocene) boundary. Abnormally high amounts of iridium within the Cretaceous-Tertiary boundary does exist and while iridium is often found in stony meteorites, it is extremely rare in the earth's crust. But doubts have been placed upon the theory of the extraterrestrial impact because additional strata layers have been found also containing iridium anomalies, but from the wrong periods of time, much earlier, and later, than when the extinctions are supposed to have occurred. Also rather devastating to the impact theory is the fact that iridium is now known to be a fairly common element that can be emitted in heavy concentrations from some, but not necessarily all, volcanoes.

There were considerable numbers of volcanoes due to the amount of tectonic activity that occurred during the Cretaceous. Iridium anomalies could have resulted from any number of these volcanoes and accounts for the strata layers containing iridium from different episodes in time. It is well known that intensive volcanism occurred in many parts of the world during the last half of the Cretaceous. Many volcanoes erupted throughout the western United States, parts of Great Britain, eastern Greenland, and areas of the western Pacific Ocean. Also of special significance is the extraordinary volcanic activity that occurred in India.

Vast lava fields known as the Deccan Traps which cover an enormous portion of the Indian peninsula are known to have occurred at about the time of the Cretaceous-Tertiary boundary. In fact, it appears that the eruptions that spewed out the awesome amounts of molten lava in India repeatedly occurred throughout a period that could have lasted for a few million years. At one point, virtually at the time when the last of the dinosaurs is thought to have died out, part of the lava flows of the Deccan Traps entombed the sediments where the last of the titanosaurs had gathered in nesting colonies and left their eggs. In the strata above this point no dinosaurs have been found.

GRADUAL EXTINCTION TECTONIC ACTIVITY AND CLIMATE CHANGES

The evidence provided by the Deccan Traps reveals a startling testimony that volcanic activity may have been a significant factor in the extinction of the dinosaurs. As with the impact theory, the accumulation of the volcanic dust that became airborne could have contributed to a cooling of the global climate. But other factors might have already instigated changes within the global climate gradually bringing the world of the dinosaurs to an end.

The movement of the continents had changed the currents of the ocean and the atmosphere. Also, the constantly growing mountain ranges might have shifted the weather patterns and in places produced extreme climates. Altogether, a chain of natural events that was set forth by the tectonic activity of the moving continents created changes in the global climate, which gradually eliminated the broad tropical and sub-tropical climates existing in the higher latitudes and in so much of the world. Along with these gradual changes in the global climate a harsher seasonality resulted in winters that were decisively cooler than throughout the Mesozoic.

The fossil record of the plant life indicates that as a result of the cooler winters many tropical plants became extinct and more temperate forms increased in numbers. The greatest losses were among the gymnosperms and evergreen angiosperms. Deciduous angiosperms that had become better adapted to the seasonal extremes survived the increasingly colder seasonal winters. This process of adaptation was a gradual one reflecting the changes in the increasingly variable climate developing during the last portion of the Cretaceous.

Tropical forms of sea life, including plankton and molluscs, were among the hardest hit by the climate changes. In contrast, the more resilient forms that were accustomed to temperate environments prevailed. This indicates that the oceans and seaways had been directly affected by the deteriorating stability of the climates, and were also cooling so much that these aquatic environments were drastically altered.

The higher latitudes were affected the most by the fluctuating weather patterns, whereas the lower latitudes nearer the equator suffered less severe drops in temperature. Nevertheless, they were significantly altered. Climatic models have suggested that the average equatorial temperatures may have cooled by as much as 5°C (9°F). Dramatic as this is, the regions within higher latitudes are believed to have suffered greater extremes with an average temperature drop that may have been as much as 15–25°C (27–45°F) less than during earlier portions of the Cretaceous.

The substantial lowering of the global climate's average temperature can certainly account for most, if not all, of the tropical forms of life that were adversely affected or became extinct during the gradual close that brought an end to the Mesozoic. Exactly how the climatic changes in temperature became so lethal to the widely varied forms of tropical life must have been different in each case. But, no doubt for many, the main cause centred upon the disruption of their environments. In response to the changing climates, the environments of the dinosaurs may have dwindled, becoming incapable of sustaining the food chain that supported them. To some extent at least, the dinosaurs probably suffered regional extinctions throughout parts of the globe, before becoming totally eradicated.

Unlike birds or mammals which have chromosomes that determine the birthing of either sex, the dinosaurs may have been more similar to reptiles such as crocodiles, and many turtles and lizards. And if this is so, then the different kinds of dinosaurs could have reached points in time when they could no longer effectively reproduce for the crucial factor depends upon temperature. After the eggs are laid, the male or female gender is determined by the influences of the temperature. This is notably the case for crocodilians, many other reptiles living today, and quite possibly, for the dinosaurs. The effects vary between reptiles, but basically different temperatures within the nest produces either males or females. The placement within the nest, how the eggs are arranged and how they are tended can all affect the incubating temperature of the eggs and produce either sex. The time of year in which the eggs are laid can produce nests of either all males or females depending on the seasonal temperature changes of the soil in which they are laid. It would not be too surprising if the eggs of dinosaurs developed either males or females by similar processes of environmental temperature influences. If the nesting grounds of the dinosaurs were special and repeatedly used because of the presence of the desired environmental conditions, then temperature changes within these areas would have had serious consequences. Under the deteriorating weather patterns and substantially cooler global climate, even vast nesting grounds may have consequently produced baby dinosaurs of only one gender. Eventually, this could have taken its toll by drastically reducing the numbers of potential mates until finally only one sex remained to live alone in a world in which they could no longer reproduce. Then, within the length of a single lifetime, the last of these solitary dinosaurs hopelessly ended the legacy of their kind.

After over 140 million years of living within a global climate that was ideal for the reptilian world of dinosaurs, their environments had become irrevocably destroyed by the ever changing forces of nature. Ironically, the cycle of world dominance that was held by the dinosaurs ended much as it had begun. Seasonal extremes with colder winters especially in the higher latitudes returned much as they had been during the Permian, long before the dinosaurs rose to power. The world that had been given to the dinosaurs was taken away, and in so doing the resilient, warm-blooded descendants of the Permian's mammal-like therapsids were given a second chance for continuance.

It has been said that nothing really dies as long as it is remembered. At least in this metaphoric view, the dinosaurs have not disappeared and will live on in the minds of people who are fascinated by these often spectacular and always mysterious prehistoric animals. In fact, with each year that passes, additional bits and pieces of the world of the dinosaurs are discovered, brought out of the entombing darkness of the earth into the light of science for Mankind to study and understand. So as time goes by, this great period of time in our earth's history will continue to be reconstructed and appreciated in fuller details of its glory.

THE WORLD OF DINOSAURS AND MAN

The Mesozoic Era lasted far longer than the so-called 'Age of Mammals' and about thirty times longer than Mankind has walked upon the earth. So by comparison, one of the greatest inaccuracies that has befallen the dinosaurs is the popular concept that they were 'failures'. Instead, it would be correct to appreciate the harmonious existence that the dinosaurs had with the world that they lived in and regard them as the highly successful animals that they were.

The study of dinosaurs is far more than a curious novelty of science. To fully appreciate the world of the dinosaurs is to understand more fully our own world with the respect and care that it deserves. The fragile balance of nature that could topple such titans has a direct bearing on the increasingly precarious existence of Mankind. Clearly, global extinctions, as with the dinosaurs, have happened repeatedly throughout the history of life. Life on this planet has been and always will be determined by the changeable global climate and the environments that it supports. The incredibly long, successful reign of the dinosaurs came crashing to an end due to natural causes that were at least not brought about by their own doing. With all of the unnatural dumping of manmade pollution, and the destruction of natural environments one can only hope that Mankind will learn the most important lesson from a global view of the dinosaurs, and that steps in the future will be taken to protect rather than destroy the climate and environments that support the very existence of Mankind. The knowledge of the consequences is quite evident, but for the first time in the history of this planet there is an opportunity for a form of life to choose not to go along the path of the dinosaurs.

Page 19. *Ichthyostega*.

Page 21. *Hylonomus*.

Page 51. *Estemmenosuchus* and *Eotitanosuchus*.

Page 55. *Titanophoneus, Venjukovia* and *Ulemosaurus*.

PLANT APPENDIX

DEVONIAN PLANTS

Vascular plants capable of populating the land had evolved by the Late Silurian period, and as a result, during the Early Devonian a great radiation onto the land took place. Early and Middle Devonian plants had vascular tissues confined to a narrow zone of the stem so they were still mechanically weak. They were also relatively low-growing forms living near water and lacked well developed roots and leaves. However, by the Late Devonian some plants had evolved proportionately more vascular tissues along with stronger roots for support and effective absorption of nutrients as well as leaves for capturing sunlight.

By the Late Devonian, flowerless seed plants had originated which further opened up the dry lands for plant expansion. Seed plants soon grew into large trees with strong woody stems and trees formed the world's first great forests.

Varieties of herbaceous lycopods, and other small vascular plants formed the understorey for the early forests. The lycopods were the ancestors of the modern day club mosses.

Ichthyostega · Page 19.

1. *Archaeopteris*, one of the very oldest kinds of large tree.
2. *Cladoxylon*, a fern-like vascular plant.
3. *Hyenia*, an early horsetail-like plant.
4. *Drepanophycus*, a lycopod.

CARBONIFEROUS PLANTS

During the Carboniferous period the small lycopods of the Devonian developed into huge plants often 30 m (97 ft) tall. These lycopods were dominant members of the Late Carboniferous coal swamps. At the feet of the tree-like plants was an undergrowth of ferns, seed-ferns, and horsetails. Giant horsetails were in abundance in the higher lands.

Hylonomus · Page 21.

1. *Sigillaria*, a giant lycopod. Within the fossilized stumps of these plants have been found the remains of the earliest type of reptile. The crown of the plant had multiple heads.
2. *Neuropteris*, a seed-fern.
3. *Callistophyton*, a vine-like plant which was a possible ancestor to the conifers.
4. *Sphenophyllum*, a sphenopsida.
5. *Calamites*, a horsetail of tree-like proportions often reaching 9 m (29 ft).
6. *Walchia*, an early conifer, shown as foliage.

PERMIAN PLANTS

The floras that flourished in the Late Carboniferous period continued to dominate into the Early Permian and then declined. Gymnosperms, including conifers, took over terrestrial environments. Having done this they continued to expand throughout the Triassic, Jurassic, and Early Cretaceous.

Estemmenosuchus **and Eotitanosuchus** · Page 51.

1. *Walchia*, a gymnosperm, and one of the early conifers that had its origin in the Late Carboniferous. The Norfolk Island pine is its living descendant.
2. *Pecopteris*, a tree-fern which forms the understorey.
3. *Phylloteheca equisetoides*, a type of horsetail.
4. *Sphenophyllum*, a sphenopsida.

Titanophoneus, **Venjukovia and Ulemosaurus** · Page 55.

1. *Calamites*, the giant tree-like horsetails.
2. *Walchia*, an araucarian conifer.

PERMIAN PLANTS OF GONDWANA

In the southern hemisphere, the flora of Gondwana was dominated by the *Glossopteris*. The glossopterids were woody plants, trees and shrubs, of all sizes adapted to different habitats, preferring low and wet lands. The leaves came in many sizes and are found in great profusion as fossils, perhaps in part because they were deciduous and shed their leaves. Southern conifers, ginkgoes, ferns, seed-ferns and horsetails were also part of the flora.

Moschops, *Eodicynodon* and *Bradysaurus* · Page 57.

1. *Glossopteris*, shown as a bush with its fruit filled with seeds. Many *Glossopteris* fruits are preserved as fossils.
2. *Glossopteris*, shown as trees.
3. *Sphenopteris*, a fern.
4. Southern conifers.

Page 57.　　*Moschops*, *Eodicynodon* and *Bradysaurus*.

Lycaenops and *Endothiodon* · Page 61.

1. *Glossopteris*, shown as a large tree.
2. *Schizoneura gondwanensis*, a horsetail.
3. *Phyllotheca equisetoides*, a horsetail.
4. *Sphenopteris*, a fern.
5. *Cordaites*, an ancestor of some of our modern conifers.
6. Southern conifers.

Page 61.　　*Lycaenops* and *Endothiodon*.

TRIASSIC PLANTS

As the Triassic became warmer and drier, plants evolved drought-resistant forms. Leaves developed a harder surface and many were needle-like to lessen the surface area thus preventing the loss of moisture. Conifers, ginkgoes, seed-ferns, ferns and cycadophytes were components of the flora.

Thrinaxodon and pups · Page 67.

1. *Dicroidium*, a seed-fern well adapted to a drier climate with a thick waxy skin.
2. *Taeniopteris*, a cycadophyte.
3. *Ginkgoites*, a ginkgo.
4. *Volziopsis*, a conifer.

Page 67.　　*Thrinaxodon* and pups.

Diarthrognathus and *Blabera altropos* · Page 119.

1. *Ginkgoites*, a ginkgo with deeply divided, strap-like leaves.
2. *Asterotheca*, a fern.

Page 119.　　*Diarthrognathus* and *Blabera atropos*.

Page 88.   *Postosuchus* and *Placerias*.

***Postosuchus* and *Placerias* · Page 88.**

1.   *Ginkgoites*, a ginkgo.
2.   *Araucarioxylon*, a wood of conifers.
3.   *Phlebopteris*, a fern.

Page 105.   *Rutiodon* and fabrosaurs.

***Rutiodon* and fabrosaurs · Page 105.**

1.   *Auracarioxylon*, a wood of conifers.
2.   *Brachyphyllum*, foliage of conifers.
3.   *Lyssoxylon*, a cycad.
4.   *Equisetites*, horsetails.
5.   *Itopsidema*, a tree-fern.
6.   *Clathropteris*, a fern shown growing on tree roots.

Page 29.   Jurassic landscape, *Ornitholestes*.

JURASSIC PLANTS

The Jurassic and Early Cretaceous periods were the age of cycads and conifers. These groups dominated the forests, while ginkgoes flourished and tree ferns were still abundant.

Jurassic landscape, *Ornitholestes* · Page 29.

1.   *Brachyphyllum*, conifer foliage.
2.   *Ginkgoites*, a ginkgo.
3.   *Pseudoctenis*, a cycad.
4.   *Marattia*, a tree-fern.
5.   *Osmundopsis*, a fern.

Page 121.   *Dilophosaurus* and *Scutellosaurus*.

***Dilophosaurus* and *Scutellosaurus* · Page 121.**

1.   *Elactocladus*, conifer foliage similar to the *Metasequoia*, the living Dawn Redwood.
2.   *Dictyophyllum*, a fern.

Dicraeosaurus **and crocodile** · Page 130.

1. *Pentoxylon*, a cycad.
2. *Marattia*, a tree-fern.
3. *Equisetites*, horsetails.
4. *Rissikia*, a podocarp conifer.
5. *Agathis*, a conifer identical to the living Kauri Pine.

CRETACEOUS PLANTS

The Cretaceous experienced the rise of a new group of plants, the angiosperms, or flowering plants. The familiar cycad and conifer forests began to dwindle and be replaced by the new group. The angiosperms are thought to have originated in West Gondwana and had dispersal routes along still existing land connections and bridges. As the continents continued their separation, some areas left in isolation evolved unique floras.

Maiasaura **herd** · Page 194.

1. *Dryophyllum* was one of the dominant leaf forms in the Upper Cretaceous floras. Because it is well defined and widespread, it is used as an index fossil. The leaves were somewhat like a willow, but the plant may have had affinities with oaks.
2. *Equisetites*, horsetails.
3. *Todites*, a fern.

Triceratops **battle** · Page 224.

1. *Ficus*, a fig tree.
2. *Sabal*, a palm.
3. *Vitis*, a grape.
4. Epiphytes, plants that grow non-parasitically upon others obtaining nutrients from the air and rain.

Cretaceous landscape · Page 31.

1. *Ficus*, a fig tree.
2. *Magnolia*, shown as a slender trunk, and as leaves in foreground.
3. *Plantanus*, a sycamore.
4. *Quercus*, an oak.
5. *Cornus*, a dogwood.
6. *Todites*, a fern.

Page 130.   *Dicraeosaurus* and crocodile.

Page 194.   *Maiasaura* herd.

Page 224.   *Triceratops* battle.

Page 31.   Cretaceous landscape, *Albertosaurus*.

241

RECOMMENDED READING

BIRD, R.T. *Bones for Barnum Brown* (Texas Christian University Press, Fort Worth, 1985. 225 pages)

BRENCHLEY, P.J. (Editor) *Fossils and Climate* (John Wiley & Sons, Chichester, New York, Brisbane, Toronto, Singapore, 1984. 352 pages)

CARROLL, R.L. *Vertebrate Paleontology and Evolution* (W.H. Freeman and Company, New York, 1988. 698 pages)

COLBERT, E.H. *Wandering Lands and Animals: The Story of continental Drift and Animal Populations* (Dover Publication, Inc. New York, 1985. 323 pages)

COX, C.B., and MOORE, P.D. *Biogeography: An Ecological and Evolutionary Approach* (Blackwell Scientific Publications, Oxford, London, Edinburgh, Boston, Palo Alto, Melbourne, 1985. 244 pages)

CZERKAS, S.J., and OLSON, E.C. (Editors) *Dinosaurs Past and Present. Volumes I and II* (Natural History Museum of Los Angeles County and University of Washington Press, Seattle and London, 1987. Volume I 161 pages, Volume II 149 pages)

FEDUCCIA, A. *The Age of Birds* (Harvard University Press, Cambridge and London, 1980. 196 pages)

GILLETTE, D.D., and LOCKLEY, M.G. (Editors) *Dinosaur Tracks and Traces* (Cambridge University Press, Cambridge, New York, New Rochelle, Melbourne, Sydney, 1989. 454 pages)

HEILMAN, G. *The Origin of Birds* (D. Appleton and Company, New York, 1927. 210 pages)

HORNER, J. R., and GORMAN, J. *Digging Dinosaurs* (Workman Publishing, New York, 1988. 210 pages)

HOTTON, N.H., MacLEAN, P.D., ROTH, J.J., and ROTH, E.C., (Editors) *The Ecology and Biology of Mammal-like Reptiles* (Smithsonian Institution Press, Washington and London, 1986. 326 pages)

KEMP. T.S. *Mammal-like Reptiles and the Origin of Mammals* (Academic Press, London, New York, Paris, San Diego, San Francisco, Sao Paolo, Sydney, Tokyo, Toronto, 1982. 363 pages)

NORMAN, D.B. *The Illustrated Encyclopedia of Dinosaurs* (Salamander and Crescent Books, London and New York, 1985. 208 pages)

OLSON, E.C. *Vertebrate Paleozoology* (John Wiley & Sons, Inc., New York, London, Sydney, and Toronto, 1971. 839 pages)

PADIAN, K. (Editor) *The Beginning of the Age of Dinosaurs: Faunal Change Across the Triassic-Jurassic Boundary* (Cambridge University Press, Cambridge, London, New York, New Rochelle, Melbourne, and Sydney, 1986. 378 pages)

RUSSELL, D.A. *A Vanished World: The Dinosaurs of Western Canada* (National Museum of Natural Sciences, National Museums of Canada, Ottawa, 1977. 142 pages)

RUSSELL, D.A. *An Odyssey in Time: The Dinosaurs of North America* (University of Toronto Press and Northword Press, Inc., Minocqua, 1989. 240 pages)

STANLEY, S.M. *Earth and Life Through Time* (W.H. Freeman and Company, New York, 1986. 690 pages)

STANLEY, S.M. *Extinction* (Scientific American Books, New York, 1987. 242 pages)

STEWART, W.N. *Paleobotany and the Evolution of Plants* (Cambridge University Press, Cambridge, New York, New Rochelle, Melbourne, and Sydney, 1983. 405 pages)

THOMAS, R.D.K., and OLSON, E.C. (Editors) *A Cold Look at the Warm-Blooded Dinosaurs* (AAAS Selected Symposium, Westview Press, Boulder, 1980)

TIDWELL, W.D. *Common Fossil Plants of Western North America* (Brigham Young University Press, Provo, 1975. 197 pages)

UYEDA, S. *The New View of the Earth: Moving Continents and Moving Oceans* (W.H. Freeman and Company, New York, 1971. 217 pages)

WHITE, M.E. *The Greening of Gondwana* (Reed Books, New South Wales, 1986. 256 pages)

BIBLIOGRAPHY

ABEL, O. (von.) *Geschichte und Methode der Rekonstruktion vorzeitlicher Wirbeltiere* (Verlag von Gustav Fischer, Jena, 1925. 325 pages)

AILING, S. *Before Dinosaurs* (China Ocean Press, Beijing, 1989. 109 pages)

ARAUJO, D.C.F. *Osteologica craniana de* Pareiasaurus americanus (*An. Acad. Brasil. Cienc*, 1985)

BAKKER, R.T. *The Dinosaur Heresies* (William Morrow and Company, Inc., New York, 1986. 481 pages)

BARSBOLD, R. and PERLE, A. 'The first record of a primitive ornithomimosaur from the Cretaceous of Mongolia'. (*Palaeont. Zh.*, Number 2, 1984. pp 121–123)

BECK, C.B. '*Archaeopteris* and its role in vascular plant evolution.' *Paleobotany, Paleoecology, and Evolution. Volume I.* Karl J. Niklas, Editor. (*Prager scientific*, 1981. pp. 193–230)

BENNETT, C.S. 'A pterodactyloid pterosaur pelvis from the Santana Formation of Brazil: Implications for terrestrial locomotion.' (*Journal of Vertebrate Paleontology*, 1990. Volume 10, Number 1. pp. 80–85)

BENTON, M.J. 'Ectothermy and the success of dinosaurs.' (*Evolution*, 1979. Volume 3, Number 3. pp. 983–997)

BENTON, M.J. 'Dinosaur success in the Triassic: a noncompetitive ecological model.' (*The Quarterly Review of Biology*, 1983. Volume 58, Number 1. pp.29–55)

BENTON, M.J., and WALKER, A.D. 'Palaeocology, taphonomy, and dating of Permo-Triassic reptiles from Elgin, north-east Scotland.' (*Palaeontology*, 1985. Volume 28, Part 2. pp. 207–234)

BENTON, M.J. 'The origins of the dinosaurs.' (*Modern Geology*, 1987. Volume 13. pp 41–56)

BENTON, M.J. 'Fossil reptiles from ancient caves.' (*Nature*, 1989. Volume 337. pp. 309–310)

BESSE, J. and COURTILLOT, V. 'Paleogeographic maps of the continents bordering the Indian Ocean since the Early Jurassic.' (*Journal of Geophysical Research*, 1988. Volume 93, Number 810. pp. 11, 791–11, 808)

BIRD, R.T. 'Did dinosaurs ever walk on land?' (*Natural History*, February 1944. Volume LIII. Number 2)

BONAPARTE, J.F. 'Los Tetrapodos Del Sector Superior De La Formacion Los Colorados, La Rioja, Argentina.' *Opera Lillonana* XXII, I Parte. (*Tucuman*, 1971. 183 paginas, 4 lamina)

BONAPARTE, J.F. 'El Mesozoico De America Del Sur Y Sus Tetrapodos.' (*Opera Lilloana 26*, 1978. Universidad National de Tucuman. 596 pages)

BONAPARTE, J.F., and VINCE, M. 'El Hallazgo Del Primer Nido De Dinosaurios Triasicos (Saurischia, Prosauropoda), Triasico Superior De Patagonia, Argentina.' (*Ameghiniana*, 1979. Tomo XVI. Numero 1–2)

BONAPARTE, J.F. 'Discripcion de *Fasolasuchus tena x* y su significado en la sistematica y evolucion de los thecondontia. Revista Del Museo Argentino De Ciencias Naturales, Bernardino Rivadavia.' (*Paleontologia*, 1981. Tomo III. No. 2)

BONAPARTE, J.F. 'Locomotion in rauisuchid thecodonts.' (*Journal of Vertebrate Paleontology*, 1984. Volume 3, Number 4. pp. 210–218).

BONAPARTE, J.F., and NOVAS, F.E. '*Abelisaurus comahuensis*, n.g. sp. carnosauria del Cretacio Tardio de Patagonia.' (*Ameghiniana*, 1985. Volume 21, Number 2–4. pp. 259–265)

BONAPARTE, J.F. (Organizador) *Simposio Evolucion De Los Vertebrados Mesozoicos. IV Congresso Argentino De Paleontologia Y Bioestratigrafia* (Actas 2, Mendoza, Perez-Companc S.A., 1986a. 218 pages)

BONAPARTE, J.F. 'Les dinosaures (Carnosaures, Allosaurides, Sauropodes, Cetiosaurides) du Jurassique Moyen de Cerro Condor (Chubut, Argentine).' (*Annales de Paleontologie*, 1986b. Volume 72, Fasciule 3. pp. 247–289)

BONAPARTE, J.F., NOVAS, F.E., and CORIA, R.A. *Carnotaurus sastrei*, Bonaparte, the horned, lightly built carnosaur from the Albian (?) of Patagonia (Natural History Museum of Los Angeles. In press)

BOONSTRA, L.D. 'Pareiasaurian studies part X. – the dermal armor.' (*Annals of the South African Museum*, 1934. Volume XXXI, Part I. pp. 39–48. Plates XXIII–XXVII)

BREED, C.S. and BREED, W.J. (Editors) Investigations in the Triassic Chinle Formation (Northland Press, Flagstaff. *Museum of Northern Arizona Bulletin*, 47, 1972. 103 pages)

BRETT-SURMAN, M.K. 'Phylogeny and palaeobiogeography of hadrosaurian dinosaurs'. (*Nature*, 1979. Volume 277. pp. 560–562)

BRINK, A.S. 'Note on a new skeleton of *Thrinaxodon liorhinus*.' (*Paleontologica Africana*, 1958–9. Volume VI. pp. 15–22)

BRINK, A.S. 'The road to endothermy – a review.' (*Mem. So. geol. France. N.S.*, 1980. Number 139. pp. 29–38)

BRIGGS, J.C. *Biogeography and Plate Tectonics* (Elsevier, Amsterdam, Oxford, New York, Tokyo, 1987.)

BRINKMAN, D.B., and SUES, H.D. 'A staurikosaurid dinosaur from the Upper Triassic Ishigualasto Formation of Argentina and the relationships of the Staurikosauridae.' (*Palaeontology*, 1987. Volume 30, Part 3. pp. 493–503)

BROOM, R.S. 'On the South African pseudosuchian *Euparkeria* and allied genera.' (*Proceedings of the Zoological Society of London*, September 1913. pp. 619–633)

BROOM, R.S. 'Catalogue of Types and Figured Specimens of Fossil Vertebrates in the American Museum of Natural History. II. – Permian, Triassic, and Jurassic Reptiles of South Africa.' (*Bulletin of the American Museum of Natural History*, 1915. Volume XXV., Part II)

BROOM, R.S. *The Mammal-Like Reptiles of South Africa: and the Origin of Mammals* (H.F. & G. Witherby, London, 1932. 258 pages)

BROSCHE, P., and SUNDERMANN, J. (Editors) *Tidal Friction and the Earth's Rotation II.* (Springer-Verlag, Berlin, Heidelberg, New York, 1982)

BROWN, B. 'A complete skeleton of the horned dinosaur *Monoclonius*, and description of a second skeleton showing skin impressions.' (*Bulletin of the American Museum of Natural History*, 1918. Volume XXXVII. pp. 281–306. With plates)

BROWN, B., and SCHLAIKJER, E.M. 'The structure and relationships of *Protoceratops*.' (*Annals of the New York Academy of Science*, 1940. Volume XL, Article 3. pp. 133–266)

BUFFETAUT, E. 'The palaeobiogeographical significance of the Mesozoic continental vertebrates from South-East Asia.' (*Mem. Soc. geol. France, N.S.*, 1984. Number 147. pp. 37–42)

BUFFETAUT, E. 'Unusual theropod dinosaur teeth from the Upper Jurassic of Phu Wiang. Northeastern Thailand.' (*Revue de Paleobiologie*, 1986. Volume 5, Number 2. pp. 217–220)

BUFFETAUT, E. 'On the age of the dinosaur fauna from the Lamenta Formation (Upper Cretaceous of Central India).' (*Newsl. stratigr*, 1987. Volume 18, Number 1. pp. 1–6)

BUFFETAUT, E. 'Un dinosaure theropode d'affinites gondwaniennes dans le Cretace Superieur de Provence.' (*C. R. Academy Science Paris*, 1988. Volume 306, Series II. pp. 153–158)

CARPENTER, K. 'Skeletal and dermal armor reconstruction of *Euoplocephalus tutus* (Ornithischia: Ankylosauridae) from the Late Cretaceous Oldman Formation of Alberta.' (*Canadian Journal of Earth Sciences*, 1982. Volume 19, Number 4. pp. 689–697)

CARPENTER, K. 'Skeletal reconstruction and life restoration of *Sauropelta* (Ankylosauria: Nodosauridae) from the Cretaceous of North America.' (*Canadian Journal of Earth Sciences*, 1984. Volume 21. pp. 1491–1498)

CARROLL, R.L., and GASKILL, P. 'The nothosaur *Pachypleurosaurus* and the origin of plesiosaurs.' (*Philosophical Transactions of the Royal Society of London, Series B*, 1985. Volume 309. pp. 343–393)

CHARIG, A.J., ATTRIDGE, J., and CROMPTON, A.W. 'On the origin of the sauropods and the classification of the Saurischia.' (*Proceedings of the Linnean Society of London*, 1965. Volume 176., 2. pp. 197–221. 1 Plate)

CHARIG, A.J., and MILNER, A.C. '*Baryonyx*, a remarkable new theropod dinosaur.' (*Nature*, 1986. Volume 324, Number 6095. pp. 359–361)

CHATTERJEE, S. 'A rhyncosaur from the Upper Triassic Maleri Formation of India.' (*Philosophical Transactions of the Royal Society of London, Series B*, 1974. Volume 267, Number 884. pp. 209–261)

CHATTERJEE, S. 'A primitive parasuchid (phytosaur) reptile from the Upper Triassic Maleri Formation of India.' (*Palaeontology*, 1978. Volume 21, Part 1. pp. 83–127)

CHATTERJEE, S. 'Phylogeny and classification of thecodontian reptiles.' (*Nature*, 1982. Volume 295. pp. 317–320)

CHATTERJEE, S. 'The drift of India: A conflict in plate tectonics.' (*Mem. Soc. geol. France. N.S.*, 1984. Number 147. pp. 43–48)

CHATTERJEE, S. '*Postosuchus*, a new thecodontian reptile from the Triassic of Texas and the origin of tyrannosaurs.' (*Philosophical Transactions of the Royal Society of London, Series B*, 1985. Volume 309, pp. 395–460)

CHATTERJEE, S., and HOTTON, H. 'The paleoposition of India.' (*Journal of Southeast Asian Earth Sciences*, 1986. Volume 1, Number 3. pp. 145–189)

CHATTERJEE, S. 'A new theropod dinosaur from India with remarks on the Gondwan-Laurasia connection in the Late Triassic. Gondwana Six: Stratigraphy, Sedimentology, and Paleontology.' (*Geophysical Monograph 41*, 1987. Garry D. McKenzie [Editor]. American Geophysical Union, Washington)

CHATTERJEE, S. 'Skull of *Protoavis* and early evolution of birds. Abstracts of Papers.' (*Journal of Vertebrate Paleontology*, 1987. Volume 7, Number 3. pp. 14 A)

CHATTERMOLE, P., and MOORE, P. *The Story of the Earth* (Cambridge University Press, Cambridge, 1985)

CLARK, J.M., JACOBS, L.L., AND DOWNS, W.R. 'Mammal-Like dentition in a Mesozoic crocodilian.' (*Science*, 1989. Volume 244. pp. 1064–1066)

CLEMENS, W., and ARCHIBALD, D. 'Evolution of terrestrial faunas during the Cretaceous-Tertiary transition.' (*Mem. soc. geol. France, N.S.*, 1980. Number 139. pp. 67–74)

COLBERT, E.H. A gigantic crocodile from the Upper Cretaceous beds of Texas. (*American Museum Novitates*. Number 1688, 1954. 22 pages)

COLBERT, E.H. *Lystrosaurus* from Antarctica. (*American Museum Novitates*. Number 2535, 1974. 43 pages)

COLBERT, E.H. A saurischian dinosaur from the Triassic of Brazil. (*American Museum Novitates*. Number 2405, 1970. 39 pages)

COLBERT, E.H. Triassic cynodont reptiles from Antarctica. (*American Museum Novitates*. Number 2611, 1977. 30 pages)

COLBERT, E.H. *Evolution of the Vertebrates* (John Wiley & Sons, New York. Chichester, Brisbane, Toronto, 1980. 510 pages)

COLBERT, E.H. A Primitive Ornithischian Dinosaur from the Kayenta Formation of Arizona. (Northland Press, Flagstaff. *Museum of Northern Arizona Bulletin* 53, 1981. 61 pages)

COLBERT, E.H. *Dinosaurs: An Illustrated History* (Hammond Incorporated, Maplewood, 1983. 224 pages)

COLBERT, E.H., and JOHNSON, R.R. (Editors) The Petrified Forest Through the Ages. (Northland Press, Flagstaff. *Museum of Northern Arizona Bulletin*, 54, 1985. 91 pages)

COLBERT, E.H. The Triassic Dinosaur *Coelophysis*. (Northland Press, Flagstaff. *Museum of Northern Arizona Bulletin*, 57, 1989. 160 pages)

COOMBS, W.P. 'Sauropod habits and habitats.' (*Paleogeography, Paleoclimatology, Paleoecology*, 1975, Volume 7. pp. 1–33)

COOMBS, W.P. 'The families of the ornithischian dinosaur order Ankylosauria.' (*Palaeontology*, 1978. Volume 1. pp. 143–170)

COOMBS, W.P. 'Juvenile ceratopsians from Mongolia – the smallest known dinosaur specimens.' (*Nature*, 1980. Volume 283. pp. 380–381)

COX, C.B. 'An outline of the biogeography of the Mesozoic world.' (*Mem. Soc. geol. France, N.S.*, 1980. pp. 75–79)

CROWLEY, T.J., HYDE, W.T., and SHORT, D.A. 'Seasonal cycle variations on the superecontinent of Pangaea.' (*Geology*, 1989. Volume 17. pp. 457–460)

CRUICKSHANK, A.R.I. 'The proterosuchian thecodonts.' (*Studies in Vertebrate Evolution* K.A. Josey and T.S. Kemp [Editors]. Oliver and Boyd, Edinburgh, 1972. pp. 89–119)

CRUICKSHANK, A.R.I. 'The pes of *Erythosuchus africanus* Broom.' (*Zoological Journal of the Linnean Society*, 1978. Volume 62. pp. 161–177, with 13 Plates and 1 Figure)

CRUSH, P.J. 'A late Upper Triassic sphenosuchid crocodilian from Wales.' (*Palaeontology*, 1984. Volume 27, Part 1. pp. 131–157)

CURRIE, P.J. 'A new haptodontine sphenacodont (Reptilia: Pelycosauria) from the Upper Pennsylvanian of North America.' (*Journal of Paleontology*, 1977. Volume 5, Number 5. pp. 927–942, 9 Text-Figures)

CURRIE, P.J. 'The osteology of haptodontine sphenacodonts (Reptilia: Pelycosauria).' (*Palaeontographica Abstract A 163*, 1979. pp. 130–188)

CURRIE, P.J. 'Hadrosaur trackways from the Lower Cretaceous of Canada.' (*Acta Palaeont. Polonica*, 1983. Volume 28, 1–2. pp. 63–73)

CURRIE, P.J. and KOSTER, E.H. 'Mesozoic Terrestrial Ecosystems.' (*Occasional Paper of the Tyrrell Museum of Palaeontology*, 1987. Number 3)

DARRAH, W.C. *Principles of Paleobotany* (The Ronald Press Company, New York, 1960)

DODSON, P. 'Comparative osteology of the American ornithopods *Camptosaurus* and *Tenontosaurus*.' (*Mem. Soc. geol. France, N.S.*, 1980. pp. 81–85)

DODSON, P., BEHRENSMEYER, A.K., and BAKKER, R.T. 'Taphonomy of the Morrison Formation (Kimmeridgian-Portlandian) and the Cloverly Formation (Aptian-Albian) of the western United States.' (*Mem. Soc. geol. France, N.S.*, 1980. Number 139)

DOTT, R.H. and BATTEN, R.L. *Evolution of the Earth* (McGraw-Hill, New York, 1971. 572 pages plus index)

BIBLIOGRAPHY

DUNCAN, R.A. and PYLE, D.G. 'Rapid eruption of the Deccan flood basalts at the Cretaceous/Tertiary boundary.' (*Nature*, 1988. Volume 333. pp. 841–843)

DUTUIT, J. and OUAZZOU, A. 'Decouverte d'une piste de dinosaure sauropode sur le site d'empreintes de Demnat (Haut-Atlas marocain).' (*Soc. geol. France, N.S.*, 1980. Number 139. pp. 96–102)

EATON, G.F. 'Osteology of *Pteranodon*.' (*Memoirs of the Connecticut Academy of Arts and Sciences*, 1910. Volume 2. pp. 1–38)

EWER, R.F. 'The anatomy of the thecodont reptile *Euparkeria capensis*.' (*Philosophical Transactions of the Royal Society of London, Series B*, 1965. Volume 248, Number 751. pp. 379–435)

FARLOW, J.O. 'Lower Cretaceous Dinosaur Tracks, Paluxy River Valley, Texas.' (*South Central G.S.A.*, Baylor University, 1987. 50 pages, 39 figs., 20 charts)

FINDLAY, G.H. 'On the scaloposaurid skull of *Oliveria parringtoni*, Brink with a note on the origin of hair.' (*Palaeontologia Africana*, 1968. Volume XI. pp. 47–59)

GALTON, P.M. 'The ornithischian dinosaur *Hypsilophodont* from the Wealden of the Isle of Wight.' (*Bulletin British Museum [Natural History] Geology*, 1974. Volume 25. pp. 1–152)

GALTON, P.M. Prosauropod Dinosaurs (Reptilia: Saurischia) of North America. (*Postilla*, Yale Peabody Museum, Yale University, 1976. Number 169. 98 pages)

GALTON P.M. 'On *Staurikosaurus pricei*, an early saurischian dinosaur from the Triassic of Brazil, with notes on the Herrerasauridae and Poposauridae.' (*Palaont. Z.*, 1977. Volume 51. pp. 234–245)

GALTON, P.M. 'Armored dinosaurs (Ornithischia: Ankylosauria) from the Middle and Upper Jurassic of England.' (*Geobios*, 1980a. Number 13, fasc. 6. pp. 825–837)

GALTON, P.M. '*Dryosaurus and Camptosaurus* intercontinental genera of Upper Jurassic ornithopod dinosaurs.' (*Mem. soc. geol. France, N.S.*, 1980b. Number 139)

GALTON, P.M. 'Diet of prosauropod dinosaurs from the Late Triassic and Early Jurassic.' (*Lethaia*, 1985. Volume 18. pp. 105–123)

GILMORE, C.W. Osteology of the armoured Dinosauria in the United States National Museum, with special reference to the Genus *Stegosaurus* (Smithsonian Institution, *United States National Museum Bulletin* 89, 1914. 142 pages)

GILMORE, C.W. Osteology of the carnivorous Dinosauria in the United States National Museum, with special reference to the genera *Antrodemus (Allosaurus)* and *Ceratosaurus* (Smithsonian Institution, *United States National Museum Bulletin* 110, 1920. 159 pages)

GILMORE, C.W. On *Troodon validus*: an orthopodus dinosaur from the Belly River Cretaceous of Alberta, Canada (*University of Alberta Bulletin Number 1, 1924. 43 pages. 15 Plates*)

GILMORE, C.W. Osteology of *Apatosaurus* with special reference to specimens in the Carnegie Museum (*Memoirs of the Carnegie Museum*, 1936. Volume XI. Number 4, 272 pages, plus Plates)

GILMORE, C.W. Reptilian fauna of the North Horn Formation of central Utah. (*Geological Survey Professional Paper 210–C*. United States Government Printing Office, 1946. 51 pages, 14 Plates)

GREGORY, W.K. 'The skeleton of *Moschops capensis* Broom, a Dinocephalian Reptile from the Permian of South Africa.' (*Bulletin of the American Museum of Natural History*, 1926. Volume LVI, Article III. pp. 179–251)

HALLAM, A. (Editor) *Atlas of Paleobiogeography* (Elsevier Scientific Publishing Company, Amsterdam, London, New York, 1973. 531 pages)

HATCHER, J.B., and LULL, R.S. *The Ceratopsia* (United States Geological Survey Government Printing Office, 1907. 300 pages)

HECTH, M.K., OSTROM, J.H., VIOHL, G., WELLNHOFER, P., (Editors) *The Beginnings of Birds: Proceeding of the International* Archaeopteryx *Conference Eichstatt* (Freunde des Jura-Museums Eichstatt, Williabaldsburg, 1984. 382 pages)

HOLLAND, W.J. 'The osteology of *Diplodocus* Marsh.' (*Memoirs of the Carnegie Museum*, 1905. Volume II, Number 6. pp. 225–264, 30 plates)

HORNER, J.R. 'A new hadrosaur (Reptilia, Ornithischia) from the Upper Cretaceous Judith River Formation of Montana.' (*Journal of Vertebrate Paleontology*, 1988. Volume 8, Number 3. pp. 314–321)

HUENE, F. (von.)'Uber *Erythosuchus*, Verteter Der Neuen Reptile-Ordnung Pelycosima.' (*Geologische und Palaeontologische Abhandlungen*, 1911. Neue Folge Band X. Heft 1. Verlag von Gustav Fischer, Jena)

HUENE, F. (von.) 'The Carnivorous Saurischia in the Jura and Cretaceous Formations.' (*De la Revista del Museuo de La Plata*, 1926a. Tomo XXIX, paginas 35 a 167)

HUENE, F. (von.) 'Los Saurisquios Y Ornitisquios Del Cretaceo Argentino.' (*Anales Del Museo Del La Plata*, 1926b. Tomo III. 133 figuras y 44 laminas. 194 paginas)

JACOBS, L.I., (Editor) *Aspects of Vertebrate History: Essays in Honor of Edwin Harris Colbert*. (Museum of Northern Arizona Press, 1980. 407 pages)

JAEGER, J., COUTILLOT, V. and TAPPONNIER, P. 'Paleontological view of the ages of the Deccan Traps, the Cretaceous/Tertiary boundary, and the India-Asia collision.' (*Geology*, 1989. Volume 17. pp. 316–319)

JAEKEL, O. 'Die Wirbeltierfunde auf dem Keuper von Halberstadt.' (*Palaeontologische Zeitschrift*, 1918. Serie II. pp. 88–214)

JAIN, S.L., KUTTY, T.S., ROY-CHOWDHURY, T., and CHATTERJEE, S. 1975. 'The sauropod dinosaur from the Lower Jurassic Kota Formation of India.' (*Proceedings of the Royal Society of London, Series A*, 1975. Volume 188. pp. 221–228)

JANENSCH, W. 'Material und formengehalt de sauropoden in der ausbeute der Tendaguru-expedition.' (*Palaeontographica*, 1929. Supplement 7, (2). pp. 2–34)

JANENSCH, W. 'Die skelettrekonstrucktion von *Brachiosaurus brancai*.' (*Paleontographica*, 1950. Supplement 7, (3). pp. 97–102)

JENSEN, J.A., and PADIAN, K. 'Small pterosaurs and dinosaurs from the Uncompahgre fauna (Brushy Basin Member, Morrison Formation: ?Tithonian), Late Jurassic, western Colorado.' (*Journal of Paleontology*, 1989. Volume 63, Number 3. pp. 364–373)

KERMAC, K.A., MUSSETT, F., and RIGNEY, H.W. 'The skull of *Morganucodon*.' (*Zoological Journal of the Linnean Society*, 1981. Volume 71. pp. 1–158)

KIELAN JAWOROWSKA, Z. 'Results of the Polish-Mongolian Palaeontological Expeditions-Part VII.' (*Palaeontologia Polonica*, 1977. Number 57. pp. 5–60. 14 Plates)

KITCHING, J.W. 'On the *Lystrosaurus* Zone and its fauna with special reference to some immature Lystrosauridae.' (*Palaeontologia Africana*, 1968. Volume XI)

KNOWLTON, F.H. *Plants of the Past*. (Princeton University Press, Princeton, 1927)

KUHN, O. *Cotylosauria. Handbuch der Palaoherpetologie. Part 6* (Gustav Fischer Verlag, Stuttgart, 1969)

LANGFORD, G. *The Wilmington Coal Flora* (Esconi Associates, Northern Illinois, 1958)

LANGSTON, W. 'Nonmammalian Comanchean tetrapods.' (*Geoscience and Man Volume VIII*, 1974 [Bob. F. Perkins, Editor] pp. 77–102. 4 Plates, 10 Text-Figures, 2 Tables)

LILLEGRAVEN, J.A., KIELAN-JAWOROWSKA, Z. and CLEMENS, W.A., (Editors) *Mesozoic Mammals* (University of California Press, Berkeley, Los Angeles, London, 1979. 311 pages)

LONGMAN, H.A. 'A giant dinosaur from Durham Downs, Queensland.' (*Memoirs of the Queensland Museum, 1926*. Volume VIII. Part III. pp. 183–194)

LULL, R.S. 'Dinosaurian Distribution.' (*American Journal of Science*, 1910. Volume XXIX. January)

LULL, R.S. The Sauropod Dinosaur *Barosaurus* Marsh (*Memoirs of the Connecticut Academy of Arts and Sciences*, December 1919. Volume VI, 42 pages, 8 plates)

LULL, R.S. A Revision of the Ceratopsia (*Memoirs of the Peabody Museum of Natural History*, 1933. Volume III, Part 3. 175 pages)

LULL, R.S., and WRIGHT, N.E. Hadrosaurian Dinosaurs of North America (*Geological Society of America. Special Papers Number 40*, 1942. 242 pages, 31 Plates)

LYDEKKER, R. Fossil Reptilia and Batrachia (*Memoirs of the Geological Survey of India*, 1879. Volume I. Part 3)

LYDEKKER, R. 'Knowledge of the Fossil Vertebrates of Argentina, Part I, The Dinosaurs of Patagonia.' (*Anales Del Museo De La Plata*, 1893. *Paleontologia Argentina* II. pp. 3–13)

MADSEN, J.H. *Allosaurus fragilis* a revised osteology (*Utah Geological and Mineral Survey. Bulletin 109*, 1976. 163 pages)

MAISONNEUVE, J. 'Contributions a la paleoecologie du Mesozoique: les vairations de teneur en oxygene de l'atmosphere.' (*Mem. Soc. geol. France, N.S.*, 1980. Number 139. pp. 123–129)

MALEEVE, E.A. 'Gigantic carnivorous dinosaurs of Mongolia (in Russian).' (*Dokladi Akad. Nauk. SSSR*, 1955. 104. pp. 634–637)

MARSH, O.C. 'The Dinosaurs of North America.' (*United States Geological Survey*, 1894–95. Sixteenth Annual Report, Part 1. pp. 143–244)

MARSH, O.C., and MOOK, C.C. *Camarasaurus, Amphicoelias*, and Other Sauropods of Cope. (*Memoirs of the American Museum of Natural History*. New Series, 1921. Volume III, Part III)

MARTIL, D.M. and UNWIN, D.M. 'Exceptionally well preserved pterosaur wing membrane from the Cretaceous of Brazil.' (*Nature*, 1989. Volume 340. pp. 138–140)

MARTIN, L.D., STEWARD, J.D., and WHETSTONE, K.N. 'The origin of birds: structure of the tarsus and teeth.' (*The Auk*, 1980. Volume 97. pp. 86–93)

MARYANSKA, T., and OSMOLSKA, H. 'Pachycephalosauria, a new suborder of ornithischian dinosaurs.' (*Palaeontologia Polonica*, 1974. Number 30. pp. 1–102. Plates XXII–XXXI)

MARYANSKA, T. 'Ankylosauridae (Dinosauria) from Mongolia.' (*Palaeontologia Polonica*, 1977. Number 37. pp. 86–151. Plates 19–36)

MATTHEW, W.D. 'The pose of sauropodous dinosaurs.' (*The American Naturalist*, 1910. Volume XLIV. pp. 547–560)

MILNER, A. 'Late extinctions of amphibians.' (*Nature*, 1989. Volume 338. p. 117)

MOHABEY, D.M. 'Juvenile sauropod dinosaur from Upper Cretaceous Lameta Formation of Panchmahals District, Gujarat, India.' (*Journal Geological Society of India*, 1987. Volume 30. pp. 210–216)

MOLNAR, R.E. 'Australian late Mesozoic terrestrial tetrapods: some implications.' (*Mem Soc. geol. France, N.S.*, 1980. Number 139. pp. 131–143)

MOLNAR, R.E., FLANNERY, T.F., and RICH, T.H. 'Aussie *Allosaurus* after all.' (*Journal of Paleontology*, 1985. Volume 59, Number 6. pp. 1511–1513)

MOLNAR, R.E. and GALTON, P.M.. 'Hypsilophodontid dinosaurs from Lighting Ridge, New South Wales, Australia.' (*Geobios*, 1986. Number 19, fasc. 2. pp. 231–239)

MOLNAR, R.E. 'A pterosaur pelvis from western Queensland, Australia.' (*Alcheringa II*, 1987. pp. 87–94)

MONBARON, M. 'Dinosauriens Du Haut Atlas Central (Maroc): Etat de recherche et precision sur la decouverte d'un squelette complet de grand Cetiosaure.' (*Societe Jurassienne D'Emulation*, 1983. Extrait des Actes. pp. 203–234)

NEILL, W.T. *The Last of the Ruling Reptiles: Alligators, Crocodiles, and Their Kin*. (Columbia University Press, New York and London, 1971)

NORMAN, D.B. 'On the ornithischian dinosaur *Iguanodon bernissartensis* from the Lower Cretaceous of Bernissart (Belgium).' (*Institut Royal Des Sciences Naturelles De Belgique*, 1980. Memoire Number 178. pp. 1–103)

OLSEN, P.E., SHUBIN, N.H., and ANDERS, M.H. 'Triassic-Jurassic extinctions.' (*Science*, 1988. Volume 214. pp. 1358–1360)

OLSON, E.C. Origin of mammals based upon cranial morphology of the therapsid suborders (*Geological Society of America Special Papers*. Number 55, 1944. 136 pages)

OLSON, E.C. 'The family Diadectidae.' (*Fieldiana: Geology*, 1947. Volume II, Number 1. pp. 1–53)

OLSON, E.C. '*Diplocaulus*. A study in growth and variation.' (*Fieldiana: Geology*, 1951. Volume II, Number 2)

OLSON, E.C., and BEERBOWER, J.R. 'The San Angelo Formation, Permian of Texas, and its vertebrates.' (*The Journal of Geology*, September 1953. Volume 61, Number 5)

OLSON, E.C. 'Catalogue of localities of Permian and Triassic terrestrial vertebrates of the territories of the U.S.S.R.' (*The Journal of Geology*, 1957. Volume 65, Number 2. pp. 196–226)

OLSON, E.C. 'The evolution of mammalian characters.' (*Evolution*, 1959. Volume XIII, Number 3. pp. 344–353)

OLSON, E.C. 'Late Permian Terrestrial Vertebrates, U.S.A. and U.S.S.R.' (*Transactions of the American Philosophical Society*, 1962. New Series – Volume 52, Part 2. 224 pages)

OLSON, E.C. Chickasha Vertebrates (*Oklahoma Geological Survey*, 1965. Circular 70. 70 pages)

OLSON, E.C. Early Permian Vertebrates (*Oklahoma Geological Survey*, 1967. Circular 74. 111 pages)

OLSON, E.C. 'The Family Casidae.' (*Fieldiana: Geology*, 1968. Volume 17, Number 3. 349 pages)

OLSON, E.C. 'The changes of terrestrial vertebrates and climates during the Permian of North America.' (*Forma et Functio*, 1970. Volume 3. pp. 113–138)

OLSON, E.C. 'A skeleton of *Lysorophus tricarinatus* (Amphibia: Lepospondyli) from the Hennessey Formation (Permian) of Oklahoma.' (*Journal of Paleontology*, 1971. Volume 45, Number 3. pp. 443–449)

OLSON, E.C. 'The habitat: climatic change and its influence on life and habitat.' (*Biology of Nutrition*, 1972. I.E.F.N. Volume 18. [R.N. Fiennes. Editor]. pp. 267–305)

OLSON, E.C. 'On the source of therapsids.' (*Annals of the South African Museum*, 1974. Volume 64. pp. 27–46)

OLSON, E.C. 'Permo-Carboniferous paleoecology and morphotypic series.' (*American Zool*, 1975a. Volume 15. pp. 371–389)

OLSON, E.C. 'Permo-Carboniferous fresh water burrows.' (*Fieldiana: Geology*, 1975b. Volume 33, Number 15. pp. 271–290)

OLSON, E.C. 'Permian lake faunas: a study in community evolution.' (*Journal of the Palaeontological Society of India*, 1975c. Volume 20. pp. 146–163)

OLSON, E.C. 'Biological and physical factors in the dispersal of Permo-Carboniferous terrestrial vertebrates.' (*Historical Biogeography, Plate Tectonics, and the Changing Environment* [Jane Gray and Arthur J. Boucot, Editors] Oregon State University Press, 1979a)

OLSON, E.C. 'Aspects of the biology of *Trimerorhachis* (Amphibia: Temnospondyli).' (*Journal of Paleontology*, 1979b. Volume 53, Number 1. pp. 1–17. 8 Text-Figures)

OLSON, E.C. 'The North American Seymouriidae.' (*Aspects of Vertebrate History* [L.I. Jacobs, Editor] Museum of Northern Arizona Press, 1980)

OLSON, E.C. 'Vertebrate paleoecology: A current perspective.' (*Paleogeography, Paleoclimatology, Paleoecology*, 1985. Volume 50. pp. 83–106)

OLSON, E.C. 'Problems of Permo-Triassic terrestrial vertebrate extinctions.' (*Historical Biology*, 1989. Volume 2. pp. 17–35)

OSBORN, H.F. Crania of *Tyrannosaurus* and *Allosaurus* . (*Memoirs of the American Museum of Natural History* [*Tyrannosaurus* Contributions Number 3], 1912. 30 pages, 2 plates)

OSBORN, H.F. 'Skeletal adaptations of *Ornitholestes, Struthiomimus, Tyrannosaurus*.' (*Bulletin American Museum of Natural History*, 1916. Volume XXXV. pp. 733–771, 3 plates)

OSMOLSKA, H., and RONIEWICZ, E. 'Deinocheiridae, a new family of theropod dinosaurs.' (*Palaeontologia Polonica, 21*, 1969. pp. 6–19. 5 plates)

OSMOLKSA, H. 'The late Cretaceous vertebrate assemblages of the Gobi Desert, Mongolia.' (*Mem. Soc. geol. France, N.S.*, 1980. Number 139. pp. 145–150)

OSTROM, J.R. '*Archaeopteryx* and the origin of birds.' (*Biological Journal of the Linnean Society*, 1967. Volume 8. pp. 91–182)

OSTROM, J.H., Osteology of *Deinonychus antirrhopus*, an unusual theropod from the Lower Cretaceous of Montana (*Peabody Museum of Natural History*, Yale University, New Haven. Bulletin 30, 1969. 165 pages)

OSTROM, J.H. 'The osteology of *Compsognathus longipes* Wagner.' (*Zitteliana*, 1978. Vol. 4. pp. 73–118, plates 7–14)

OWEN, R. *A History of British Fossil Reptiles. Volume IV* (Cassell & Company Limited, London, 1849–84)

PADIAN, K. 'Presence of the dinosaur *Scelidosaurus* indicates Jurassic age for the Kayenta Formation (Glen Canyon Group, northern Arizona).' (*Geology*, 1989. Volume 17. pp. 438–441)

PADIAN, K., and CHURE, D.J., Conveners. CULVER, S.J., (Editor) *The Age of Dinosaurs: Short Courses in Paleontology* (The Paleontological Society, University of Tennessee, Knoxville, 1989. 210 pages)

PARRISH, J.M., PARRISH, J.T., HUTCHINSON, J.H., SPICER R.A. 'Late Cretaceous vertebrate fossils from the North Slope of Alaska and implications for dinosaur ecology.' (*Palaios*, 1987. Volume 2. pp. 377–389)

PAUL, G.S. *Predatory Dinosaurs of the World* (Simon and Schuster, New York, London, Toronto, Sydney, and Tokyo, 1988. 464 pages)

POWELL, E.J. 'Revision de los titanosauridos de America Del Sur.' (Tesis presentada para optar al titulo de Doctor en Ciencias Geologicas. Universidad Nacional de Tucuman, 1986)

PRESS, F., and SIEVER, R. *Earth* (W.H. Freeman and Company, New York, 1982)

RAATH, M.A. 'Fossil vertebrate studies in Rhodesia: a new dinosaur (Reptilia: Saurischia) from near the Trias-Jurassic boundary.' (*Arnoldia*, 1972. Volume 5, Number 30. pp. 1–37)

READ, C.B. and MAMAY, S.H. 'Upper Paleozoic floral zones and floral provinces of the United States.' (*United States Geological Survey Professional Papers*, 454 K, 1964. pp. 1–35, 19 plates)

REIF, W.F., and WESTPHAL, F. (Editors) *Third Symposium on Mesozoic Terrestrial Ecosystems, Tubingen, 1984* (Tubingen University Press, Tubingen. 259 pages)

REISZ, R.R. 'A diapsid reptile from the Pennsylvanian of Kansas.' (*University of Kansas, Museum of Natural History, Special Publications Number 7*, 1981. pp. 1–74)

REISZ, R.R., and BERMAN, D.S. '*Ianthasaurus hardestii* new species, a primitive edaphosaur (Reptilia: Pelycosauria) from the Upper Pennsylvanian Rock Lake Shale near Garnett, Kansas.' (*Canadian Journal of Earth Sciences*, 1986. pp. 71–91)

ROMER, A.S. 'The locomotor apparatus of certain primitive and mammal-like reptiles.' (*Bulletin of the American Museum of Natural History*, 1922. Vol. XLVI, Art. X, pp. 517–606)

ROMER, A.S. 'An ophiacodont reptile from the Permian of Kansas.' (*The Journal of Geology*, 1925. Volume XXXIII, Number 2)

ROMER, A.S. 'Notes on the Permo-Carboniferous reptile *Dimetrodon*.' (*The Journal of Geology*, 1927a. Volume XXXV, Number 8)

ROMER, A.S. 'The Pelvic Musculature of Ornithischian Dinosaurs.' (*Acta Zoologica*, 1927b. BD 8)

ROMER, A.S. 'A skeletal model of the primitive reptile *Seymouria*, and the phylogenetic position of that type.' (*The Journal of Geology*, 1928. Volume XXXVI, Number 3)

ROMER, R.S., and PRICE, L.W. 'Review of the Pelycosauria.' (*Geological Society of America*, 1940. Special Papers Number 28. 538 pages)

ROMER, R.S. 'The Chanares (Argentina) Triassic reptile fauna. XIII. An early orithosuchid pseudosuchian, *Gracilisuchus stipanicicorum*.' (*Breviora*, 1972a. Number 389)

ROMER, R.S. 'A Carboniferous labyrinthodont amphibian with complete dermal armor.' (*Kirtlandia*, 1972b. Number 16. 8 pages)

ROMER, R.S. *Vertebrate Paleontology* (The University of Chicago Press, Chicago and London, 1974. 468 pages)

ROMER, R.S. *Osteology of the Reptiles* (The University of Chicago Press, Chicago and London, 1976. 772 pages)

ROSS, C.A. (Editor) *Crocodiles and Alligators* (Facts on File, New York and Oxford, 1989. 240 pages)

ROWE, T. 'A new species of the theropod dinosaur *Syntarsus* from the Early Jurassic Kayenta Formation of Arizona.' (*Journal of Vertebrate Paleontology*, 1989. Volume 9, Number 2. pp. 125–136)

RUSSELL, D.A. 'Reconstruction of *Leptoceratops gracilis* from the Upper Edmonton Formation (Cretaceous) of Alberta.' (*Canadian Journal of Earth Sciences*, 1970. Volume 7. pp. 181–184)

RUSSELL, D.A. 'Ostrich dinosaurs from the Late Cretaceous of Western Canada.' (*Canadian Journal of Earth Sciences*, 1972. Volume 9, Number 375. pp. 376–401)

RUSSELL, D.A., BELAND, P., and McINTOSH, J.S. 'Paleoecology of the dinosaurs of Tendaguru (Tanzania).' (*Mem. Soc. geol. France, N.S.*, 1980. Number 139. pp. 169–175)

SANTA LUCA, A.P., CROMPTON, A.W., and CHARIG, A.J. 'A complete skeleton of the Late Triassic ornithischian *Heterodontosaurus tucki*.' (*Nature*, 1976. Volume 264. pp. 324–328)

SANTA LUCA, A.P. 'The postcranial skeleton of *Heterodontosaurus tucki* (Reptilia: Ornithischia) from the Stormberg of South Africa.' (*Annals of the South African Museum*, 1980. Volume 79, Number 7. pp. 159–211)

SCHMIDT-NIELSEN, K. 'How birds breathe.' (*Scientific American*, 1971. Volume 225 (6). pp. 72–79)

SCOTESE, C.R., BAMBACH, K., BARTON, C., VAN DER VOO, R., and ZIEGLER, M. 'Paleozoic base maps.' (*Journal of Geology*, 1979. Volume 87, Number 3. pp. 217–277)

SERENO, P.C., and SHICHIN, C. '*Psittacosaurus xinjiangensis* (Ornithischia: Ceratopsia), a new psittacosaur from the Lower Cretaceous of northwestern China.' (*Journal of Vertebrate Paleontology*, 1988. Volume 8, Number 4. pp. 353–365)

SERENO, P.C., SHICHIN, C., ZHENGWU, C., and CHANGGANG, R. '*Psittacosaurus meileyingensis* (Ornithischia: Ceratopsia) a new psittacosaur from the Lower Cretaceous of northeastern China.' (*Journal of Vertebrate Paleontology*, 1988. Volume 8, Number 4. pp. 366–377)

SEELEY, H.G. *Dragons of the Air: An Account of Extinct Flying Reptiles* (D. Appleton & Company and Methuen & Company, New York and London, 1901. 237 pages)

SHAROV, A.G. 'An unusual reptile from the Lower Triassic of Fergana. (*Paleontological Journal*, 1970. Number 1. pp. 112–116)

SHAROV, A.G. 'A new flying reptile from the Mesozoic of Kazakhstan and Kirgizia (in Russian).' (*Trudy Paleontologicheskogo Instituta*, 1971. *Akad. Nauk S.S.S.R.* 130. pp. 104–113)

SHUONAN, Z., BAIMING, Z., MATEER, N.J. and LUCAS, S.G. 'The Mesozoic reptiles of China. Studies of Chinese fossil vertebrates.' S.G. Lucas and N.J. Mateer (Editors) (*Bulletin of the Geological Institutions of the University of Uppsala, N.S.*, 1985. Volume 11. pp 133–150)

SIMMONS, D.J. 'The Non-Therapsid Reptiles of the Lufeng Basin, Yunnan, China.' (*Fieldiana: Geology*, 1965. Volume 15, Number 1. 93 pages)

SKINNER, B.J. (Editor) *Paleontology and Paleoenvironments* (William Kaufmann, Inc. Los Altos, 1981. 205 pages)

SMITH, A.G. and BRIDEN, J.C. *Mesozoic and Cenozoic paleocontinental maps* (Cambridge University Press, Cambridge, 1977. 63 pages)

SRIVASTAVA, S., MOHABEY, D.M., SAHNI, A., and PANT, S.C. 'Upper Cretaceous dinosaur egg clutches from Kheda District (Gujarat, India). (*Palaeontographica*, 1986. Abt. A. Band 193. pp. 220–233. 3 Plates)

SUES, H.D. and TAQUET, P. 'A pacycephalosaurid dinosaur from Madagascar and a Laurasia-Gondwanaland connection in the Cretaceous.' (*Nature*, 1979. Volume 279. pp. 733–735)

TAQUET, P. 'Geologie et paleontologie du gisement de Gadoufaoua (Aptien du Niger).' (*Cahiers du Paleontologie*, C.N.R.S., 1976)

THULBORN, R.A. 'The post-cranial skeleton of the Triassic ornithischian dinosaur *Fabrosaurus australis*,' (*Palaeontology*, 1972. Volume 15, Part 1. pp. 29–60)

TUCKER, M.E. and BENTON, M.J. 'Triassic environments, climates and reptile evolution.' (*Paleogeography, Paleoclimatology, Paleoecology*, 1982. Volume 40. pp. 361–379)

UNWIN, D.N. 'New remains of the pterosaur *Dimorphodon* (Pterosauria: Rhamphorhynchoidea) and the terrestrial ability of early pterosaurs.' (*Modern Geology*, 1988. Volume 13. pp. 57–68)

VAN ANDEL, T.H. *New Views of an Old Planet: Continental Drift and the History of the Earth* (Cambridge University Press, Cambridge, London, New York, New Rochelle, Melbourne, Sydney, 1985)

WALKER, A.D. 'Triassic reptiles from the Elgin area: *Stagonolepis, Dasygnathus* and their allies.' (*Philosophical Transactions of the Royal Society of London, Series B*, 1961. Volume 244. pp. 103–204)

WALKER, A.D. 'A Triassic Reptile from the Elgin area: *Ornithosuchus* and the origin of carnosaurs.' (*Philosophical Transactions of the Royal Society of London, Series B*, 1964. Number 744. Volume 248. pp. 53–134)

WALKER, A.D. 'New light on the origin of birds and crocodiles.' (*Nature*, 1972. Volume 237. pp. 257–263)

WEISHAMPEL, D.B., and WEISHAMPEL, J.B. 'Annotated localities of ornithopod dinosaurs: Implication to Mesozoic paleobiogeography' (*The Mosasaur*, 1983. Volume 1. pp. 43–87)

WELLS, S.P. '*Dilophosaurus wetherilli* (Dinosauria, Theropoda) osteology and comparisons.' (*Paleontographica, Abt. B*, 1984. Volume 185. pp. 85–180)

WHEELER, P.E. 'Elaborate CNS cooling structures in large dinosaurs.' (*Nature*, 1978. Volume 275. pp. 441–443)

WILD, R. 'Flugsaurier aus der Obertrias von Italien.' (*Naturwissenschaften*, 1984. 71. pp. 1–11, 2 figures)

WILLISTON, S.W. *American Permian Vertebrates* (The University of Chicago Press, Chicago, 1911)

WILLISTON, S.W. *Water Reptiles of the Past and Present* (The University of Chicago Press, Chicago, 1914)

WILSON, J.T. Introduction. *Continents Adrift and Continents Aground* (W.H. Freeman and Company, San Francisco, 1976)

ZHIMING, D., and TANG, Z. 'Note on a new Mid-Jurassic sauropod (*Datousaurus bashanensis* gen. et. sp. nov.) from Sichuan Basin, China.' (*Vertebrata Pal Asiatica*, 1984. Volume XXII, Number 1)

ZHIMING, D., and MILNER, A.C. *Dinosaurs from China* (British Museum [Natural History] and China Ocean Press, 1988. 114 pages)

ZHOU, S. *The Middle Jurassic Dinosaurian Fauna from Dashanpu, Ziegong, Sichuan. Volume II Stegosaurs* (Sichuan Scientific and Technological Publishing House, 1984. 52 pages, 45 text-figures, and 13 plates)

XINGXUE, L., and ZHAOQI, Y. 'Fructifications of Gigantopterids from South China.' (*Paleontographica Abt. B*. 1953. Volume 185. pp. 11–26)

GLOSSARY

A

Abelisaurs Gondwanic theropods.
Abelisaurus A large carnosaur from South America.
Acetabulum A cup-shaped depression in the pelvis into which the ball joint of the femur fits. Perforated in dinosaurs.
Adaptation The modification of organisms in response to environmental change.
Adaptive radiation The expansion of organisms into new environments as a result of the acquisition of new characteristics.
Aestivate To burrow into mud and become inactive during periods of drought.
Aetosaurs Heavily armoured, semi-aquatic herbivorous thecodonts of the Triassic Period.
Air sacs An extension of the respiratory system additional to the lungs in birds, pterosaurs, and some dinosaurs. Hollow bones of these animals indicate the presence of air sacs.
Allosaurus (*allos* strange + *sauros* reptile) A large Jurassic bipedal carnosaur.
Alluvial fan A low, cone-shaped accumulation of soil that forms by sediments being washed down from a steep highland in to a broad valley.
Altricial An animal that is helpless at birth and requires parental care to survive.
Ambient heat Heat from the surrounding environment that a cold-blooded animal uses to warm itself.
Ammonites Molluscs with a coiled shell which were common in the Mesozoic seas. They are relatives of today's *Nautilus*, and squid.
Amniote egg Named for the sac that contains the embryo, the amnion. This is the type of egg laid by reptiles and birds which has a hard outer shell to protect the embryo from drying out and a nutritious yoke inside.
Amphibious Capable of living both in the water and on the land.
Anapsid A group of reptiles characterized by having no skull openings behind the eyes.
Anatosaurus (*anatos* harmless + *sauros* reptile) A Late Cretaceous hadrosaur from western North America.
Angiosperms Flowering plants.
Ankylosaurus (*ankylos* to grow together + *sauros* reptile) A heavily armoured quadrupedal ornithischian from the Cretaceous with a tail club.
Apatosaurus (*apate* deceit, illusory + *sauros* reptile) Commonly known as *Brontosaurus*. It is a large sauropod from western North America.
Archaeopteryx (*archaeos* primitive + *pteros* wing) A Jurassic bird with dinosaurian characteristics from central Europe.
Archosaurs The group of reptiles which includes the extinct dinosaurs, thecodonts, pterosaurs, and the living crocodiles.
Arthropods Invertebrates with jointed legs such as insects, spiders, crabs, and shrimps.
Articulated Segments that are joined together such as the bones of a skeleton.
Articular surface The surface where bones are joined together such as the shoulder and knee joints of the body.

B

Barapasaurus (*bara* big + *saurus* reptile) An Early Jurassic sauropod from India.
Biped A creature that walks on two legs.
Bolide A large brilliant meteor, especially one that explodes.
Brachiosaurus (*brachion* arm + *sauros* reptile) An extremely large sauropod with longer forelimbs than hind limbs. From the Late Jurassic of western North America and Africa.
Brontosaurus (*bronte* thunder + *sauros* reptile) See *Apatosaurus*.

C

Cacops A small labyrinthodont amphibian which comes from the Early Permian of North America.
Caliche nodules Calcium carbonate that accumulates in nodules in warm climate soils that are dry for part of the year.
Camarasaurus (*kamara* chamber, vault + *sauros* reptile) A spatulate-toothed sauropod from the Late Jurassic.
Camptorhinus A primitive cotylosaur reptile from the Early Permian.
Camptosaurus (*kamptos* bent + *sauros* reptile) A primitive ornithopod from the Late Jurassic of western North America and Europe.
Carapace A bony or chitinous shell covering the back or part of the back of an animal, such as the upper shell of a turtle.
Carnivore An animal that feeds on other animals.
Carnosauria (*carnis* flesh + *sauros* reptile). A suborder of the theropod dinosaurs, large heavily built reptiles with short necks.
Carnotaurus (*carnis* flesh + *taurus* bull). A South American abelisaur with two stout bull-like horns projecting from its skull.
Cartilage A firm elastic connective tissue that surrounds bony joints.
Caudal Situated in or near the tail or hind end of the body, such as caudal vertebrae.
Centrosaurus (*kentron* spike or spur + *sauros* reptile) A Late Cretaceous ceratopsian with a distinctly large nasal horn.
Ceratopsia The suborder of Cretaceous horned dinosaurs.
Ceratosaurus (*keratos* horn + *sauros* reptile) A Late Jurassic North American carnosaur distinguished by a prominent nasal horn.
Cetiosaurs The basal group of sauropods.
Cetiosaurus (*keteios* large + *sauros* reptile) A large sauropod from the Late Jurassic of Morocco with long forelimbs and a comparatively short neck.
Chasmosaurus (*chasma* space + *sauros* reptile) A very long-frilled ceratopsian from the Late Cretaceous of Alberta, Canada.
Chevrons Extensions of small bones from the bottom of the tail vertebrae.
Coelophysis (*koilos* hollow + *physa* bag) A gracile Late Triassic coelurosaur from North America.
Coelurosaur Lightly built theropods with long necks and slender skulls.
Collagenous tissues Elastic connective tissue containing collagen found within the facia which underlies the skin, as well as in cartilage.
Community An interdependent group of plants and animals.
Compsognathus (*kompsos* elegant + *gnathos* jaw) A small coelurosaur from Germany.
Condyle A rounded articular prominence on a bone such as the head of the femur or a knuckle joint.
Conifers A cone-bearing plant, such as pines, firs and yews.
Continental drift The movement of the continents over the surface of the earth.
Coracoid The bone that in reptiles, birds and monotremes, together with the scapula (shoulder blades), forms the articular surface for the front limbs. In higher mammals, it is a reduced bony process of the scapula.
Coriolis effect Deflection of wind or ocean currents due to the spin of the earth, so that the currents follow curved rather than straight paths and bend to the right in the northern hemisphere and to the left in the southern hemisphere.
Corprolite Fossil dung.
Corythosaurus (*korythos* helmet + *sauros* reptile) A crested lambeosaur from the Late Cretaceous of Alberta, Canada.
Cotylosauria An order of primitive reptiles descended from certain labyrinthodont amphibians. The cotylosaurs were probably the stem reptiles, from which other reptilian orders evolved.
Cycads Cone-bearing woody Gymnosperm plants that have survived from the Triassic to present day.
Cynodonts Advanced mammal-like reptiles from the Triassic.

D

Deinocheirus (*deinos* terrible + *cheiros* hand) This theropod from Mongolia is known only by its gigantic forelimbs.
Deinonychus (*deinos* terrible + *onychos* claw) A moderate-sized Early Cretaceous coelurosaur with a large claw on its foot.
Dermal armour Small plates or nodules of bone embedded in the skin of some dinosaurs.
Desmatosuchus (*desmatos* bond + *souchos* crocodile) An armoured herbivorous, semi-aquatic Triassic thecodont.
Diadectes A large Permian amphibian with so many reptilian characteristics that it is often considered a cotylosaurian reptile.
Diapsid A group of reptiles that include the dinosaurs, crocodiles, lizards, and snakes which are characterized by having a pair of openings immediately behind the eye socket.
Dicroidium A common index fossil of the Triassic adapted to dry climatic conditions.
Dicynodontia (*di* two + *kynos* dog + *odon* tooth) A suborder of therapsids somewhat hippopotamus-like in shape and often with tusks in their beaked jaws. They were widely distributed throughout the world during the Permian and Triassic.
Digitigrade Walking on the digits or toes of the foot with the ankle raised from the ground.
Dilophosaurus (*di* two + *lophos* crest + *sauros* reptile) An Early Jurassic coelurosaur with two blade-like crests on its skull.
Dimetrodon A carnivorous pelycosaur characterized by a large longitudinal sail on its back.
Dimorphism Having two forms of the same species usually related to the differences between males and females.
Dinosauria (*deinos* terrible + *sauros* reptile) A general term including the Mesozoic reptiles now classified in two orders, Saurischia and Ornithischia.
Diplocaulus An Early Permian amphibian with a broad, flat, crescent-shaped skull.
Diplodocus (*diplos* double + *dokos* beam) An elongated, peg-toothed sauropod from the Late Jurassic.
Disarticulated Separated or pulled apart.

E

Ecology The inter-relationships between animal and plant life and their environment.
Ecological niche An area occupied by organisms that have specially adapted to that habitat.
Ecological replacement The filling of a vacated habitat by the evolution of a new species or the migration of a different species.
Ecosystem The plants and animals of a community together with the physical environment they occupy.
Ectothermic 'Cold blooded': the condition in which an organism relies on external sources of heat to control its body temperature.
Edaphosaurus (*edaphos* earth + *sauros* reptile) An Early Permian herbivorous pelycosaur noted for the large sail on its back.
Edmontosaurus (from the Edmonton Formation + *sauros* reptile) A Late Cretaceous hadrosaur from the Edmonton Formation of Alberta.
Endothermic 'Warm blooded': the condition in which an organism is able to generate heat internally by means of chemical reactions to control its body temperature.
Endothiodon A dicynodont from the Late Permian.
Epicontinental seas (*epi* above + continental). Shallow seas that flood low lying continental interiors.
Erect posture A stance in which the hindlimbs are aligned directly beneath the body. Used by dinosaurs, birds, and mammals.
Eryops A large labyrinthodont amphibian from the Early Permian.
Euryapsid An extinct group of aquatic reptiles which included plesiosaurs and ichthyosaurs, characterized by a single opening high up on the side of the skull behind each eye socket.
Evaporites Sedimentary layers such as salt and gypsum formed by the evaporation of sea water.
Evolution The continuous adaptation of organisms to a changing environment by natural selection.

F

Fauna The animals within an ecosystem.
Femur The bone of the upper leg or thigh bone.
Fenestra An opening in the skull.
Fibula The smaller bone of the lower leg. (See also tibia.)
Flora The plants within an ecosystem.
Food web The nutritional structure of an ecosystem in which there are levels of producer species and consumer species.
Foraminifer A small marine creature having a shell perforated with small holes or pores.
Fossil Any record of past life preserved in sedimentary rock such as bones, teeth, egg shells, and also including impressions of skin, footprints and burrows.

G

Gastric mill A muscular part of the stomach used to grind up food with the assistance of swallowed stones, or gastroliths.
Gastroliths Stones swallowed by reptiles and birds and used to help grind the food in the stomach or gizzard.
Ginkgo The modern gymnosperm tree related to the once abundant fossil group of ginkgophytes.
Glacial till Sediments ploughed up and deposited by a glacier as it moves.
Glacier A large mass of ice that creeps over the earth's surface.
Glossopteris One of main Permian fossil plants throughout all of Gondwana. They had strap-like leaves, woody trunks and grew in either tree or shrub form.
Gondwana The southern supercontinent which was composed of South America, Africa, Antarctica, Australia and India.
Gorgonopsids Therapsids, or mammal-like reptiles, from the Late Permian often having large, sabre-like canine teeth.
Gracile Graceful, slender, thin.
Gymnosperms (*gymnos* naked + *sperma* seed) Vascular plants whose seeds are unprotected by any covering, such as conifers.

H

Habitat The physical place an organism occupies.
Hadrosaur Flat-headed or solid-crested 'duckbilled' dinosaurs.
Hadrosaurus (*hadros* bulky + *sauros* reptile) A Late Cretaceous ornithischian dinosaur.
Herbivore An animal that feeds on plants.
Heterodontosaurus (*heteros* different + *odon* tooth + *sauros* reptile). An early ornithischian dinosaur with grinding teeth.
Humerus The bone of the upper arm.
Hypacrosaurus (*hypakros* nearly the highest + *sauros* reptile). A hollow crested lambeosaur from the Late Cretaceous.
Hypsilophodon (*hypsi* high + *lophos* crest + *odon* tooth). An early ornithopod with abrading teeth.

I

Ichthyosaurs Mesozoic marine reptiles of porpoise-like form.
Ichthyostega One of the first land-living vertebrates and most primitive of the labyrinthodont amphibians.
Ictidosaur Advanced mammal-like reptiles widely distributed throughout the Late Triassic world.

Iguanodon (*iguana* lizard + *odon* tooth) A large ornithopod dinosaur from the Early Cretaceous. The first dinosaur to be scientifically described.
Illium One of the bones of the pelvis. It is connected to the vertebral column.
Index fossil A fossil that provides precise correlations of time between various places. It is distinct and easily recognized, widespread, and common in a limited time zone.
Inostrancevia A gigantic gorgonopsid from the Late Permian of Russia.
Insectivore Animals that eat insects.
Ischium One of the bones of the pelvis. It points downwards and backwards from the hip socket.
Isolation The separation of part of a species from another part so that there is no longer a gene flow between them.

K *Kentrosaurus* (*kentron* spike + *sauros* reptile) A Late Jurassic stegosaur found in association with numerous long spikes.
Kritosaurus (*kritos* chosen + *sauros* reptile) A Late Cretaceous hadrosaur.

L **Labyrinthodontia** (*labyrinthos* labyrinth + *odon* tooth) A major group of early amphibians widely distributed throughout the world from the Late Devonian through the Late Triassic.
Lambeosaur Duckbilled dinosaurs with hollow crests.
Lambeosaurus (*Lambe* Lawrence Lambe, Canadian palaeontologist + *sauros* reptile) A Late Cretaceous hollow crested duckbilled dinosaur.
Land bridge A strip of land connecting two continents which allows organisms to migrate back and forth.
Laramide orogeny See Orogeny.
Laurasia The northern supercontinent including North America, Asia and Europe; separated from Gondwana by the Tethys seaway.
Lepidosaurs Lizards and snakes.
Lesothosaurus (*Lesotho* a nation in South Africa + *sauros* reptile) A primitive ornithischian with non-grinding teeth from the Late Triassic.
Ligaments Tough sheets or threads of tissue which connect bones and hold organs in place.
Lithosphere The ridged outer portion of the earth which includes the continental and oceanic crust in its top part. It is divided into plates.
Lycaenops A gorgonopsid from the Late Permian.
Lycopods Clubmosses. Among the earliest vascular land plants dating back 420 million years. Some forms still exist today.
Lystrosaurus An Early Triassic dicynodont found in South Africa, Antarctica, India and China.

M *Maiasaura* (*maia* nurse + *sauros* reptile) A Cretaceous hadrosaur which exhibited parental care.
Mamenchisaurus (*Mamenchi* an area in Szechuan, China + *sauros* reptile) A Late Jurassic sauropod with an extremely long neck.
Mantel The region of the Earth's interior between the outer crust and the core.
Megalosaurus (*megale* giant + *sauros* reptile) A large carnosaur of Jurassic to Early Cretaceous age.
Mesosaurus A small aquatic Permian reptile found in South Africa and Brazil.
Metoposaurus (*metapon* forehead + *sauros* reptile) A Late Triassic labyrinthodont amphibian with a very wide broad head found in North America, Europe, Africa, and India.

N **Natural selection** The process which results in the survival of those organisms best adapted for particular changes in the environment.
Neural spine A spine, or projection, arising from the top of a vertebra.
Nodosaurs Heavily armoured quadrupedal ornithischians without tail clubs.
Nuchal ligaments Ligaments that strengthen and support the neck.

O **Omnivore** Animals that eat both plants and animals.
Orbit The bony socket which holds the eye.
Ornithischian One of the two major orders of dinosaurs based on hip structure. In this group the pelvis has the pubic bone rotated back to lie parallel to the ischium in a bird-like fashion. The group is herbivorous and includes ornithopods, stegosaurs, ceratopsians, ankylosaurs, nodosaurs and pachycephalosaurs.
Ornitholestes (*ornithos* bird + *lestes* robber) A Late Jurassic coelurosaur.
Ornithopod (*ornithos* bird + *podos* foot) A suborder of ornithischian dinosaurs, including hypsilophodonts, iguanodonts, hadrosaurs and lambeosaurs.
Orogeny Mountain building, especially a mountain building event in history, such as the Laramide orogeny.

P *Pachycephalosaurus* (*pachys* thick + *kephale* head + *saurus* reptile) A Late Cretaceous ornithischian with an extremely thick, dome-shaped skull.
Pachyrhinosaurus (*pachys* thick + *rhinos* nose + *sauros* reptile) A Late Cretaceous ceratopsian which has a thick boss instead of a horn on its nasal area.
Palatal teeth Teeth located in the plate or roof of the mouth.
Pangaea The single vast supercontinent in which all the continents of the earth were combined.
Parasaurolophus (*para* beside + *sauros* reptile + *lophos* crest) A lambeosaur with a long, hollow, crest extending from the back of its skull.
Pareiasaurs Very large cotylosaurs, primitive reptiles from the Late Permian.
Pelvis The hip region of the skeleton.
Pelycosaurs An order of reptiles from the Carboniferous and Permian, directly antecedent to the therapsids, or mammal-like reptiles. Some pelycosaurs have distinctive 'sails' on their backs.
Phylogeny The evolutionary history of a group of related organisms.
Phytosaur (*phyton* plant + *sauros* reptile) Thecodonts from the Triassic which are similar in appearance to modern gavials.
Placerias (*plankos* wide) A wide-bodied dicynodont from the Late Triassic.
Plateosaurus (*plate* blade of an ore + *sauros* reptile) A Late Triassic prosauropod.
Plate tectonics The movements and interactions of the earth's lithospheric plates.
Plesiosaurs Mesozoic marine reptiles.
Precocial An organism that, upon birth, is active and able to move about freely.
Predentary bone A beak-like bone on the front of the lower jaw in ornithischians.
Procolophonids Small primitive reptiles from the Early Triassic.
Prosauropods Triassic saurischians close to the ancestry of the sauropods.
Proterosuchian A long-jawed thecodont similar to crocodiles in appearance.
Protoceratops (*protos* first + *keros* horn + *ops* face) A small early ceratopsian without a definite horn, but possessing instead a raised nasal area.
Psittacosaurus (*psittakos* parrot + *sauros* reptile) The most primitive ceratopsian.
Pterosauria (*pteron* wing + *sauros* reptile) The flying reptiles of the Mesozoic.
Pubis One of the bones of the pelvis which points forward in saurischians and backward in ornithischians.
Pygostyle (*pyge* rump + *stylos* pillar) The bone at the posterior end of the spinal column in birds formed by the fusion of several caudal vertebrae.

Q **Quadruped** A creature that walks on four legs.

R **Radius** One of the bones of the lower arm (see also ulna).
Raptorial Adapted for seizing prey, as the bills or claws of certain carnivorous birds.
Respiration The metabolic process by which organisms supply their cells with the oxygen needed to produce energy.
Rhamphorhynchus (*ramphos* bill + *rhynchos* snout) A Late Jurassic pterosaur.
Rhoetosaurus (*Rhoetus* one of the giants in Greek mythology + *sauros* reptile) An Early Jurassic sauropod from Australia.
Rhynchocephalia An order of reptiles which include the Triassic rhynchosaurs and the living *sphenodon* (tuatara) of New Zealand.
Rostral bone The beak-like bone on the front of the upper jaw in ceratopsians.
Rugose Rough and wrinkled.
Rutiodon (*rhytis* wrinkle + *odon* tooth) A Late Triassic phytosaur.

S **Sacrum** A bone formed by the fusion of two or more vertebrae which forms part of the pelvis.
Saurischian One of the two major orders of dinosaurs based on hip structure. In this group the pubis is long and points forward and downward from the hip socket in reptilian fashion. This group includes the carnivorous theropods and the herbivorous sauropods.
Saurolophine Hadrosaurs with slender solid spikes projecting from their skulls.
Saurolophus (*sauros* reptile + *lophos* crest) A Late Cretaceous hadrosaur from North America and Asia.
Sauropod A suborder of long-necked saurischian dinosaurs which are quadrupedal, herbivorous, and usually gigantic.
Scelidosaurus (*skeidos* rib + *sauros* reptile) A primitive armoured Early Jurassic ornithischian.
Scutellosaurus (*scutellum* little shield + *sauros* reptile. A small armoured ornithischian from the Early Jurassic.
Scutes Plates of bone embedded in the skin of some dinosaurs and reptiles.
Seymouria A small Early Permian amphibian with so many reptilian characteristics that it is often considered a cotylosaurian reptile.

Shantungosaurus (*Shantung* a Chinese province + *sauros* reptile) One of the largest hadrosaurs from the Late Cretaceous of China.
Sphenosuchian The thecodont ancestors of the modern crocodiles.
Spinosaurus (*spina* spine + *sauros* reptile) This Late Cretaceous theropod has extremely elongated neural spines on its vertebrae.
Stegoceras (*stegos* roof + *keras* horn) A small Late Cretaceous dome-headed ornithischian.
Stegosaurs Ornithischians with plates arranged on their backs.
Stegosaurus (*stegos* roof + *sauros* reptile) Late Jurassic stegosaur with a single row of plates along its back.
Struthiomimus (*struthion* ostrich + *mimos* mimic) A Late Cretaceous bipedal coelurosaur with a long neck and toothless jaws.
Styracosaurus (*styrakion* end of a spear + *sauros* reptile) A Late Cretaceous ceratopsian with long spikes projecting from its frill.
Subduction The process where one lithospheric plate meets another and descends beneath it.
Supernova The explosion of a dying star.
Sprawling posture The stance of an animal that has its legs projecting out to the sides like a lizard.
Synapsid A group of reptiles which are characterized by having a single opening low down on the skull behind the eyes to which the mammals are related.
Syntarsus (*syn* together + *tarsos* flat of the foot). A Late Triassic African coelurosaur closely related to the North American *Coelophysis*.

T *Tapinocephalus* A large herbivorous therapsid from the Permian of South Africa.
Tarbosaurus (*tarbos* fear + *sauros* reptile) A huge carnosaur from the Late Cretaceous of Mongolia, closely related to the North American *Tyrannosaurus*.
Tectonic Pertaining to the deformation of the earth's crust.
Temporal openings Openings between the bones of the skull which determine the classification of reptile groups.
Tendons Cord or rod-like fibrous tissue which connects muscle with bone, often ossified in ornithischian dinosaurs.
Tenontosaurus (*tenontos* sinew + *sauros* reptile) An Early Cretaceous ornithopod.
Tethys sea The seaway which separated the supercontinents of Laurasia and Gondwana which contained a distinctive and diverse tropical fauna.
Thecodontia (*theke* sheath + *odon* tooth) The order of Triassic archosaurian reptiles ancestral to dinosaurs, pterosaurs, and crocodiles.
Therapsida (*theros* wild beast + *apsidos* arch) The mammal-like reptiles, the therapsids.
Theriodontia Mammal-like reptiles which were very advanced.
Theropodia (*theros* wild beast + *podos* foot) A sub-order of saurischian dinosaurs, most of which were bipedal and carnivorous. The theropods are often divided into two types, the coelurosaurs and the carnosaurs.
Thrinaxodon An Early Triassic therapsid from South Africa and Antarctica.
Tibia The larger bone of the lower leg (see also fibula).
Titanosaurs Gondwanic sauropods.
Toujiangosaurus (*Toujiang* a river in Szechuan, China + *sauros* reptile) A Late Jurassic stegosaur.
Trade winds Winds that in each hemisphere blow diagonally westwards towards the equator.
Triceratops (*treis* three + *keratos* horn + *ops* face) Late Cretaceous ceratopsian with three large horns.
Tropical climate A climate in which the average annual temperature is in the range of 18–20°C (64–68°F).
Typothorax (*typos* impression + *thorax* breast plate) An armoured aetosaur from the Late Triassic.
Tyrannosaurus (*tyrannos* tyrant + *sauros* reptile). A huge Late Cretaceous theropod.

U **Ulna** One of the bones of the lower arm (see also radius).
Ungual A claw, hoof, or nail.
Uplift The raising of regions of the earth from structural forces such as the upward flow of masses of magma through the earth's crust, or the compression of the crust by subduction or continental collision.

V **Varanid** A term relating to the Monitor lizards.
Vascular plant A plant that has vessels in its stem for transporting nutrients and water.
Velociraptor (*velocis* swift + *rapere* to plunder or rob) A small Late Cretaceous theropod suspected of robbing nests.
Vertebra(e) One of the bones or the set of bones that form the vertebral column or backbone.

Z **Zygapophyses** Projections from the front and back of the vertebrae which form articular surfaces in the vertebral column.

246